John Henry Newman, William Samuel Lilly

Characteristics from the Writings of John Henry Newman

Being selections personal, historical, philosophical, and religious, from his various works

John Henry Newman, William Samuel Lilly

Characteristics from the Writings of John Henry Newman
Being selections personal, historical, philosophical, and religious, from his various works

ISBN/EAN: 9783337068899

Printed in Europe, USA, Canada, Australia, Japan

Cover: Foto ©ninafisch / pixelio.de

More available books at **www.hansebooks.com**

CHARACTERISTICS

FROM THE WRITINGS OF

JOHN HENRY NEWMAN.

CHARACTERISTICS

FROM THE WRITINGS OF

JOHN HENRY NEWMAN

BEING SELECTIONS

PERSONAL, HISTORICAL, PHILOSOPHICAL, AND
RELIGIOUS, FROM HIS VARIOUS WORKS

ARRANGED BY

WILLIAM SAMUEL LILLY

OF THE INNER TEMPLE, BARRISTER-AT-LAW

WITH THE AUTHOR'S APPROVAL

Ille velut fidis arcana sodalibus olim
Credebat libris, neque si male cesserat unquam
Decurrens alio, neque si bene; quo fit ut omnis
Votiva pateat veluti descripta tabella
Vita senis.

EIGHTH EDITION

LONDON
KEGAN PAUL, TRENCH & CO., 1, PATERNOSTER SQUARE
1888

[The rights of translation and of reproduction are reserved.]

I DEDICATE THIS VOLUME TO

S. L. L.

WHO HAS DONE SO MUCH TO LIGHTEN MY LABOUR AND TO ENHANCE MY PLEASURE IN COMPILING IT.

PREFACE.

It may be well by way of introduction to this volume, to state, as simply and in as few words as possible, the aim and scope which I proposed to myself in compiling it.

My end has been to contribute, as far as I could, to the wider and more accurate knowledge of a writer concerning whom an amount of ignorance and misunderstanding still prevails, which is especially surprising, considering the high place he admittedly holds, both as a thinker and a master of style. A recent critic has described him, as "the man in the working of whose individual mind the intelligent portion of the English public is more interested than in that of any other living person."[1] This description is, I think, correct: and yet, although Dr. Newman's inner life has from various circumstances been laid completely bare to the world, there is probably no living person who has been so strangely and so persistently misconceived. Into the cause of those misconceptions it is not necessary for me to inquire. It is sufficient to remark that for the last ten years they have been gradually clearing away, and

[1] Austin: Poetry of the Period, p. 178.

that he has himself provided the best means for their removal in the books to which the verses quoted on my title-page so aptly apply. In the following pages I have endeavoured to give an account through extracts from those books, of his present views on the chief matters of general interest on which he has written from time to time. I have sought especially to present his mind on the great religious questions which have so largely exercised the intellect of this age, and which, even in the judgment of those who are unable to accept his conclusions, he has faced, investigated, and determined for himself with an unflinching courage, and an unswerving steadfastness of purpose, almost as rare, perhaps, as the high mental endowments which he has brought to the task.

Dr. Newman's writings, most of them of an occasional character, extend to thirty-four volumes, and in making my selections from them, I have been careful to choose passages which, while suffering the least by severance from the context, would present the ideas I was desirous to exhibit in their completeness and maturity. Hence the title I have given it—a title, I may observe, which does not altogether satisfy me, but for which I have been unable to find any better substitute in English. Hence, too, it is, that I have drawn chiefly from his later writings, for it is, of course, in his Catholic works that his views are found in their full development and final resolution.

Such has been the principle upon which I have proceeded in making my selections. In classifying them, my task was less difficult, as each seemed naturally to fall under one of the four divisions of Personal, Philosophical, Historical, and Religious. Part I., denominated Personal

Preface.

with the exception of the letter appended to it, is taken entirely from the Apologia. Part IV., which is termed "Religious," is subdivided into three sections, styled respectively Protestantism, Anglicanism, and Catholicism, and is intended to exhibit Dr. Newman's views on the more salient characteristics of those systems. Omissions in the text—they are always immaterial—are[1] duly noted, and a few words which I have been obliged to introduce for the sake of continuity, are enclosed in brackets,[2] as are also any notes added by me. The notes printed without brackets are Dr. Newman's, and, with[3] one exception, will be found in the original text.

In compiling my volume I have primarily endeavoured to consult for readers who, from want of leisure or from other reasons, are unable to procure and peruse for themselves Dr. Newman's writings at large, and who desire to possess, in a compendious form, a summary, prepared with his approval, of his ultimate judgments on the most important matters of which he has written during the last half century. There is, however, another class to whom also my volume may possibly be of service. It may, I think, prove sometimes useful to persons more or less acquainted with Dr. Newman's works, but not always able to find, just when they want it, some striking passage which dwells vaguely in their memories. For the convenience of such readers I have taken care to make the index as copious as I could. On the whole I may, perhaps, say, that I have endeavoured to construct my volume on much the same principles as those which Lord Bacon lays down for the compilation of a book

---

[1] By the marks . . .   [2] Thus [ ].   [3] At p. 437.

of "Institutions" of the law.[1] "Principally," he says, "it ought to have two properties, the one a perspicuous and clear order or method, and the other an universal latitude or comprehension, that the student may have a little prenotion of everything."

And now, perhaps, I have said enough or more than enough in explanation of the manner in which I have discharged my very subordinate part in this work. But I must not omit to record my thanks to my revered friend, Dr. Newman, for the readiness with which he assented to my undertaking it, and for the unwearied patience with which he has allowed me to encroach upon his time by the questions which I have occasionally found it necessary to put to him; nay, more than that, for the thoughtful kindness with which he has himself, in many cases, anticipated difficulties and favoured me with suggestions. I should, however, remark that, in claiming for my compilation his approval, I refer only to the sanction he has given for the statement, that it correctly represents his present opinions on the subjects of which it treats. For the actual selection of the passages, and the order in which they are placed, as well as for the headings prefixed to them, I am solely responsible.

It only remains for me to express my acknowledgments to the various firms which have published for Dr. Newman for the permission readily accorded me by them to make extracts from the works in which they are respectively interested, and to Mr. R. W. Thrupp, Photographer to the Queen, Birmingham, for allowing the portrait which faces

---

[1] Proposal for amending the Laws of England. Works. Bohn's edition, Vol. I. p. 669.

the title-page to be engraved from a photograph executed by him. I subjoin a catalogue of the editions of Dr. Newman's works which I have had before me. They are, I believe, in all cases the latest.

W. S. L.

London: June 11th, 1874.

---

* 1—8. PAROCHIAL AND PLAIN SERMONS. (*Rivingtons.*) Ed. of 1873.
* 9. SERMONS ON SUBJECTS OF THE DAY. (*Rivingtons.*) Ed. of 1871.
* 10. UNIVERSITY SERMONS. (*Rivingtons.*) 3rd Ed.
* 11. SERMONS TO MIXED CONGREGATIONS. (*Burns and Oates.*) 4th Ed.
* 12. OCCASIONAL SERMONS. (*Burns and Oates.*) 3rd Ed.
  13. LECTURES ON THE PROPHETICAL OFFICE OF THE CHURCH. (*Rivingtons*). (*Out of print.*)
* 14. LECTURES ON JUSTIFICATION. (*Rivingtons.*) 3rd Ed.
* 15. LECTURES ON THE DIFFICULTIES OF ANGLICANS, with Letter to Dr. Pusey. (*Burns and Oates.*) 4th Ed.
* 16. LECTURES ON THE PRESENT POSITION OF CATHOLICS. (*Burns and Oates.*) 4th Ed.
* 17. ESSAY IN AID OF A GRAMMAR OF ASSENT. (*Burns and Oates.*) 4th Ed.
* 18. TWO ESSAYS ON MIRACLES. (*Pickering.*) 3rd Ed.
* 19, 20. ESSAYS CRITICAL AND HISTORICAL, WITH NOTES. 1. Poetry. 2. Rationalism. 3. De la Mennais. 4. Palmer on Faith and Unity. 5. St. Ignatius. 6. Prospects of the Anglican Church. 7. The Anglo-American Church. 8. Countess of Huntingdon. 9. Catholicity of the Anglican Church. 10. The Antichrist of Protestants. 11. Milman's Christianity. 12. Reformation of the Eleventh Century. 13. Private Judgment. 14. Davison. 15. Keble. (*Pickering.*)

* 21. DISCUSSIONS AND ARGUMENTS. 1. How to accomplish it. 2. Antichrist of the Fathers. 3. Scripture and the Creed. 4. Tamworth Reading Room. 5. Who's to Blame? 6. An Argument for Christianity. (*Pickering.*)
22. PAMPHLETS. 1. Suffragan Bishops. 2. Letter to a Magazine. 3. Letter to Faussett. 4. Letter to Jelf. 5. Letter to the Bishop of Oxford. (*Out of print.*)
* 23. IDEA OF A UNIVERSITY. 1. Nine Discourses. 2. Occasional Lectures and Essays. (*Pickering.*) 3rd Ed.
24. ESSAY ON THE DEVELOPMENT OF CHRISTIAN DOCTRINE. (*Toovey.*) 2nd Ed.
25. ANNOTATED TRANSLATION OF ATHANASIUS. (*Parker.*)
* 26. THEOLOGICAL TRACTS. 1. Dissertatiunculae. 2. Doctrinal Causes of Arianism. 3. Apollinarianism. 4. St. Cyril's Formula. 5. Ordo de Tempore. 6. Douay Version of Scripture. (*Pickering.*)
* 27. THE ARIANS OF THE FOURTH CENTURY. (*Lumley.*) 3rd Ed.
* 28—30. HISTORICAL SKETCHES. 1. The Turks. 2. Cicero. 3. Apollonius. 4. Primitive Christianity. 5. Church of the Fathers. 6. St. Chrysostom. 7. Theodoret. 8. St. Benedict. 9. Benedictine Schools. 10. Universities. 11. Northmen and Normans. 12. Medieval Oxford. 13. Convocation of Canterbury. (*Pickering.*)
* 31. LOSS AND GAIN. (*Burns and Oates.*) 6th Ed.
* 32. CALLISTA. (*Pickering.*) 2nd Ed.
* 33. VERSES ON VARIOUS OCCASIONS. (*Burns and Oates.*) 4th Ed.
* 34. APOLOGIA PRO VITA SUA. (*Longmans.*) 3rd Ed.

The volumes marked with an asterisk have already appeared in the new and uniform edition of Dr. Newman's Works, now in course of publication.

CONTENTS.

PART I.—PERSONAL.

	PAGE
Early Religious Impressions	3
First Years of Residence at Oriel	9
Mr. Keble's Teaching	12
Hurrell Froude	15
The Teaching of Antiquity	18
Travels in the South of Europe	23
The Tracts for the Times	26
Dr. Pusey	33
The Via Media	36
Growth of the "Anglo-Catholic" Party	38
Tract Ninety	39
"Securus Judicat Orbis Terrarum"	43
Three further Blows	50
From 1841 to 1845	52
Reception	59
Since 1845	61
The Anglican Church seen from Without	62
Letter to Father Coleridge on Anglican Orders	66

PART II.—PHILOSOPHICAL.

Intellectual Education pre-eminently a Discipline in Accuracy of Mind	71
The Popular Conception of an "Intellectual Man"	74
The Origin of Political and Religious Watchwords	76
Real Apprehension of the Affections and Passions possible only by Experience	77
Realization	78

	PAGE
Our Notions of Things merely Aspects of them	80
How Men really Reason in Concrete Matters	82
Intellectual Obstructions	92
The Laws of the Mind the Expression of the Divine Will	93
First Principles	94
The Ethics of Culture	96
Culture and Vice	103
The World's Philosophy of Religion	105
The Doctrine of Retributive Punishment	109
What is Theology?	111
Physical Philosophy and Theology	117
The Baconian Philosophy	119
Rationalism	122
The God of Monotheism and the God of Rationalism	126
The "Duty of Scepticism"	130
Apprehension of God through the Conscience	131
Hume's Argument against the Jewish and Christian Miracles	139
Gibbon's "Five Causes"	141
The Principle of Faith	146

PART III.—HISTORICAL.

English Jealousy of Church and Army	153
Irish Discontent	157
The Northman Character	162
Northman and Norman	165
Athens	167
Oxford	173
St. Benedict and Early Monachism	175
The Death of St. Bede	179
Abelard	182
Pope Liberius	187
Death of St. Gregory VII.	188
Rome and Constantinople in 1566	189
The Election of St. Pius V.	190
The Battle of Lepanto	194
The Religious History of England	197
Catholicism in England from the Sixteenth to the Nineteenth Century	209
The Re-establishment of the Hierarchy	213

Contents.

Part IV.—Religious.

Section I.—Protestantism.

	PAGE
Protestantism and Historical Christianity	223
Bible Religion	225
Puritanism	227
Muscular Christianity	228
English Religious Ideas	229
A Protestant View of Conversions	236
Protestant Texts	239
Protestant Image Worship	242
The Right of Private Judgment or the Private Right of Judgment	243
The Rationale of Protestant Persecution	245
Protestantism drifting into Scepticism	247

Section II.—Anglicanism.

The Anglican View of the Visible Church	250
The Branch Theory	252
The Church of England	254
Anglican Orders	258
Anglican Ordinances	271
The High Church Party	284
The Christian Year	286
The Tractarian Movement	290
Anglo-Catholic or Patristico-Protestant?	294
The Non-jurors and the Lesson they Teach	299
The Anglican Argument from Differences among Catholics	304
Anglican Objections from Antiquity	306
Invincible Ignorance and Anglicanism	313
Fundamental Difference between Catholicism and Anglicanism	319

Section III.—Catholicism.

Catholicism and the Religions of the World	320
Faith in the Catholic Church	324
Faith in any other Religious Body than the Catholic Church impossible	332
Dispositions for joining the Catholic Church	334

	PAGE
No Logical Alternative between Catholicism and Scepticism	338
A Convert	340
Faith and Devotion	341
Private Judgment among Catholics	345
The Aim of the Catholic Church	347
The Religion of Catholics	356
The Privileges of Catholics	359
Integrity of Catholic Doctrine	361
Transubstantiation	363
Mass	364
Benediction	366
Confession	367
Counsels of Perfection	368
Relics and Miracles	370
The Earliest Recorded Apparition of the Blessed Virgin	379
The Antecedent Argument for an Infallible Arbiter of Faith and Morals	381
The Practical Wisdom of the Holy See	385
The Obligations of Catholics to the Holy See	387
English Catholics and Pius IX.	391
Scandals in the Catholic Church	393
"Popular" Catholics	395
A Bad Catholic	398
The Idea of a Saint	402
Lingering Imperfections of Saints; Personal and Temporary Errors of Popes	403
St. John Baptist	404
St. John Evangelist	406
St. Mary Magdalen	407
St. Augustine	410
St. Philip Neri	413
Mater Dei	416
Mater Purissima	419
Refugium Peccatorum	423
Sine Labe Originali Concepta	424
Maria Assumpta	432
Growth of the Cultus of Mary	435

PART I.

PERSONAL.

I.

EARLY RELIGIOUS IMPRESSIONS.

WHEN I was fifteen (in the autumn of 1816), I fell under the influences of a definite creed, and received into my intellect impressions of dogma, which, through God's mercy, have never been effaced or obscured. Above and beyond the conversations and sermons of the excellent man, long dead, the Rev. Walter Mayers, of Pembroke College, Oxford, who was the human means of this beginning of divine faith in me, was the effect of the books which he put into my hands, all of the school of Calvin. One of the first books I read was a book of Romaine's; I neither recollect the title nor the contents, except one doctrine, which, of course, I do not include among those which I believe to have come from a divine source, viz. the doctrine of final perseverance. I received it at once, and believed that the inward conversion of which I was conscious (and of which I am still more certain than that I have hands or feet) would last into the next life, and that I was elected to eternal glory. I have no consciousness that this belief had any tendency whatever to lead me to be careless about pleasing God. I retained it until the age of twenty-one, when it gradually faded away; but I believe that it had some influence on my opinions, in . . isolating me from the objects which surrounded me . . and making me rest in the thought of two and two only absolute and luminously self-evident beings, myself and my Creator; —for while I considered myself predestined to salvation my mind did not dwell upon others, as fancying them simply passed over, not predestined to eternal death. I only thought of the mercy to myself.

The detestable doctrine last mentioned is simply denied and abjured, unless my memory strangely deceives me, by the writer who made a deeper impression on my mind than any other, and to whom (humanly speaking) I almost owe my soul—Thomas Scott of Aston Sandford . . What, I suppose, will strike any reader of Scott's history and writings is his bold unworldliness and vigorous independence of mind. He followed truth wherever it led him, beginning with Unitarianism, and ending in a zealous faith in the Holy Trinity. . . It was he who first planted deep in my mind that fundamental truth of religion. . .

Besides his unworldliness, what I also admired in Scott was his resolute opposition to Antinomianism, and the minutely practical character of his writings. They show him to be a true Englishman, and I deeply felt his influence; and for years I used almost as proverbs what I considered to be the scope and issue of his doctrine, "Holiness rather than peace," and "Growth the only true evidence of life." . .

Of the Calvinistic tenets, the only one which took root in my mind was the fact of heaven and hell, divine favour and divine wrath, of the justified and the unjustified. The notion that the regenerate and the justified were one and the same, and that the regenerate, as such, had the gift of perseverance, remained with me not many years, as I have said already.

The main Catholic doctrine of the warfare between the city of God and the powers of darkness was also deeply impressed upon my mind by a work of a character very opposite to Calvinism, Law's "Serious Call."

From this time I have held with a full assent and belief the doctrine of eternal punishment, as delivered by our Lord himself, in as true a sense as I hold that of eternal happiness, though I have tried in various ways to make that truth less terrible to the intellect.

Now I come to two other works which produced a deep impression on me in the same autumn of 1816, when I was fifteen years old, each contrary to each, and planting in me the seeds of an intellectual inconsistency which disabled me for a long course of years. I read Joseph Milner's Church History, and was nothing short of enamoured with the long extracts from St. Augustine, St. Ambrose, and the other Fathers which I found there. I read them as being the religion of the Primitive Christians, but simultaneously with Milner I read Newton on the Prophecies, and, in consequence, became most firmly convinced that the Pope was the Anti-Christ predicted by Daniel, St. Paul, and St. John. My imagination was stained by the effects of this doctrine up to the year 1843; it had been obliterated from my reason and judgment at an earlier date. . .

In 1822 I came under very different influences from those to which I had hitherto been subjected. At that time, Mr. Whately, as he was then, afterwards Archbishop of Dublin, for the few months he remained in Oxford, which he was leaving for good, showed great kindness to me. He renewed it in 1825, when he became Principal of Alban Hall, making me his Vice-Principal and Tutor. Of Dr. Whately I will speak presently; for from 1822 to 1825 I saw most of the present Provost of Oriel, Dr. Hawkins, at that time

Vicar of St. Mary's; and, when I took orders in 1824, and had a curacy in Oxford, then, during the long vacations, I was especially thrown into his company... He was the first who taught me to weigh my words, and to be cautious in my statements. He led me to that mode of limiting and clearing my sense in discussion and in controversy, and of distinguishing between cognate ideas, and of obviating mistakes by anticipation, which to my surprise has been since considered, even in quarters friendly to me, to savour of the polemics of Rome. He is a man of most exact mind himself, and he used to snub me severely on reading, as he was kind enough to do, the first Sermons that I wrote, and other compositions which I was engaged upon. Then as to doctrine, he was the means of great additions to my belief. As I have noticed elsewhere, he gave me the "Treatise on Apostolical Preaching," by Sumner, afterwards Archbishop of Canterbury, from which I was led to give up my remaining Calvinism, and to receive the doctrine of Baptismal Regeneration. In many other ways, too, he was of use to me on subjects semi-religious and semi-scholastic... One principle which I gained from him more directly bearing upon Catholicism, than any I have mentioned, is the doctrine of Tradition...

It was about the year 1823, I suppose, that I read Bishop Butler's "Analogy," the study of which has been to so many, as it was to me, an era in their religious opinions. Its inculcation of a visible Church, the oracle of truth and a pattern of sanctity, of the duties of external religion, and of the historical character of Revelation, are characteristics of this great work which strike the reader at once; for myself, if I may attempt to determine what I most gained from it, it lay in two points, which are the underlying principles of a great portion of my teaching. First, the very idea of an analogy between the separate works of God leads to the conclusion that the system which is of less importance is economically or sacramentally connected with the more momentous system, and of this conclusion the theory, to which I was inclined as a boy, viz. the unreality of material phenomena, is an ultimate resolution. At this time I did not make the distinction between matter itself and its phenomena, which is so necessary and so obvious in discussing the subject. Secondly, Butler's doctrine that Probability is the guide of life, led me, at least, under the teaching to which a few years later I was introduced, to the question of the logical cogency of faith, on which I have written so much. Thus to Butler I trace those two principles of my teaching which have led to a charge against me both of fancifulness and of scepticism.

And now as to Dr. Whately. I owe him a great deal... He, emphatically, opened my mind, and taught me to think and to use my reason. After being first noticed by him in 1822 I became very intimate with him in 1825, when I was his Vice-Principal at Alban Hall. I gave up that office in 1826, when I became Tutor of my College, and his hold upon me gradually relaxed. He had done his work towards me, or nearly so, when he had taught me to see with my own eyes and to walk with my own feet. His mind was too different from mine for us to remain long on one line. When I was diverging from him in opinion (which he did not like), I thought of dedicating my first book to him, in words to the effect that he had not only taught me to think, but to think for myself. .. What he did for me in point of religious opinion, was, first, to teach me the existence of the Church, as a substantive body or corporation; next, to fix in me those anti-Erastian views of church polity, which were one of the most prominent features of the Tractarian movement.

.. I am not aware of any other religious opinion which I owe to Dr. Whately. In his special theological tenets I had no sympathy. In the year 1827 he told me he considered I was Arianizing. The case was this: though at that time I had not read Bishop Bull's "Defensio," nor the Fathers, I was just then very strong for that ante-Nicene view of the Trinitarian doctrine, which some writers, both Catholic and non-Catholic, have accused of wearing a sort of Arian exterior. This is the meaning of a passage in Froude's Remains, in which he seems to accuse me of speaking against the Athanasian Creed. I had contrasted the two aspects of the Trinitarian doctrine, which are respectively presented by the Athanasian Creed and the Nicene. My criticisms were to the effect that some of the verses of the former Creed were unnecessarily scientific. This is a specimen of a certain disdain for Antiquity which had been growing on me now for several years. . . The truth is, I was beginning to prefer intellectual excellence to moral. I was drifting in the direction of the Liberalism[1] of the day. I was rudely awakened from my dream at the end of 1827 by two great blows—illness and bereavement. ("Apologia," pp. 4–14.)

[1] [Dr. Newman, in a note on this passage, explains that by Liberalism he means "false liberty of thought, or the exercise of thought upon matters in which, from the constitution of the human mind, thought cannot be brought to any successful issue, and, therefore, is out of place. Among such matters," he continues, "are first principles of whatever kind; and of these the most sacred and momentous are especially to be reckoned, the truths of Revelation." He observes that this explanation is "the more necessary, because such great Catholics and distinguished writers as Count Montalembert and Father Lacordaire use the word in a favourable sense, and claim to be Liberals themselves," and adds, " I do not believe that it is possible for me to differ in any important matter from two men whom I so highly admire.

II.

FIRST YEARS OF RESIDENCE AT ORIEL.

DURING the first years of my residence at Oriel, though proud of my college, I was not quite at home there. I was very much alone, and I used often to take my daily walk by myself. I recollect once meeting Dr. Copleston, then Provost, with one of the Fellows. He turned round, and with the kind courteousness which sat so well on him, made me a bow and said, *Nunquam minus solus, quam cum solus.* At that time, indeed—(from 1823)—I had the intimacy of my dear and true friend Dr. Pusey, and could not fail to admire and revere a soul so devoted to the cause of religion, so full of good works, so faithful in his affections; but he left residence when I was getting to know him well. As to Dr. Whately himself, he was too much my superior to allow of my being at my ease with him; and to no one in Oxford at this time did I open my heart fully and familiarly. But things changed in 1826. At that time I became one of the Tutors of my College, and this gave me position; besides, I had written one or two Essays which had been well received. I began to be known. I preached my first University Sermon. Next year I was one of the Public Examiners for the B.A. degree. In 1828 I became Vicar of St. Mary's. It was to me like the feeling of spring weather after winter; and,

In their general line of thought and conduct I enthusiastically concur. . . If I hesitate to adopt their language about Liberalism, I impute the necessity of such hesitation, to some difference between us in the use of words or in the circumstances of country."—Ib. pp. 288 and 285.]

if I may so speak, I came out of my shell. I remained out of it until 1841.

The two persons who knew me best at that time are still alive, beneficed clergymen, no longer my friends. They could tell better than any one else what I was in those days. From this time my tongue was, as it were, loosened, and I spoke spontaneously and without effort. One of the two, a shrewd man, said of me, I have been told, "Here is a Fellow who, when he is silent, will never begin to speak, and when he once begins to speak will never stop." It was at this time that I began to have influence, which steadily increased for a course of years. I gained upon my pupils, and was in particular intimate and affectionate with two of our Probationer Fellows, Robert Isaac Wilberforce (afterwards Archdeacon), and Richard Hurrell Froude. Whately then, an acute man, perhaps saw around me the signs of an incipient party of which I was not conscious myself. And thus we discern the first elements of that movement afterwards called Tractarian. The true and primary author of it, however, as is usual with great motive powers, was out of sight. Having carried off, as a mere boy, the highest honours of the University, he had turned from the admiration which haunted his steps, and sought for a better and holier satisfaction in pastoral work in the country. Need I say that I am speaking of John Keble? The first time that I was in a room with him was on the occasion of my election to a Fellowship at Oriel, when I was sent for into the Tower, to shake hands with the Provost and Fellows. How is that hour fixed in my memory after the changes of forty-two years; forty-two this very day on which I write! I have lately had a letter in my hands which I sent at the time to my great friend, John William Bowden, with whom I passed almost exclusively my Undergraduate years. "I had to hasten to the Tower," I say to him, "to receive the congratulations of all the Fellows. I bore it till Keble took my hand, and then felt so abashed and unworthy of the honour done to me, that I seemed desirous of quite sinking into the ground." His had been the first name which I had heard spoken of, with reverence rather than admiration, when I came up to Oxford. When one day I was walking in High Street with my dear earliest friend just mentioned, with what eagerness did he cry out, "There's Keble!" and with what awe did I look at him! Then at another time I heard a Master of Arts of my college give an account how he had just then had occasion to introduce himself on some business to Keble, and how gentle, courteous, and unaffected Keble had been, so as almost to put him out of countenance. Then, too, it was reported, truly or falsely, how a rising man of brilliant reputation, the present Dean of St. Paul's, Dr. Milman, admired and loved him, adding, that somehow he was strangely unlike any one else. However, at the time when I was elected Fellow of Oriel, he was not in residence, and he was shy of me for years, in consequence of the marks which I bore upon me of the Evangelical and Liberal schools, at least so I have ever thought. Hurrell Froude brought us together about 1828: it is one of the sayings preserved in his "Remains"—"Do you know the story of the murderer who had done one good thing in his life? Well, if I was ever asked what good thing I had ever done, I should say I had brought Keble and Newman to understand each other." ("Apologia," pp. 15–18.)

III.

MR. KEBLE'S TEACHING.

"THE Christian Year" made its appearance in 1827. It is not necessary, and scarcely becoming, to praise a book which has already become one of the classics of the language. When the general tone of religious literature was so nerveless and impotent, as it was at that time, Keble struck an original note, and woke up in the hearts of thousands a new music, the music of a school long unknown in England. Nor can I pretend to analyze, in my own instance, the effects of religious teaching so deep, so pure, so beautiful. I have never till now tried to do so, yet I think I am not wrong in saying, that the two main intellectual truths it brought home to me, were the same two which I had learned from Butler, though recast in the creative mind of my new master. The first of these was what may be called, in a large sense of the word, the sacramental system; that is, the doctrine that material phenomena are both the types and the instruments of real things unseen,—a doctrine, which embraces in its fulness, not only what Anglicans as well as Catholics believe about the Sacraments, properly so called, but also the article of the "Communion of Saints," and likewise the Mysteries of the Faith. The connection of this philosophy of religion with what is sometimes called "Berkeleyism" has been mentioned above. I knew little of Berkeley at this time, except by name; nor have I ever studied him.

On the second intellectual principle which I gained from Mr. Keble, I could say a great deal, if this were the place for it. It runs through very much that I have written, and has gained for me many hard names. Butler teaches us that probability is the guide of life. The danger of this doctrine, in the case of many minds, is, its tendency to destroy in them absolute certainty, leading them to consider every conclusion as doubtful, and resolving truth into an opinion, which it is safe, indeed, to obey or to profess, but not possible to embrace with true internal assent. If this were to be allowed, then the celebrated saying, "O God, if there be a God, save my soul, if I have a soul," would be the highest measure of devotion; but who can really pray to a Being, about whose existence he is seriously in doubt?

I considered that Mr. Keble met this difficulty by ascribing the firmness of assent which we give to religious doctrine, not to the probabilities which introduced it, but to the living power of faith and love which accepted it. In matters of religion, he seemed to say, it is not merely probability which makes us intellectually certain, but probability as it is put to account by faith and love. It is faith and love which give to probability a force which it has not in itself. Faith and love are directed towards an Object; in the vision of that Object they live; it is that Object, received in faith and love, which renders it reasonable to take probability as sufficient for internal conviction. Then the argument from Probability, in the matter of religion, becomes an argument from Personality, which, in fact, is one form of the argument from Authority.

In illustration, Mr. Keble used to quote the words of the Psalm: "I will guide thee with mine *eye*. Be ye not like to horse and mule, which have no understanding; whose mouths must be held with bit and bridle, lest they fall upon thee." This is the very difference, he used to say, between slaves and friends or children. Friends do not ask for literal commands, but, from their knowledge of the speaker, they understand his half-words, and from love of him they anticipate his wishes. Hence it is, that in his poem for St. Bartholomew's Day, he speaks of the "Eye of God's Word"; and in the note quotes Mr. Miller, of Worcester College, who remarks, in his Bampton Lectures, on the special power of Scripture, as having "this Eye, like that of a portrait, uniformly fixed upon us turn where we will." The view thus suggested by Mr. Keble, is brought forward in one of the earliest of the "Tracts for the Times." In No. 8 I say: "The Gospel is a Law of Liberty. We are treated as sons, not as servants; not subjected to a code of formal commandments, but addressed as those who love God, and wish to please Him."

I did not at all dispute this view of the matter, for I made use of it myself; but I was dissatisfied, because it did not go to the root of the difficulty. It was beautiful and religious, but it did not even profess to be logical, and accordingly I tried to complete it by considerations of my own, which are to be found in my University Sermons, Essay on Ecclesiastical Miracles, and Essay on Development of Doctrine. My[1] argument is, in outline, as follows: that that absolute certitude which we were able to possess, whether as to the truths of natural theology, or as to the fact of a revelation, was the result of an assemblage of concurring and converging probabilities, and that, both according to the constitution of the human mind and the will of its Maker; that certitude was a habit of mind; that certainty was a quality of propositions; that probabilities which did not reach to logical certainty might suffice for a mental certitude; that the certitude thus brought about might equal in measure and strength the certitude which was created by the strictest scientific

[1] [This argument is worked out in the "Grammar of Assent."]

demonstration; and that to possess such certitude might in given cases, and to given individuals, be a plain duty, though not to others, in other circumstances :—

Moreover, that as there were probabilities which sufficed for certitude, so there were other probabilities which were legitimately adapted to create opinion; that it might be quite as much a matter of duty in given cases, and to given persons, to have about a fact an opinion of a definite strength and consistency, as in the case of greater or of more numerous probabilities it was a duty to have a certitude; that accordingly we were bound to be more or less sure, on a sort of (as it were) graduated scale of assent, viz. according as the probabilities attaching to a professed fact were brought home to us, and as the case might be, to entertain it about a pious belief, or a pious opinion, or a religious conjecture, or, at least, a tolerance of such belief, or opinion, or conjecture in others; that, on the other hand, as it was a duty to have a belief of more or less strong texture, in given cases, so, in other cases, it was a duty not to believe, not to opine, not to conjecture, not even to tolerate the notion that a professed fact was true, inasmuch as it would be credulity, or superstition, or some other moral fault to do so. This was the region of Private Judgment in religion; that is, of a Private Judgment, not formed arbitrarily and according to one's fancy or liking, but conscientiously, and under a sense of duty. ("Apologia," pp. 18-21.)

IV.

HURRELL FROUDE.

HURRELL FROUDE was a pupil of Keble, formed by him and in turn reacting upon him. I knew him first in 1826, and was in the closest and most affectionate friendship with him from about 1829 till his death in 1836. He was a man of the highest gifts,—so truly many-sided that it would be presumptuous for me to describe him, except under those aspects in which he came before me. Nor have I here to speak of the gentleness and tenderness of nature, the playfulness, the free elastic force and graceful versatility of mind, and the patient winning considerateness in discussion which endeared him to those to whom he opened his heart, for I am all along engaged upon matters of belief and opinion, and am introducing others into my narrative, not for their own sake, or because I love and have loved them, so much as because, and so far as, they have influenced my theological views. In this respect, then, I speak of Hurrell Froude,—in his intellectual aspect— as a man of high genius, brimful, and overflowing with ideas and views, in him original, which were too many and strong even for his bodily strength, and which crowded and jostled against each other in their effort after distinct shape and expression. And he had an intellect as critical and logical as it was speculative and bold. Dying prematurely, as he did, and in the conflict and transition-state of opinion, his religious views never reached their ultimate conclusion, by the very reason of their multitude and their depth. His opinions arrested and influenced me, even when they did not gain my assent. He professed openly his admiration of the Church of Rome, and his hatred of the Reformers. He delighted in the notion of an hierarchical system, of sacerdotal power, and of full ecclesiastical liberty. He felt scorn of the maxim, "The Bible and the Bible only is the religion of Protestants;" and he gloried in accepting Tradition as a main instrument of religious teaching. He had a high, severe idea of the intrinsic excellence of Virginity; and he considered the

Blessed Virgin its great pattern. He delighted in thinking of the Saints; he had a vivid appreciation of the idea of sanctity, its possibility and its heights; and he was more than inclined to believe a large amount of miraculous interference as occurring in the early and middle ages. He embraced the principle of penance and mortification. He had a deep devotion to the Real Presence, in which he had a firm faith. He was powerfully drawn to the Medieval Church, but not to the Primitive.

He had a keen insight into abstract truth; but he was an Englishman to the back-bone in his severe adherence to the real and the concrete. He had a most classical taste, and a genius for philosophy and art, and he was fond of historical inquiry, and the politics of religion. He had no turn for theology as such. He set no sufficient value on the writings of the Fathers, on the detail or development of doctrine, on the definite traditions of the Church viewed in their matter, on the teaching of the Ecumenical Councils, or on the controversies out of which they arose. He took an eager courageous view of things on the whole. I should say that his power of entering into the minds of others did not equal his other gifts; he could not believe, for instance, that I really held the Roman Church to be anti-Christian. On many points he would not believe but that I agreed with him, when I did not. He seemed not to understand my difficulties. His were of a different kind, the contrariety between theory and fact. He was a high Tory of the Cavalier stamp, and was disgusted with the Toryism of the opponents of the Reform Bill. He was smitten with the love of the Theocratic Church; he went abroad, and was shocked by the degeneracy which he thought he saw in the Catholics of Italy.

It is difficult to enumerate the precise additions to my theological creed which I derived from a friend to whom I owe so much. He taught me to look with admiration towards the Church of Rome, and in the same degree to dislike the Reformation. He fixed deep in me the idea of devotion to the Blessed Virgin, and he led me gradually to believe in the Real Presence. ("Apologia," pp. 23-25.)

V.

THE TEACHING OF ANTIQUITY.

THERE is one remaining source of my opinions to be mentioned, and that far from the least important. In proportion as I moved out of the shadow of that Liberalism which had hung over my course, my early devotion towards the Fathers returned, and in the long vacation of 1828 I set about to read them chronologically, beginning with St. Ignatius and St. Justin. About 1830 a proposal was made to me to furnish a History of the Principal Councils. I accepted it, and at once set to work on the Council of Nicæa. It was to launch myself on an ocean with currents innumerable, and I was drifted back first to the ante-Nicene history, and then to the Church of Alexandria. The work at last appeared under the title of "The Arians of the Fourth Century," and of its 422 pages the first 117 consisted of introductory matter, and the Council of Nicæa did not appear till the 254th, and then occupied at most twenty pages.

I do not know when I first learnt to consider that Antiquity was the true exponent of the doctrines of Christianity and the basis of the Church of England; but I take it for granted that the works of Bishop Bull, which

Blessed Virgin its great pattern. He delighted in thinking of the Saints; he had a vivid appreciation of the idea of sanctity, its possibility and its heights; and he was more than inclined to believe a large amount of miraculous interference as occurring in the early and middle ages. He embraced the principle of penance and mortification. He had a deep devotion to the Real Presence, in which he had a firm faith. He was powerfully drawn to the Medieval Church, but not to the Primitive.

He had a keen insight into abstract truth; but he was an Englishman to the back-bone in his severe adherence to the real and the concrete. He had a most classical taste, and a genius for philosophy and art, and he was fond of historical inquiry, and the politics of religion. He had no turn for theology as such. He set no sufficient value on the writings of the Fathers, on the detail or development of doctrine, on the definite traditions of the Church viewed in their matter, on the teaching of the Ecumenical Councils, or on the controversies out of which they arose. He took an eager courageous view of things on the whole. I should say that his power of entering into the minds of others did not equal his other gifts; he could not believe, for instance, that I really held the Roman Church to be anti-Christian. On many points he would not believe but that I agreed with him, when I did not. He seemed not to understand my difficulties. His were of a different kind, the contrariety between theory and fact. He was a high Tory of the Cavalier stamp, and was disgusted with the Toryism of the opponents of the Reform Bill. He was smitten with the love of the Theocratic Church; he went abroad, and was shocked by the degeneracy which he thought he saw in the Catholics of Italy.

It is difficult to enumerate the precise additions to my theological creed which I derived from a friend to whom I owe so much. He taught me to look with admiration towards the Church of Rome, and in the same degree to dislike the Reformation. He fixed deep in me the idea of devotion to the Blessed Virgin, and he led me gradually to believe in the Real Presence. ("Apologia," pp. 23–25.)

V.

THE TEACHING OF ANTIQUITY.

THERE is one remaining source of my opinions to be mentioned, and that far from the least important. In proportion as I moved out of the shadow of that Liberalism which had hung over my course, my early devotion towards the Fathers returned, and in the long vacation of 1828 I set about to read them chronologically, beginning with St. Ignatius and St. Justin. About 1830 a proposal was made to me to furnish a History of the Principal Councils. I accepted it, and at once set to work on the Council of Nicæa. It was to launch myself on an ocean with currents innumerable, and I was drifted back first to the ante-Nicene history, and then to the Church of Alexandria. The work at last appeared under the title of "The Arians of the Fourth Century," and of its 422 pages the first 117 consisted of introductory matter, and the Council of Nicæa did not appear till the 254th, and then occupied at most twenty pages.

I do not know when I first learnt to consider that Antiquity was the true exponent of the doctrines of Christianity and the basis of the Church of England; but I take it for granted that the works of Bishop Bull, which at this time I read, were my first introduction to this principle. The course of reading which I pursued in the composition of my volume was directly adapted to develop it in my mind. What principally attracted me in the ante-Nicene period was the great Church of Alexandria, the historical centre of teaching in those times. Of Rome for some centuries comparatively little is known. The battle of Arianism was first fought in Alexandria. Athanasius, the champion of the truth, was Bishop of Alexandria; and in his writings he refers to the great religious names of an earlier date, to Origen, Dionysius, and others, who were the glory of its see, or of its school. The broad philosophy of Clement and Origen carried me away; the philosophy, not the theological doctrine; and I have drawn out some portions of it in my volume, with the zeal and freshness, but with the partiality, of a Neophyte. Some portions of their teaching, magnificent in themselves, came like music on my inward ear, as if the response to ideas, which, with little external to encourage them, I had cherished so long. They were based on the mystical or sacramental principle, and spoke of the various Economies or Dispensations of the Eternal. I understood these passages to mean that the exterior world, physical and historical, was but the manifestation to our senses of realities greater than itself. Nature was a parable; Scripture was an allegory; pagan literature, philosophy, and mythology, properly understood, were but a preparation for the Gospel. The Greek poets and sages were in a certain sense prophets, for "thoughts beyond their thought to those high bards were given." There had been a directly divine dispensation granted to the Jews; but there had been, in some sense, a dispensation carried on in favour of the Gentiles. He who had taken the seed of Jacob for His elect people, had not therefore cast the rest of mankind out of His sight. In the fulness of time, both Judaism and Paganism had come to nought; the outward framework which concealed yet suggested the Living Truth, had never been intended to last, and it was dissolving under the beams of the Sun of Justice which shone behind it and through it. The process of change had been slow; it had been done, not rashly, but by rule and measure, "at sundry times and in divers manners," first one disclosure and then another, till the whole evangelical doctrine was brought into full manifestation. And thus room was made for the anticipation of further and deeper disclosures, of truths still under the veil of the letter, and in their season to be revealed. The visible world still remains without its divine interpretation; Holy Church, in her sacraments and her hierarchical appointments, will remain, even unto the end of the world, after all but a symbol of those heavenly facts which fill eternity. Her mysteries are but the expressions in human language of truths to which the human mind is unequal. It is evident how much there was in all this in correspondence with the thoughts which had attracted me when I was young, and with the doctrine which I have already associated with the "Analogy" and the "Christian Year."

It was, I suppose, to the Alexandrian school and to the early Church that I owe in particular what I definitely held about the Angels. I viewed them, not only as the ministers employed by the Creator in the Jewish and Christian dispensations, as we find on the face of Scripture, but as carrying on, as Scripture also implies, the Economy of the Visible World. I considered them as the real causes of motion, life, and light, and of those elementary principles of the physical universe, which, when offered in their developments to our senses, suggest to us the notion of cause and effect, and of what are called the laws of nature. This doctrine I have drawn out in my Sermon for Michaelmas Day, written in 1831.[1] I say of the Angels, "Every breath of air, and ray of light and heat, every beautiful prospect, is, as it were, the skirts of their garments, the waving of the robes of those whose faces see God.". .

While I was engaged in writing my work upon the Arians, great events were happening at home and abroad, which brought out into form and passionate expression the various beliefs which had so gradually been winning their way into my mind. Shortly before, there had been a Revolution in France. . . The great Reform agitation was going on around me as I wrote. . . Lord Grey had told the Bishops to set their house in order, and some of the Prelates had been insulted and threatened in the streets of London. The vital question was, how were we to keep the Church from being liberalized? There was such apathy on the subject in some quarters, such imbecile alarm in others; the true principles of Churchmanship seemed so radically decayed, and there was such distraction in the counsels of the Clergy. Blomfield, the Bishop of London of the day, an active and open-hearted man, had been for years engaged in diluting the high orthodoxy of the Church by the introduction of members of the Evangelical body into places of influence and trust. He had deeply offended men who agreed in opinion with myself, by an off-hand saying (as it was reported) to the effect that belief in the Apostolical succession had gone out with the Non-jurors. "We can count you," he said to some of the gravest and most venerated persons of the old school. And the Evangelical party itself, with their late successes, seemed

[1] [Parochial and Plain Sermons, Vol. II. p. 362.]

to have lost that simplicity and unworldliness which I admired so much in Milner and Scott. It was not that I did not venerate such men as Ryder, the then Bishop of Lichfield, and others of similar sentiments, who were not yet promoted out of the ranks of the Clergy, but I thought little of the Evangelicals as a class. I thought they played into the hands of the Liberals. With the Establishment thus divided and threatened, thus ignorant of its true strength, I compared that fresh, vigorous power of which I was reading in the first centuries. In her triumphant zeal on behalf of that Primeval Mystery, to which I had had so great a devotion from my youth, I recognized the movement of my Spiritual Mother. " Incessu patuit dea." The self-conquest of her Ascetics, the patience of her Martyrs, the irresistible determination of her Bishops, the joyous swing of her advance, both exalted and abashed me. I said to myself, " Look on this picture and on that." I felt affection for my own Church, but not tenderness; I felt dismay at her prospects, anger and scorn at her do-nothing perplexity. I thought that if Liberalism once got a footing within her, it was sure of the victory in the event. I saw that Reformation principles were powerless to rescue her. As to leaving her, the thought never crossed my imagination; still I ever kept before me that there was something greater than the Established Church, and that that was the Church Catholic and Apostolic, set up from the beginning, of which she was but the local presence and the organ. She was nothing, unless she was this. She must be dealt with strongly or she would be lost. There was need of a second Reformation. ("Apologia," pp. 25-32.)

VI.

TRAVELS IN THE SOUTH OF EUROPE.

[My "History of the Arians"] was ready for the press in July, 1832, though not published till the end of 1833. My health had suffered from the labour involved in the composition of [the] volume, [and] I was easily persuaded to join Hurrell Froude and his father, who were going to the south of Europe for the health of the former.

We set out in December, 1832. It was during this expedition that my Verses which are in the "Lyra Apostolica" were written; a few, indeed, before it, but not more than one or two of them after it. Exchanging, as I was, definite Tutorial work, and the literary quiet and pleasant friendships of the last six years, for foreign countries and an unknown future, I naturally was led to think that some inward changes, as well as some larger course of action, were coming upon me. At Whitchurch, while waiting for the down mail to Falmouth, I wrote the verses about my Guardian Angel,[1] which begin with these words, "Are these the tracks of some unearthly Friend?" and which go on to speak of "the vision" which haunted me :—that vision is more or less brought out in the whole series of these compositions.

I went to various coasts of the Mediterranean; parted with my friends in Rome; went down for the second time to Sicily without companion at the end of April, and got back to England by Palermo in the early part of July. The strangeness of foreign life threw me back into myself; I found pleasure in historical sights and beautiful scenes, not in men and manners. We kept clear of Catholics

[1] [See "Verses on Various Occasions," p. 69.]

throughout our tour. I had a conversation with the Dean of Malta, a most pleasant man, lately dead; but it was about the Fathers, and the Library of the great church. I knew the Abbate Santini at Rome, who did no more than copy for me the Gregorian tones. Froude and I made two calls upon Monsignore (now Cardinal) Wiseman, at the Collegio Inglese, shortly before we left Rome. Once we heard him preach at a church in the Corso. I do not recollect being in a room with any other ecclesiastics, except a priest at Castro Giovanni, in Sicily, who called on me when I was ill, and with whom I wished to hold a controversy. As to Church Services, we attended the Tenebræ, at the Sistine, for the sake of the Miserere, and that was all. My general feeling was, "All, save the spirit of man, is divine." I saw nothing but what was external; of the hidden life of Catholics I knew nothing. I was still more driven back into myself, and felt my isolation. England was in my thoughts solely, and the news from England came rarely and imperfectly. The Bill for the Suppression of the Irish Sees was in progress, and filled my mind. I had fierce thoughts against the Liberals. The motto [prefixed to] the "Lyra Apostolica," [which we] began at Rome, shows the feeling of both Froude and myself at this time. We borrowed from M. Bunsen a Homer, and Froude chose the words in which Achilles, on returning to the battle, says, "You shall know the difference, now that I am back again."

Especially when I was left by myself, the thought came upon me that deliverance is wrought, not by the many, but by the few; not by bodies, but by persons. Now it was, I think, that I repeated to myself the words which had ever been dear to me from my school days, "Exoriare aliquis!" —now, too, that Southey's beautiful poem of "Thalaba," for which I had an immense liking, came forcibly to my mind.

I began to think that I had a mission. There are sentences of my letters to my friends to this effect, if they are not destroyed. When we took leave of Monsignore Wiseman he had courteously expressed a wish that we might make a second visit to Rome. I said with great gravity, "We have a work to do in England." I went down at once to Sicily, and the presentiments grew stronger. I struck into the middle of the island, and fell ill of a fever at Leonforte. My servant thought that I was dying, and begged for my last directions. I gave them, as he wished; but I said, "I shall not die." I repeated, "I shall not die, for I have not sinned against light, I have not sinned against light." I never have been able to make out at all what I meant.

I got to Castro Giovanni, and was laid up there for nearly three weeks. Towards the end of May I left for Palermo, taking three days for the journey. Before starting from my inn, in the morning of May 26th or 27th, I sat down on my bed, and began to sob bitterly. My servant, who had acted as my nurse, asked me what ailed me. I could only answer him, "I have a work to do in England."

I was aching to get home; yet, for want of a vessel, I was kept at Palermo for three weeks. I began to visit the Churches, and they[1] calmed my patience, though I did

---

[1] [The subjoined verses, dated Palermo, June 13th, 1833, are interesting, not only as a record of this soothing influence, but also as affording, in the judgment of many, the first indication found in Dr. Newman's writings of what are called "tendencies to Rome," tendencies of which, it is needless to add, he was then wholly unconscious :—

"Oh that thy creed were sound!
    For thou dost soothe the heart, thou Church of Rome,
By thy unwearied watch and varied round
    Of service in thy Saviour's holy home.

not attend any services. I knew nothing of the Presence of the Blessed Sacrament there. At last I got off in an orange boat, bound for Marseilles. Then it was that I wrote the lines, "Lead, Kindly Light," which have since become well known. We were becalmed a whole week in the Straits of Bonifaccio. I was writing verses the whole time of my passage. At length I got to Marseilles, and set off for England. The fatigue of travelling was too much for me, and I was laid up for several days at Lyons. At last I got off again, and did not stop, night or day, (except a compulsory delay at Paris,) till I reached England and my mother's house. My brother had arrived from Persia only a few hours before. This was on the Tuesday. The following Sunday, July 14th, Mr. Keble preached the Assize Sermon in the University Pulpit. It was published under the title of "National Apostacy." I have ever considered and kept the day, as the start of the religious movement of 1833. ("Apologia," pp. 32–35.)

VII.

THE TRACTS FOR THE TIMES.

WHEN I got back from abroad I found that already a movement had commenced in opposition to the specific

> I cannot walk the city's sultry streets,
> But the wide porch invites to still retreats,
> Where passion's thirst is calm'd, and care's unthankful gloom.
> " There, on a foreign shore,
>   The homesick solitary finds a friend ;
> Thoughts, prison'd long for lack of speech, outpour
>   Their tears ; and doubts in resignation end.
> I almost fainted from the long delay
> That tangles me within this languid bay,
> When comes a foe, my wounds with oil and wine to tend."
>
> *Verses on Various Occasions*, p. 146.]

danger which at that time was threatening the religion of the nation and its Church. Several zealous and able men had united their counsels, and were in correspondence with each other. The principal of them were Mr. Keble, Hurrell Froude, who had reached home long before me, Mr. William Palmer of Dublin and Worcester College (not Mr. William Palmer of Magdalen, who is now a Catholic), Mr. Arthur Perceval, and Mr. Hugh Rose. . .

Out of my own head I began the Tracts [for the Times]. . . I had the consciousness that I was employed in that work which I had been dreaming about, and which I felt to be so momentous and inspiring. I had a supreme confidence in our cause; we were upholding that Primitive Christianity which was delivered for all time by the early teachers of the Church, and which was registered and attested in the Anglican Formularies and by the Anglican divines. That ancient religion had wellnigh faded out of the land, through the political changes of the last 150 years, and it must be restored. It would be in fact a second Reformation;—a better Reformation, for it would be a return not to the sixteenth century, but to the seventeenth. No time was to be lost, for the Whigs had come to do their worst, and the rescue might come too late. Bishoprics were already in course of suppression; Church property was in course of confiscation; Sees would soon be receiving unsuitable occupants. We knew enough to begin preaching upon, and there was no one else to preach. I felt as on board a vessel, which first gets under weigh, and then the deck is cleared out, and luggage and live stock stowed away into their proper receptacles.

Nor was it only that I had confidence in our cause, both in itself, and in its polemical force; but also, on the other hand, I despised every rival system of doctrine and its arguments too. As to the High Church and the Low

Church, I thought that the one had no more a logical basis than the other; while I had a thorough contempt for the controversial position of the latter. I had a real respect for the character of many of the advocates of each party, but that did not give cogency to their arguments; and I thought, on the contrary, that the Apostolical form of doctrine was essential and imperative, and its grounds of evidence impregnable. . . And now let me state more definitely what the position was which I took up, and the propositions about which I was so confident. These were three.

1. First was the principle of dogma : my battle was with Liberalism ; by Liberalism I meant the anti-dogmatic principle and its developments. This was the first point on which I was certain. Here I make a remark : persistence in a given belief is no sufficient test of its truth, but departure from it is at least a slur upon the man who has felt so certain about it. In proportion, then, as I had in 1832 a strong persuasion of the truth of opinions which I have since given up, so far a sort of guilt attaches to me, not only for that vain confidence, but for all the various proceedings which were the consequence of it. But under the first head I have the satisfaction of feeling that I have nothing to retract, and nothing to repent of. The main principle of the movement is as dear to me now as it ever was. I have changed in many things, in this I have not. From the age of fifteen, dogma has been the fundamental principle of my religion. I know no other religion. I cannot enter into the idea of any other sort of religion; religion, as a mere sentiment, is to me a dream and a mockery. As well can there be filial love without the fact of a father, as devotion without the fact of a Supreme Being. What I held in 1816 I held in 1833, and I hold in 1864. Please God, I shall hold it to the end. Even when

I was under Dr. Whately's influence I had no temptation to be less zealous for the great dogmas of the faith, and at various times I used to resist such trains of thought on his part as seemed to me (rightly or wrongly) to obscure them. Such was the fundamental principle of the movement of 1833.

2. Secondly, I was confident in the truth of a certain definite religious teaching, based upon this foundation of dogma, viz. that there was a visible Church, with sacraments and rites, which are the channels of invisible grace. I thought that this was the doctrine of Scripture, of the early Church, and of the Anglican Church. Here, again, I have not changed in opinion; I am as certain now on this point as I was in 1833, and have never ceased to be certain. In 1834 and the following years I put this ecclesiastical doctrine on a broader basis, after reading Laud, Bramhall, and Stillingfleet, and other Anglican divines, on the one hand, and after prosecuting the study of the Fathers on the other; but the doctrine of 1833 was strengthened in me, not changed. When I began the "Tracts for the Times" I rested the main doctrine, of which I am speaking, upon Scripture, on the Anglican Prayer Book, and on St. Ignatius' Epistles. (1.) As to the existence of a visible Church, I especially argued out the point from Scripture in Tract II., viz. from the Acts of the Apostles and the Epistles. (2.) As to the Sacraments and Sacramental rites, I stood on the Prayer Book. . . (3.) And as to the Episcopal system, I founded it upon the Epistles of St. Ignatius. . . One passage especially impressed itself upon me: speaking of cases of disobedience to ecclesiastical authority, he says, "A man does not deceive that Bishop whom he sees, but he practises rather with the Bishop Invisible, and so the question is not with flesh, but with God, who knows the

secret heart." I wished to act on this principle to the letter, and I may say with confidence that I never consciously transgressed it. I loved to act as feeling myself in my Bishop's sight, as if it were the sight of God. It was one of my special supports and safeguards against myself; I could not go very wrong while I had reason to believe that I was in no respect displeasing him. It was not a mere formal obedience to rule that I put before me, but I desired to please him personally, as I considered him set over me by the Divine Hand. I was strict in observing my clerical engagements, not only because they *were* engagements, but because I considered myself simply as the servant and instrument of my Bishop. I did not care much for the Bench of Bishops, except as they might be the voice of my Church; nor should I have cared much for a Provincial Council, nor for a Diocesan Synod, presided over by my Bishop; all these matters seemed to me to be *jure ecclesiastico;* but what to me was *jure divino,* was the voice of my Bishop in his own person. My own Bishop was my Pope; I knew no other; the successor of the Apostles, the Vicar of Christ. This was but a practical exhibition of the Anglican theory of Church Government, as I had already drawn it out myself, after various Anglican Divines. This continued all through my course. When at length, in 1845, I wrote to Bishop Wiseman, in whose Vicariate I found myself, to announce my conversion, I could find nothing better to say to him than that I would obey the Pope as I had obeyed my own Bishop in the Anglican Church.

And now, in concluding my remarks on the second point on which my confidence rested, I repeat, that here again I have no retractation to announce as to its main outlines. While I am now as clear in my acceptance of the principle of dogma, as I was in 1833 and 1816, so again

I am now as firm in my belief of a visible Church, of the authority of Bishops, of the grace of the Sacraments, of the religious worth of works of penance, as I was in 1833. I have added Articles to my Creed, but the old ones, which I then held with a Divine faith, remain.

3. But now, as to the third point on which I stood in 1833, and which I have utterly renounced and trampled upon since,—my then view of the Church of Rome,—I will speak about it as exactly as I can. When I was young, as I have said already, and after I was grown up, I thought the Pope to be anti-Christ. At Christmas, 1824-5, I preached a sermon to that effect. But in 1827 I accepted eagerly the stanza in the "Christian Year," which many people thought too charitable, "Speak *gently* of thy sister's fall." From the time I knew Froude I got less and less bitter on the subject... When it was that in my deliberate judgment I gave up the notion altogether in any shape, that some special reproach was attached to the name [of the Church of Rome], I cannot tell; but I had a shrinking from renouncing it, even when my reason so ordered me, from a sort of conscience or prejudice, I think up to 1843. Moreover, at least during the Tract Movement, I thought the essence of her offence to consist in the honours which she paid to the Blessed Virgin and the Saints; and the more I grew in devotion, both to the Saints and to our Lady, the more impatient was I at the Roman practices, as if those glorified creations of God must be gravely shocked, if pain could be theirs, at the undue veneration of which they were the objects.

On the other hand, Hurrell Froude, in his familiar conversations, was always tending to rub the idea out of my mind. In a passage of one of his letters from abroad, alluding, I suppose, to what I used to say in opposition to him, he observes: "I think people are injudicious who talk against the Roman Catholics for worshipping saints, and honouring the Virgin and images, &c. These things may perhaps be idolatrous; I cannot make up my mind about it; but to my mind it is the Carnival that is real practical idolatry, as it is written, 'the people sat down to eat and drink, and rose up to play.'" The Carnival, I observe in passing, is, in fact, one of those very excesses to which, for at least three centuries, religious Catholics have ever opposed themselves, as we see in the life of St. Philip, to say nothing of the present day; but this we did not then know. Moreover, from Froude I learnt to admire the great Medieval Pontiffs. . . Then, when I was abroad, the sight of so many great places, venerable shrines, and noble churches, much impressed my imagination, and my heart was touched also. Making an expedition on foot across some wild country in Sicily, at six in the morning I came upon a small church; I heard voices, and I looked in. It was crowded, and the congregation was singing. Of course it was the Mass, though I did not know it at the time. And, in my weary days at Palermo, I was not ungrateful for the comfort which I had received in frequenting the churches; nor did I ever forget it. Then, again, her zealous maintenance of the doctrine and the rule of celibacy which I recognized as Apostolic, and her faithful agreement with Antiquity in so many other points which were dear to me, was an argument as well as a plea in favour of the great Church of Rome. Thus I learnt to have tender feelings towards her; but still my reason was not affected at all. My judgment was against her, when viewed as an institution, as truly as it had ever been. . .

As a matter, then, of simple conscience, though it went against my feelings, I felt it to be a duty to protest against the Church of Rome. And besides this, it was a duty, because the prescription of such a protest was a living principle of my own Church, as expressed not simply in a *catena*, but by a consensus of her divines, and by the voice of her people. Moreover, such a protest was necessary as an integral portion of her controversial basis; for I adopted the argument of Bernard Gilpin, that Protestants "were *not able* to give any *firm and solid* reason of the separation, besides this, to wit, that the Pope is anti-Christ." But while I thus thought such a protest to be based upon truth, and to be a religious duty, and a rule of Anglicanism, and a necessity of the case, I did not at all like the work. ("Apologia," pp. 36–55.)

VIII.

Dr. PUSEY.

DURING the first year of the Tracts the attack [of the Liberals] upon the University began. In November, 1834, was sent to me, by Dr. Hampden, the second edition of his Pamphlet, entitled, "Observations on Religious Dissent; with particular reference to the use of Theological Tests in the University." In this pamphlet it was maintained that Religion is distinct from Theological Opinion; that it is but a common prejudice to identify theological propositions, methodically deduced and stated, with the simple religion of Christ, and that under Theological Opinion were to be placed the Trinitarian doctrine and the Unitarian; that a dogma was a theological opinion formally insisted on; that speculation always left an opening for improvement; that the Church of England was not dogmatic in its spirit, though the wording of its formularies might often carry the sound of dogmatism. . . Since that time Phaeton has got into the chariot of the sun; we, alas! can only look on, and watch him down the steep of heaven. Meanwhile, the lands which he is passing over, suffer from his driving.

Such was the commencement of the assault of Liberalism upon the old orthodoxy of Oxford and England, and it could not have been broken, as it was, for so long a time, had not a great change taken place in the circumstances of that counter-movement which had already started with the view of resisting it. For myself, I was not the person to take the lead of a party; I never was, from first to last, more than a leading author of a school; nor did I ever wish to be anything else. . . I felt great impatience at our being called a party, and would not allow that we were such. I had a lounging, free-and-easy way of carrying things on. I exercised no sufficient censorship upon the Tracts. . .

It was under these circumstances that Dr. Pusey joined us. I had known him well since 1827-8, and had felt for him an enthusiastic admiration. I used to call him ὁ μέγας. His great learning, his immense diligence, his scholar-like mind, his simple devotion to the cause of religion, overcame me, and great of course was my joy, when, in the last days of 1833, he showed a disposition to make common cause with us. . . He at once gave to us a position and a name. Without him we should have had little chance, especially at the early date of 1834, of making any serious resistance to the Liberal aggression. But Dr. Pusey was a Professor and Canon of Christ Church; he had a vast influence in consequence of his deep religious seriousness, the munificence of his charities, his Professorship, his family connexions, and his easy relations with the University authorities. . . He was, to use the common expression, a host in himself. He was able to give a name, a form, and a personality, to what was without him a sort of mob; and when various parties had to meet together in order to resist the liberal acts of the Government, we of the Movement took our place by right among them.

Such was the benefit which he conferred on the Movement externally, nor were the internal advantages at all inferior to it. He was a man of large designs. He had a hopeful, sanguine mind; he had no fear of others; he was haunted by no intellectual perplexities. People are apt to say that he was once nearer to the Catholic Church than he is now. I pray God he may one day be far nearer to the Catholic Church than he was then, for I believe that, in his reason and judgment, all the time that I knew him, he never was near to it at all. When I became a Catholic I was often asked, "What of Dr. Pusey?" When I said that I did not see symptoms of his doing as I had done, I was sometimes thought uncharitable. If confidence in his position is (as it is) a first essential in the leader of a party, this Dr. Pusey possessed pre-eminently. The most remarkable instance of this, was his statement, in one of his subsequent defences of the Movement, when moreover it had advanced a considerable way in the direction of Rome, that among its more hopeful peculiarities was its "stationariness." He made it in good faith; it was his subjective view of it. ("Apologia," pp. 57–62.)

IX.

THE VIA MEDIA.

I SUSPECT it was Dr. Pusey's influence and example which set me, and made me set others, on the larger and more careful works in defence of the principles of the Movement which followed in a course of years,—some of them demanding and receiving from their authors such elaborate treatment that they did not make their appearance till both its temper and its fortunes had changed. I set about a work at once; one in which was brought out with precision the relation in which we stood to the Church of Rome. We could not move a step in comfort till this was done. It was of absolute necessity and a plain duty from the first, to provide as soon as possible a large statement, which would encourage and reassure our friends, and repel the attacks of our opponents. A cry was heard on all sides of us that the Tracts and the writings of the Fathers would lead us to become Catholics, before we were aware of it. . . There was another reason still, and quite as important. Monsignore Wiseman, with the acuteness and zeal which might be expected from that great Prelate, had anticipated what was coming, had returned to England by 1836, had delivered Lectures in London on the doctrines of Catholicism, and created an impression through the country, shared in by ourselves, that we had for our opponents in controversy, not only our brethren, but our hereditary foes. These were the circumstances which led to my publication of "The Prophetical Office of the Church viewed relatively to Romanism and Popular Protestantism." This work employed me for three years, from the beginning of 1834 to the end of 1836. It was composed after a careful consideration and comparison of the principal Anglican Divines of the 17th century. . . . Its subject is the doctrine of the Via Media, a name which had already been applied to the Anglican system by writers of name. It is an expressive title, but not altogether satisfactory, because it is at first sight negative. This had been the reason of my dislike to the word "Protestant"; viz. it did not denote the profession of any particular religion at all, and was compatible with infidelity. A Via Media was but a receding from extremes,—therefore it needed to be drawn out into a definite shape and character; before it could have any definite claims on our respect, it must first be shown to be one, intelligible, and consistent. This was the first condition of any reasonable treatise on the Via Media. The second condition, and necessary too, was not in my power. . . Even if the Via Media were ever so positive a religious system, it was not as yet objective and real; it had no original anywhere of which it was the representative. It was at present a paper religion. This I confess in my Introduction: I say, "Protestantism and Popery are real religions . . but the Via Media, viewed as an integral system, has scarcely had existence except on paper." I grant the objection, though I endeavour to lessen it:—"It still remains to be tried, whether what is called Anglo-Catholicism, the religion of Andrewes, Laud, Hammond, Butler, and Wilson, is capable of being professed, acted on, and maintained on a large sphere of action, or whether it be a mere modification or transition-state of either Romanism or popular Protestantism." I trusted that some day it would prove to be a substantive religion.

Lest I should be misunderstood, let me observe that this hesitation about the validity of the theory of the Via Media implied no doubt of the three fundamental points on which it was based, as I have described them above: dogma, the sacramental system, and anti-Romanism. ("Apologia," pp. 63–69.)

X.

GROWTH OF THE "ANGLO-CATHOLIC" PARTY.

So I went on for years up to 1841. It was, in a human point of view, the happiest of my life. I was truly at home. I had in one of my volumes appropriated to myself the words of Bramhall, "Bees, by the instinct of nature, do love their hives, and birds their nests." I did not suppose that such sunshine would last, though I knew not what would be its termination. It was the time of plenty, and, during its seven years, I tried to lay up as much as I could for the dearth which was to follow it. We prospered and spread. I have spoken of the doings of these years, since I was a Catholic, in a passage, part of which I will here quote:

"From beginnings so small," I said, "from elements of thought so fortuitous, with prospects so unpromising, the Anglo-Catholic party suddenly became a power in the National Church, and an object of alarm to her rulers and friends. Its originators would have found it difficult to say what they aimed at of a practical kind; rather, they put forth views and principles for their own sake, because they were true, as if they were obliged to say them; and, as they might be themselves surprised at their earnestness in uttering them, they had as great cause to be surprised at the success which attended their propagation. And, in fact, they could only say, that those doctrines were in the air; that to assert was to prove, and that to explain was to persuade; and that the Movement in which they were taking part was the birth of a crisis rather than of a place. In a very few years, a school of opinion was formed, fixed in its principles, indefinite and progressive in their range, and it extended itself into every part of the country. If we enquire what the world thought of it, we have still more to raise our wonder; for, not to mention the excitement it caused in England, the Movement and its party-names were known to the police of Italy and to the back-woodmen of America. And so it proceeded, getting stronger and stronger every year, till it came into collision with the Nation, and that Church of the Nation, which it began by professing especially to serve." ("Apologia," pp. 75, 76.)

XI.

TRACT NINETY.

From the time that I had entered upon the duties of Public Tutor at my College, when my doctrinal views were very different from what they were in 1841, I had meditated a comment upon the Articles. Then, when the Movement was in its swing, friends had said to me, "What will you make of the Articles?" But I did not share the apprehension which their question implied. Whether, as time went on, I should have been forced, by the necessities of the original theory of the Movement, to put on paper the speculations which I had about them, I am not able to conjecture. The actual cause of my doing so, in the beginning of 1841, was the restlessness, actual and prospective, of those who neither liked the Via Media nor my strong judgment against Rome. I had been enjoined, I think by my Bishop, to keep these men straight, and I wished so to do; but their tangible difficulty was subscription to the Articles, and thus the question of the Articles came before me. It was thrown in our teeth, "How can you manage to sign the Articles? they are directly against Rome." "Against Rome?" I made answer, "what do you mean by 'Rome'?" And then I proceeded to make distinctions, of which I shall now give an account.

By "Roman doctrine" might be meant one of three things: 1. The *Catholic teaching* of the early centuries; or 2, the *formal dogmas of Rome*, as contained in the later Councils, especially the Council of Trent, and as condensed in the Creed of Pope Pius IV. 3. The *actual popular beliefs and usages sanctioned by Rome* in the countries in communion with it, over and above the dogmas; and these I called "dominant errors." Now Protestants commonly thought, that in all three senses "Roman doctrine" was condemned in the Articles; I thought that the *Catholic teaching* was not condemned, that the *dominant errors* were; and as to the *formal dogmas*, that some were, some were not, and that the line had to be drawn between them. Thus: 1. The use of prayers for the dead was a Catholic doctrine,—not condemned in the Articles; 2. The prison of Purgatory was a Roman dogma, which was condemned in them; but the infallibility of Ecumenical Councils was a Roman dogma,—not condemned; and 3. The fire of Purgatory, was an authorized and popular error, not a dogma,—which was condemned.

Further, I considered that the difficulties, felt by the persons whom I have mentioned, mainly lay in their mistaking, 1. Catholic teaching, which was not condemned in the Articles, for Roman dogma, which was condemned; and 2, Roman dogma, which was not condemned in the Articles, for dominant error, which was. If they went further than this, I had nothing more to say to them.

A further motive which I had for my attempt, was the desire to ascertain the ultimate points of contrariety between the Roman and Anglican creeds, and to make them as few as possible. I thought that each creed was obscured and misrepresented by a dominant circumambient "Popery" and "Protestantism."

The main thesis then of my Essay was this:—the Articles do not oppose Catholic teaching; they but partially oppose Roman dogma; they for the most part oppose the dominant errors of Rome. And the problem was, as I have said, to draw the line as to what they allowed and what they condemned. . .

In the sudden storm of indignation with which the Tract was received throughout the country on its appearance, I recognize much of real religious feeling, much of honest and true principle, much of straightforward, ignorant, common sense. In Oxford there was genuine feeling too; but there had been a smouldering, stern, energetic animosity, not at all unnatural, partly rational, against its author. A false step had been made; now was the time for action. I am told that, even before the publication of the Tract, rumours of its contents had got into the hostile camp in an exaggerated form, and not a moment was lost in proceeding to action, when I was actually fallen into the hands of the Philistines. I was quite unprepared for the outbreak, and was startled at its violence. I do not think I had any fear. Nay, I will add, I am not sure that it was not, in one point of view, a relief to me.

I saw indeed, clearly, that my place in the Movement was lost. Public confidence was at an end; my occupation was gone. It was simply an impossibility that I could say anything henceforth to good effect, when I had been posted up by the marshal on the buttery-hatch of every College of my University, after the manner of discommoned pastrycooks; and when, in every part of the country and every class of society, through every organ and opportunity of opinion, in newspapers, in periodicals, at meetings, in pulpits, at dinner-tables, in coffee-rooms, in railway carriages, I was denounced as a traitor who had laid his train, and was detected in the very act of firing it against the time-honoured Establishment. There were indeed men, besides my own immediate friends, men of name and position, who gallantly took my part, as Dr. Hook, Mr. Palmer, and Mr. Perceval; it must have been a grievous trial for themselves, yet what, after all, could they do for me? Confidence in me was lost; but I had already lost full confidence in myself. Thoughts had passed over me a year and a half before in respect to the Anglican claims, which for the time had profoundly troubled me. They had gone: I had not less confidence in the power of the Apostolical movement than before; not less confidence than before in the grievousness of what I called the " dominant errors " of Rome; but how was I any more to have absolute confidence in myself? How was I to have confidence in my present confidence? How was I to be sure that I should always think as I thought now? I felt that by this event a kind Providence had saved me from an impossible position in the future.

First, if I remember right, they wished me to withdraw the Tract. This I refused to do; I would not do so for the sake of those who were unsettled, or in danger of unsettlement. I would not do so for my own sake, for how could I acquiesce in a mere Protestant interpretation of the Articles? How could I range myself among the professors of a theology, of which it put my teeth on edge even to hear the sound?

Next they said, "Keep silence, do not defend the Tract." I answered, "Yes, if you will not condemn it,—if you will allow it to continue on sale." They pressed me whenever I gave way; they fell back when they saw me obstinate. Their line of action was to get out of me as much as they could; but upon the point of their tolerating the Tract I *was* obstinate. So they let me continue it on sale, and they said they would not condemn it. But they said that this was on condition that I did not defend it, that I stopped the series, and that I myself published my own condemnation in a letter to the Bishop of Oxford. I impute nothing whatever to him, he was ever most kind to me. Also they said they could not answer for what some individual Bishops might perhaps say about the Tract in their own charges. I agreed to their conditions. My one point was to save the Tract.

Not a line in writing was given me as a pledge of the observance of the main article on their side of the engagement. Parts of letters from them were read to me, without being put into my hands. It was an "understanding." A clever man had warned me against "understandings" some six years before: I have hated them ever since. ("Apologia," pp. 77-90.)

XII.

"SECURUS JUDICAT ORBIS TERRARUM."

THE Long Vacation of 1839 began early. There had been a great many visitors to Oxford from Easter to Commemoration, and Dr. Pusey's party had attracted attention, more, I think, than in any former year. I had put away from me the controversy with Rome for more than two years. In my Parochial Sermons the subject had at no time been introduced; there had been nothing for two years, either in my Tracts or in the "British Critic," of a polemical character. I was returning for the Vacation to the course of reading which I had many years before chosen as especially my own. I have no reason to suppose that the thoughts of Rome came across my mind at all. About the middle of June I began to study and master the history of the Monophysites. I was absorbed in the doctrinal question. This was from about June 13th to August 30th. It was during this course of reading that for the first time a doubt came upon me of the tenableness of Anglicanism. I recollect on the 30th of July mentioning to a friend, whom I had accidentally met, how remarkable the history was; but by the end of August I was seriously alarmed.

I have described in a former work,[1] how the history affected me. My stronghold was Antiquity; now here, in the middle of the fifth century, I found, as it seemed to me, Christendom of the sixteenth and the nineteenth centuries reflected. I saw my face in that mirror, and I was a Monophysite. The Church of the Via Media was in the position of the Oriental Communion. Rome was, where she now is; and the Protestants were the Eutychians. Of all passages of history, since history has been, who would have thought of going to the sayings and doings of Eutyches, that *delirus senex*, as (I think) Petavius calls him, and to the enormities of the unprincipled Dioscorus, in order to be converted to Rome. Now let it be simply understood that I am not writing controversially, but with the one object of relating things as they happened to me in the course of my conversion. With this view I will quote a passage from the account, which I gave in 1850[2] of my reasonings and feelings in 1839.

---

[1] [For an account of the Monophysites see "Essay on Development," p. 293.]
[2] [In Lectures on Ang. Dif., pp. 338.]

"It was difficult to make out how the Eutychians or Monophysites were heretics, unless Protestants and Anglicans were heretics also; difficult to find arguments against the Tridentine Fathers, which did not tell against the Fathers of Chalcedon; difficult to condemn the Popes of the sixteenth century, without condemning the Popes of the fifth. The drama of religion, and the combat of truth and error, were ever one and the same. The principles and proceedings of the Church now, were those of the Church then; the principles and proceedings of heretics then, were those of Protestants now. I found it so, —almost fearfully; there was an awful similitude, more awful, because so silent and unimpassioned, between the dead records of the past, and the feverish chronicle of the present. The shadow of the fifth century was on the sixteenth. It was like a spirit rising from the troubled waters of the old world, with the shape and lineaments of the new. The Church then, as now, might be called peremptory and stern, resolute, overbearing, and relentless; and heretics were shifting, changeable, reserved, and deceitful, ever courting civil power, and never agreeing together, except by its aid; and the civil power was ever aiming at comprehensions, trying to put the invisible out of view, and substituting expediency for faith. What was the use of continuing the controversy, or defending my position, if, after all, I was forging arguments for Arius or Eutyches, and turning devil's-advocate against the much-enduring Athanasius and the majestic Leo? Be my soul with the Saints! and shall I lift up my hand against them? Sooner may my right hand forget her cunning and wither out-right, as his who once stretched it out against a prophet of God! anathema to a whole tribe of Cranmers, Ridleys, Latimers, and Jewels; perish the names of Bramhall, Ussher, Taylor, Stillingfleet, and Barrow, from the face of the earth, ere I should do aught but fall at their feet in love and in worship, whose image was continually before my eyes, and whose musical words were ever in my ears and on my tongue."

Hardly had I brought my course of reading to a close, when the "Dublin Review" of that same August was put into my hands, by friends who were more favourable to the cause of Rome than I was myself. There was an article in it on "the Anglican Claim," by Dr. Wiseman. This was about the middle of September. It was on the Donatists, with an application to Anglicanism. I read it, and did not see much in it. The Donatist controversy was known to me for some years... The case was not parallel to that of the Anglican Church. St. Augustine in Africa wrote against the Donatists in Africa. They were a furious party who made a schism within the African Church, and not beyond its limits. It was a case of Altar against Altar, of two occupants of the same see, as that between the Non-jurors in England and the Established Church; not the case of one Church against another, as of Rome against the Oriental Monophysites. But my friend, an anxiously religious man, now, as then, very dear to me, a Protestant still, pointed out the palmary words of St. Augustine, which were contained in one of the extracts made in the "Review," and which had escaped my observation, "Securus judicat orbis terrarum." He repeated these words again and again, and, when he was gone, they kept ringing in my ears. "Securus judicat orbis terrarum;" they were words which went beyond the occasion of the Donatists, they applied to that of the Monophysites. They gave a cogency to the Article which had escaped me at first. They decided ecclesiastical questions on a simpler rule than that of Antiquity. Nay St. Augustine was one of the prime oracles of Antiquity;

here then Antiquity was deciding against itself. What a light was hereby thrown upon every controversy in the Church! not that, for the moment, the multitude may not falter in their judgment,—not that, in the Arian hurricane, Sees more than can be numbered did not bend before its fury, and fall off from St. Athanasius,—not that the crowd of Oriental Bishops did not need to be sustained during the contest by the voice and the eye of St. Leo; but that the deliberate judgment, in which the whole Church at length rests and acquiesces, is an infallible prescription, and a final sentence, against such portions of it as protest and secede. Who can account for the impressions which are made on him? For a mere sentence, the words of St. Augustine, struck me with a power which I never had felt from any words before. To take a familiar instance, they were like the "Turn again Whittington" of the chime; or, take a more serious one, they were like the "Tolle, lege,—Tolle, lege," of the child, which converted St. Augustine himself. "Securus judicat orbis terrarum!" By those great words of the ancient Father, interpreting and summing up the long and varied course of ecclesiastical history, the theory of the Via Media was absolutely pulverized.

I became excited at the view thus opened upon me. I was just starting on a round of visits; and I mentioned my state of mind to two most intimate friends: I think to no others. After a while, I got calm, and at length the vivid impression upon my imagination faded away. What I thought about it on reflection, I will attempt to describe presently. I had to determine its logical value, and its bearing upon my duty. Meanwhile, so far as this was certain—I had seen the shadow of a hand upon the wall. It was clear that I had a good deal to learn on the question of the Churches, and that perhaps some new light was coming upon me. He who has seen a ghost, cannot be as if he had never seen it. The heavens had opened and closed again. The thought for the moment had been "The Church of Rome will be found right after all;" and then it had vanished. My old convictions remained as before.

At this time, I wrote my Sermon on Divine Calls, which I published in my volume of Plain Sermons. It ends thus :—

"O that we could take that simple view of things, as to feel that the one thing which lies before us is to please God! What gain is it to please the world, to please the great, nay even to please those whom we love, compared with this? What gain is it to be applauded, admired, courted, followed, —compared with this one aim, of not being 'disobedient to a heavenly vision?' What can this world offer comparable with that insight into spiritual things, that keen faith, that heavenly peace, that high sanctity, that everlasting righteousness, that hope of glory, which they have, who in sincerity love and follow our Lord Jesus Christ? Let us beg and pray Him day by day to reveal Himself to our souls more fully, to quicken our senses, to give us sight and hearing, taste and touch of the world to come; so to work within us, that we may sincerely say, 'Thou shalt guide me with thy counsel, and after that receive me with glory. Whom have I in heaven but Thee? and there is none upon earth that I desire in comparison of Thee. My flesh and my heart faileth, but God is the strength of my heart, and my portion for ever.'"

Now to trace the succession of thoughts, and the conclusions, and the consequent innovations on my previous belief, and the general conduct to which I was led, . . upon this sudden visitation. And first, I will say, whatever comes of saying it, for I leave inferences to others, that for years I must have had something of an habitual notion, though it was latent, and had never led me to distrust my own convictions, that my mind had not found its ultimate rest, and that in some sense or other I was on journey. During the same passage across the Mediterranean in which I wrote, "Lead Kindly Light," I also wrote the verses which are found in the "Lyra" under the head of "Providences,"[1] beginning: "When I look back." This was in 1833; and, since I have begun this narrative, I have found a memorandum under the date of Sept. 7, 1829, in which I speak of myself as "now in my rooms in Oriel College slowly advancing, &c., and led on by God's hand blindly, not knowing whither he is taking me." But, whatever this presentiment be worth, it was no protection against the dismay and disgust, which I felt, in consequence of the dreadful misgiving, of which I have been relating the history. The one question was, What was I to do? I had to make up my mind for myself, and others could not help me. I determined to be guided, not by my imagination, but by my reason. And this I said over and over again in the years which followed, both in conversation and in private letters. Had it not been for this severe resolve, I should have been a Catholic sooner than I was. Moreover, I felt on consideration a positive doubt, on the other hand, whether the suggestion did not come from below. Then I said to myself, Time alone can solve that question. It was my business to go on as usual, to obey those convictions to which I had so long surrendered myself, which still had possession of me, and on which my new thoughts had no direct bearing. That new conception of things should only so far influence me, as it had a logical claim to do so. If it came from above, it would come again;—so I trusted, —and with more definite outlines and greater cogency and

---

[1] [They will be found at p. 178 of "Verses on Various Occasions," under the title of "Semita Justorum."]

consistency of proof. I thought of Samuel, before he "knew the word of the Lord;" and therefore I went and lay down to sleep again. ("Apologia," pp. 114-120.)

XIII.

THREE FURTHER BLOWS

IN the summer of 1841, I found myself at Littlemore, without any harrass or anxiety on my mind. I had determined to put aside all controversy, and I set myself down to my translation of St. Athanasius; but, between July and November, I received three blows which broke me.

1. I had got but a little way in my work, when my trouble returned on me. The ghost had come a second time. In the Arian history I found the very same phenomenon, in a far bolder shape, which I had found in the Monophysite. I had not observed it in 1832. Wonderful that this should come upon me! I had not sought it out. I was reading and writing in my own line of study, far from the controversies of the day, on what is called a "metaphysical" subject; but I saw clearly, that in the history of Arianism, the pure Arians were the Protestants, the semi-Arians were the Anglicans, and that Rome now was what it was then. The truth lay, not with the Via Media, but with what was called "the extreme party." As I am not writing a work of controversy, I need not enlarge upon the argument; I have said something on the subject in a volume from which I have already quoted.

2. I was in the misery of this new unsettlement when a

second blow came upon me. The Bishops, one after another, began to charge against me. It was a formal, determinate movement. This was the real understanding; that on which I had acted on the first appearance of Tract Ninety, had come to nought. I think the words which had then been used to me were, that "perhaps two or three of them might think it necessary to say something in their charges;" but by this time they had tided over the difficulty of the Tract, and there was no one to enforce the understanding. They went on in this way, directing charges at me, for three whole years. I recognized it as a condemnation; it was the only one that was in their power. . .

3. As if this were not enough, there came the affair of the Jerusalem Bishopric. . . At the very time that the Anglican Bishops were directing their censures upon me for avowing an approach to the Catholic Church not closer than I believed the Anglican formularies would allow, they were, on the other hand, fraternizing, by their act or by their sufferance, with Protestant bodies, and allowing them to put themselves under an Anglican Bishop, without any renunciation of their errors, or regard to their due reception of Baptism and Confirmation; while there was great reason to suppose that the said Bishop was intended to make converts from the orthodox Greeks and the schismatical Oriental bodies, by means of the influence of England. This was the third blow, which finally shattered my faith in the Anglican Church. That Church was not only forbidding any sympathy or concurrence with the Church of Rome, but it actually was courting an intercommunion with Protestant Prussia and the heresy of the Orientals. The Anglican Church might have the Apostolical succession, as had the Monophysites, but such acts as were in progress led me to the gravest

suspicion, not that it would soon cease to be a Church, but that, since the 16th century, it had never been a Church all along. . .

Looking back two years afterwards, on the above-mentioned and other acts, on the part of Anglican Ecclesiastical authorities, I observed: "Many a man might have held an abstract theory about the Catholic Church, to which it was difficult to adjust the Anglican,—might have admitted a suspicion, or even painful doubts, about the latter,—yet never have been impelled onwards, had our rulers preserved the quiescence of former years; but it is the corroboration of a present, living, and energetic heterodoxy which realizes and makes them practical; it has been the recent speeches and acts of authorities, who had so long been tolerant of Protestant error, which have given to enquiry and to theory its force and its edge."

As to the project of a Jerusalem Bishopric, I never heard of any good or harm it has ever done, except what it has done for me, which many think a great misfortune, and I one of the greatest of mercies. It brought me on to the beginning of the end. ("Apologia," pp. 139–146.)

XIV.

FROM 1841 TO 1845.

From the end of 1841, I was on my death-bed, as regards my membership with the Anglican Church, though at the time I became aware of it only by degrees. . . My dear friend, Dr. Russell, the present President of Maynooth, had perhaps more to do with my conversion than any one else. He called upon me in passing through Oxford in the summer of 1841, and I think I took him over some of the buildings of the University. He called again another summer, on his way from Dublin to London. I do not recollect that he said a word on the subject of religion on either occasion. He sent me at different times several letters; he was always gentle, mild, unobtrusive, uncontroversial. He let me alone. He also gave me one or two books. Veron's Rule of Faith and some Treatises of the Wallenburghs, was one; a volume of St. Alphonso Liguori's Sermons, was another.

Now it must be observed that the writings of St. Alphonso, as I knew them by the extracts commonly made from them, prejudiced me as much against the Roman Church as anything else, on account of what was called their "Mariolatry;" but there was nothing of the kind in this book. I wrote to ask Dr. Russell whether anything had been left out in the translation; he answered that there certainly were omissions in one Sermon about the Blessed Virgin. This omission, in the case of a book intended for Catholics, at least showed that such passages as are found in the works of Italian Authors were not acceptable to every part of the Catholic world. Such devotional manifestations in honour of Our Lady had been my great *crux* as regards Catholicism; I say frankly, I do not fully enter into them now; I trust I do not love her the less, because I cannot enter into them. They may be fully explained and defended, but sentiment and taste do not run with logic; they are suitable for Italy, but they are not suitable for England. But, over and above England, my own case was special: from a boy I had been led to consider that my Maker and I, His creature, were the two beings, luminously such, *in rerum naturâ*. I will not here speculate, however, about my own feelings. Only this I know full well now, and did not know then, that the Catholic Church allows no image of any sort, material or immaterial, no dogmatic symbol, no rite, no sacrament, no Saint, not even the Blessed Virgin herself, to come between the soul and its Creator. It is face to face, "solus cum solo," in all matters between man and his God. He alone creates; He alone has redeemed; before His awful eyes we go in death; in the vision of Him is our eternal beatitude.

1. Solus cum solo:—I recollect but indistinctly what I gained from the volume of which I have been speaking, but it must have been something considerable. At least I had got a key to a difficulty; in these Sermons (or rather heads of sermons, as they seem to be, taken down by a hearer), there is much of what would be called legendary illustration, but the substance of them is plain, practical, awful preaching upon the great truths of salvation. What I can speak of with greater confidence is the effect produced on me, a little later, by studying the Exercises of St. Ignatius. For here again, in a matter consisting in the purest and most direct acts of religion,—in the intercourse between God and the soul, during a season of recollection, of repentance, of good resolution, of enquiry into vocation, —the soul was "sola cum solo;" there was no cloud interposed between the creature and the Object of his faith and love. The command practically enforced was, "My son, give Me thy heart?" The devotions then to Angels and Saints as little interfered with the incommunicable glory of the Eternal, as the love which we bear our friends and relations, our tender human sympathies, are inconsistent with that supreme homage of the heart to the Unseen, which really does but sanctify and exalt, not jealously destroy, what is of earth. At a later date Dr. Russell sent me a large bundle of penny or halfpenny books of devotion, of all sorts, as they are found in the booksellers' shops in Rome, and, on looking them over, I was quite astonished

to find how different they were from what I had fancied, how little there was in them to which I could really object. I have given an acoount of them in my "Essay on the Development of Doctrine." Dr. Russell sent me St. Alphonso's book at the end of 1842 ; however, it was still a long time before I got over my difficulty, on the score of the devotions paid to the Saints ; perhaps, as I judge from a letter I have turned up, it was some way into 1844 before I could be said fully to have got over it.

2. I am not sure that I did not also at this time feel the force of another consideration. The idea of the Blessed Virgin was, as it were, *magnified* in the Church of Rome, as time went on,—but so were all the Christian ideas ; as that of the Blessed Eucharist. The whole scene of pale, faint, distant Apostolic Christianity is seen in Rome, as through a telescope or magnifier. The harmony of the whole, however, is, of course, what it was. It is unfair then to take one Roman idea, that of the Blessed Virgin, out of what may be called its context.

3. Thus I am brought to the principle of development of doctrine in the Christian Church, to which I gave my mind at the end of 1842. I had made mention of it in "Home Thoughts Abroad," published in 1836, and, even at an earlier date, I had introduced it into my "History of the Arians," in 1832; nor had I ever lost sight of it in my speculations. And it is certainly recognized in the Treatise of Vincent of Lerins, which has so often been taken as the basis of Anglicanism. In 1843 I began to consider it attentively. I made it the subject of my last University Sermon, on February 2; and the general view to which I came is stated thus, in a letter to a friend, of the date of July 14, 1844. It will be observed, that now, as before, my *issue* is still Creed *versus* Church :—

"The kind of considerations which weighs with me are

such as the following: 1. I am far more certain (according to the Fathers) that we *are* in a state of culpable separation, *than* that developments do *not* exist under the Gospel, and that the Roman developments are not the true ones. 2. I am far more certain, that *our* (modern) doctrines are wrong, *than* that the *Roman* (modern) doctrines are wrong. 3. Granting that the Roman (special) doctrines are not found drawn out in the early Church, yet I think there is sufficient trace of them in it, to recommend and prove them, *on the hypothesis* of the Church having a divine guidance, though not sufficient to prove them by itself. So that the question simply turns on the nature of the promise of the Spirit made to the Church. 4. The proof of the Roman (modern) doctrine is as strong (or stronger) in Antiquity as that of certain doctrines which both we and Romans hold: e.g. there is more of evidence in Antiquity for the necessity of Unity, than for the Apostolical succession; for the Supremacy of the See of Rome, than for the Presence in the Eucharist; for the practice of Invocation, than for certain books in the present Canon of Scripture, &c., &c. 5. The analogy of the Old Testament, and also of the New, leads to the acknowledgment of doctrinal developments."

4. And thus I was led on to a further consideration. I saw that the principle of development not only accounted for certain facts, but was in itself a remarkable philosophical phenomenon, giving a character to the whole course of Christian thought. It was discernible from the first years of the Catholic teaching up to the present day, and gave to that teaching a unity and individuality. It served as a sort of test, which the Anglican could not exhibit, that modern Rome was in truth ancient Antioch, Alexandria, and Constantinople, just as a mathematical curve has its own law and expression.

5. And thus I was led on to examine more attentively what I doubt not was in my thoughts long before, viz. the concatenation of argument by which the mind ascends from its first to its final religious idea, and I came to the conclusion that there was no medium, in true philosophy, between Atheism and Catholicity, and that a perfectly consistent mind, under those circumstances in which it finds itself here below, must embrace either the one or the other. And I hold this still: I am a Catholic by virtue of my believing in a God; and if I am asked why I believe in a God, I answer, that it is because I believe in myself, for I find it impossible to believe in my own existence (and of that fact I am quite sure) without believing also in the existence of Him, who lives as a Personal, All-seeing, All-judging Being in my conscience. Now, I daresay, I have not expressed myself with philosophical correctness, because I have not given myself to the study of what metaphysicians have said on the subject, but I think I have a strong true meaning in what I say, which will stand examination.

6. Moreover, I found a corroboration of the fact of the logical connection of Theism with Catholicism in a consideration parallel to that which I had adopted on the subject of development of doctrine. The fact of the operation, from first to last, of that principle of development in the truths of Revelation, is an argument in favour of the identity of Roman and primitive Christianity; but as there is a law which acts upon the subject-matter of dogmatic theology, so there is a law in the matter of religious faith. In a [former portion][1] of this narrative I spoke of certitude as the consequence, divinely intended and enjoined upon us, of the accumulative force of certain given reasons which, taken one by one, were only pro-

[1] [See page 14.]

babilities. Let it be recollected that I am historically relating my state of mind, at the period of my life which I am surveying. I am not speaking theologically, nor have I any intention of going into controversy: but, speaking historically of what I held in 1843-4, I say, that I believed in a God on a ground of probability, that I believed in Christianity on a probability, and that I believed in Catholicism on a probability, and that these three grounds of probability, distinct from each other of course in subject-matter, were still, all of them, one and the same in nature of proof, as being probabilities—probabilities of a special kind, a cumulative, a transcendent probability, but still probability; inasmuch as He who has made us has so willed, that in mathematics, indeed, we should arrive at certitude by rigid demonstration, but in religious enquiry we should arrive at certitude by accumulated probabilities; —He has willed, I say, that we should so act, and, as willing it, He co-operates with us in our acting, and thereby enables us to do that which He wills us to do, and carries us on, if our will does but co-operate with His, to a certitude which rises higher than the logical force of our conclusions. And thus I came to see clearly, and to have a satisfaction in seeing, that, in being led on into the Church of Rome, I was not proceeding on any secondary or isolated grounds of reason, or by controversial points in detail, but was protected and justified, even in the use of those secondary or particular arguments, by a great and broad principle. But, let it be observed that I am stating a matter of fact, not defending it, and if any Catholic says in consequence that I have been converted in a wrong way, I cannot help that now.

I have nothing more to say on the subject of the change in my religious opinions. On the one hand I came gradually to see that the Anglican Church was formally in the wrong, on the other that the Church of Rome was formally in the right;[1] then, that no valid reasons could be assigned for continuing in the Anglican, and again that no valid objections could be taken to joining the Roman. Then, I had nothing more to learn; what still remained for my conversion, was, not further change of opinion, but to change opinion itself into the clearness and firmness of intellectual conviction. ("Apologia," pp. 147-200.)

XV.

RECEPTION.

IN 1843, I took two very significant steps:—1. In February I made a formal retraction of all the hard things which I had said against the Church of Rome. 2. In September I resigned the living of St. Mary's, Littlemore, included. . . I [began] my Essay on the Development of Doctrine in the beginning of 1845, and I was hard at it all through the year until October. As I advanced, my difficulties so cleared away that I ceased to speak of "the Roman Catholics," and called them boldly Catholics. Before I got to the end, I resolved to be received, and the book remains in the state which it was then, unfinished.

One of my friends at Littlemore had been received into the Church on Michaelmas day, at the Passionist House, at Aston, near Stone, by Father Dominic, the Superior. At the beginning of October the latter was passing through London to Belgium, and, as I was in some perplexity what steps to take for being received myself, I assented to the proposition made to me, that the good priest should

---

[1] [As to "what it was that converted Dr. Newman," see p. 308.]

take Littlemore in his way, with a view to his doing for me the same charitable service as he had done to my friend.

On October the 8th I wrote to a number of friends the following letter:—

"Littlemore, October 8th, 1845. I am this night expecting Father Dominic, the Passionist, who, from his youth, has been led to have distinct and direct thoughts, first of the countries of the north, then of England. After thirty years' (almost) waiting, he was, without his own act, sent here. But he has had little to do with conversions. I saw him here for a few minutes on St. John Baptist's day last year.

"He is a simple, holy man; and withal gifted with remarkable powers. He does not know of my intention; but I mean to ask of him admission into the One Fold of Christ..."

For a while after my reception, I proposed to betake myself to some secular calling... [But] soon, Dr. Wiseman, in whose Vicariate Oxford lay, called me to Oscott; and I went there with others; afterwards he sent me to Rome, and finally placed me in Birmingham... I left Oxford for good on Monday, February 23, 1846. On the Saturday and Sunday before I was in my house at Littlemore, simply by myself, as I had been for the first day or two when I had originally taken possession of it. I slept on Sunday night at my dear friend's, Mr. Johnson's, at the Observatory. Various friends came to see the last of me; Mr. Copeland, Mr. Church, Mr. Buckle, Mr. Pattison, and Mr. Lewis. Dr. Pusey, too, came up to take leave of me; and I called on Dr. Ogle, one of my very oldest friends, for he was my private Tutor, when I was an Undergraduate. In him I took leave of my first College, Trinity, which was so dear to me, and which held on its foundation so many who had been kind to me, both when I was a boy, and all through my Oxford life. Trinity had never been unkind to me. There used to be much snap-dragon growing on the walls opposite my freshman's rooms there, and I had for years taken it as the emblem of my own perpetual residence even unto death in my University. On the morning of the 23rd I left the Observatory. I have never seen Oxford since, excepting its spires, as they are seen from the railway. ("Apologia," pp. 200-237.)

XVI.

SINCE 1845.

FROM the time that I became a Catholic, of course I have no further history of my religious opinions to relate. In saying this I do not mean to say that my mind has been idle, or that I have given up thinking on theological subjects, but that I have had no variations to record, and have had no anxiety of heart whatever. I have been in perfect peace and contentment. I never have had one doubt. I was not conscious to myself, on my conversion, of any change, intellectual or moral, wrought in my mind. I was not conscious of firmer faith in the fundamental truths of Revelation, or of more self-command; I had not more fervour; but it was like coming into port after a rough sea, and my happiness on that score remains to this day without interruption.

Nor had I any difficulty about receiving those additional articles which are not found in the Anglican creed. Some of them I believed already, but not any one of them was a trial to me. I made a profession of them upon my reception with the greatest ease, and I have the same ease in believing them now. I am far, of course, from denying that every article of the Christian Creed, whether as held by Catholics or by Protestants, is beset with intellectual difficulties, and it is simple fact, that, for myself, I cannot answer those difficulties. Many persons are very sensitive of the difficulties of religion. I am as sensitive of them as any one, but I have never been able to see a connection between apprehending those difficulties, however keenly, and multiplying them to any extent, and, on the other hand, doubting the doctrines to which they are attached. Ten thousand difficulties do not make one doubt, as I understand the subject; difficulty and doubt are incommensurate. There of course may be difficulties in the evidence, but I am speaking of difficulties intrinsic to the doctrines themselves, or to their relations with each other. A man may be annoyed that he cannot work out a mathematical problem, of which the answer is or is not given him, without doubting that it admits of an answer, or that a certain particular answer is the true one. Of all points of faith, the being of a God is, to my own apprehension, encompassed with most difficulty, and yet borne in upon our minds with most power. ("Apologia," pp. 238-239.)

XVII.

THE ANGLICAN CHURCH SEEN FROM WITHOUT.

I SAID, in a former page, that, on my conversion, I was not conscious of any change in me of thought or feeling, as regards matters of doctrine. This, however, was not the case as regards some matters of fact, and, unwilling as I am to give offence to religious Anglicans, I am bound to confess that I felt a great change in my view of the Church of England. I cannot tell how soon there came on me—but very soon—an extreme astonishment that I had ever imagined it to be a portion of the Catholic Church. For the first time, I looked at it from without, and (as I should myself say) saw it as it was. Forthwith I could not get myself to see in it anything else, than what I had so long fearfully suspected, from as far back as 1836,—a mere national institution. As if my eyes were suddenly opened, so I saw it—spontaneously, apart from any definite act of reason or any argument; and so I have seen it ever since. I suppose, the main cause of this lay in the contrast which was presented to me by the Catholic Church. Then I recognized at once a reality which was quite a new thing with me. Then I was sensible that I was not making for myself a Church by an effort of thought. I needed not to make an act of faith in her; I had not painfully to force myself into a position, but my mind fell back upon itself in relaxation and peace, and I gazed at her almost passively as a great objective fact. I looked at her;—at her rites, her ceremonial, and her precepts, and I said, "This *is* a religion;" and then, when I looked back upon the poor Anglican Church, for which I had laboured so hard, and upon all that appertained to it, and thought of our various attempts to dress it up doctrinally and æsthetically, it seemed to me to be the veriest of nonentities. Vanity of vanities, all is vanity! How can I make a record of what passed within me without seeming to be satirical? But I speak plain, serious words. As people call me credulous for acknowledging Catholic claims, so they call me satirical for disowning Anglican pretensions; to them it *is* credulity. to them it *is* satire; but it is not so in me. What they think exaggeration, I think truth. I am not speaking of the Anglican Church with any disdain, though to them I seem contemptuous. To them of course it is "Aut Cæsar aut nullus," but not to me. It may be a great creation though it *be* not divine, and this is how I judge of it. Men who abjure the divine right of kings would be very indignant, if on that account they were considered disloyal. And so I recognize in the Anglican Church[1] a time-honoured institution, of noble historical memories, a monument of ancient wisdom, a momentous arm of political strength, a great national organ, a source of vast popular advantage, and, to a certain point, a witness and teacher of religious truth. I do not think that, if what I have written about it since I have been a Catholic, be equitably considered as a whole, I shall be found to have taken any other view than this; but that it is something sacred, that it is an oracle of revealed doctrine, that it can claim a share in St. Ignatius or St. Cyprian, that it can take the rank, contest the teaching, and stop the path of the Church of St. Peter, that it can call itself "the Bride of the Lamb," this is the view of it which simply disappeared from my mind on my conversion, and which it would be almost a miracle to reproduce. "I went by, and lo! it was gone; I sought it, but its place could nowhere be found;" and nothing can bring it back to me. And, as to its possession of an episcopal succession from the time of the Apostles, well, it may have it, and if the Holy See ever so decide, I will believe it, as being the decision of a higher judgment than my own; but, for myself, I must have St. Philip's gift, who saw the sacerdotal character on the forehead of a gaily-attired youngster, before I can by my own wit acquiesce in it, for antiquarian arguments are altogether unequal to the urgency of visible facts. Why is it that I must pain dear friends by saying

---

[1] [See page 254.]

so, and kindle a sort of resentment against me in the kindest of hearts? But I must, though to do it be not only a grief to me, but most impolitic at the moment. Anyhow, this is my mind, and, if to have it, if to have betrayed it, before now, involuntarily, by my words or my deeds, if on a fitting occasion, as now, to have avowed it, if all this be a proof of the justice of the charge brought against me, of having "turned round upon my Mother-Church with contumely and slander," in this sense, but in no other sense, do I plead guilty to it without a word in extenuation.

In no other sense, surely. The Church of England has been the instrument of Providence in conferring great benefits on me;—had I been born in Dissent perhaps I should never have been baptized; had I been born an English Presbyterian, perhaps I should never have known our Lord's divinity; had I not come to Oxford, perhaps I never should have heard of the visible Church, or of Tradition, or other Catholic doctrines. And as I have received so much good from the Anglican Establishment itself, can I have the heart, or rather the want of charity, considering that it does for so many others, what it has done for me, to wish to see it overthrown? I have no such wish while it is what it is, and while we are so small a body. Not for its own sake, but for the sake of the many congregations to which it ministers, I will do nothing against it. While Catholics are so weak in England, it is doing our work; and though it does no harm in a measure, at present the balance is in our favour. What our duty would be at another time, and in other circumstances, supposing, for instance, the Establishment lost its dogmatic faith, or at least did not preach it, is another matter altogether. In secular history we read of hostile nations having long truces, and renewing them from time to time, and that seems to be the position which the Catholic Church may fairly take up at present in relation to the Anglican Establishment.

Doubtless the National Church has hitherto been a serviceable breakwater against doctrinal errors more fundamental than its own. How long this will last in the years now before us, it is impossible to say, for the Nation drags down its Church to its own level; but still the National Church has the same sort of influence over the nation that a periodical has upon the party which it represents, and my own idea of a Catholic's fitting attitude towards the National Church, in this its supreme hour, is that of assisting and sustaining it, if it be in our power, in the interest of dogmatic truth. I should wish to avoid everything (except, indeed, under the direct call of duty, and this is a material exception,) which went to weaken its hold upon the public mind, or to unsettle its establishment, or to embarrass and lessen its maintenance of those great Christian and Catholic principles and doctrines which it has, up to this time, successfully preached. ("Apologia," pp. 339–342.)

LETTER TO FATHER COLERIDGE ON ANGLICAN ORDERS.

The Oratory, Birmingham,
August 5, 1868.

MY DEAR FATHER COLERIDGE,—

You ask me what I precisely mean, in my "Apologia," .. by saying, *apropos* of Anglican Orders, that "antiquarian arguments are altogether unequal to the urgency of visible facts"[1] I will try to explain :—

---

[1] [Vide page 64.]

I. The inquiry into Anglican orders has ever been to me of the class which I must call dreary, for it is dreary, surely, to have to grope into the minute intricate passages and obscure corners of past occurrences in order to ascertain whether this man was ever consecrated; whether that man used a valid form; whether a certain sacramental intention came up to the mark; whether the report or register of an ecclesiastical act can be cleared of suspicion. On giving myself to consider the question, I never have been able to arrive at anything higher than a probable conclusion, which is most unsatisfactory, except to antiquarians, who delight in researches into the past for their own sake.

II. Now, on the other hand, what do I mean by "visible facts?" I mean such definite facts as throw a broad antecedent light upon what may be presumed, in a case in which sufficient evidence is not forthcoming. For instance :—

1. The Apostolical Succession, its necessity, and its grace, is not an Anglican tradition, though it is a tradition found in the Anglican Church. By contrast, our Lord's divinity *is* an Anglican tradition—every one, high and low, holds it. It is not only in Prayer Book and Catechism, but in the mouths of all professors of Anglicanism. Not to believe it, is to be no Anglican; and any persons in authority, for three hundred years, who were suspected to doubt or explain it away, were marked men, as Dr. Colenso is now marked. And they have been so few that they could be counted. Not such is the Apostolic Succession; and considering that the Church is the "*columna et firmamentum veritatis*," and is ever bound to stir up the gift that is in her, there is surely a strong presumption that the Anglican body has not, what it does not profess to have. I wonder how many of its bishops and deans hold the doctrine at this time; some who do not, occur to the mind at once. One knows what was the case thirty or forty years ago by the famous saying[1] of Blomfield, Bishop of London.

2. If there is a true Succession, there is a true Eucharist; if there is not a true Eucharist, there is no true Succession. Now, what is the presumption here? I think it is Mr. Alexander Knox who says or suggests, that if so great a gift be given, it must have a rite. I add, if it has a rite, it must have a *custos* of the rite. Who is the *custos* of the Anglican Eucharist? The Anglican clergy? Could I, without distressing or offending an Anglican, describe what sort of custodes they have been, and are to their Eucharist? "O bone custos," in the words of the poet, "cui commendavi Filium Meum!"

[1] [Vide page 21.]

Is it not charitable towards the bulk of the Anglican clergy to hope, to believe, that so great a treasure has not been given to their keeping? And, would our Lord leave Himself for centuries in such hands? Inasmuch, then, as "the Sacrament of the body and blood of Christ," in the Anglican communion is without protective ritual and jealous guardianship, there seems to me a strong presumption that neither the real gift, nor its appointed guardians, are to be found in that communion.

3. Previous baptism is the condition of the valid administration of the other sacraments. When I was in the Anglican Church I saw enough of the lax administration of baptism, even among High Churchmen, though they did not, of course, intend it, to fill me with great uneasiness. Of course there are definite persons, whom one might point out, whose baptisms are sure to be valid. But my argument has nothing to do with present baptisms. Bishops were baptized, not lately, but as children; the present bishops were consecrated by other bishops, they again by others. What I have seen in the Anglican Church makes it very difficult for me to deny that every now and then a bishop was a consecrator who had never been baptized. Some bishops have been brought up in the north as Presbyterians, others as Dissenters, others as Low Churchmen, others have been baptized in the careless perfunctory way once so common. There is, then, much reason to believe that some consecrators were not bishops for the simple reason that, formally speaking, they were not Christians. But, at least, there is a great presumption that where evidently our Lord has not provided a rigid rule of baptism, he has not provided a valid ordination.

By the light of such presumptions as these, I interpret the doubtful issues of the antiquarian argument, and feel deeply that if Anglican orders are unsafe with reference to the actual evidence producible for their validity, much more unsafe are they when considered in their surroundings.[1]

Most sincerely yours,
JOHN H. NEWMAN.

(Essays Crit. and Hist. vol. ii. p. 109.)

[1] [The question of "Anglican Orders" is discussed more fully at p. 258.]

PART II.

PHILOSOPHICAL.

INTELLECTUAL EDUCATION PRE-EMINENTLY A DISCIPLINE IN ACCURACY OF MIND.

It has often been observed that, when the eyes of the infant first open upon the world, the reflected rays of light which strike them from the myriad of surrounding objects presents to him no image, but a medley of colours and shadows. They do not form into a whole; they do not rise into foregrounds and melt into distances; they do not divide into groups; they do not coalesce into unities; they do not combine into persons; but each particular hue and tint stands by itself, wedged in amid a thousand others upon the vast and flat mosaic, having no intelligence, and conveying no story, any more than the wrong side of some rich tapestry. The little babe stretches out his arms and fingers, as if to grasp or to fathom the many-coloured vision; and thus he gradually learns the connection of part with part, separates what moves from what is stationary, watches the coming and going of figures, masters the idea of shape and of perspective, calls in the information conveyed through the other senses to assist him in his mental process, and thus gradually converts a kaleidoscope into a picture. The first view was the more splendid, the second the more real; the former more poetical, the latter more philosophical. Alas! what are we doing all through life, both as a necessity and as a duty, but unlearning the world's poetry, and attaining to its prose! This is our education, as boys and as men, in the action of life, and in the closet or library; in our affections, in our aims, in our hopes, and in our memories. And in like manner it is the education of our intellect; I say, that one main portion of intellectual education, of the labours of both school and university, is to remove the original dimness of the mind's eye; to strengthen and perfect its vision; to enable it to look out into the world right forward, steadily and truly; to give the mind clearness, accuracy, precision; to enable it to use words aright, to understand what it says, to conceive justly what it thinks about, to abstract, compare, analyze, divide, define, and reason, correctly. There is a particular science which takes these matters in hand, and it is called logic; but it is not by logic, certainly not by logic alone, that the faculty I speak of is acquired. The infant does not learn to spell and read the hues upon his retina by any scientific rule; nor does the student learn accuracy of thought by any manual or treatise. The instruction given him, of whatever kind, if it be really instruction, is mainly, or at least pre-eminently, this,—a discipline in accuracy of mind.

Boys are always more or less inaccurate, and too many, or rather the majority, remain boys all their lives. When, for instance, I hear speakers at public meetings declaiming about "large and enlightened views," or about "freedom of conscience," or about "the Gospel," or any other popular subject of the day, I am far from denying that some among them know what they are talking about; but it would be satisfactory, in a particular case, to be sure of the fact; for it seems to me that those household words may stand in a man's mind for a something or other, very glorious indeed, but very misty, pretty much like the idea of "civilization" which floats before the mental vision of a

Turk,—that is, if, when he interrupts his smoking to utter the word, he condescends to reflect whether it has any meaning at all. Again, a critic, in a periodical, dashes off, perhaps, his praises of a new work, as "talented, original, replete with intense interest, irresistible in argument, and, in the best sense of the word, a very readable book;"—can we believe that he cares to attach any definite sense to the words of which he is so lavish? nay, that, if he had a habit of attaching sense to them, he could ever bring himself to so prodigal and wholesale an expenditure of them?

To a short-sighted person, colours run together and intermix, outlines disappear, blues and reds and yellows become russets or browns; the lamps and candles of an illumination spread into an unmeaning glare, or dissolve into a milky way. He takes up an eye-glass, and the mist clears up, every image stands out distinct, and the rays of light fall back upon their centres. It is this haziness of intellectual vision which is the malady of all classes of men by nature, of those who read and write and compose, quite as well as of those who cannot,—of all who have not had a really good education. Those who cannot read or write may, nevertheless, be in the number of those who have remedied and got rid of it; those who can, are too often under its power. It is an acquisition quite separate from miscellaneous information, or knowledge of books. ("Idea of a University," p. 331.)

THE POPULAR CONCEPTION OF AN "INTELLECTUAL MAN."

An intellectual man, as the world now conceives of him, is one who is full of "views" on all subjects of philosophy, on all matters of the day. It is almost thought a disgrace not to have a view at a moment's notice on any question from the Personal Advent to the Cholera or Mesmerism. This is owing in great measure to the necessities of periodical literature, now so much in request. Every quarter of a year, every month, every day there must be a supply, for the gratification of the public, of new and luminous theories on the subjects of religion, foreign politics, home politics, civil economy, finance, trade, agriculture, emigration, and the colonies. Slavery, the gold fields, German philosophy, the French Empire, Wellington, Peel, Ireland, must all be practised on, day after day, by what are called original thinkers. As the great man's guest must produce his good stories or songs at the evening banquet, as the platform orator exhibits his telling facts at mid-day, so the journalist lies under the stern obligation of extemporizing his lucid views, leading ideas, and nutshell truths for the breakfast-table. The very nature of periodical literature, broken into small wholes, and demanded punctually to an hour, involves the habit of this extempore philosophy. "Almost all the Ramblers," says Boswell of Johnson, "were written just as they were wanted for the press; he sent a certain portion of the copy of an essay, and wrote the remainder while the former part of it was printing." Few men have the gifts of Johnson, who to great vigour and resource of intellect, when it was fairly roused, united a rare common-sense and a conscientious regard for veracity, which preserved him from flippancy or extravagance in writing. Few men are Johnsons; yet how many men at this day are assailed by incessant demands on their mental powers, which only a productiveness like his could suitably supply! There is a demand for a reckless originality of thought, and a sparkling plausibility of argument, which he would have despised, even if he could have displayed; a demand for crude theory and unsound philosophy, rather than none at all. It is a sort of repetition of the "Quid novi?" of the Areopagus, and it must have an answer. Men must be found who can treat, where it is necessary, like the Athenian sophist, *de omni scibili*,

> "Grammaticus, Rhetor, Geometres, Pictor, Aliptes,
>   Augur, Schœnobates, Medicus, Magus, omnia novit."

I am speaking of such writers with a feeling of real sympathy for men who are under the rod of a cruel slavery. I have never indeed been in such circumstances myself, nor in the temptations which they involve; but most men who have had to do with composition must know the distress which at times it occasions them to have to write—a distress sometimes so keen and so specific that it resembles nothing else than bodily pain. That pain is the token of the wear and tear of mind; and, if works done comparatively at leisure involve such mental fatigue and exhaustion, what must be the toil of those whose intellects are to be flaunted daily before the public in full dress, and that dress ever new and varied, and spun, like the silk-worm's, out of themselves! Still, whatever true sympathy we may feel for the ministers of this dearly purchased luxury, and whatever sense we may have of the great intellectual power which the literature in question displays, we cannot honestly close our eyes to its direct evil. ("Idea of a University," Pref. xx.)

THE ORIGIN OF POLITICAL AND RELIGIOUS WATCHWORDS.

MANY a disciple of a philosophical school, who talks fluently, does but assert, when he seems to assent to the *dicta* of his master, little as he may be aware of it. Nor is he secured against this self-deception by knowing the arguments on which those *dicta* rest, for he may learn the arguments by heart, as a careless schoolboy gets up his Euclid. This practice of asserting simply on authority, with the pretence and without the reality of assent, is what is meant by formalism. To say "I do not understand a proposition, but I accept it on authority," is not formalism; it is not a direct assent to the proposition, still it *is* an assent to the authority which enunciates it; but what I here speak of is professing to understand without understanding. It is thus that political and religious watchwords are created; first one man of name and then another adopts them, till their use becomes popular, and then every one professes them, because every one else does. Such words are "liberality," "progress," "light," "civilization;" such are "justification by faith only," "vital religion," "private judgment," "the Bible, and nothing but the Bible." Such, again, are "Rationalism," "Gallicanism," "Jesuitism," "Ultramontanism"—all of which, in the mouths of conscientious thinkers, have a definite meaning, but are used by the multitude as war-cries, nicknames, and shibboleths, with scarcely enough of the scantiest grammatical apprehension of them to allow of their being considered really more than assertions. ("Grammar of Assent," p. 41.)

REAL APPREHENSION OF THE AFFECTIONS AND
PASSIONS POSSIBLE ONLY BY EXPERIENCE.

THE affections and passions of our nature are *sui generis* respectively, and incommensurable, and must be severally experienced in order to be apprehended really.[1] I can understand the *rabbia* of a native of Southern Europe, if I am of a passionate temper myself; and the taste for speculation or betting found in great traders or on the turf, if I am fond of enterprise or games of chance; but, on the other hand, not all the possible descriptions of headlong love will make me comprehend the *delirium*, if I have never had a fit of it; nor will ever so many sermons about the inward satisfaction of strict conscientiousness create the image of a virtuous action in my mind, if I have been brought up to lie, thieve, and indulge my appetites. Thus we meet with men of the world who cannot enter into the very idea of devotion, and think, for instance, that, from the nature of the case, a life of religious seclusion must be either one of unutterable dreariness or abandoned sensuality, because they know of no exercise of the affections but what is merely human; and with others again, who, living in the home of their own selfishness, ridicule as something fanatical and pitiable the self-sacrifices of generous high-mindedness and chivalrous honour. They cannot create images of these things, any more than children can on the contrary of vice, when they ask where and who the bad men are; for they have no personal memories, and have to content themselves with notions drawn from books or the intercourse of life. ("Grammar of Assent," p. 27.)

[1] [Really: *i.e.*, as *things*, not as *notions*.]

REALIZATION.

Let us consider, too, how differently young and old are affected by the words of some classic author, such as Homer or Horace. Passages which to a boy are but rhetorical commonplaces, neither better nor worse than a hundred others which any clever writer might supply, which he gets by heart and thinks very fine, and imitates, as he thinks, successfully, in his own flowing versification, at length come home to him, when long years have passed, and he has had experience of life, and pierce him, as if he had never before known them, with their sad earnestness and vivid exactness. Then he comes to understand how it is that lines, the birth of some chance morning or evening at an Ionian festival, or among the Sabine hills, have lasted generation after generation, for thousands of years, with a power over the mind, and a charm, which the current literature of his own day, with all its obvious advantages, is utterly unable to rival. Perhaps this is the reason of the mediæval opinion about Virgil, as if a prophet or magician; his single words and phrases, his pathetic half lines, giving utterance, as the voice of Nature herself, to that pain and weariness, yet hope of better things, which is the experience of her children in every time.

And what the experience of the world effects for the illustration of classical authors, that office the religious sense, carefully cultivated, fulfils towards Holy Scripture. To the devout and spiritual, the Divine Word speaks of things, not merely of notions. And, again, to the disconsolate, the tempted, the perplexed, the suffering, there comes, by means of their very trials, an enlargement of thought, which enables them to see in it what they never saw before. Henceforth there is to them a reality in its teachings, which they recognize as an argument, and the best of arguments, for its divine origin. Hence the practice of meditation on the Sacred Text, so highly thought of by Catholics. Reading, as we do, the gospels from our youth up, we are in danger of becoming so familiar with them as to be dead to their force, and to view them as a mere history. The purpose, then, of meditation is to realize them; to make the facts which they relate stand out before our minds as objects, such as may be appropriated by a faith as living as the imagination which apprehends them.

It is obvious to refer to the unworthy use made of the more solemn parts of the sacred volume by the mere popular preacher. His very mode of reading, whether warnings or prayers, is as if he thought them to be little more than fine writing, poetical in sense, musical in sound, and worthy of inspiration. The most awful truths are to him but sublime or beautiful conceptions, and are adduced and used by him, in season, and out of season, for his own purposes, for embellishing his style or rounding his periods. But let his heart at length be ploughed by some keen grief or deep anxiety, and Scripture is a new book to him. This is the change which so often takes place in what is called religious conversion, and it is a change so far simply for the better, by whatever infirmity or error it is in the particular case accompanied. And it is strikingly suggested to us, to take a saintly example, in the confession of the patriarch Job, when he contrasts his apprehension of the Almighty before and after his afflictions. He says he had indeed a true apprehension of the Divine Attributes before them as well as after; but with the trial came a great change in the character of that apprehension:—
"With the hearing of the ear," he says, "I have heard

Thee, but now mine eye seeth Thee; therefore I reprehend myself, and do penance in dust and ashes." ("Grammar of Assent," p. 75.)

OUR NOTIONS OF THINGS MERELY ASPECTS OF THEM.

OUR notions of things are never simply commensurate with the things themselves; they are aspects of them, more or less exact, and sometimes a mistake *ab initio*. Take an instance from arithmetic :—We are accustomed to subject all that exists to numeration; but, to be correct, we are bound first to reduce to some level of possible comparison the things which we wish to number. We must be able to say, not only that they are ten, twenty, or a hundred, but so many different somethings. For instance, we could not without extravagance throw together Napoleon's brain, ambition, hand, soul, smile, height, and age at Marengo, and say that there were seven of them, though there are seven words; nor will it even be enough to content ourselves with what may be called a negative level, viz. that these seven were an un-English or are a departed seven. Unless numeration is to issue in nonsense, it must be conducted on conditions. This being the case, there are, for what we know, collections of beings to whom the notion of number cannot be attached, except catachrestically, because, taken individually, no positive point of real agreement can be found between them, by which to call them. If, indeed, we can denote them by a plural noun, then we can measure that plurality; but if they agree in nothing, they cannot agree in bearing a common name, and to say that they amount to a thousand these or those, is not to number them, but to count up a certain number of names or words which we have written down.

Thus, the Angels have been considered by divines to have each of them a species to himself; and we may fancy each of them so absolutely *sui similis* as to be like nothing else, so that it would be as untrue to speak of a thousand Angels as of a thousand Hannibals or Ciceros. It will be said, indeed, that all beings but One at least will come under the notion of creatures, and are dependent upon that One; but that it is true of the brain, smile, and height of Napoleon, which no one would call three creatures. But, if all this be so, much more does it apply to our speculations concerning the Supreme Being, whom it may be unmeaning, not only to number with other beings, but to subject to number in regard to His own intrinsic characteristics. That is, to apply arithmetical notions to Him may be as unphilosophical as it is profane. Though He is at once Father, Son, and Holy Ghost, the word "Trinity" belongs to those notions of Him which are forced on us by the necessity of our finite conceptions, the real and immutable distinction which exists between Person and Person, implying in itself no infringement of His real and numerical Unity. And if it be asked how, if we cannot speak of Him as Three, we can speak of Him as One, I reply that He is not One in the way in which created things are severally units; for one, as applied to ourselves, is used in contrast to two or three and a whole series of numbers; but of the Supreme Being it is safer to use the word "monad" than unit, for He has not even such relation to His creatures as to allow, philosophically speaking, of our contrasting Him with them. ("Grammar of Assent," p. 47.)

HOW MEN REALLY REASON IN CONCRETE MATTERS.

(I.)

It is plain that formal logical sequence is not in fact the method by which we are enabled to become certain of what is concrete; and it is equally plain what the real and necessary method is. It is the cumulation of probabilities, independent of each other, arising out of the nature and circumstances of the particular case which is under review; probabilities too fine to avail separately, too subtle and circuitous to be convertible into syllogisms, too numerous and various for such conversion, even were they convertible. As a man's portrait differs from a sketch of him in having, not merely a continuous outline, but all its details filled in, and shades and colours laid on and harmonized together, such is the multiform and intricate process of ratiocination, necessary for our reaching him as a concrete fact, compared with the rude operation of syllogistic treatment.

Let us suppose I wish to convert an educated, thoughtful Protestant, and accordingly present for his acceptance a syllogism of the following kind:—"All Protestants are bound to join the Church; you are a Protestant: ergo." He answers, we will say, by denying both premisses; and he does so by means of arguments, which branch out into other arguments, and those into others, and all of them severally requiring to be considered by him on their own merits, before the syllogism reaches him, and in consequence mounting up, taken altogether, into an array of inferential exercises large and various beyond calculation. Moreover, he is bound to submit himself to this complicated process from the nature of the case; he would act rashly, if he did not; for he is a concrete individual unit, and being so, is under so many laws, and is the subject of so many predications all at once, that he cannot determine, off-hand, his position and his duty by the law and the predication of one syllogism in particular. I mean, he will fairly say, "Distinguo," to each of its premisses: he says, "Protestants are bound to join the Church—under circumstances," and "I am a Protestant—in a certain sense;" and therefore the syllogism, at first sight, does not touch him at all.

Before, then, he grants the major, he asks whether all Protestants really are bound to join the Church—are they bound in case they do not feel themselves bound; if they are satisfied that their present religion is a safe one; if they are sure it is true; if, on the other hand, they have grave doubts as to the doctrinal fidelity and purity of the Church; if they are convinced that the Church is corrupt; if their conscience instinctively rejects certain of its doctrines; if history convinces them that the Pope's power is not *jure divino*, but merely in the order of Providence? if, again, they are in a heathen country where priests are not? or where the only priest who is to be found exacts of them, as a condition of their reception, a profession, which the Creed of Pope Pius IV. says nothing about; for instance, that the Holy See is fallible even when it teaches, or that the Temporal Power is an anti-Christian corruption? On one or other of such grounds he thinks he need not change his religion; but presently he asks himself, can a Protestant be in such a state as to be really satisfied with his religion, as he has just now been professing? Can he possibly believe Protestantism came from above as a whole? how much of it can he believe came from above? and, as to that portion which he feels did come from above, has it not all been derived to him from the Church, when traced to its source? Is not Protestantism in itself a negation? Did not the Church exist before it? and can he be sure, on the other hand, that any one of the Church's doctrines is not from above? Further, he finds he has to make up his mind what is a corruption, and what are the tests of it; what he means by a religion; whether it is obligatory to profess any religion in particular; what are the standards of truth and falsehood in religion; and what are the special claims of the Church.

And so, again, as to the minor premiss, perhaps he will answer, that he is not a Protestant; that he is a Catholic of the early undivided Church; that he is a Catholic, but not a Papist. Then he has to determine questions about division, schism, visible unity, what is essential, what is desirable; about provisional states; as to the adjustment of the Church's claims with those of personal judgment and responsibility; as to the soul of the Church contrasted with the body; as to degrees of proof, and the degree necessary for his conversion; as to what is called his providential position, and the responsibility of change; as to the sincerity of his purpose to follow the Divine Will, whithersoever it may lead him; as to his intellectual capacity of investigating such questions at all.

None of these questions, as they come before him, admit of simple demonstration; but each carries with it a number of independent probable arguments, sufficient, when united, for a reasonable conclusion about itself. And first he determines that the questions are such as he personally, with such talents or attainments as he has, may fairly entertain; and then he goes on, after deliberation, to form a definite judgment upon them; and determines them, one way or another, in their bearing on the bald syllogism which was originally offered to his acceptance. And, we will say, he comes to the conclusion, that he ought to accept it as true in his case; that he is a Protestant in such a sense, of such a complexion, of such knowledge, under such circumstances, as to be called upon by duty to join the Church; that this is a conclusion of which he can be certain, and ought to be certain, and that he will be incurring grave responsibility, if he does not accept it as certain, and act upon the certainty of it. And to this conclusion he comes, as is plain, not by any possible verbal enumeration of all the considerations, minute but abundant, delicate but effective, which unite to bring him to it; but by a mental comprehension of the whole case, and a discernment of its upshot, sometimes after much deliberation, but, it may be, by a clear and rapid act of the intellect, always, however, by an unwritten summing-up, something like the summation of the terms of an algebraical series. ("Grammar of Assent," p. 281.)

(II.)

THIS is the mode in which we ordinarily reason, dealing with things directly, and as they stand, one by one, in the concrete, with an intrinsic and personal power, not a conscious adoption of an artificial instrument or expedient; and it is especially exemplified both in uneducated men, and in men of genius—in those who know nothing of intellectual aids and rules, and in those who care nothing for them—in those who are either without or above mental discipline. As true poetry is a spontaneous outpouring of thought, and therefore belongs to rude as well as to gifted minds, whereas no one becomes a poet merely by the canons of criticism, so this unscientific reasoning, being sometimes a natural, uncultivated faculty, sometimes approaching to a gift, sometimes an acquired habit and second nature, has a higher source than logical rule—"nascitur, non fit." When it is characterized by precision, subtlety, promptitude, and truth, it is of course a gift and a rarity: in ordinary minds it is biassed and degraded by prejudice, passion, and self-interest; but still, after all, this divination comes by nature, and belongs to all of us in a measure, to women more than to men, hitting or missing, as the case may be, but with a success on the whole sufficient to show that there is a method in it, though it be implicit.

A peasant who is weather-wise may be simply unable to assign intelligible reasons why he thinks it will be fine to-morrow, and if he attempts to do so he may give reasons wide of the mark; but that will not weaken his own confidence in his prediction. His mind does not proceed step by step, but he feels all at once the force of various combined phenomena, though he is not conscious of them. Again, there are physicians who excel in the *diagnosis* of complaints; though it does not follow from this, that they could defend their decision in a particular case against a brother physician who disputed it. They are guided by natural acuteness and varied experience; they have their own idiosyncratic modes of observing, generalizing, and concluding; when questioned, they can but rest on their own authority, or appeal to the future event. In a popular novel[1] a lawyer is introduced who "would know, almost by instinct, whether an accused person was or was not guilty; and he had already perceived by instinct" that the heroine was guilty. "I've no doubt she's a clever woman,' he said, and at once named an attorney practising at the Old Bailey. So, again, experts and detectives, when employed to investigate mysteries, in cases whether of the

"Orley Farm."

civil or criminal law, discern and follow out indications which promise solution with a sagacity incomprehensible to ordinary men. A parallel gift is the intuitive perception of character possessed by certain men, while others are as destitute of it, as others again are of an ear for music. What common measure is there between the judgments of those who have this intuition, and those who have not? What but the event can settle any difference of opinion with which they regard a third person? These are instances of a natural capacity, or of nature improved by practice and habit, enabling the mind to pass promptly from one set of facts to another, not only, I say, without conscious media, but without conscious antecedents.

Sometimes, I say, this illative faculty is nothing short of genius. Such seems to have been Newton's perception of truths mathematical and physical, though proof was absent. At least that is the impression left on my own mind by various stories which are told of him, one of which was stated in the public papers a few years ago. "Professor Sylvester," it was said, "has just discovered the proof of Sir Isaac Newton's rule for ascertaining the imaginary roots of equations. . . This rule has been a Gordian-knot among algebraists for the last century and a half. The proof being wanting, authors became ashamed at length of advancing a proposition, the evidence for which rested on no other foundation than belief in Newton's sagacity."[1]

Such is the gift of the calculating boys who now and then make their appearance, who seem to have certain short cuts to conclusions which they cannot explain to themselves. Some are said to have been able to determine off-hand what numbers are prime—numbers, I think, up to seven places.

[1] *Guardian*, June 28, 1865.

In a very different subject-matter, Napoleon supplies us with an instance of a parallel genius in reasoning, by which he was enabled to look at things in his own province, and to interpret them truly, apparently without any ratiocinative media. "By long experience," says Alison, "joined to great natural quickness and precision of eye, he had acquired the power of judging, with extraordinary accuracy, both of the amount of the enemy's force opposed to him in the field, and the probable result of the movements, even the most complicated, going forward in the opposite armies. . . He looked around him for a little while with his telescope, and instantly formed a clear conception of the position, forces, and intention of the whole hostile array. In this way he could, with surprising accuracy, calculate in a few minutes, according to what he could see of their formation and the extent of the ground which they occupied, the numerical force of armies of 60,000 or 80,000 men; and if their troops were at all scattered, he knew at once how long it would require for them to concentrate, and how many hours must elapse before they could make their attack."[1]

It is difficult to avoid calling such clear presentiments by the name of instinct; and I think they may be so called, if by instinct be understood, not a natural sense, one and the same in all, and incapable of cultivation, but a perception of facts without assignable media of perceiving. There are those who can tell at once what is conducive or injurious to their welfare, who are their friends, who their enemies, what is to happen to them, and how they are to meet it. Presence of mind, fathoming of motives, talent for repartee, are instances of this gift. As to that divination of personal danger which is found in the young and

---

[1] History, vol. x. pp. 286, 287.

innocent, we find a description of it in one of Scott's romances, in which the heroine, "without being able to discover what was wrong either in the scenes of unusual luxury with which she was surrounded, or in the manner of her hostess," is said nevertheless to have felt "an instinctive apprehension that all was not right—a feeling in the human mind," the author proceeds to say, "allied perhaps to that sense of danger which animals exhibit when placed in the vicinity of the natural enemies of their race, and which makes birds cower when the hawk is in the air, and beasts tremble when the tiger is abroad in the desert." [1]

A religious biography, lately published, affords us an instance of this spontaneous perception of truth in the province of revealed doctrine. "Her firm faith," says the Author of the Preface, "was so vivid in its character, that it was almost like an intuition of the entire prospect of revealed truth. Let an error against faith be concealed under expressions however abstruse, and her sure instinct found it out. I have tried this experiment repeatedly. She might not be able to separate the heresy by analysis, but she saw, and felt, and suffered from its presence." [2]

And so of the great fundamental truths of religion, natural and revealed, and as regards the mass of religious men: these truths, doubtless, may be proved and defended by an array of invincible logical arguments, but such is not commonly the method in which they make their way into our minds. The grounds, on which we hold the divine origin of the Church, and the previous truths which are taught us by nature—the being of a God, and the immortality of the soul—are felt by most men to

---

[1] "Peveril of the Peak."
[2] "Life of Mother Margaret M. Hallahan," p. vii.

be recondite and impalpable, in proportion to their depth and reality. As we cannot see ourselves, so we cannot well see intellectual motives which are so intimately ours, and which spring up from the very constitution of our minds; and while we refuse to admit the notion that religion has not irrefragable arguments in its behalf, still the attempts to argue, in the case of an individual *hic et nunc*, will sometimes only confuse his apprehension of sacred objects, and subtracts from his devotion quite as much as it adds to his knowledge.

This is found in the case of other perceptions besides that of faith. It is the case of nature against art: of course, if possible, nature and art should be combined, but sometimes they are incompatible. Thus, in the case of calculating boys, it is said, I know not with what truth, that to teach them the ordinary rules of arithmetic is to endanger or to destroy the extraordinary endowment. And men who have the gift of playing on an instrument by ear, are sometimes afraid to learn by rule, lest they should lose it.

There is an analogy, in this respect, between Ratiocination and Memory, though the latter may be exercised without antecedents or media, whereas the former requires them in its very idea. At the same time association has so much to do with memory, that we may not unfairly consider that memory, as well as reasoning, depends on certain conditions. Writing is a *memoria technica*, or logic of memory. Now it will be found, I think, that, indispensable as is the use of letters, still, in fact, we weaken our memory in proportion as we habituate ourselves to commit all that we wish to remember to memorandums. Of course, in proportion as our memory is weak or overburdened, and thereby treacherous, we cannot help ourselves; but in the case of men of strong memory, in any particular subject-matter, as in that of dates, all artificial expedients, from the "Thirty days has September," &c., to the more formidable formulas in use, are as difficult and repulsive as the natural exercise of memory is healthy and easy to them; just as the clear-headed and practical reasoner, who sees conclusions at a glance, is uncomfortable under the drill of a logician, being oppressed and hampered, as David in Saul's armour, by what is intended to be a benefit.

I need not say more on this part of the subject. What is called reasoning is often only a peculiar and personal mode of abstraction, and so far, like memory, may be said to exist without antecedents. It is a power of looking at things in some particular aspect, and of determining their internal and external relations thereby. And according to the subtlety and versatility of their gift, are men able to read what comes before them justly, variously, and fruitfully. Hence, too, it is that in our intercourse with others, in business and family matters, social and political transactions, a word or an act on the part of another is sometimes a sudden revelation; light breaks in upon us, and our whole judgment of a course of events, or of an undertaking, is changed. We determine correctly, or otherwise, as it may be; but in either case, by a sense proper to ourselves, for another may see the objects which we are thus using, and give them quite a different interpretation, inasmuch as he abstracts another set of general notions from those same phenomena which present themselves to us. ("Ibid," p. 324.)

INTELLECTUAL OBSTRUCTIONS.

As even Saints may suffer from imaginations in which they have no part, so the shreds and tatters of former controversies, and the litter of an argumentative habit, may beset and obstruct the intellect—questions which have been solved without their solutions, chains of reasoning with missing links, difficulties which have their roots in the nature of things, and which are necessarily left behind in a philosophical enquiry because they cannot be removed, and which call for the exercise of good sense and for strength of will to put them down with a high hand, as irrational or preposterous. Whence comes evil? why are we created without our consent? how can the Supreme Being have no beginning? how can He need skill, if He is Omnipotent? if He is Omnipotent, why does He permit suffering? if He permits suffering, how is He all-loving? if He is all-loving, how can He be just? if He is infinite, what has He to do with the finite? how can the temporary be decisive of the eternal?—these, and a host of like questions, must arise in every thoughtful mind, and, after the best use of reason, must be deliberately put aside, as beyond reason, as (so to speak) no-thoroughfares, which, having no outlet themselves, have no legitimate power to divert us from the King's highway, and to hinder the direct course of religious enquiry from reaching its destination. A serious obstruction, however, they will be now and then to particular minds, enfeebling the faith which they cannot destroy—being parallel to the uncomfortable association with which we regard one whom we have fallen in with, acquaintance or stranger, arising from some chance word, look, or action of his which we have witnessed and which prejudices him in our imagination, though we are angry with ourselves that it should do so. ("Grammar of Assent," p. 210.)

THE LAWS OF THE MIND THE EXPRESSION OF THE DIVINE WILL.

As the structure of the universe speaks to us of Him who made it, so the laws of the mind are the expression, not of mere constituted order, but of His will. I should be bound by them even were they not His laws; but since one of their very functions is to tell me of Him, they throw a reflex light upon themselves, and, for resignation to my destiny, I substitute a cheerful concurrence in an over-ruling Providence. We may gladly welcome such difficulties as there are in our mental constitution, and in the inter-action of our faculties, if we are able to feel that He gave them to us, and He can overrule them for us. We may securely take them as they are, and use them as we find them. It is He who teaches us all knowledge; and the way by which we acquire it is His way. He varies that way according to the subject-matter; but whether He has set before us in our particular pursuit the way of observation or of experiment, of speculation or of research, of demonstration or of probability, whether we are enquiring into the system of the universe, or into the elements of matter and of life, or into the history of human society and past times, if we take the way proper to our subject-matter, we have His blessing upon us, and shall find, besides abundant matter for mere opinion, the materials in due measure of proof and assent.

And especially, by this disposition of things, shall we learn, as regards religious and ethical inquiries, how little we can effect, however much we exert ourselves, without that blessing; for, as if on set purpose, He has made this path of thought rugged and circuitous above other investigations, that the very discipline inflicted on our minds in finding Him, may mould them into due devotion to Him when He is found. "Verily, Thou art a hidden God, the God of Israel, the Saviour," is the very law of His dealings with us. Certainly we need a clue into the labyrinth which is to lead us to Him; and who among us can hope to seize upon the true starting-points of thought for that enterprise, and upon all of them, to understand their right direction, to follow them out to their just limits, and duly to estimate, adjust, and combine the various reasonings in which they issue, so as safely to arrive at what is worth any labour to secure, without a special illumination from Himself? Such are the dealings of Wisdom with the elect soul. "She will bring upon him fear, and dread, and trial; and She will torture him with the tribulation of Her discipline, till she try him by Her laws, and trust his soul. Then She will strengthen him, and make Her way straight to him, and give him joy." ("Grammar of Assent," p. 344.)

FIRST PRINCIPLES.

THIS is what we call an enlightened age; we are to have large views of things; everything is to be put on a philosophical basis; reason is to rule; the world is to begin again; a new and transporting set of views is about to be exhibited to the great human family. Well and good; have them, preach them, enjoy them, but deign to recollect the while, that there have been views in the world before you; that the world has not been going on up to this day without any principles whatever; that the Old Religion was based on principles, and that it is not enough to flourish about your " new lamps," if you would make us give up our " old " ones. Catholicism, I say, had its First Principles before you were born; you say they are false; very well, prove them to be so; they are false, indeed, if yours are true; but not false merely because yours are yours. While yours are yours it is self-evident, indeed, to you, that ours are false; but it is not the common way of carrying on business in the world, to value English goods by French measures, or to pay a debt in paper which was contracted in gold. Catholicism has its First Principles. Overthrow them, if you can; endure them, if you cannot. It is not enough to call them effete, because they are old, or antiquated because they are ancient. It is not enough to look into our Churches, and cry "It is all a form, *because* divine favour cannot depend on external observances;" or, " It is all a bondage, *because* there is no such thing as sin;" or, " a blasphemy, *because* the Supreme Being cannot be present in ceremonies;" or; " a mummery, *because* prayer cannot move Him ;" or, "a tyranny, *because* vows are unnatural;" or, " hypocrisy, *because* no rational man can credit it at all?" I say here is endless assumption, unmitigated hypothesis, reckless assertion. Prove your, "because," " because," " because;" prove your First Principles, and if you cannot, learn philosophic moderation. Why may not my First Principles contest the prize with yours? they have been longer in the world, they have lasted longer, they have done harder work, they have seen rougher service! You sit in your easy-chairs, you dogmatize in your lecture-rooms, you wield your pens: it all looks well on paper: you write exceedingly well: there never was an age in which there was better writing, logical, nervous, eloquent, and pure,—go and carry it all out in the world. Take your First Principles, of which you are so proud, into the crowded streets of our cities, into the formidable classes which make up the bulk of our population; try to work society by them. You think you can; I say you cannot— at least, you have not as yet; it is to be seen if you can. "Let not him that putteth on his armour boast as he who taketh it off." Do not take it for granted that that is certain which is waiting the test of reason and experiment. Be modest until you are victorious. My principles, which I believe to be eternal, have at least lasted eighteen hundred years; let yours live as many months. That man can sin, that he has duties, that the Divine Being hears prayer, that He gives His favours through visible ordinances, that He is really present in the midst of them, these principles have been the life of nations; they have shown they could be carried out; let any single nation carry out yours, and you will have better claim to speak contemptuously of Catholic rites, of Catholic devotions, of Catholic belief. ("Present Position of Catholics," p. 293.)

THE ETHICS OF CULTURE.

(I.)

THE embellishment of the exterior is almost the beginning and the end of philosophical morality. This is why it aims at being modest rather than humble; this is how it can be proud at the very time that it is unassuming. To humility indeed it does not even aspire; humility is one of the most difficult of virtues, both to attain and to ascertain. It lies close upon the heart itself, and its tests are exceedingly delicate and subtle. Its counterfeits abound; however, we are little concerned with them here, for, I repeat, it is hardly professed, even by name, in the code of ethics which we are reviewing. As has been often observed, ancient civilization had not the idea, and had no word to express it; or rather, it had the idea, and considered it a defect of mind, not a virtue, so that the word which denoted it conveyed a reproach. As to the modern world, you may gather its ignorance of it by its perversion of the somewhat parallel term "condescension." Humility, or condescension, viewed as a virtue of conduct, may be said to consist, as in other things, so in our placing ourselves in our thoughts on a level with our inferiors. It is not only a voluntary relinquishment of the privileges of our own station, but an actual participation or assumption of the condition of those to whom we stoop. This is true humility, to feel and to behave as if we were low; not to cherish a notion of our importance while we affect a low position. Such was St. Paul's humility, when he called himself "the least of the saints;" such the humility of those many holy men who have considered themselves the greatest of sinners. It is an abdication, as far as their own thoughts are concerned, of those prerogatives or privileges to which others deem them entitled. Now it is not a little instructive to contrast with this idea,—with this theological meaning of the word "condescension,"—its proper English sense; put them in juxtaposition, and you will at once see the difference between the world's humility and the humility of the Gospel. As the world uses the word, "condescension" is a stooping indeed

of the person, but a bending forward unattended with any
the slightest effort to leave by a single inch the seat in
which it is so firmly established. It is the act of a superior, who protests to himself, while he commits it, that he
is superior still, and that he is doing nothing else but an
act of grace towards those on whose level, in theory, he is
placing himself. And this is the nearest idea which the
philosopher can form of the virtue of self-abasement; to
do more than this is, to his mind, a meanness, or an hypocrisy, and at once excites his suspicion and disgust. What
the world is, such it has ever been; we know the contempt
which the educated pagans had for the martyrs and confessors of the Church, and it is shared by the anti-Catholic
bodies of this day.

Such are the ethics of Philosophy, when faithfully represented; but an age like this, not pagan, but professedly
Christian, cannot venture to reprobate humility in set
terms, or to make a boast of pride. Accordingly, it looks
out for some expedient by which it may blind itself to the
real state of the case. Humility, with its grave and self-
denying attributes, it cannot love; but what is more beautiful, what more winning, than modesty? What virtue, at
first sight, simulates humility so well? Though what, in
fact, is more radically distinct from it? In truth, great as
is its charm, modesty is not the deepest or the most religious of virtues. Rather it is the advanced guard or
sentinel of the soul militant, and watches continually over
its nascent intercourse with the world about it. It goes
the round of the senses; it mounts up into the countenance; it protects the eye and ear; it reigns in the voice
and gesture. Its province is the outward deportment, as
other virtues have relation to matters theological, others
to society, and others to the mind itself. And being more
superficial than other virtues, it is more easily disjoined

from their company; it admits of being associated with principles or qualities naturally foreign to it, and is often made the cloak of feelings or ends for which it was never given to us. So little is it the necessary index of humility, that it is even compatible with pride. The better for the purpose of philosophy; humble it cannot be, so forthwith modesty becomes its humility.

Pride, under such training, instead of running to waste in the education of the mind, is turned to account; it gets a new name; it is called self-respect, and ceases to be the disagreeable, uncompanionable quality which it is in itself. Though it be the motive principle of the soul, it seldom comes to view; and when it shows itself, then delicacy and gentleness are its attire, and good sense and sense of honour direct its motions. It is no longer a restless agent without definite aim; it has a large field of exertion assigned to it, and it subserves those social interests which it would naturally trouble. It is directed into the channel of industry, frugality, honesty, and obedience; and it becomes the very staple of the religion and morality held in honour in a day like our own. It becomes the safeguard of chastity, the guarantee of veracity, in high and low; it is the very household god of society, as at present constituted, inspiring neatness and decency in the servant-girl, propriety of carriage and refined manners in her mistress, uprightness, manliness, and generosity in the head of the family. It diffuses a light over town and country; it covers the soil with handsome edifices and smiling gardens; it tills the field, it stocks and embellishes the shop. It is the stimulating principle of providence on the one hand, and of free expenditure on the other; of an honourable ambition, and of elegant enjoyment. It breathes upon the face of the community, and the hollow sepulchre is forthwith beautiful to look upon.

Refined by the civilization which has brought it into activity, this self-respect infuses into the mind an intense horror of exposure, and a keen sensitiveness of notoriety and ridicule. It becomes the enemy of extravagances of any kind; it shrinks from what are called scenes; it has no mercy on the mock-heroic, on pretence or egotism, on verbosity in language, or what is called prosiness in conversation. It detests gross adulation; not that it tends at all to the eradication of the appetite to which the flatterer ministers, but it sees the absurdity of indulging it, it understands the annoyance thereby given to others, and if a tribute must be paid to the wealthy or the powerful, it demands greater subtlety and art in the preparation. Thus vanity is changed into a more dangerous self-conceit, as being checked in its natural eruption. It teaches men to suppress their feelings and to control their tempers, and to mitigate both the severity and the tone of their judgments. It prefers playful wit and satire in putting down what is objectionable, as a more refined and good-natured, as well as a more effectual method, than the expedient which is natural to uneducated minds. It is from this impatience of the tragic and the bombastic that it is now quietly but energetically opposing itself to the unchristian practice of duelling, which it brands as simply out of taste, and as the remnant of a barbarous age; and certainly it seems likely to effect what Religion has aimed at abolishing in vain.

(II.)

HENCE it is that it is almost a definition of a gentleman to say he is one who never inflicts pain. This description is both refined and, as far as it goes, accurate. He is mainly occupied in merely removing the obstacles which hinder the free and unembarrassed action of those about him; and he concurs with their movements rather than takes the initiative himself. His benefits may be considered as parallel to what are called comforts or conveniences in arrangements of a personal nature: like an easy-chair or a good fire, which do their part in dispelling cold and fatigue, though nature provides both means of rest and animal heat without them. The true gentleman in like manner carefully avoids whatever may cause a jar or a jolt in the minds of those with whom he is cast; all clashing of opinion, or collision of feeling, all restraint, or suspicion, or gloom, or resentment; his great concern being to make every one at their ease and at home. He has his eyes on all his company; he is tender towards the bashful, gentle towards the distant, and merciful towards the absurd; he can recollect to whom he is speaking; he guards against unseasonable allusions or topics which may irritate; he is seldom prominent in conversation, and never wearisome. He makes light of favours while he does them, and seems to be receiving when he is conferring. He never speaks of himself except when compelled, never defends himself by a mere retort; he has no ears for slander or gossip, is scrupulous in imputing motives to those who interfere with him, and interprets everything for the best. He is never mean or little in his disputes, never takes unfair advantage, never mistakes personalities or sharp sayings for arguments, or insinuates evil which he dare not say out. From a long-sighted prudence, he observes the maxim of the ancient sage, that we should ever conduct ourselves towards our enemy as if he were one day to be our friend. He has too much good sense to be affronted at insults, he is too well employed to remember injuries, and too indolent to bear malice. He is patient, forbearing, and resigned, on philosophical principles; he submits to pain, because it is inevitable, to bereavement, because it is irreparable, and to death, because it is his destiny. If he engages in controversy of any kind, his disciplined intellect preserves him from the blundering discourtesy of better, perhaps, but less educated minds, who, like blunt weapons, tear and hack instead of cutting clean, who mistake the point in argument, waste their strength on trifles, misconceive their adversary, and leave the question more involved than they find it. He may be right or wrong in his opinion, but he is too clear-headed to be unjust; he is as simple as he is forcible, and as brief as he is decisive. Nowhere shall we find greater candour, consideration, indulgence: he throws himself into the minds of his opponents, he accounts for their mistakes. He knows the weakness of human reason as well as its strength, its province and its limits. If he be an unbeliever, he will be too profound and large-minded to ridicule religion or to act against it; he is too wise to be a dogmatist or fanatic in his infidelity. He respects piety and devotion; he even supports institutions as venerable, beautiful, or useful, to which he does not assent; he honours the ministers of religion, and it contents him to decline its mysteries without assailing or denouncing them. He is a friend of religious toleration, and that, not only because his philosophy has taught him to look on all forms of faith with an impartial eye, but also from the gentleness and effeminacy of feeling, which is the attendant on civilization.

Not that he may not hold a religion too, in his own way, even when he is not a Christian. In that case his religion is one of imagination and sentiment; it is the embodiment of those ideas of the sublime, majestic, and beautiful, without which there can be no large philosophy. Sometimes he acknowledges the being of God, sometimes he invests an unknown principle or quality with the attributes of perfection. And this deduction of his reason, or creation of his fancy, he makes the occasion of such excellent thoughts, and the starting-point of so varied and systematic a teaching, that he even seems like a disciple of Christianity itself. From the very accuracy and steadiness of his logical powers, he is able to see what sentiments are consistent in those who hold any religious doctrine at all, and he appears to others to feel and to hold a whole circle of theological truths, which exist in his mind no otherwise than as a number of deductions.

Such are some of the lineaments of the ethical character, which the cultivated intellect will form, apart from religious principle. ("Idea of a University," p. 204.)

CULTURE AND VICE.

I SPOKE just now of the scorn and hatred which a cultivated mind feels for some kinds of vice, and the utter disgust and profound humiliation which may come over it, if it should happen in any degree to be betrayed into them. Now this feeling may have its root in faith and love, but it may not; there is nothing really religious in it, considered by itself. Conscience indeed is implanted in the breast by nature, but it inflicts upon us fear as well as shame; when the mind is simply angry with itself and nothing more, surely the true import of the voice of nature and the depth of its intimations have been forgotten, and a false philosophy has misinterpreted emotions which ought to lead to God. Fear implies the transgression of a law, and a law implies a lawgiver and judge ; but the tendency of intellectual culture is to swallow up the fear in the self-reproach, and self-reproach is directed and limited to our mere sense of what is fitting and becoming. Fear carries us out of ourselves, shame confines us within the round of our own thoughts. Such, I say, is the danger which awaits a civilized age; such is its besetting sin (not inevitable, God forbid! or we must abandon the use of God's own gifts), but still the ordinary sin of the Intellect; conscience becomes what is called a moral sense; the command of duty is a sort of taste; sin is not an offence against God, but against human nature.

The less amiable specimens of this spurious religion are those which we meet not unfrequently in my own country. I can use with all my heart the poet's words,

"England, with all thy faults, I love thee still;"

but to those faults no Catholic can be blind. We find these men possessed of many virtues, but proud, bashful, fastidious, and reserved. Why is this? it is because they think and act as if there were really nothing objective in their religion; it is because conscience to them is not the word of a lawgiver, as it ought to be, but the dictate of their own minds and nothing more; it is because they do not look out of themselves, because they do not look through and beyond their own minds to their Maker, but are engrossed in notions of what is due to themselves, to their own dignity, and their own consistency. Their conscience has become a mere self-respect. Instead of doing one thing and then another, as each is called for, in faith and obedience, careless of what may be called the *keeping* of deed with deed, and leaving Him who gives the command to blend the portions of their conduct into a whole, their one object, however unconscious to themselves, is to paint a smooth and perfect surface, and to be able to say to themselves that they have done their duty. When they do wrong, they feel, not contrition, of which God is the object, but remorse, and a sense of **degradation**. They call themselves fools, not sinners; they are angry and impatient, not humble. They **shut** themselves up in themselves; it **is** misery to them to think or to speak of their own feelings; it is misery to suppose that others see them, **and their** shyness and sensitiveness often become morbid. As to confession, which is so natural to the Catholic, to them it is impossible; unless, indeed, in cases where they have been guilty, an apology is due to their own character, is expected of them, and will be satisfactory to look back upon. They are victims of an intense self-contemplation. ("Idea of a University," p. 191.)

THE WORLD'S PHILOSOPHY OF RELIGION.

THE world considers that all men are pretty much on a level, or that, differ **though** they may, they differ by such fine shades from each other, that it is impossible, because it would be untrue **and** unjust, **to** divide them into two bodies, or to **divide them** at all. Each man is like himself and **no one else**; each man has his **own** opinions, his own rule of faith and conduct, his own worship; if a number join together in a religious form, this is an accident, for the sake of convenience; for each is complete in himself; religion is simply a personal concern; there is no such thing really as a common or joint religion, that is, one in which a number of men, strictly speaking, partake; it is all matter of private judgment. Hence, as men sometimes proceed even to avow, there is **no** such thing as a true religion **or** a false; that is true to each, which each sincerely believes to be true; and what is true to one, is not true to his neighbour. There are no special doctrines necessary to be believed in order to salvation; it is not very difficult to be saved; and most men may take it for granted that they shall be saved. All men are in God's favour, except so far as, and while, they commit acts of sin; but when the sin is over, they get back into His favour again, naturally, and as a thing of course, no one knows how, owing to God's infinite indulgence, unless indeed they persevere and die in a course of sin, and perhaps even then. There is no such place as hell, or at least punishment is not eternal. Predestination, election, grace, perseverance, faith, sanctity, unbelief, and reprobation are strange ideas, and, as they think, very false ones. This is the cast of opinion of men in general, in proportion as they exercise their minds on the subject of religion, and think for themselves; and if in any respect they depart from the easy, cheerful, and tranquil temper of mind which it expresses, it is when they are led to think of those who presume to take the contrary view, that is, who take the view set forth by Christ and His Apostles. On these they are commonly severe, that is, on the very persons whom God acknowledges as His, and is training heavenward—on Catholics, who are the witnesses and preachers of those awful doctrines of grace, which condemn the world, and which the world cannot endure.

In truth the world does not know of the existence of grace; nor is it wonderful, for it is ever contented with itself, and has never turned to account the supernatural aids bestowed upon it. Its highest idea of man lies in the order of nature; its pattern man is the natural man; it thinks it wrong to be anything else than a natural man. It sees that nature has a number of tendencies, inclinations, and passions; and because these are natural, it thinks that each of them may be indulged for its own sake, so far as it does no harm to others, or to a person's bodily, mental, and temporal well-being. It considers that want of moderation, or excess, is the very definition of sin, if it goes so far as to recognize that word. It thinks that he is the perfect man who eats, and drinks, and sleeps, and walks, and diverts himself, and studies, and writes, and attends to religion in moderation. The devotional feeling, and the intellect, and the flesh, have each its claim upon us, and each must have play, if the Creator is to be duly honoured. It does not understand, it will not admit, that impulses and propensities which are found in our nature, as God created it, may nevertheless, if indulged, become sins, on the ground that He has subjected them to higher principles, whether these principles be in our nature, or be superadded to our nature. Hence it is very slow to believe that evil thoughts are really displeasing to God, and incur punishment. Works, indeed, tangible actions, which are seen and which have influence, it will allow to be wrong; but it will not believe even that deeds are sinful, or that they are more than reprehensible, if they are private or personal; and it is blind utterly to the malice of thoughts, of imaginations, of wishes, and of words. Because the wild emotions of anger, desire, greediness, craft, cruelty, are no sin in the brute creation, which has neither the means nor the command to repress them, therefore they are no sins in a being who has a diviner sense and a controlling power. Concupiscence may be indulged, because it is in its first elements natural.

Behold here the true origin and fountain-head of the warfare between the Church and the world; here they join issue, and diverge from each other. The Church is built upon the doctrine that impurity is hateful to God, and that concupiscence is its root; with the Prince of the Apostles, her visible Head, she denounces "the corruption of concupiscence which is in the world," or, that corruption in the world which comes of concupiscence; whereas the corrupt world defends, nay, I may even say, sanctifies that very concupiscence which is the world's corruption. Its bolder and more consistent teachers make the laws of this physical creation so supreme, as to disbelieve the existence of miracles, as being an unseemly violation of them; and in like manner, it deifies and worships human nature and its impulses, and denies the power and the grant of grace. This is the source of the hatred which the world bears to the Church; it finds a whole catalogue of sins brought into light and denounced, which it would fain believe to be no sins at all; it finds itself, to its indignation and impatience, surrounded with sin, morning, noon, and night; it finds that a stern law lies against it, where it believed that it was its own master and need not think of God; it finds guilt accumulating upon it hourly, which nothing can prevent, nothing remove, but a higher power, the grace of God. It finds itself in danger of being humbled to the earth as a rebel, instead of being allowed to indulge its self-dependence and self-complacency. Hence it takes its stand on nature, and denies or rejects divine grace. Like the proud spirit in the beginning, it wishes to find its supreme good in its own self, and nothing above it; it undertakes to be sufficient for its own happiness; it has no desire for the supernatural, and therefore does not believe in it. And as nature cannot rise above nature, it will not believe that the narrow way is possible; it hates those who enter upon it as if pretenders and hypocrites, or laughs at their aspirations as romance and fanaticism, lest it should have to believe in the existence of grace. ("Discourses to Mixed Congregations," p. 148.)

THE DOCTRINE OF RETRIBUTIVE PUNISHMENT.

I ALLUDED just now to those who consider the doctrine of retributive punishment, or of divine vengeance, to be incompatible with the true religion; but I do not see how they can maintain their ground. In order to do so, they have first to prove that an act of vengeance must be a sin in our own instance; but even this is far from clear. Anger and indignation against cruelty and injustice, resentment of injuries, desire that the false, the ungrateful, and the depraved should meet with punishment, these, if not in themselves virtuous feelings, are at least not vicious; but, first, from the certainty that it will run into excess and become sin, and, next, because the office of punishment has not been committed to us; and, further, because it is a feeling unsuitable to those who are themselves so laden with imperfection and guilt, therefore vengeance, in itself allowable, is forbidden to us. These exceptions do not hold in the case of a perfect being, and certainly not in the instance of the Supreme Judge. Moreover, we see that even men have different duties, according to their personal qualifications and their positions in the community. The rule of morals is the same for all; and yet, notwithstanding, what is right in one is not necessarily right in another. What would be a crime in a private man to do, is a crime in a magistrate not to have done: still wider is the difference between man and his Maker. Nor must it be forgotten, that . . retributive justice is the very attribute under which God is primarily brought before us in the teachings of our natural conscience.

And further, we cannot determine the character of particular actions till we have the whole case before us out of which they arise; unless, indeed, they are in themselves distinctively vicious. We all feel the force of the maxim, "Audi alteram partem." It is difficult to trace the path and to determine the scope of Divine Providence. We read of a day when the Almighty will condescend to place His actions in their completeness before His creatures, and "will overcome when He is judged." If, till then, we feel it to be a duty to suspend our judgment concerning certain of His actions or precepts, we do no more than what we do every day in the case of an earthly friend or enemy, whose conduct in some point requires explanation. It surely is not too much to expect of us that we should act with parallel caution, and be "memores conditionis nostræ" as regards the acts of our Creator. There is a poem of Parnell's which strikingly brings home to us how differently the divine appointments will look in the light of day, from what they appear to be in our present twilight. An Angel, in disguise of a man, steals a golden cup, strangles an infant, and throws a guide into the stream, and explains to his horrified companion, that acts which would be enormities in man are in him, as God's minister, deeds of merciful correction or of retribution.

Moreover, when we are about to pass judgment on the dealings of Providence with other men, we shall do well to consider first His dealings with ourselves. We cannot know about others, about ourselves we do know something; and we know that He has ever been good to us, and not severe. Is it not wise to argue from what we actually know, to what we do not know? It may turn out in the day of account that unforgiven souls, while charging His laws with injustice in the case of others, may be unable to find fault with His dealings severally towards themselves.

As to those various religions which, together with Christianity, teach the doctrine of eternal punishment, here again we ought, before we judge, to understand, not only the whole state of the case, but what is meant by the doctrine itself. Eternity, or endlessness, is in itself only a negative idea, though punishment is positive. Its fearful force, as added to punishment, lies in what it is not; it means no change of state, no annihilation, no restoration. But it cannot become a quality of punishment, any more than a man's living seventy years is a quality of his mind, or enters into the idea of his virtues or talents. If punishment be attended by continuity, or by sense of succession, this must be because it is endless and something more; such inflictions are an addition to its endlessness, and do not necessarily belong to it because it is endless. As I have already said, the great mystery is, not that evil has no end, but that it had a beginning. But I submit the whole subject to the Theological School. ("Grammar of Assent," p. 414.)

WHAT IS THEOLOGY?

Now what is Theology? First, I will tell you what it is not. And here, in the first place (though of course I speak on the subject as a Catholic) observe, that, strictly speaking, I am not assuming that Catholicism is true, while I make myself the champion of Theology. Catholicism has not formally entered into my argument hitherto, nor shall I just now assume any principle peculiar to it, for reasons which will appear in the sequel, though of course I shall use Catholic language. Neither, secondly, will I fall into the fashion of the day, of identifying Natural Theology with Physical Theology; which said Physical Theology is a most jejune study, considered as a science, and really is no science at all, for it is ordinarily nothing more than a series of pious or polemical remarks upon the physical world viewed religiously, whereas the word "Natural" properly comprehends man and society, and all that is involved therein, as the great Protestant writer, Dr. Butler, shows us. Nor, in the third place, do I mean by Theology polemics of any kind; for instance, what are called "the Evidences of Religion," or "the Christian Evidences;" for, though these constitute a science supplemental to Theology and are necessary in their place, they are not Theology itself, unless an army is synonymous with the body politic. Nor, fourthly, do I mean by Theology that vague thing called "Christianity," or "our common Christianity," or "Christianity the law of the land," if there is any man alive who can tell what it is. I discard it, for the very reason that it cannot throw itself into a proposition. Lastly, I do not understand by Theology acquaintance with the Scriptures; for, though no person of religious feelings can read Scripture but he will find those feelings roused, and gain much knowledge of history into the bargain, yet historical reading and religious feeling are not science. I mean none of these things by Theology, I simply mean the Science of God, or the truths we know about God put into system; just as we have a science of the stars, and call it astronomy, or of the crust of the earth, and call it geology.

For instance, I mean, for this is the main point, that, as in the human frame there is a living principle, acting upon it, and through it, by means of volition, so, behind the veil of the visible universe, there is an invisible, intelligent

Being, acting on and through it, as and when He will. Further, I mean that this invisible Agent is in no sense a soul of the world, after the analogy of human nature, but, on the contrary, is absolutely distinct from the world, as being its Creator, Upholder, Governor, and Sovereign Lord. Here we are at once brought into the circle of doctrines which the idea of God embodies. I mean, then, by the Supreme Being, one who is simply self-dependent, and the only Being who is such; moreover, that He is without beginning or Eternal, and the only Eternal; that in consequence He has lived a whole eternity by Himself; and hence that He is all-sufficient, sufficient for His own blessedness, and all-blessed, and ever-blessed. Further, I mean a Being, who, having these prerogatives, has the Supreme Good, or rather is the Supreme Good, or has all the attributes of Good in infinite intenseness; all wisdom, all truth, all justice, all love, all holiness, all beautifulness; who is omnipotent, omniscient, omnipresent; ineffably one, absolutely perfect; and such, that what we do not know and cannot even imagine of Him, is far more wonderful than what we do and can. I mean One who is sovereign over His own will and actions, though always according to the eternal Rule of right and wrong, which is Himself. I mean, moreover, that He created all things out of nothing, and preserves them every moment, and could destroy them as easily as He made them; and that, in consequence, He is separated from them by an abyss, and is incommunicable in all His attributes. And further, He has stamped upon all things, in the hour of their creation, their respective natures, and has given them their work and mission and their length of days, greater or less, in their appointed place. I mean, too, that He is ever present with His works, one by one, and confronts everything He has made by His particular and most loving Providence, and manifests

Himself to each according to its needs; and has on rational beings imprinted the moral law, and given them power to obey it, imposing on them the duty of worship and service, searching and scanning them through and through with His omniscient eye, and putting before them a present trial and a judgment to come.

Such is what Theology teaches about God, a doctrine, as the very idea of its subject-matter presupposes, so mysterious as in its fulness to lie beyond any system, and in particular aspects to be simply external to nature, and to seem in parts even to be irreconcilable with itself, the imagination being unable to embrace what the reason determines. It teaches of a Being infinite, yet personal; all-blessed, yet ever operative; absolutely separate from the creature, yet in every part of the creation at every moment; above all things, yet under everything. It teaches of a Being who, though the highest, yet in the work of creation, conservation, government, retribution, makes Himself, as it were, the minister and servant of all; who, though inhabiting eternity, allows Himself to take an interest, and to have a sympathy, in the matters of space and time. His are all beings, visible and invisible, the noblest and the vilest of them. His are the substance, and the operation, and the results of that system of physical nature into which we are born. His too are the powers and achievements of the intellectual essences, on which He has bestowed an independent action and the gift of origination. The laws of the universe, the principles of truth, the relation of one thing to another, their qualities and virtues, the order and harmony of the whole, all that exists, is from Him; and, if evil is not from Him, as assuredly it is not, this is because evil has no substance of its own, but is only the defect, excess, perversion, or corruption, of that which has substance. All we see, hear, and touch the remote sidereal firmament, as well as our own sea and land, and the elements which compose them, and the ordinances they obey, are His. The primary atoms of matter, their properties, their mutual action, their disposition and collocation, electricity, magnetism, gravitation, light, and whatever other subtle principles or operations the wit of man is detecting or shall detect, are the work of His hands. From Him has been every movement which has convulsed and refashioned the surface of the earth. The most insignificant or unsightly insect is from Him, and good in its kind; the ever-teeming, inexhaustible swarms of animalculæ, the myriads of living motes invisible to the naked eye, the restless ever-spreading vegetation which creeps like a garment over the whole earth, the lofty cedar, the umbrageous banana, are His. His are the tribes and families of birds and beasts, their graceful forms, their wild gestures, and their passionate cries.

And so in the intellectual, moral, social, and political world. Man, with his motives and works, his languages, his propagation, his diffusion, is from Him. Agriculture, medicine, and the arts of life, are His gifts. Society, laws, government, He is their sanction. The pageant of earthly royalty has the semblance and the benediction of the Eternal King. Peace and civilization, commerce and adventure, wars when just, conquest when humane and necessary, have His co-operation and His blessing upon them. The course of events, the revolution of empires, the rise and fall of states, the periods and eras, the progresses and the retrogressions of the world's history, not indeed the incidental sin, over-abundant as it is, but the great outlines and the results of human affairs, are from His disposition. The elements and types and seminal principles and constructive powers of the moral world, in ruins though it be, are to be referred to Him. He "enlighteneth every man that cometh into this world." His are the dictates of the moral sense, and the retributive reproaches of conscience. To Him must be ascribed the rich endowments of the intellect, the irradiation of genius, the imagination of the poet, the sagacity of the politician, the wisdom (as Scripture calls it) which now rears and decorates the Temple, now manifests itself in proverb or in parable. The old saws of nations, the majestic precepts of philosophy, the luminous maxims of law, the oracles of individual wisdom, the traditionary rules of truth, justice, and religion, even though imbedded in the corruption, or alloyed with the pride, of the world, betoken His original agency, and His long-suffering presence. Even where there is habitual rebellion against Him, or profound far-spreading social depravity, still the undercurrent, or the heroic outburst, of natural virtue, as well as the yearnings of the heart after what it has not, and its presentiment of its true remedies, are to be ascribed to the Author of all good. Anticipations or reminiscences of His glory haunt the mind of the self-sufficient sage, and of the pagan devotee; His writing is upon the wall, whether of the Indian fane, or of the porticoes of Greece. He introduces Himself, He all but concurs, according to His good pleasure, and in His selected season, in the issues of unbelief, superstition, and false worship, and He changes the character of acts by His over-ruling operation. He condescends, though He gives no sanction, to the altars and shrines of imposture, and He makes His own fiat the substitute for its sorceries. He speaks amid the incantations of Balaam, raises Samuel's spirit in the witch's cavern, prophesies of the Messias by the tongue of the Sibyl, forces Python to recognize His ministers, and baptizes by the hand of the misbeliever. He is with the heathen dramatist in his denunciations of injustice and tyranny, and his auguries of divine vengeance upon crime. Even on the unseemly legends of a popular mythology He casts His shadow, and is dimly discerned in the ode or the epic, as in troubled water or in fantastic dreams. All that is good, all that is true, all that is beautiful, all that is beneficent, be it great or small, be it perfect or fragmentary, natural as well as supernatural, moral as well as material, comes from Him. ("Idea of a University," p. 60.)

PHYSICAL PHILOSOPHY AND THEOLOGY.

ONE reason for the prejudice of physical philosophers against theology is to be found in the difference of method by which truths are gained in theology and in physical science. Induction is the instrument of Physics, and deduction only is the instrument of Theology. There the simple question is, What is revealed? all doctrinal knowledge flows from one fountain head. If we are able to enlarge our view and multiply our propositions, it must be merely by the comparison and adjustment of the original truths; if we would solve new questions, it must be by consulting old answers. The notion of doctrinal knowledge absolutely novel, and of simple addition from without, is intolerable to Catholic ears, and never was entertained by any one who was even approaching to an understanding of our creed. Revelation is all in all in doctrine; the Apostles its sole depository, the inferential method its sole instrument, and ecclesiastical authority its sole sanction. The Divine Voice has spoken once for all, and the only question is about its meaning. Now this process, as far as it was reasoning, was the very mode of, reasoning which, as regards physical knowledge, the school of Bacon has superseded by the inductive method : no wonder, then, that that school should be irritated and indignant to find that a subject-matter remains still, in which their favourite instrument has no office ; no wonder that they rise up against this memorial of an antiquated system, as an eyesore and an insult ; and no wonder that the very force and dazzling success of their own method in its own departments should sway or bias unduly the religious sentiments of any persons who come under its influence. They assert that no new truth can be gained by deduction ; Catholics assent, but add, that, as regards religious truth, they have not to seek at all, for they have it already. Christian Truth is purely of revelation ; that revelation we can but explain, we cannot increase, except relatively to our own apprehensions ; without it we should have known nothing of its contents, with it we know just as much as its contents, and nothing more. And, as it was given by a divine act independent of man, so will it remain in spite of man. Niebuhr may revolutionize history, Lavoisier chemistry, Newton astronomy ; but God Himself is the author as well as the subject of Theology. When Truth can change, its Revelation can change ; when human reason can outreason the Omniscient, then may it supersede His work.

Avowals such as these fall strange upon the ear of men whose first principle is the search after truth, and whose starting-points of search are things material and sensible. They scorn any process of enquiry not founded on experiment ; the Mathematics indeed they endure, because that science deals with ideas, not with facts, and leads to conclusions hypothetical rather than real ; "Metaphysics" they even use as a by-word of reproach ; and Ethics they admit only on condition that it gives up conscience as its scientific ground, and bases itself on tangible utility: but as to Theology, they cannot deal with it, they cannot master it, and so they simply outlaw it and ignore it. Catholicism, forsooth, "confines the intellect," because it holds that God's intellect is greater than theirs, and that what He has done, man cannot improve. And what, in some sort, justifies them to themselves in this extravagance, is the circumstance that there is a religion close at their doors which, discarding so severe a tone, has actually adopted their own principle of enquiry. Protestantism treats Scripture just as they deal with Nature; it takes the sacred text as a large collection of phenomena, from which, by an inductive process, each individual Christian may arrive at just those religious conclusions which approve themselves to his own judgment. It considers faith a mere modification of reason, as being an acquiescence in certain probable conclusions till better are found. Sympathy, then, if no other reason, throws experimental philosophers into alliance with the enemies of Catholicism. ("Idea of a University," p. 222.)

THE BACONIAN PHILOSOPHY.

THE Philosophy of Utility has at least done its work; it aimed low, but it has fulfilled its aim. If that man of great intellect who has been its prophet in the conduct of life played false to his own professions, he was not bound by his philosophy to be true to his friend or faithful in his trust. Moral virtue was not the line in which he undertook to instruct men; and though, as the poet calls him, he were the "meanest" of mankind, he was so in what may be called his private capacity and without any prejudice to the theory of induction. He had a right to be so, if he chose, for anything that the Idols of the den or the theatre had to say to the contrary. His mission was the increase of physical enjoyment and social comfort;[1] and most wonderfully, most awfully has he fulfilled his conception and his design. Almost day by day have we fresh and fresh shoots, and buds, and blossoms, which are to ripen into fruit, on that magical tree of Knowledge which he planted, and to which none of us, perhaps, except the very poor, but owes, if not his present life, at least his daily food, his health, and general well-being. He was the divinely provided minister of temporal benefits to all of us so great, that, whatever I am forced to think of him as a man, I have not the heart, from mere gratitude, to speak of him severely. And, in spite of the tendencies of his philosophy, which are, as we see at this day, to depreciate, or to trample on Theology, he has himself, in his writings, gone out of his way, as if with a prophetic misgiving of those tendencies, to insist on it as the instrument of that beneficent Father,[2] who, when He came on earth in visible form, took on Him first and most

---

[1] It will be seen that on the whole I agree with Lord Macaulay in his Essay on Bacon's Philosophy. I do not know whether he would agree with me.

[2] De Augment. iv. 2, vid. Macaulay's Essay; vid. also "In principio operis ad Deum Patrem, Deum Verbum, Deum Spiritum, preces fundimus humillimas et ardentissimas, ut humani generis ærumnarum memores, et peregrinationis istius vitæ, in quâ dies paucos et malos terimus, *novis suis eleemosynis, per manus nostras,* familiam humanam dotare dignentur. Atque illud insuper supplices rogamus, ne *humana divinis officiant;* neve *ex reseratione viarum sensûs,* et accensione majore luminis naturalis, *aliquid incredulitatis* et noctis, animis nostris erga divina mysteria oboriatur," etc. ("Præf. Instaur. Magn.")

prominently the office of assuaging the bodily wounds of human nature. And truly, like the old mediciner in the tale, "he sat diligently at his work, and hummed, with cheerful countenance, a pious song;" and then in turn "went out singing into the meadows so gaily that those who had seen him from afar might well have thought it was a youth gathering flowers for his beloved, instead of an old physician gathering healing herbs in the morning dew."[1]

Alas, that men, in the action of life or in their heart of hearts, are not what they seem to be in their moments of excitement, or in their trances or intoxications of genius—so good, so noble, so serene! Alas, that Bacon too, in his own way, should after all be but the fellow of those heathen philosophers who in their disadvantages had some excuse for their inconsistency, and who surprise us rather in what they did say than in what they did not do! Alas, that he too, like Socrates or Seneca, must be stripped of his holy-day coat, which looks so fair, and should be but a mockery amid his most majestic gravity of phrase; and, for all his vast abilities, should, in the littleness of his own moral being, but typify the intellectual narrowness of his school! However, granting all this, heroism after all was not his philosophy: I cannot deny he has abundantly achieved what he proposed. He is simply a Method whereby bodily discomforts and temporal wants are to be most effectually removed from the greatest number; and already, before it has shown any signs of exhaustion, the gifts of nature, in their most artificial shapes and luxurious profusion and diversity, from all quarters of the earth, are, it is undeniable, by its means brought even to our doors, and we rejoice in them. ("Idea of a University," p. 117.)

---

[1] Fouqué's "Unknown Patient."

RATIONALISM.

RATIONALISM is a certain abuse of reason; that is, a use of it for purposes for which it never was intended, and is unfitted. To rationalize in matters of Revelation is to make our reason the standard and measure of the doctrines revealed; to stipulate that those doctrines should be such as to carry with them their own justification; to reject them if they come in collision with our existing opinions or habits of thought, or are with difficulty harmonized with our existing stock of knowledge. And thus a rationalistic spirit is the antagonist of faith, for faith is, in its very nature, the acceptance of what our reason cannot reach, simply and absolutely upon testimony.

There is, of course, a multitude of cases in which we allowably and rightly accept statements as true, partly on reason, and partly on testimony. We supplement the information of others by our own knowledge, by our own judgment of probabilities; and if it be very strange or extravagant we suspend our assent. This is undeniable; still, after all, there are truths which are incapable of reaching us except on testimony, and there is testimony, which, by and in itself, has an imperative claim on our acceptance.

As regards Revealed Truth, it is not Rationalism to set about to ascertain by the exercise of reason what things are attainable by reason and what are not; nor, in the absence of an express Revelation, to enquire into the truths of religion, as they come to us by nature; nor to determine what proofs are necessary for the acceptance of a Revelation, if it be given; nor to reject a Revelation on the plea of insufficient proof; nor, after recognizing it as divine, to investigate the meaning of its declarations, and to interpret its language; nor to use its doctrines, as far as they can be fairly used, in enquiring into its divinity; nor to compare and connect them with our previous knowledge, with a view of making them parts of a whole; nor to bring them into dependence on each other, to trace their mutual relations, and to pursue them to their legitimate issues. This is not Rationalism, but it is Rationalism to accept the Revelation and then to explain it away; to speak of it as the Word of God, and to treat it as the word of man; to refuse to let it speak for itself; to claim to be told the *why* and the *how* of God's dealings with us, as therein described, and to assign to Him a motive and scope of our own; to stumble at the partial knowledge which He may give us of them; to put aside what is obscure, as if it had not been said at all; to accept one half of what has been told us, and not the other half; to assume that the contents of Revelation are also its proof; to frame some gratuitous hypothesis about them, and then to garble, gloss, and colour them, to trim, clip, pare away, and twist them, in order to bring them into conformity with the idea to which we have subjected them.

When the rich lord in Samaria said, "Though God shall make windows in heaven, shall this thing be?" he rationalized, as professing his inability to discover *how* Elisha's prophecy was to be fulfilled, and thinking in this way to excuse his unbelief. When Naaman, after acknowledging the prophet's supernatural power, objected to bathe in Jordan, it was on the ground of his not seeing the *means* by which Jordan was to cure his leprosy above the rivers of Damascus. "*How* can these things be?" was the objection of Nicodemus to the doctrine of regeneration; and when the doctrine of the Holy Communion was first announced, "the Jews strove among themselves," in answer to their Divine Informant, saying, "*How* can this man give us His flesh to eat?" When St. Thomas, believing in our

Lord, doubted of our Lord's resurrection, though his reason for so doing is not given, it plainly lay in the astonishing, unaccountable nature of such an event. A like desire of judging for oneself is discernible in the original fall of man. Eve did not believe the tempter, any more than God's word, till she perceived that "the fruit was good for food."

So, again, when men who profess Christianity ask *how* prayer can really influence the course of God's Providence, or *how* everlasting punishment, as such, consists with God's infinite mercy, they rationalize.

The same spirit shows itself in the restlessness of others to decide *how* the sun was stopped at Joshua's word, *how* the manna was provided, and the like, forgetting what our Saviour suggests to the Sadducees—"*the power* of God."

Conduct such as this, on so momentous a matter, is, generally speaking, traceable to one obvious cause—the Rationalist makes himself his own centre, not his Maker; he does not go to God, but he implies that God must come to him. And this, it is to be feared, is the spirit in which multitudes of us act at the present day. Instead of looking out of ourselves, and trying to catch glimpses of God's workings, from any quarter,—throwing ourselves forward upon Him and waiting on Him,—we sit at home, bringing everything to ourselves, enthroning ourselves in our own views, and refusing to believe anything that does not force itself upon us as true. Our private judgment is made everything to us,—is contemplated, recognized, and consulted, as the arbiter of all questions, and as independent of everything external to us. Nothing is considered to have an existence except so far forth as our own minds discern it. The notion of half views and partial knowledge, of guesses, surmises, hopes and fears, of truths faintly apprehended and not understood, of isolated facts in the great scheme of Providence, in a word, the idea of mystery is discarded.

Hence, a distinction is drawn between what is called Objective and Subjective Truth, and Religion is said to consist in the reception of the latter. By Objective Truth is meant the Religious System considered as existing in itself, external to this or that particular mind. By Subjective is meant that which each mind receives in particular, and considers to be such. To believe in Objective Truth is to throw ourselves forward upon that which we have but partially mastered or made subjective; to embrace, maintain, and use general propositions which are larger than our own capacity, of which we cannot see the bottom, which we cannot follow out into their multiform details; to come before and bow before the import of such propositions, as if we were contemplating what is real and independent of human judgment. Such a belief, implicit, and symbolized as it is in the use of creeds, seems to the Rationalist superstitious and unmeaning, and he consequently confines faith to the province of Subjective Truth, or to the reception of doctrine, as, and so far as, it is met and apprehended by the mind, which will be differently, as he considers, in different persons, in the shape of orthodoxy in one, heterodoxy in another. That is, he professes to *believe* in that which he *opines*, and he avoids the obvious extravagance of such an avowal by maintaining that the moral trial involved in Faith does not lie in the submission of the reason to external realities partially disclosed, but in what he calls that candid pursuit of truth which ensures the eventual adoption of that opinion on the subject, which is best for us individually, which is most natural, according to the constitution of our minds, and therefore divinely intended for us. I repeat, he owns that faith, viewed with reference to its objects, is never more than an opinion, and is pleasing to God, not as an active principle, apprehending definite doctrines, but as a result and fruit, and therefore an evidence of past diligence, independent enquiry, dispassionateness, and the like. Rationalism takes the words of Scripture as signs of ideas: Faith, of things or realities. ("Essays Crit. and Hist.," vol. I., p. 31.)

THE GOD OF MONOTHEISM AND THE GOD OF RATIONALISM.

WITH us Catholics, as with the first race of Protestants, as with Mahometans, and all Theists, the word God contains a theology in itself. According to the teaching of Monotheism God is an Individual, Self-dependent, All-perfect, Unchangeable Being; intelligent, living, personal, and present; Almighty, all-seeing, all-remembering; between whom and His creatures there is an infinite gulf; who has no origin, who is all-sufficient for Himself; who created and upholds the universe; who will judge every one of us, sooner or later, according to that law of right and wrong which He has written on our hearts. He is One who is sovereign over, operative amidst, independent of the appointments which He has made. One in whose hands are all things, who has a purpose in every event, and a standard for every deed, and thus has relations of His own towards the subject-matter of each particular science which the book of knowledge unfolds; who has with an adorable, never-ceasing energy, implicated Himself in all the history of creation, the constitution of nature, the course of the world, the origin of society, the fortunes of nations, the action of the human mind; and who thereby necessarily becomes the subject-matter of a science far wider and more noble than any of those which are included in the circle of secular education.

This is the doctrine which belief in a God implies in the mind of a Catholic: if it means anything it means all this, and cannot keep from meaning all this, and a great deal more; and even though there were nothing in the religious tenets of the last three centuries to disparage dogmatic truth, still, even then, I should have difficulty in believing that a doctrine so mysterious, so peremptory, approved itself as a matter of course to educated men of this day, who gave their minds attentively to consider it. Rather, in a state of society such as ours, in which authority, prescription, tradition, habit, moral instinct, and the divine influences, go for nothing; in which patience of thought, and depth and consistency of view, are scorned as subtle and scholastic; in which free discussion and fallible judgment are prized as the birthright of each individual, I must be excused if I exercise towards this age, as regards its belief in this doctrine, some portion of that scepticism which it exercises itself towards every received but unscrutinized assertion whatever. I cannot take it for granted, I must have it brought home to me by tangible evidence, that the spirit of the age means by the Supreme Being what Catholics mean. Nay, it would be a relief to my mind to gain some ground of assurance that the parties influenced by that spirit had, I will not say a true apprehension of God, but even so much as the idea of what a true apprehension is.

Nothing is easier than to use the word, and mean nothing by it. The heathens used to say, "God wills," when they meant "Fate;" "God provides," when they meant "Chance;" "God acts," when they meant "Instinct" or

"Sense ;" and "God is everywhere," when they meant "the Soul of Nature." The Almighty is something infinitely different from a principle, or a centre of action, or a quality, or a generalization of phenomena. If, then, by the word, you do but mean a Being who keeps the world in order, who acts in it, but only in the way of general Providence, who acts towards us but only through what are called laws of Nature, who is more certain not to act at all than to act independent of those laws, who is known and approached indeed, but only through the medium of those laws; such a God it is not difficult for any one to conceive, not difficult for any one to endure. If, I say, as you would revolutionize society, so you would revolutionize heaven, if you have changed the divine sovereignty into a sort of constitutional monarchy, in which the Throne has honour and ceremonial enough, but cannot issue the most ordinary command except through legal forms and precedents, and with the counter-signature of a minister, then belief in a God is no more than an acknowledgment of existing, sensible powers and phenomena, which none but an idiot can deny. If the Supreme Being is powerful or skilful, just so far forth as the telescope shows power, and the microscope shows skill, if His moral law is to be ascertained simply by the physical processes of the animal frame, or His will gathered from the immediate issues of human affairs, if His Essence is just as high and deep and broad and long as the universe, and no more; if this be the fact, then will I confess that there is no specific science about God, that Theology is but a name, and a protest in its behalf an hypocrisy. Then is He but coincident with the laws of the universe; then is He but a function, or correlative, or subjective reflection and mental impression, of each phenomenon of the material or moral world, as it flits before us. Then, pious as it is to think of Him, while the pageant of experiment or abstract reasoning passes by, still, such piety is nothing more than a poetry of thought or an ornament of language, and has not even an infinitesimal influence upon philosophy or science, of which it is rather the parasitical production.

I understand, in that case, why Theology should require no specific teaching, for there is nothing to mistake about ; why it is powerless against scientific anticipations, for it merely is one of them ; why it is simply absurd in its denunciations of heresy, for heresy does not lie in the region of fact and experiment. I understand, in that case, how it is that the religious sense is but a "sentiment," and its exercise a "gratifying treat," for it is like the sense of the beautiful or the sublime. I understand how the contemplation of the universe "leads onwards to *divine* truth," for divine truth is not something separate from Nature, but it is Nature with a divine glow upon it. I understand the zeal expressed for Physical Theology, for this study is but a mode of looking at Physical Nature, a certain view taken of Nature, private and personal, which one man has, and another has not, which gifted minds strike out, which others see to be admirable and ingenious, and which all would be the better for adopting. It is but the theology of Nature, just as we talk of the *philosophy* or the *romance* of history, or the *poetry* of childhood, or the picturesque, or the sentimental, or the humorous, or any other abstract quality, which the genius or the caprice of the individual, or the fashion of the day, or the consent of the world, recognizes in any set of objects which are subjected to its contemplation. ("Idea of a University," p. 36.)

THE "DUTY OF SCEPTICISM."

THE right of making assumptions has been disputed; but, when the objections are examined, I think they only go to show that we have no right in argument to make any assumption we please. Thus, in historical researches, it seems fair to say that no testimony should be received, except such as comes to us from competent witnesses, while it is not unfair to urge, on the other side, that tradition, though unauthenticated, being (what is called) in possession, has a prescription in its favour, and may, *primâ facie,* or provisionally, be received. Here are the materials of a fair dispute; but there are writers who seem to have gone far beyond this reasonable scepticism, laying down as a general proposition that we have no right in philosophy to make any assumption whatever, and that we ought to begin with a universal doubt. This, however, is of all assumptions the greatest, and to forbid them is to forbid it. Doubt itself is a positive state, and implies a definite habit of mind, and thereby necessarily involves a system of principles and doctrines of its own. Again, if nothing is to be assumed, what is our very method of reasoning but an assumption? and what our nature itself? The very sense of pleasure and pain, which is one of the most intimate portions of ourselves, inevitably translates itself into intellectual assumptions.

Of the two, I would rather have to maintain that we ought to begin with believing every thing that is offered to our acceptance, than that it is our duty to doubt of every thing. This, indeed, seems the true way of learning. In that case, we soon discover and discard what is contradictory; and error having always some portion of truth in it, and the truth having a reality which error has not, we may expect, that when there is an honest purpose and fair talents, we shall somehow make our way forward, the error falling off from the mind, and the truth developing and occupying it. ("Grammar of Assent," p. 370.)

APPREHENSION OF GOD THROUGH THE CONSCIENCE.

CONSCIENCE, considered as a moral sense, an intellectual sentiment, is a sense of admiration and disgust, of approbation and blame: but it is something more than a moral sense; it is always, what the sense of the beautiful is only in certain cases—it is always emotional. No wonder then that it always implies what that sense only sometimes implies; that it always involves the recognition of a living object, towards which it is directed. Inanimate things cannot stir our affections; these are correlative with persons. If, as is the case, we feel responsibility, are ashamed, are frightened, at transgressing the voice of conscience, this implies that there is One to whom we are responsible, before whom we are ashamed, whose claims upon us we fear. If, on doing wrong, we feel the same tearful, broken-hearted sorrow which overwhelms us on hurting a mother; if, on doing right, we enjoy the same sunny serenity of mind, the same soothing, satisfactory delight which follows on our receiving praise from a father, we certainly have within us the image of some person, to whom our love and veneration look, in whose smile we find our happiness, for whom we yearn, towards whom we direct our pleadings, in whose anger we are troubled and waste away. These feelings in us are such as require for their exciting cause an intelligent being: we are not affectionate towards a stone, nor do we feel shame before a horse or a dog; we have no remorse or compunction in breaking mere human law: yet, so it is, conscience excites all these painful emotions, confusion, foreboding, self-condemnation; and, on the other hand, it sheds upon us a deep peace, a sense of security, a resignation, and a hope, which there is no sensible, no earthly object to elicit. "The wicked flees, when no one pursueth;" then why does he flee? whence his terror? Who is it that he sees in solitude, in darkness, in the hidden chambers of his heart? If the cause of these emotions does not belong to this visible world, the Object to which his perception is directed must be Supernatural and Divine; and thus the phenomena of Conscience, as a dictate, avail to impress the imagination with the picture of a Supreme Governor, a Judge, holy, just, powerful, all-seeing, retributive, and is the creative principle of religion, as the Moral Sense is the principle of ethics.

And let me here refer to the fact that this instinct of the mind, recognizing an external Master in the dictate of conscience, and imaging the thought of Him in the definite impressions which conscience creates, is parallel to that other law of, not only human, but of brute nature, by which the presence of unseen individual beings is discerned under the shifting shapes and colours of the visible world. Is it by sense, or by reason, that brutes understand the real unities, material and spiritual, which are signified by the lights and shadows, the brilliant, ever-changing kaleidoscope, as it may be called, which plays upon their *retina?* Not by reason, for they have not reason; not by sense, because they are transcending sense; therefore it is an instinct. This faculty on the part of brutes, unless we were used to it, would strike us as a great mystery. It is one peculiarity of animal natures to be susceptible of phenomena through the channels of sense; it is another to have in those sensible phenomena a perception of the individuals to which certain groups of them belong. This perception of individual things is given to brutes in large measures, and that, apparently from the moment of their birth. It is by no mere physical instinct, such as that which leads him to his mother for milk, that the new-dropped lamb recognizes each of his fellow lambkins as a whole, consisting of many parts bound up in one, and, before he is an hour old, makes experience of his and their rival individualities. And much more distinctly do the horse and dog recognize even the personality of their masters. How are we to explain this apprehension of things, which are one and individual, in the midst of a world of pluralities and transmutations, whether in the instance of brutes or of children? But until we account for the knowledge which an infant has of his mother or his nurse, what reason have we to take exception at the doctrine, as strange and difficult, that in the dictate of conscience, without previous experiences or analogical reasoning, he is able gradually to perceive the voice, or the echoes of the voice, of a Master, living, personal, and sovereign?

I grant, of course, that we cannot assign a date, ever so early, before which he had learned nothing at all, and formed no mental associations, from the words and conduct of those who have the care of him. But still, if a child of five or six years old, when reason is at length fully awake, has already mastered and appropriated thoughts and beliefs, in consequence of their teaching, in such sort as to be able to handle and apply them familiarly, according to the occasion, as principles of intellectual action, those beliefs at the very least must be singularly congenial to his mind, if not connatural with its initial action. And that such a spontaneous reception of religious truths is common with children, I shall take for granted, till I am convinced that I am wrong in so doing. The child keenly understands that there is a difference between right and wrong; and when he has done what he believes to be wrong, he is conscious that he is offending One to whom he is amenable, whom he does not see, who sees him. His mind reaches forward with a strong presentiment to the thought of a Moral Governor, sovereign over him, mindful, and just. It comes to him like an impulse of nature to entertain it.

It is my wish to take an ordinary child, but one who is safe from influences destructive of his religious instincts. Supposing he has offended his parents, he will all alone and without effort, as if it were the most natural of acts, place himself in the presence of God, and beg of Him to set him right with them. Let us consider how much is contained in this simple act. First, it involves the impression on his mind of an unseen Being with whom he is in immediate relation, and that relation so familiar that he can address Him whenever he himself chooses; next, of One whose goodwill towards him he is assured of, and can take for granted—nay, who loves him better, and is nearer to him, than his parents; further, of One who can hear him, wherever he happens to be, and who can read his thoughts, for his prayer need not be vocal; lastly, of One who can effect a critical change in the state of feeling of others towards him. That is, we shall not be wrong in holding that this child has in his mind the image of an Invisible Being, who exercises a particular providence among us, who is present everywhere, who is heart-reading, heart-changing, ever-accessible, open to impetration. What a strong and intimate vision of God must he have already attained, if, as I have supposed, an ordinary trouble of mind has the spontaneous effect of leading him for consolation and aid to an Invisible Personal Power!

Moreover, this image brought before his mental vision is the image of One who by implicit threat and promise commands certain things which he, the same child, coincidently, by the same act of his mind, approves; which receive the adhesion of his moral sense and judgment, as right and good. It is the image of One who is good, inasmuch as enjoining and enforcing what is right and good, and who, in consequence, not only excites in the child hope and fear—nay (it may be added), gratitude towards Him, as giving a law and maintaining it by reward and punishment, but kindles in him love towards Him, as giving him a good law, and therefore as being good Himself, for it is the property of goodness to kindle love, or rather the very object of love is goodness; and all those distinct elements of the moral law, which the typical child, whom I am supposing, more or less consciously loves and approves—truth, purity, justice, kindness, and the like—are but shapes and aspects of goodness. And having in his degree a sensibility towards them all, for the sake of them all he is moved to love the Lawgiver, who enjoins them upon him. And, as he can contemplate these qualities and their manifestations under the common name of goodness, he is prepared to think of them as indivisible, correlative, supplementary of each other in one and the same Personality, so that there is no aspect of goodness which God is not; and that the more, because the notion of a perfection embracing all possible excellences, both moral and intellectual, is especially congenial to the mind, and there are in fact intellectual attributes, as well as moral, included in the child's image of God, as above represented.

Such is the apprehension which even a child may have of his Sovereign, Lawgiver, and Judge; which is possible in the case of children, because, at least, some children possess it, whether others possess it or no; and which, when it is found in children, is found to act promptly and keenly, by reason of the paucity of their ideas. It is an image of the good God, good in Himself, good relatively to the child, with whatever incompleteness; an image before it has been reflected on, and before it is recognized by him as a notion. Though he cannot explain or define the word "God," when told to use it, his acts show that to him it is far more than a word. He listens, indeed, with wonder and interest to fables or tales; he has a dim, shadowy sense of what he hears about persons and matters of this world; but he has that within him which actually vibrates, responds, and gives a deep meaning to the lessons of his first teachers, about the will and the providence of God.

How far this initial religious knowledge comes from without, and how much from within, how much is natural, how much implies a special divine aid which is above nature, we have no means of determining, nor is it necessary for my present purpose to determine. I am not engaged in tracing the image of God in the mind of a child or a man to its first origins, but showing that he can become possessed of such an image, over and above all mere notions of God, and in what that image consists. Whether its elements, latent in the mind, would ever be elicited without extrinsic help is very doubtful; but whatever be the actual history of the first formation of the divine image within us, so far is certain, that, by informations external to ourselves as time goes on, it admits of being strengthened and improved. It is certain too[1], that, whether it grows brighter and stronger, or, on the other hand, is dimmed, distorted, or obliterated, depends on each of us individually, and on his circumstances. It is more than probable that, in the event, from neglect, from the temptations of life, from bad companions, or from the urgency of secular occupations, the light of the soul will fade away and die out. Men transgress their sense of duty, and gradually lose those sentiments of shame and fear, the natural supplements of transgression, which, as I have said, are the witnesses of the Unseen Judge. And, even were it deemed impossible that those who had in their first youth a genuine apprehension of Him, could ever utterly lose it, yet that apprehension may become almost undistinguishable, from an inferential acceptance of the great truth, or may dwindle into a mere notion of their intellect. On the contrary, the image of God, if duly cherished, may expand, deepen, and be completed with the growth of their powers, and in the course of life, under the varied lessons, within and without them, which are brought home to them concerning that same God, One and Personal, by means of education, social intercourse, experience, and literature.

To a mind thus carefully formed upon the basis of its natural conscience, the world, both of nature and of man, does but give back a reflection of those truths about the One Living God, which have been familiar to it from childhood. Good and evil meet us daily as we pass through life, and there are those who think it philosophical to act towards the manifestations of each with some sort of impartiality, as if evil had as much right to be there as good, or even a better, as having more striking triumphs and a broader jurisdiction. And

[1] [Compare the passage in Book IV. of the "Excursion," beginning:—
"Alas! the endowment of immortal power."]

because the course of things is determined by fixed laws, they consider that those laws preclude the present agency of the Creator in the carrying out of particular issues. It is otherwise with the theology of a religious imagination. It has a living hold on truths which are really to be found in the world, though they are not upon the surface. It is able to pronounce by anticipation, what it takes a long argument to prove—that good is the rule, and evil the exception. It is able to assume that, uniform as are the laws of nature, they are consistent with a particular Providence. It interprets what it sees around it by this previous inward teaching, as the true key of that maze of vast complicated disorder; and thus it gains a more consistent and luminous vision of God from the most unpromising materials. Thus conscience is a connecting principle between the creature and his Creator; and the firmest hold of theological truths is gained by habits of personal religion. When men begin all their works with the thought of God, acting for His sake and to fulfil His will, when they ask His blessing on themselves and their life, pray to Him for the objects they desire, and see Him in the event, whether it be according to their prayers or not, they will find everything that happens tend to confirm them in the truths about Him which live in their imagination, varied and unearthly as those truths may be. Then they are brought into His presence as a Living Person, and are able to hold converse with Him, and that with a directness and simplicity, with a confidence and intimacy, *mutatis mutandis*, which we use towards an earthly superior; so that it is doubtful whether we realize the company of our fellow-men with greater keenness than these favoured minds are able to contemplate and adore the Unseen Incomprehensible Creator. ("Grammar of Assent," p. 106.)

HUME'S ARGUMENT AGAINST THE JEWISH AND CHRISTIAN MIRACLES.

It is argued by Hume against the actual occurrence of the Jewish and Christian miracles, that whereas "it is experience only which gives authority to human testimony, and it is the same experience which assures us of the laws of nature," therefore, "when these two kinds of experience are contrary" to each other, "we are bound to subtract the one from the other;" and, in consequence, since we have no experience of a violation of natural laws, and much experience of the violation of truth, "we may establish it as a maxim that no human testimony can have such force as to prove a miracle, and make it a just foundation for any such system of religion."[1]

I will accept the general proposition, but I resist its application. Doubtless it is abstractedly more likely that men should lie than that the order of nature should be infringed; but what is abstract reasoning to a question of concrete fact? To arrive at the fact of any matter, we must eschew generalities, and take things as they stand, with all their circumstances. *À priori*, of course the acts of men are not so trustworthy as the order of nature, and the pretence of miracles is in fact more common than the occurrence. But the question is not about miracles in general, or men in general, but definitely, whether these particular miracles, ascribed to the particular Peter, James, and John, are more likely to have been or not; whether they are unlikely, supposing that there is a Power, external to the world, who can bring them about; supposing

---

[1] Works, vol. iii. p. 17; ed. 1770.

they are the only means by which He can reveal Himself to those who need a revelation ; supposing He is likely to reveal Himself; that He has a great end in doing so; that the professed miracles in question are like His natural works, and such as He is likely to work, in case He wrought miracles ; that great effects, otherwise unaccountable, in the event followed upon the acts said to be miraculous ; that they were from the first accepted as true by large numbers of men against their natural interests; that the reception of them as true has left its mark upon the world, as no other event ever did ; that, viewed in their effects, they have—that is, the belief of them has—served to raise human nature to a high moral standard, otherwise unattainable: these and the like considerations are parts of a great complex argument, which so far can be put into propositions, but which, between, and around, and behind these, is implicit and secret, and cannot by any ingenuity be imprisoned in a formula, and packed into a nut-shell. These various conditions may be decided in the affirmative or in the negative. That is a further point ; here I only insist upon the nature of the argument, if it is to be philosophical. It must be no smart antithesis which may look well on paper, but the living action of the mind on a great problem of fact; and we must summon to our aid all our powers and resources, if we would encounter it worthily, and not as if it were a literary essay. ("Grammar of Assent," p. 298.)

GIBBON'S "FIVE CAUSES."

GIBBON has mentioned five causes in explanation of [the rise and establishment of Christianity], viz. the zeal of Christians, inherited from the Jews; their doctrine of a future state; their claim to miraculous power; their virtues; and their ecclesiastical organization. Let us briefly consider them.

He thinks these five causes, when combined, will fairly account for the event; but he has not thought of accounting for their combination. If they are ever so available for his purpose, still that availableness arises out of their coincidence, and out of what does that coincidence arise? Until this is explained, nothing is explained, and the question had better have been let alone. These presumed causes are quite distinct from each other, and, I say, the wonder is, what made them come together. How came a multitude of Gentiles to be influenced with Jewish zeal? How came zealots to submit to a strict, ecclesiastical *régime*? What connexion has such a *régime* with the immortality of the soul? Why should immortality, a philosophical doctrine, lead to belief in miracles, which is a superstition of the vulgar? What tendency had miracles and magic to make men austerely virtuous? Lastly, what power had a code of virtue, as calm and enlightened as that of Antoninus, to generate a zeal as fierce as that of Maccabæus? Wonderful events before now have apparently been nothing but coincidences, certainly; but they do not become less wonderful by cataloguing their constituent causes, unless we also show how these came to be constituent.

However, this by the way; the real question is this—

are these historical characteristics of Christianity, also in matter of fact, historical causes of Christianity? Has Gibbon given proof that they are? Has he brought evidence of their operation, or does he simply conjecture in his private judgment that they operated? Whether they were adapted to accomplish a certain work, is a matter of opinion; whether they did accomplish it is a question of fact. He ought to adduce instances of their efficiency before he has a right to say that they are efficient. And the second question is, what is this effect, of which they are to be considered as causes? It is no other than this, the conversion of bodies of men to the Christian faith. Let us keep this in view. We have to determine whether these five characteristics of Christianity were efficient causes of bodies of men becoming Christians? I think they neither did effect such conversions, nor were adapted to do so, and for these reasons:—

1. For first, as to zeal, by which Gibbon means, party spirit, or *esprit de corps;* this doubtless is a motive principle when men are already members of a body, but does it operate in bringing them into it? The Jews were born in Judaism, they had a long and glorious history, and would naturally feel and show *esprit de corps;* but how did party spirit tend to bring Jew or Gentile out of his own place into a new society, and that a society which as yet scarcely was formed into a society? Zeal, certainly, may be felt for a cause, or for a person; on this point I shall speak presently; but Gibbon's idea of Christian zeal is nothing better than the old wine of Judaism decanted into new Christian bottles, and would be too flat a stimulant, even if it admitted of such a transference, to be taken as a cause of conversion to Christianity without definite evidence, in proof of the fact. Christians had zeal for Christianity after they were converted, not before.

2. Next, as to the doctrine of a future state. Gibbon seems to mean by this doctrine the fear of hell; now certainly in this day there are persons converted from sin to a religious life by vivid descriptions of the future punishment of the wicked; but then it must be recollected that such persons already believe in the doctrine thus urged upon them. On the contrary, give some tract upon hell-fire to one of the wild boys in a large town, who has had no education, has no faith; and, instead of being startled by it, he will laugh at it as something frightfully ridiculous. The belief in Styx and Tartarus was dying out of the world at the time that Christianity came, as the parallel belief now seems to be dying out in all classes of our own society. The doctrine of eternal punishment does only anger the multitude of men in our large towns now, and make them blaspheme; why should it have had any other effect on the heathen populations in the age when our Lord came? Yet it was among those populations that He and His made their way from the first. As to the hope of eternal life, that doubtless, as well as the fear of hell, was a most operative doctrine in the case of men who had been actually converted, of Christians brought before the magistrate, or writhing under torture; but the thought of eternal glory does not keep bad men from a bad life now, and why should it convert them then from their pleasant sins, to a heavy, mortified, joyless existence, to a life of ill-usage, fright, contempt, and desolation?

3. That the claim to miracles should have any wide influence in favour of Christianity among heathen populations, who had plenty of portents of their own, is an opinion in curious contrast with the objection against Christianity which has provoked an answer from Paley, viz. that " Christian miracles are not recited or appealed to, by early Christian writers themselves, so fully or so

frequently as might have been expected." Paley[1] solves the difficulty as far as it is a fact, by observing, as I have suggested, that "it was their lot to contend with magical agency, against which the mere production of these facts was not sufficient for the convincing of their adversaries:" "I do not know," he continues, "whether they themselves thought it quite decisive of the controversy." A claim to miraculous power on the part of Christians, which is so unfrequent as to become an objection to the fact of their possessing it, can hardly have been a principal cause of their success.

4. And how is it possible to imagine with Gibbon that what he calls the "sober and domestic virtues" of Christians, their "aversion to the luxury of the age," their "chastity, temperance, and economy," that these dull qualities were persuasives of a nature to win and melt the hard heathen heart, in spite too of the dreary prospect of the *barathrum*, the amphitheatre, and the stake? Did the Christian morality by its severe beauty make a convert of Gibbon himself? On the contrary, he bitterly says, "It was not in this world that the primitive Christians were desirous of making themselves either agreeable or useful." "The virtue of the primitive Christians, like that of the first Romans, was very frequently guarded by poverty and ignorance." "Their gloomy and austere aspect, their abhorrence of the common business and pleasures of life, and their frequent predictions of impending calamities, inspired the Pagans with the apprehension of some danger which would arise from the new sect." Here we have not only Gibbon hating their moral and social bearing, but his heathen also. How then were those heathen overcome by the amiableness of that which they viewed with such

---

[1] [See note at p. 147.]

disgust? We have here plain proof that the Christian character repelled the heathen; where is the evidence that it converted them?

5. Lastly, as to the ecclesiastical organization, this, doubtless, as time went on, was a special characteristic of the new religion; but how could it directly contribute to its extension? Of course it gave it strength, but it did not give it life. We are not born of bones and muscles. It is one thing to make conquests, another to consolidate an empire. Before Constantine, Christians made their great conquests. Rules are for settled times, not for time of war. So much is this contrast felt in the Catholic Church now, that, as is well known, in heathen countries and in countries which have thrown off her yoke she suspends her diocesan administration and her Canon Law, and puts her children under the extraordinary, extra-legal jurisdiction of Propaganda.

This is what I am led to say on Gibbon's Five Causes. I do not deny that they might have operated now and then; Simon Magus came to Christianity in order to learn the craft of miracles, and Peregrinus from love of influence and power; but Christianity made its way, not by individual, but by broad, wholesale conversions, and the question is, how they originated?

It is very remarkable that it should not have occurred to a man of Gibbon's sagacity to enquire, what account the Christians themselves gave of the matter. Would it not have been worth while for him to have let conjecture alone, and to have looked for facts instead? Why did he not try the hypothesis of faith, hope, and charity? Did he never hear of love towards God, and faith in Christ? Did he not recollect the many words of Apostles, Bishops, Apologists, Martyrs, all forming one testimony? No; such thoughts are close upon him, and close upon the truth; but he cannot sympathize with them, he cannot believe in them, he cannot even enter into them, *because* he needs the due preparation of mind. ("Grammar of Assent," p. 451.)

THE PRINCIPLE OF FAITH.

THE Gospel, as contrasted with all religious systems which have gone before and come after, even those in which God has spoken, is specially the system of faith and "the law of faith," and its obedience is the "obedience of faith," and its justification is "by faith," and it is a "power of God unto salvation to every one that believeth." For at the time of its first preaching the Jews went by sight and the Gentiles by reason; both might believe, but on a belief resolvable into sight or reason—neither went simply by faith. The Greeks sought after "wisdom," some original and recondite philosophy, which might serve as an "evidence" or ground of proof for "things not seen." The Jews, on the other hand, "required a sign," some sensible display of God's power, a thing of sight and touch, which might be "the substance," the earnest and security "of things hoped for." Such was the state of the world, when it pleased Almighty God, in furtherance of his plan of mercy, to throw men's minds upon the next world, without any other direct medium of evidence than the word of man claiming to be His; to change the face of the world by what the world called "the foolishness of preaching" and the unreasoning zeal and obstinacy of faith, using a principle in truth's behalf which in the world's evil history has ever been the spring of great events and strange achievements. Faith, which in the natural man has manifested itself in the fearful energy of superstition and fanaticism, is in the Gospel grafted on the love of God, and made to mould the heart of man into His image.

The Apostles then proceeded thus:—they did not rest their cause on argument; they did not rely on eloquence, wisdom, or reputation; nay, nor did they make miracles necessary to the enforcement of their claims.[1] They did not resolve faith into sight or reason; they contrasted it with both, and bade their hearers believe, sometimes in spite, sometimes in default, sometimes in aid, of sight and reason. They exhorted them to make trial of the Gospel, since they would find their account in so doing. They appealed to men's hearts, and, according to their hearts, so they answered them. They appealed to their secret belief in a superintending Providence, to their hopes and fears thence resulting; and they professed to reveal to them the nature, personality, attributes, will, and works of Him "whom they ignorantly worshipped." They came as commissioned from Him, and declared that mankind was a guilty and outcast race,—that sin was a misery,—that the world was a

---

[1] Vid. Acts xvii. 23, xxiv. 25. Paley, whose work on the Evidences is founded on the notion that the miracles wrought by Christ and His Apostles are to be *the ground* of our faith, feels the difficulty that *in fact* they were not so accounted in early times. After quoting passages of the Fathers in his favour, he adds, " I am ready, however, to admit that the ancient Christian advocates did not insist upon the miracles in argument *so frequently as I should have done.* It was their lot to contend with notions of magical agency, against which the mere production of the facts was not sufficient for the convincing of their adversaries. *I do not know whether they themselves thought it quite decisive of the controversy.*"—Part iii. c. 5, fin. Then on what *did* they believe? Again: Are not philosophical objections as cogent now against miracles as the belief in magic then?

snare,—that life was a shadow,—that God was everlasting, —that His Law was holy and true, and its sanctions certain and terrible ;—that He also was all-merciful,—that He had appointed a Mediator between Him and them, who had removed all obstacles, and was desirous to restore them, and that He had sent themselves to explain how. They said that that Mediator had come and gone ; but had left behind Him what was to be His representative till the end of all things, His mystical Body, the Church, in joining which lay the salvation of the world.

So they preached, and so they prevailed ; using indeed persuasives of every kind as they were given them, but resting at bottom on a principle higher than the senses or the reason. They used many arguments, but as outward forms of something beyond argument. Thus they appealed to the miracles they wrought, as sufficient signs of their power, and assuredly divine, in spite of those which other systems could show or pretended. They expostulated with the better sort on the ground of their instinctive longings and dim visions of something greater than the world. They awed and overcame the passionate by means of what remained of heaven in them, and of the involuntary homage which such men pay to the more realized tokens of heaven in others. They asked the more generous-minded whether it was not worth while to risk something on the chance of augmenting and perfecting those precious elements of good which their hearts still held ; and they could not hide what they cared not to "glory in," their own disinterested sufferings, their high deeds, and their sanctity of life. They won over the affectionate and gentle by the beauty of holiness, and the embodied mercies of Christ as seen in the ministrations and ordinances of His Church. Thus they spread their nets for disciples, and caught thousands at a cast ; thus they roused and inflamed their hearers into enthusiasm, till "the Kingdom of Heaven suffered violence, and the violent took it by force."

And when these had entered it, many of them, doubtless, would wax cold in love, and fall away; for many had entered only on impulse; many, with Simon Magus, on wonder or curiosity; many from a mere augmentative belief, which leads as readily into heresy as into the Truth. But still, those who had the seed of God within them, would become neither offences in the Church, nor apostates, nor heretics; but would find day by day, as love increased, increased experience that what they had ventured boldly, amid conflicting evidence, of sight against sight, and reason against reason, with many things against it, but more things for it, they had ventured well. The examples of meekness, cheerfulness, contentment, silent endurance, private self-denial, fortitude, brotherly love, perseverance in well-doing, which would from time to time meet them in their new kingdom,—the sublimity and harmony of the Church's doctrine,—the touching and subduing beauty of her services and appointments,—their consciousness of her virtue, divinely imparted, upon themselves, in subduing, purifying, changing them,—the bountifulness of her alms-giving,—her power, weak as she was and despised, over the statesmen and philosophers of the world,—her consistent and steady aggression upon it, moving forward in spite of it on all sides at once, like the wheels in the Prophet's vision, and this in contrast with the ephemeral and variable outbreaks of sectarianism,—the unanimity and intimacy existing between her widely-separated branches, — the mutual sympathy and correspondence of men of hostile nations and foreign languages,—the simplicity of her ascetics, the gravity of her Bishops, the awful glory shed around her Martyrs, and the mysterious and recurring traces of miraculous agency here and there, once and again according as the Spirit willed,—these and the like persuasives acted on them day by day, turning the whisper of their hearts into an habitual conviction, and establishing in the reason what had been begun in the will. And thus has the Church been upheld ever since by an appeal to the People,—to the necessities of human nature, the anxieties of conscience, and the instincts of purity; forcing upon Kings a sufferance or protection which they fain would dispense with, and upon Philosophy a grudging submission and a reserved and limited recognition. ("Lectures on Justification," pp. 267–272.)

PART III.

HISTORICAL.

ENGLISH JEALOUSY OF CHURCH AND ARMY.

EVERY Sovereign State will naturally feel a jealousy of an *imperium in imperio*, though not every State is in a condition to give expression to it. England has indulged that jealousy to the full, and has assumed a bearing towards the military profession much the same as she shows towards the ecclesiastical. There is, indeed, a close analogy between the two powers, both in themselves and in their relation to the State; and, in order to explain the position of the army in England, I cannot do better than refer to the position which in this country has been assigned to the Church. The Church and the Army are respectively the instruments of moral and material force, and are real powers in their own respective fields of operation. They necessarily have common sympathies and an intense *esprit de corps*. They are, in consequence, the strongest supports or the most formidable opponents of the State to which they belong, and require to be subjected, beyond any mistake, to its sovereignty. In England, sensitively suspicious of combination and system, three precautions have been taken in dealing with the soldier and the parson—(I hope I may be familiar without offence)—precautions borrowed from the necessary treatment of wild animals— (1) to tie him up; (2) to pare his claws; and (3) to keep him low; then he will be both safe and useful;—the result is a National Church, and a Constitutional Army.

1. In the first place we tie both parson and soldier up, by forbidding each to form one large organization. We prohibit an organized religion and an organized force. Instead of one corporation in religion, we only allow of a multitude of small ones, as chapters and rectories, while we ignore the Establishment as a whole, deny it any legal status, and recognize the Dissenting bodies. For Universities we substitute Colleges with rival interests, that the intellect may not be too strong for us, as is the case with some other countries; we freely multiply local schools, for they have no political significance. And in like manner we are willing to perfect the discipline and appointment of regiments, but we instinctively recoil from the idea of an army. We toast, indeed, "The Army," but as an abstraction, as we used to drink to "The Church," before the present substitution of "The Clergy of all Denominations," which has much more of reality in it. Moreover, while we have a real reason for sending our troops all over the world, shifting them about, using them for garrison duty, and for the defence of dependencies, we are thereby able also to hide and divide them from one another. Nor is this all; if any organization requires a directing mind at the head of it, it is an army; but, faithful to our Constitutional instincts, we have committed its command, *ex abundanti cautelâ*, to as many, I believe, as five independent boards, whose concurrence is necessary for a practical result. Nay, as late occurrences have shown, we have thought it a less evil that our troops should be starved in the Crimea for for want of the proper officer to land the stores, and that clothing and fuel shall oscillate to and fro between Balaklava and Malta, than that there should be the chance for the smallest opening into our political system of a power

formidable to nationalism. Thus we tie up both parson and soldier.

2. Next, in all great systems and agencies of any kind, there are certain accessories, absolutely necessary for their efficiency, yet hardly included in their essential idea. Such, to take a very small matter, is the use of the bag in making a pudding. Material edifices are no part of religion, but you cannot have religious services without them; nor can you move field-pieces without horses, nor get together horses without markets and transports. The greater part of these supplemental articles the English Constitution denies to its religious establishment altogether, and to its army, when not on active service. Fabrics of worship, it encourages; but it gives no countenance to such ecclesiastical belongings as the ritual and ceremonial of religion, synods, religious orders, sisters of charity, and the like necessary instruments of Christian faith, which zealous Churchmen in times of spiritual danger, decay, or promise, make vain endeavours to restore. And such in military matters are the commissariat, transport, and medical departments, which are jealously suppressed in time of peace, and hastily and grudgingly restored on the commencement of hostilities. The Constitutional spirit allows to the troops arms and ammunition, as it allows to the clergy ordination and two sacraments, neither being really dangerous, while the supplements which I have spoken of are withheld. Then it cuts their claws.

3. And lastly, it keeps them low. Though lawyers are educated for the law, and physicians for medicine, it is felt among us to be dangerous to the Constitution to have real education either in the clerical or military profession. Neither theology nor the science of war is compatible with a military *régime*. Military and naval science is, in the ordinary Englishman's notion, the bayonet and the broad-

side. Religious knowledge comes by nature ; and so far is true, that Anglican divines thump away, in exhortation or in controversy, with a manliness, good sense, and good will as thoroughly John Bullish as the stubbornness of the Guards at Inkermann. Not that they are forbidden to cultivate theology in private as a personal accomplishment, but that they must not bring too much of it into the pulpit, for then they become extreme men, Calvinists or Papists, as it may be. A general good education, a public school, a knowledge of the classics, makes a parson ; and he is chosen for a benefice or a dignity, not on any abstract ground of merit, but by the great officers of the State, by members of the aristocracy, and by country gentlemen, or by their nominees, men who by their position are a sufficient guarantee that the nation will continually flow into the Establishment, and give it its own colour. And so of the army ; it is not so many days ago that a gentleman in office assured the House of Commons (if he was correctly reported) that the best officers were those who had a University education ; and I doubt not it is far better for the troops to be disciplined and commanded by good scholars than by incapables and dunces. But in each department professional education is eschewed, and it is thought enough that the functionary be a gentleman. A clergyman is the "resident gentleman" in his parish ; and no soldier must rise from the ranks, because he is not "company for gentlemen."

Let no man call this satire, for it is most seriously said ; nor have I intentionally coloured one sentence in the parallel which I have been drawing out ; nor do I speak as grumbling at things as they are ;—I merely want to look facts in the face. I have been exposing what I consider the weak side in our Constitution, not exactly because I want it altered, but because people should not consider it the strong side. I think it a necessary weakness. I do not see how it can be satisfactorily set right without dangerous innovations. ("Discussions and Arguments," p. 356.)

IRISH DISCONTENT.

(I.)

[AN English visitor to Ireland] if he happens to be a Catholic, has in consequence a trial to sustain of his own of which the continental tourist has no experience from Austrian police, or Russian douane, or Turkish quarantine. He has turned his eyes to a country bound to him by the ties of a common faith; and, when he lands at Cork or Kingstown, he breathes more freely from the thought that he has left a Protestant people behind him, and is among his co-religionists. He has but this one imagination before his mind, that he is in the midst of those who will not despise him for his faith's sake, who name the same sacred names, and utter the same prayers, and use the same devotions, as he does himself; whose churches are the houses of his God, and whose numerous clergy are the physicians of the soul. He penetrates into the heart of the country; and he recognizes an innocence in the young face, and a piety and patience in the aged voice, which strikingly and sadly contrast with the habits of his own rural population. Scattered over these masses of peasantry, and peasants themselves, he hears of a number of lay persons who have dedicated themselves to a religious celibate, and who, by their superior knowledge as well as sanctity, are the natural and ready guides of their humble brethren. He finds the population as munificent as it is pious, and doing greater works for God out of their poverty, than the rich and noble elsewhere accomplish in their abundance. He finds them characterized by a love of kindred so tender and faithful as to lead them, on their compulsory expatriation, to send back from their first earnings in another hemisphere incredible sums, with the purpose of bringing over to it those dear ones whom they have left in the old country. And he finds himself received with that warmth of hospitality which ever has been Ireland's boast; and, as far as he is personally concerned, his blood is forgotten in his baptism. How shall he not, under such circumstances, exult in his new friends, and feel words deficient to express both his deep reverence for their virtues, and his strong sympathy in their heavy trials?

But, alas, feelings which are so just and natural in themselves, which are so congruous in the breast of Frenchman or Italian, are impertinent in him. He does not at first recollect, as he ought to recollect, that he comes among the Irish people as a representative of persons, and actions, and catastrophes, which it is not pleasant to any one to think about; that he is responsible for the deeds of his forefathers, and of his contemporary Parliaments and Executive; that he is one of a strong, unscrupulous, tyrannous race, standing upon the soil of the injured. He does not bear in mind that it is as easy to forget injuring, as it is difficult to forget being injured. He does not admit, even in his imagination, the judgment and the sentence which the passed history of Erin sternly pronounces upon him. He has to be recalled to himself, and to be taught by what he hears around him, that an Englishman has no right to open his heart, and indulge his honest affection towards the Irish race, as if nothing had happened between him and them. The voices, so full of blessings for their Maker and their own kindred, adopt a very different strain and cadence when the name of England is mentioned; and, even when he is most warmly and generously received by those whom he falls in with, he will be repudiated by those who are at a distance. Natural amiableness, religious principle, education, reading, knowledge of the world, and the charities of civilization, repress or eradicate these bitter feelings in the class in which he finds his friends; but, as to the population, one sentiment of hatred against the oppressor, *manet altâ mente repostum*. The wrongs which England has inflicted are faithfully remembered; her services are viewed with incredulity or resentment; her name and fellowship are abominated; the news of her prosperity heard with disgust; the anticipation of her possible reverses nursed and cherished as the best of consolations. The success of France and Russia over her armies, of Yankee or Hindoo, is fervently desired as the first instalment of a debt accumulated through seven centuries; and that, even though those armies are in so large a proportion recruited from the Irish soil. If he ventures at least to ask for prayers for England, he receives one answer—a prayer that she may receive her due. It is as if the air rang with the old Jewish words, "O daughter of Babylon, blessed shall he be who shall repay thee as thou has paid to us!"

(II.)

It is remarkable that the Holy See, to whose initiative the union of the two countries is historically traceable, is in no respect made chargeable by the Irish people with the evils which have resulted to them from it. And the fact itself is remarkable that the Holy See really should be responsible for that initiative. There are other nations in the world ill-matched besides the English and Irish. There are other instances of the rule of strangers, and of the compulsory submission of the governed; but the Pope cannot be called to account for such political arrangements. The Pope did not give Greece to the Sublime Porte, or Warsaw to Russia, or Venice to Austria, or Belgium to Holland, or Norway to Sweden, or the cities of the Rhine to Prussia, the Septinsular Republic to England; but, even had he done so, still in some of these instances, he would have but united together members of one race—German to German, Fleming to Fleming, Slave to Slave. But it is certainly most remarkable that a power so authoritative, even when not divine, so sagacious, even when not supernatural; whose acts are so literally the personal acts of the Pontiff who represents it for the time being, yet of such solemn force and such tremendous permanence; which, by appealing to its present prerogatives, involves itself in its past decisions, which "openeth, and no man shutteth, and shutteth and no man openeth;"—it does we say require some explanation[1]

---

[1] [The explanation Dr. Newman offers is, that the "*object*" of the Holy See in annexing Ireland to the English crown in the twelfth century was "a *religious* one," while "the circumstantial evils in which it had no real part were *temporal.*" The Irish were "lapsing back to bar-

how an oracle so high and irrefragable should have given
its religious sanction to a union apparently so unblessed,
and which at the end of seven centuries is as devoid of
moral basis or of effective accomplishment, as it was at the
commencement. What time German and Italian, Turk
and Greek, shall be contented with each other; when "the
lion and the sheep shall abide together," and "the calf and
the bear shall feed,"—then, it will be argued, will there be
a good understanding between two nations so contradictory
the one of the other—the one an old immemorial race, the
other the composite of a hundred stocks; the one possessed
of an antique civilization, the other civilized by Christianity;
the one glorying in its schools and its philosophy, the other
in its works and institutions; the one subtle, acute, speculative, the other wise, patient, energetic; the one ad-
miring and requiring the strong arm of despotic rule,
the other spontaneously developing itself in methods of
self-government and of individual competition. And yet,
not once or twice only has the Holy See recognized in
Ireland a territory of the English Crown. Adrian IV.,
indeed, the first Pope who countenanced the invasion of
Henry II., was an Englishman; but not on his bull did
Henry rely for the justification of his proceedings. He
did not publish it in Ireland till he had received a confirmatory brief from Alexander III. Nor was Alexander the

barism," and "it was surely incumbent on the power which had converted them to interfere." The remedy the Pope applied was to send
against them the Normans—"the soldiers of a young and ambitious
power, first to reform, then secondly to unite them together." "In
matter of fact, the policy which he pursued towards Ireland, is precisely that which he had adopted towards England a century earlier,
except that its concomitants in the case of England were far more
penal, in severity at least if not in duration." See the paper (unfortu-
nately unfinished) from which the above extract is taken, "The
Northmen and Normans in England and Ireland."]

only Pope who distinctly recognized it; John XXII., a hundred and sixty years afterwards, refers to it in his brief addressed to Edward II.[1]

Such have been the dealings of the Holy See in times past with Ireland; yet it has not thereby roused against itself any resentful feelings in the minds of its natives. Doubtless, their good sense understands well that, whatever be decided about the expedience of the act of annexation itself, its serious evils did not begin until the English monarchy was false to the Pope as well as to Ireland. Up to that date the settlers in the conquered soil became so attached and united to it and its people, that, according to the proverb, they were *Hibernis hiberniores*. It is Protestantism which has been the tyrannical oppressor of the Irish; and we suppose that Protestantism neither asked nor needed letters apostolic or consecrated banner to encourage it in the war it waged against Irish Catholicism. Neither Cromwell nor William of Nassau waited for the Pope's leave or sought his blessing in his military operations against Ireland, any more than Queen Victoria appeals to the Pope's grant for her title of Defender of the Faith, though from the Pope it was originally derived. The Tudor, not the Plantagenet, introduced the iron age of Ireland. ("Hist. Sketches," vol. III. p. 257.)

THE NORTHMAN CHARACTER.

THOUGH of the same stock as the Saxons, the Northmen were gifted with a more heroic cast of soul. Perhaps it was the peculiar scenery and climate of their native

[1] Lanigan, vol. IV. pp. 165-6.

homes which suggested to them such lofty aspirations, and such enthusiastic love of dangers and hardship. The stillness of the desert may fill the fierce Arab with a rapturous enjoyment,[1] and the interminable forests of Britain or Germany might breathe profound mystery; but the icy mountains and the hoarse resounding waves of the North nurtured warriors of a princely stature, both in mind and body, befitting the future occupants of European thrones. Cradled in the surge and storm, they were spared the temptation of indolence and luxury; they neither worshipped the vivifying powers of nature with the Greek, nor with the Sabean did they kiss the hand to the bright stars of heaven; but while they gave a personal presence and volition to the fearful or the beautiful spirits which haunted the mountains, or lay in ambush in the mist, they understood by daily experience that good could not be had by the mere wishing, and they made it a first article in their creed that their reward was future, and that their present must be toil.

The light and gloom, the nobleness, the sternness, and the fancifulness of the Northman character, are admirably portrayed in the romantic tales of Fouqué. At one time he brings before us the honour-loving Froda, the friend of the Skalds, who had been taught in the book of a learned Icelander how the Lady Aslauga, a hundred years and more before, had, in her golden veil of flowing hair, won the love of King Ragnar Lodbrog, and who, smit with devotion to her, saw from time to time the sudden apparition of his bright queen in the cloudy autumn sky, animating him to great and warlike deeds. At another

---

[1] "A young French renegade confessed to Chateaubriand that he never found himself alone, galloping in the desert, without a sensation approaching to rapture, which was indescribable." (Notes to "The Bride of Abydos.")

time it is the Lady Minnetrost, the good Druda, far up upon the shores of the Baltic, on her high, moonlit tower, with her long white finger lifted up and pointing to the starry sky. Then, again, we have the tall slim form of the beautiful Sigrid, with her large blue eyes, singing her charm, gathering witch-herbs, and brewing her witch-draught, which makes heroes invincible in fight, and works in the banquet a black mysterious woe. Then we have the gigantic forms of men on the islands of the lake, with massive breastplates and huge brazen bucklers, and halberts so high that they seemed like the masts of vessels. And then the vessel comes in sight, ready for the use of the sea-knights in their pirate expeditions, and off they go over the bounding waves, on their terrible errands of blood and fire, to gain immortal glory by inflicting untold pain. And suddenly appears one of them at a marriage-feast in Normandy, the sea-king Arinbiorn, one of those warriors in the high coast country who own little or nothing on the main land, but who sail round the earth in their light barks, in the company of brave and devoted followers, passing from one side of the North Cape, nay, even from distant Iceland down to imperial Constantinople, or along the coast of blooming Asia, or of burning Africa, where almost all other seamen are at fault. And at another time we are shown the spectres of remorse, and death and judgment; and the living forms of pride, passion, and temptation, in the history of the troubled child of the fierce warrior of Drontheim. And, on the other hand, the pattern knight and his lady bright coming back to their old country from the plains of Frank-land, and presenting to the savage northern race the very ideal which they vaguely sought after, but could not adumbrate; and the pale, dark-haired Sintram, calmed and vanquished by the voice and lute of the fair Gabrielle.

This of course is romance; but it may be taken as an anticipation of what the Northmen became in the Normans. ("Historical Sketches," vol. III. p. 290.)

NORTHMAN AND NORMAN.

THE most obvious and prominent point of character common to the Northman and Norman is the peculiarity of their warlike heroism. War was their life; it was almost their *summum bonum;* good in itself, though nothing came of it.

The impetuosity of the Norman relieved itself in extravagancies, and raises a smile from its very intensity; at one time becoming a religious fanaticism, at another a fantastic knight-errantry. His very worship was to do battle; his rite of sacrifice was a passage of arms. He couched his lance to prove the matter-of-fact that his lady was the beautifullest of all conceivable women; he drew his sword on the blasphemer to convince him of the sanctity of the Gospel; and he passed abruptly from demolishing churches and burning towns to the rescue of the holy Sepulchre from the unclean infidel. In the Northmen, too, this pride of demolition had been their life-revel. They destroyed for destroying-sake; because it was good to destroy; it was a display of power, and power made them gods. They seemed as though they were possessed by some inward torment which needed outlet, and which degraded them to the madness of their own Berserkirs in the absence of some nobler satisfaction. Their fearful activity was their mode of searching out something great, they knew not what, the idea of which haunted them. It impelled them to those sudden descents and rapid careerings about a country, of which we have already spoken, and which, even in modern times, have their parallels in the characteristic energy of Gustavus and Charles XII. of Sweden. Hence, too, when they had advanced some steps in the path of civilization, from this nature or habit of restlessness, they could not bear neutrality; they interfered actively in the cause of right, in proportion as they gave up the practice of wrong. When they began to find out that piracy was criminal, instead of having recourse to peaceful occupations, they found an occupation cognate to piracy itself in putting piracy down. Kings, indeed, would naturally undertake such a mission, for piracy interfered with their sovereign power, and would not die of itself. It was not wonderful that Harold, Haco the Good and St. Olaf should hang the pirates and destroy their vessels, but the point of our remark is this, that they pursued the transgressors with the same furious zeal with which they had heretofore committed the same transgressions themselves. It is sometimes said that a reformed profligate is the sternest of moralists; and these northern rovers, on their conversion, did penance for their own piracy by a relentless persecution of pirates. They became knight-errants on water, devoting themselves to hardship and peril in the protection of the peaceful merchant. Under Canute of Denmark, a confraternity was formed with this object. Its members characteristically began by seizing on vessels not their own for its prosecution, and imposing compulsory loans on the wealthy trader for their outfit, though they professed to indemnify their owners out of the booty ultimately secured. Before they went on board they communicated; they lived soberly and severely, restricting themselves to as few followers as possible. When they found Christians in the captured ships, they set them at liberty, clothed them, and sent them home. In this way as many as eight hundred pirate vessels were destroyed.

Sometimes, in spite of their reformation, they still pursued a pirate's trade; but it was a modified piracy. They put themselves under laws in the exercise of it, and waged war against those who did not observe them. The objects of their hostility were what Turner calls "indiscriminate" pirates. "Their peculiar and self-chosen task," he says, "was to protect the defenceless navigator, and to seek and assail the *indiscriminate* plunderer. The pirate gradually became hunted down as the general enemy of the human race." He goes on to mention some of the laws imposed by Hialmar upon himself and some other discriminating pirates, to the effect that they would protect trade and agriculture, that they would not force women into their ships against their will, and that they would not eat raw flesh.

Now in what we have been drawing out there is enough to show both the elementary resemblance of character, and yet the vast dissimilitude, between the Scandinavian and the Norman. ("Hist. Sketches," vol. III. p. 295.)

ATHENS.

IF we would know what a University is, considered in its most elementary idea, we must betake ourselves to the first and most celebrated home of European civilization, to the bright and beautiful Athens,—Athens, whose schools drew to her bosom, and then sent back to the business of life, the youth of the western world for a long thousand years. Seated on the verge of the continent, the city seemed hardly suited for the duties of a central metropolis of knowledge; yet what it lost in convenience of approach, it gained in its neighbourhood to the traditions of the mysterious East, and in the loveliness of the region in which it lay. Hither, then, as to a sort of ideal land, where all the archetypes of the great and the fair were found in substantial being, and all departments of truth explored, and all diversities of intellectual power exhibited; where taste and philosophy were majestically enthroned as in a royal court; where there was no sovereignty but that of mind, and no nobility but that of genius; when professors were rulers and princes did homage,—hither flocked continually from the very corners of the *orbis terrarum*, the many-tongued generation, just rising or just risen into manhood, in order to gain wisdom.

Pisistratus had in an early age discovered and nursed the infant genius of his people, and Cimon, after the Persian war, had given it a home; that war had established the naval supremacy of Athens; she had become an imperial state; and the Ionians, bound to her by the double chain of kindred and of subjection, were importing into her both their merchandize and their civilization. The arts and philosophy of the Asiatic Court were easily carried across the sea, and there was Cimon, as I have said, with his ample fortune, ready to receive them with due honour. Not content with patronizing their profession, he built the first of those noble porticos, of which we hear so much in Athens, and he formed the groves, which in process of time formed the celebrated academy. Planting is one of the most graceful, as in Athens it was one of the most beneficent, of employments. Cimon took in hand the wild wood, pruned and dressed it, and laid it out with handsome walks and welcome fountains. Nor, while hospitable to the authors of the city's civilization, was he ungrateful to the instruments of her prosperity. His trees extended their cool, umbrageous branches over the merchants who assembled in the Agora, for many generations.

Those merchants certainly had deserved that act of bounty; for all the while their ships had been carrying forth the intellectual fame of Athens to the western world. Then commenced what may be called her University existence. Pericles, who succeeded Cimon, both in the Government and in the patronage of art, is said by Plutarch to have entertained the idea of making Athens the capital of federated Greece; in this he failed; but his encouragement of such men as Phidias and Anaxagoras led the way to her acquiring a far more lasting sovereignty over a far wider empire. Little understanding the sources of her own greatness, Athens would go to war; peace is the interest of a seat of commerce and the arts; but to war she went; yet to her, whether peace or war, it mattered not. The political power of Athens waned and disappeared; kingdoms rose and fell; centuries rolled away,—they did but bring fresh triumphs to the city of the poet and the sage. There at length the swarthy Moor and Spaniard were seen to meet the blue-eyed Gaul; and the Cappadocian, late subject of Mithridates, gazed without alarm at the haughty conquering Roman. Revolution after revolution passed over the face of Europe, as well as of Greece, but still she was there,—Athens, the city of the mind, as radiant, as splendid, as delicate, as young, as ever she had been.

Many a more fruitful coast or isle is washed by the blue Ægean, many a spot is there more beautiful or sublime to see, many a territory more ample; but there was one charm in Attica, which in the same perfection was nowhere else. The deep pastures of Arcadia, the plain of Argos, the Thessalian vale, these had not the gift; Bœotia which lay to its immediate north was notorious for the very want of it. The heavy atmosphere of that Bœotia might be good for vegetation, but it was associated in popular belief with the dullness of the Bœotian intellect; on the contrary, the special purity, elasticity, clearness, and salubrity of the air of Attica, fit concomitant and emblem of its genius, did that for it which earth did not;—it brought out every bright line and tender shade of the landscape over which it was spread, and would have illuminated the face even of a more barren and rugged country.

A confined triangle, perhaps fifty miles its greatest length, and thirty its greatest breadth; two elevated rocky barriers meeting at an angle; three prominent mountains, commanding the plain,—Parnes, Pentelicus, and Hymettus; an unsatisfactory soil; some streams, not always full;—such is about the report which the agent of a London company would have made of Attica. He would report that the climate was mild, the hills were limestone; there was plenty of good marble; more pasture land than at first survey might have been expected, sufficient certainly for sheep and goats; fisheries productive; silver mines once, but long since worked out; figs fair; oil first-rate; olives in profusion. But what he would not think of noting down was, that that olive tree was so choice in nature and so noble in shape, that it excited a religious veneration, and that it took so kindly to the light soil, as to expand into woods upon the open plain, and to climb up and fringe the hills. He would not think of writing word to his employer, how that clear air, of which I have spoken, brought out, yet blended and subdued, the colours on the marble, till they had a softness and harmony, for all their richness, which in a picture looks exaggerated, yet is after all within the truth. He would not tell how that same delicate and brilliant atmosphere freshened up the pale olive, until the

olive forgot its monotony, and its cheek glowed like the
arbutus or beech of the Umbrian hills. He would say
nothing of the thyme and thousand fragrant herbs which
carpeted Hymettus; he would hear nothing of the hum of
its bees, nor take much account of the rare flavour of its
honey, since Sozo and Minorca were sufficient for the
English demand. He would look over the Ægean from
the height he had ascended; he would follow with his eye
the chain of islands, which, starting from the Sunian head-
land, seemed to offer the fabled divinities of Attica, when
they would visit their Ionian cousins, a sort of viaduct
thereto across the sea; but that fancy would not occur to
him, nor any admiration of the dark violet billows with
their white edges down below; nor of those graceful, fan-
like jets of silver upon the rocks, which slowly rise aloft
like water spirits from the deep, then shiver and break, and
spread, and shroud themselves, and disappear, in a soft
mist of foam; nor of the gentle, incessant heaving and
panting of the whole liquid plain; nor of the long waves,
keeping steady time, like a line of soldiery, as they resound
upon the hollow shore—he would not deign to notice that
restless living element at all, except to bless his stars that
he was not upon it. Nor the distinct detail, nor the refined colouring, nor the graceful outline and roseate golden
line of the jutting crags, nor the bold shadows cast from
Otus or Laurium by the declining sun—our agent of a
mercantile firm would not value these matters even at a
low figure. Rather we must turn for the sympathy we
seek to yon pilgrim student, come from a semi-barbarous
land to that small corner of the earth, as to a shrine, where
he might take his fill of gazing on those emblems and cor-
uscations of invisible, unoriginate perfection. It was the
stranger from a remote province, from Britain or from
Mauritania, who in a scene so different from that of his

chilly, woody swamps, or of his fiery, choking sands, learned at once what a real University must be, by coming to understand the sort of country which was its suitable home.

Nor was this all that a University required and found in Athens. No one, not even there, could live on poetry. If the students at that famous place had nothing better than bright hues and soothing sounds they would not have been able or disposed to turn their residence there to much account. Of course they must have the means of living, nay, in a certain sense, of enjoyment, if Athens was to be an *alma mater* at the time, or to remain afterwards a pleasant thought in their memory. And so they had: be it recollected Athens was a port and a mart of trade, perhaps the first in Greece, and strangers were ever flocking to it, whose combat was to be with intellectual, not physical difficulties, and who claimed to have their bodily wants supplied that they might be at leisure to set about furnishing their minds. Now barren as was the soil of Attica, and bare the face of the country, yet it had only too many resources for an elegant, nay, luxurious abode there. So abundant were the imports of the place, that it was a common saying, that the productions which were found singly elsewhere were brought altogether in Athens. Corn and wine, the staple of existence in such a climate, came from the islands of the Ægean; fine wool and carpeting from Asia Minor; slaves, as now, from the Euxine; and timber too, and iron and brass, from the coasts of the Mediterranean. The Athenian did not condescend to manufactures himself, but encouraged them in others, and a population of foreigners caught at the lucrative occupation, both for home consumption and for exportation. Their cloth and other textures for dress and furniture, and their hardware—for instance, armour—were in great request. Labour was cheap; stone and marble in plenty; and the taste and skill, which at first were devoted to public buildings, as temples and porticos, were in course of time applied to the mansions of public men. If nature did much for Athens, it is undeniable that art did much more. ("Hist. Sketches," vol. III. p. 18.)

OXFORD.

ALAS! for centuries past that city has lost its prime honour and boast as a servant and soldier of the truth. Once named the second school of the Church, second only to Paris, the foster-mother of St. Edmund, St. Richard, St. Thomas Cantilupe; the theatre of great intellects; of Scotus the subtle doctor, of Hales the irrefragable, of Occam the special, of Bacon the admirable, of Middleton the solid, and of Bradwardine the profound, Oxford has now lapsed to the level of mere human loveliness, which, in its highest perfection, we admire in Athens. Nor would it have a place, now or hereafter, in these pages, nor would it occur to me to speak its name, except that—even in its sorrowful deprivation—it still retains so much of that outward lustre which, like the brightness on the prophet's face, ought to be a ray from an illumination within, as to afford me an illustration of the point on which I am engaged, viz. what should be the material dwelling-place and appearance, the local circumstances and the secular concomitants, of a great University. Pictures are drawn in tales of romance of spirits seemingly too beautiful in their fall to be really fallen; and the holy Pope at Rome,

Gregory, in fact and not in fiction, looked upon the blue eyes and golden hair of the fierce Saxon youth in the slave market, and pronounced them Angels, not Angles; and the spell which this once loyal daughter of the Church still exercises upon the foreign visitor, even now, when her true glory is departed, suggests to us how far more majestic and more touching, how brimful of indescribable influence would be the presence of a University, which was planted within, not without Jerusalem,—an influence, potent as her truth is strong, wide as her sway is world-wide, and growing, not lessening, by the extent of space over which its attraction would be exerted. . . . . . .

There are those who, having felt the influence of this ancient school, and being smit with its splendour and its sweetness, ask wistfully, if never again it is to be Catholic, or whether, at least, some footing for Catholicity may not be found there. All honour and merit to the charitable and zealous hearts who so enquire! Nor can we dare to tell what in time to come may be the inscrutable purposes of that grace, which is ever more comprehensive than human hope and aspiration. But for me, from the day I left its walls, I never, for good or bad, have had anticipation of its future; and never for a moment have I had a wish to see again a place, which I have never ceased to love, and where I lived for nearly thirty years. ("Hist. Sketches," vol. III. p. 28.)

ST. BENEDICT AND EARLY MONACHISM.

ST. BENEDICT had taken up for the most part what he found, and his Rule was but the expression of the genius of Monachism in those first times of the Church, with a more exact adaptation to their needs than could elsewhere be found. So uniform, indeed, had been the Monastic idea before his time, and so little stress had been laid by individual communities on their respective peculiarities, that religious men passed at pleasure from one body to another. St. Benedict provides in his Rule for the case of strangers coming to one of his houses and wishing to remain there. If such a one came from any Monastery with which the Monks had existing relations, then he was not to be received without letters from his Abbot; but, in the instance of "a foreign Monk from distant parts," who wished to dwell with them as a guest, and was content with their ways, and conformed himself to them, and was not troublesome, "should he in the event wish to stay for good," says St. Benedict, "let him not be refused; for there has been room to make trial of him during the time that hospitality has been shown to him: nay, let him even be invited to stay, that others may gain a lesson from his example; for in every place we are servants of one Lord, and soldiers of one King."

The unity of idea, which, as these words imply, is to be found in all Monks in every part of Christendom, may be described as a unity of object, of state, and of occupation. Monachism was one and the same everywhere, because it was a reaction from that secular life which has everywhere the same structure and the same characteristics. And, since that secular life contained in it many objects, many states, and many occupations, here was a special reason, as a matter of principle, why the reaction from it should bear the badge of unity, and should be in outward appearance one and the same everywhere. Moreover, since that same secular life was, when Monachism arose, more than ordinarily marked by variety, perturbation, and confusion, it seemed on that very account to justify emphatically a rising and revolt against itself, and a recurrence to some state which, unlike itself, was constant and unalterable. It was indeed an old, decayed, and moribund world, into which Christianity had been cast. The social fabric was overgrown with the corruptions of a thousand years, and was held together, not so much by any common principle, as by the strength of possession and the tenacity of custom. It was too large for public spirit, and too artificial for patriotism, and its many religions did but foster in the popular mind division and scepticism. Want of mutual confidence would lead to despondency, inactivity, and selfishness. Society was in the slow fever of consumption, which made it restless in proportion as it was feeble. It was powerful, however, to seduce and to deprave ; nor was there any *locus standi* from which to combat its evils ; and the only way of getting on with it, was to abandon principle and duty, to take things as they came, and to do as the world did. Worse than all, this encompassing, entangling system of things, was, at the time we speak of, the seat and instrument of a Paganism, and then of heresies, not simply contrary, but bitterly hostile, to the Christian profession. Serious men not only had a call, but every inducement which love of life and freedom could supply, to escape from its presence and its sway.

Their one idea, then, their one purpose, was to be quit of it ; too long had it enthralled them. It was not a question of this or that vocation, of the better deed, of the higher state; but of life or death. In later times a variety of holy objects might present themselves for devotion to choose from, such as the care of the poor, or of the sick, or of the young, the redemption of captives, or the conversion of the barbarians, but early Monachism was flight from the world, and nothing else. The troubled, jaded, weary heart, the stricken, laden conscience, sought a life free from corruption in its daily work, free from distraction in its daily worship; and it sought employments as contrary as possible to the world's employments,—employments, the end of which would be in themselves, in which each day, each hour, would have its own completeness;—no elaborate undertakings, no difficult aims, no anxious ventures, no uncertainties to make the heart beat or the temples throb, no painful combination of efforts, no extended plan of operations, no multiplicity of details, no deep calculations, no sustained machinations, no suspense, no vicissitudes, no moments of crisis or catastrophe;—nor, again, any subtle investigations, nor perplexities of proof, nor conflicts of rival intellects, to agitate, harass, depress, stimulate, weary, or intoxicate the soul.

Hitherto I have been using negatives to describe what the primitive Monk was seeking; in truth, Monachism was, as regards the secular life and all that it implies, emphatically a negation, or, to use another word, a *mortification*; a mortification of sense and a mortification of reason. Here a word of explanation is necessary. The Monks were too good Catholics to deny that reason is a divine gift, and had too much common sense to think to do without it. What they denied themselves was the various and manifold exercises of the reason; and on this account, because such exercises were excitements. When the reason is cultivated, it at once begins to combine, to centralize, to look forward, to look back, to view things as a whole, whether for speculation or for action; it practises synthesis and analysis, it discovers, it invents. To these exercises of the intellect is opposed simplicity, which is the state of mind which does not combine, does not deal with premises and conclusions, does not recognize means and their end, but lets each work, each place, each occurrence stand by itself,—which acts towards each as it comes before it, without a thought of anything else. This simplicity is the temper of children, and it is the temper of Monks. This was their mortification of the intellect; every man who lives, must live by reason, as every one must live by sense; but, as it is possible to be content with the bare necessities of animal life, so is it possible to confine ourselves to the bare ordinary use of reason, without caring to improve it or make the most of it. These Monks held both sense and reason to be the gifts of heaven; but they used each of them as little as they could help, reserving their full time and their whole selves for devotion;—for, if reason is better than sense, so devotion they thought to be better than either; and, as even a heathen might deny himself the innocent indulgences of sense in order to give his time to the cultivation of the reason, so did the Monks give up reason, as well as sense, that they might consecrate themselves to divine meditation.

Now, then, we are able to understand how it was that the Monks had a unity, and in what it consisted. It was a unity, I have said, of object, of state, and of occupation. Their object was rest and peace; their state was retirement; their occupation was some work that was simple, as opposed to intellectual, viz. prayer, fasting, meditation, study, transcription, manual labour, and other unexciting, soothing employments. Such was their institution all over the world; they had eschewed the busy mart, the craft of gain, the money-changer's bench, and the merchant's cargo. They had turned their backs upon the wrangling forum, the political assembly, and the pantechnicon of trades. They had had their last dealings with architect and habit-maker, with butcher and cook; all they wanted, all they desired, was the sweet soothing presence of earth, sky, and sea, the hospitable cave, the bright running stream, the easy gifts which mother earth, "justissima tellus," yields on very little persuasion. "The monastic institute," says the biographer of St. Maurus, "demands *summa quies*, the most perfect quietness;" and where was quietness to be found, if not in reverting to the original condition of man, as far as the changed circumstances of our race admitted; in having no wants, of which the supply was not close at hand; in the *nil admirari;* in having neither hope nor fear of anything below; in daily prayer, daily bread, and daily work, one day being just like another, except that it was one step nearer than the day before it to that great day, which would swallow up all days, the day of everlasting rest? ("Hist. Sketches," vol. II. p. 372.)

THE DEATH OF ST. BEDE.

HERE the beautiful character in life and death of St. Bede naturally occurs to the mind, who is, in his person and his writings, as truly the pattern of a Benedictine, as is St. Thomas of a Dominican; and with an extract from the letter of Cuthbert to Cuthwin concerning his last hours, which, familiarly as it is known, is always pleasant to read, I break off my subject for the present.

"He was exceedingly oppressed," says Cuthbert of St. Bede, "with shortness of breathing, though without pain, before Easter Day, for about a fortnight; but he rallied, and was full of joy and gladness, and gave thanks to Almighty God day and night, and every hour, up to Ascension Day; and he gave us, his scholars, daily lectures, and passed the rest of the day in singing the Psalms, and the night, too, in joy and thanksgiving, except the scanty time which he gave to sleep. And as soon as he woke he was busy in his customary way, and he never ceased, with uplifted hands, giving thanks to God. I solemn'y protest, never have I seen or heard of any one who was so diligent in thanksgiving.

"He sang that sentence of the Blessed Apostle Paul, 'It is a dreadful thing to fall into the hands of the Living God,' and many other passages of Scripture, in which he warned us to shake off the slumber of the soul, by anticipating our last hour. And he sang some verses of his own in English also, to the effect that no one could be too well prepared for his end, viz. in calling to mind, before he departs hence, what good or evil he has done, and how his judgment will lie. And he sang too the antiphons, of which one is, 'O King of glory, Lord of Angels, who this day hast ascended in triumph above all the heavens, leave us not orphans, but send the promise of the Father upon us, the Spirit of Truth. Alleluia.' And when he came to the words, 'leave us not orphans,' he burst into tears, and wept much. He said, too, 'God scourgeth every son whom He receiveth,' and, with St. Ambrose, 'I have not so lived as to be ashamed to have been among you, nor do I fear to die, for we have a good Lord.'

"In those days, besides our lectures and the Psalmody, he was engaged in two works; he was translating into English the Gospel of St. John, as far as the words, 'But what are those among so many,' and some extracts from the 'Notæ of Isidore.' On the Tuesday before Ascension Day, he began to suffer still more in his breathing, and his feet were slightly swollen. However, he went through the day, dictating cheerfully, and he kept saying from time to time, 'Take down what I say quickly, for I know not how long I am to last, or whether my Maker will not take me soon.' He seemed to us to be quite aware of the time of his going, and he passed that night in giving of thanks, without sleeping. As soon as morning broke, that is on the Wednesday, he urged us to make haste with the writing which we had begun. We did so till nine o'clock, when we walked in procession with the Relics of the Saints, according to the usage of that day. But one of our party said to him, 'Dearest master, one chapter is still wanting ; can you bear our asking you about it?' He answered, 'I can bear it ; take your pen and be ready, and write quickly.' At three o'clock he said to me, 'Run fast, and call our priests, that I may divide among them some little gifts, which I have in my box.' When I had done this in much agitation, he spoke to each, urging and entreating them all to make a point of saying masses and prayers for him. Thus he passed the day in joy until the evening, when the above-named youth said to him, 'Dear master, there is yet one sentence not written!' He answered, 'Write quickly.' Presently the youth said, 'Now it is written ;' he replied, 'Good, thou hast said the truth, *consummatum est;* take my head into thy hands, for it is very pleasant to me to sit facing my old praying place, and thus to call upon my Father.' And so, on the floor of his cell, he sang, 'Glory be to the Father, Son, and Holy Ghost,' and just as he had said, ' Holy Ghost,' he breathed his last, and went to the realms above."

It is remarkable that this flower of the Benedictine school

died on the same day as St. Philip Neri, May 26; Bede on Ascension Day, and Philip on the early morning, after the feast of *Corpus Christi.* It was fitting that two Saints should go to heaven together, whose mode of going thither was the same ; both of them singing, praying, working, and guiding others, in joy and exultation till their very last hour. ("Hist. Sketches," vol. II. p. 428.)

ABELARD.

As the inductive method rose in Bacon, so did the logical in the mediæval schoolmen, and Aristotle, the most comprehensive intellect of antiquity, as the one who had conceived the sublime idea of mapping the whole field of knowledge, and subjecting all things to one profound analysis, became the presiding master in their lecture halls. It was at the end of the eleventh century that William of Champeaux founded the celebrated Abbey of St. Victor, under the shadow of St. Geneviève. . . . Of this William of Champeaux, Abelard was the pupil. He had studied the dialectic art elsewhere, before he offered himself for his instructions, and in the course of two years, when as yet he had only reached the age of twenty-two, he made such progress as to be capable of quarrelling with his master, and setting up a school for himself. . .

Great things are done by devotion to one idea; there is one class of geniuses who would never be what they are could they grasp a second. The calm philosophical mind, which contemplates parts without denying the whole, and the whole without confusing the parts, is notoriously indisposed to action whereas single and simple views arrest the mind, and hurry it on to carry them out. Thus men of one idea and nothing more, whatever their merit, must be, to a certain extent, narrow-minded, and it is not wonderful that Abelard's devotion to the new [scholastic] philosophy made him undervalue the seven arts out of which it had grown. He felt it impossible so to honour what was now to be added, as not to dishonour what existed before. He would not suffer the arts to have their own use, since he had found a new instrument for a new purpose; so he opposed the reading of the classics. The monks had opposed them before him; but this is little to our present purpose. It was the duty of men who abjured the gifts of this world, on the principle of mortification, to deny themselves literature, just as they would deny themselves particular friendships, or figured music. The doctrine which Abelard introduced and represents, was founded on a different basis. He did not recognize in the poets of antiquity any other merit than that of furnishing an assemblage of elegant phrases and figures, and accordingly he asks why they should not be banished from the city of God, since Plato banished them from his commonwealth. The animus of this language is clear when we turn to the pages of John of Salisbury, and Peter of Blois, who were champions of the ancient learning. We find them complaining that the careful "getting up," as we now call it, "of books" was growing out of fashion. Youths once studied critically the text of poets and philosophers; they got them by heart; they analyzed their arguments; they noted down their fallacies; they were closely examined in the matters which had been brought before them in lectures; they composed. But now, another teaching was coming in; students were promised truth in a nut-shell; they intended to get possession of the sum-total of philosophy in less than two or three years; and facts were apprehended, not in their substance and details, by means of living, and, as it were, personal documents, but in dead abstracts and tables. Such were the declamations to which the new logic gave occasion.

These, however, are lesser matters; we have a graver quarrel with Abelard than that of his undervaluing the classics. . . Wisdom, says the inspired writer, is *desursum*, is *pudica*, is *pacifica*,—"from above, chaste, peaceable." We have already seen enough of Abelard's career to understand that his wisdom, instead of being *pacifica*, was ambitious and contentious. An Apostle speaks of the tongue both as a blessing and as a curse. It may be the beginning of a fire; he says, a "Universitas iniquitatis;" and, alas! such it became in the mouth of the gifted Abelard. His eloquence was wonderful; he dazzled his contemporaries, says Fulco, "by the brilliancy of his genius, the sweetness of his eloquence, the ready flow of his language, and the subtlety of his knowledge." People came to him from all quarters;—from Rome, in spite of mountains and robbers; from England, in spite of the sea; from Flanders and Germany; from Normandy, and the remote districts of France; from Angers and Poitiers; from Navarre by the Pyrenees, and from Spain, besides the students of Paris itself; and among those who sought his instructions, now or afterwards, were the great luminaries of the schools in the next generation. Such were Peter of Poitiers, Peter Lombard, John of Salisbury, Arnold of Brescia, Ivo and Geoffrey of Auxerre. It was too much for a weak head and heart; weak in spite of intellectual power; for vanity will possess the head, and worldliness the heart, of the man, however gifted, whose wisdom is not an effluence of the Eternal Light.

True wisdom is not only "pacifica," it is also "pudica;"

chaste as well as peaceable. Alas for Abelard! a second disgrace, deeper than ambition, is his portion now. The strong man,—the Samson of the schools in the wildness of his course, the Solomon in the fascination of his genius,—shivers and falls before the temptation which overcame that mighty pair, the most excelling in body and in mind.

> Desire of wine, and all delicious drinks,
> Which many a famous warrior overturns,
> Thou could'st repress; nor did the dancing ruby,
> Sparkling outpoured, the flavour or the smell,
> Or taste, that cheers the heart of gods and men,
> Allure thee from the cool crystalline stream.
> But what availed this temperance not complete
> Against another object more enticing?
> What boots it at one gate to make defence,
> And at another to let in the foe,
> Effeminately vanquished?

In a time when Colleges were unknown, and the young scholar was thrown upon the dubious hospitality of a great city, Abelard might even be thought careful of his honour that he went to lodge with an old ecclesiastic, had not his host's niece, Eloisa, lived with him. A more subtle snare was laid for him than beset the heroic champion, or the all-accomplished monarch of Israel; for sensuality came upon him, under the guise of intellect, and it was the high mental endowments of Eloisa, who became his pupil, speaking in her eyes, and thrilling on her tongue, which were the intoxication and the delirium of Abelard. . . He is judged: he is punished: but he is not reclaimed. True wisdom is not only "pacifica," not only "pudica," it is "desursum" too. It is a revelation from above; it knows heresy as little as it knows strife or licence. But Abelard, who had run the career of earthly wisdom in two of its phases, now is destined to represent its third. It is at the famous Abbey of St. Denis that we find him languidly rising from his dream of sin, and the suffering that followed. The bad dream is cleared away; clerks come to him, and the Abbot, begging him to lecture still, for love now, as for gain before. Once more his school is thronged by the curious and the studious; but at length the rumour spreads that Abelard is exploring the way to some novel view on the subject of the Most Holy Trinity. Wherefore is hardly clear, but about the same time the monks drive him away from the place of refuge he had gained. He betakes himself to a cell, and thither his pupils follow him. "I betook myself to a certain cell," he says, "wishing to give myself to the schools, as was my custom. Thither so great a multitude of scholars flocked, that there was neither room to house them, nor fruits of the earth to feed them." Such was the enthusiasm of the student, such the attraction of the teacher, when knowledge was advertised freely, and its market opened.

Next he is in Champagne, in a delightful solitude near Nogent, in the diocese of Troyes. Here the same phenomenon presents itself which is so frequent in his history. "When the scholars knew it," he says, "they began to crowd thither from all parts; and leaving other cities and strongholds, they were content to dwell in the wilderness For spacious houses, they framed for themselves small tabernacles, and for delicate food they put up with wild herbs. Secretly did they whisper among themselves: 'Behold the whole world is gone out after him!' When, however, my Oratory could not hold even a moderate portion of them, then they were forced to enlarge it, and to build it up with wood and stone." He called the place his "Paraclete," because it had been his consolation.

I do not know why I need follow his life further. I have said enough to illustrate the course of one who may be called the founder, or at least the first great name of the Parisian schools. After the events I have mentioned, he is found in Lower Britanny then, being about forty years of age, in the Abbey of St. Gildas; then with St. Geneviève again. He had to sustain the fiery eloquence of a Saint, directed against his novelties; he had to present himself before two Councils; he had to burn the book which had given offence to pious ears. His last two years were spent at Clugni, on his way to Rome. The home of the weary, the school of the erring, the tribunal of the penitent, is the city of St. Peter. He did not reach it; but he is said to have retracted what had given scandal in his writings, and to have made an edifying end. He died at the age of sixty-two, in the year of grace 1142.

In reviewing his career, the career of so great an intellect so miserably thrown away, we are reminded of the famous words of the dying scholar and jurist, which are a lesson to us all: "Heu, vitam perdidi, operosè nihil agendo." A happier lot be ours! ("Hist. Sketches," vol. III. p. 195.)

POPE LIBERIUS.

WHEN Arianism broke out, it was Athanasius and the Egyptians who were "faithful found among the faithless;" even the Infallible See .. [was] not happy in the man who filled it. Liberius .. anathematized Athanasius on a point on which Athanasius was right and Liberius was wrong. [But] it is astonishing to me how any one can fancy that Liberius, in subscribing the Arian confessions, promulgated them *ex cathedrâ*, considering he was not his own master when he signed them, and that they were not his drawing up. Who would say that it would be a judgment of the Queen's Bench, or a judicial act of any kind, if ribbon-men in Ireland seized on one of her Majesty's Judges, hurried him into the wilds of Connemara, and there made him, under terror of his life, sign a document in the very teeth of an award which he had lately made in Court in a question of property. Surely for an *ex cathedrâ* decision of the Pope is required his formal initiation of it, his authorship of its wording, and his utterance amid his Court, with solemnities parallel to those of an Ecumenical Council. It is not a transaction that can be done in his travelling dress, in some hedge-side inn, or town tavern, or imperial servant's-hall. Liberius' subscription can only claim a Nag's Head's sort of infallibility. ("Hist. Sketches," vol. II. p. 340.)

DEATH OF ST. GREGORY VII.

On the 25th of May, 1085, he peacefully closed his earthly career; just rallying strength, amid the exhaustion of his powers, to utter with his departing breath the words, "I have loved justice and hated iniquity, and therefore I die in exile."

"In exile!" said a prelate who stood by his bed, . . "in exile thou can'st not die! Vicar of Christ and His Apostles, thou hast received the nations for thine inheritance, and the uttermost parts of the earth for thy possession."[1]

Gregory thought he had failed: so it is; often a cause seems to decline as its champion grows in years, and to die in his death; but this is to judge hastily; others are destined to complete what he began. No man is given to see his work through. "Man goeth forth unto his work and to his labour until the evening," but the evening falls before it is done. There was One alone who began and finished, and died. ("Essays, Crit. and Hist.," vol. II. p. 316.)

ROME AND CONSTANTINOPLE IN 1566.

ST. PIUS V. became Pope in 1566, and Selim became Sultan in that very same year. What a strange contrast did Rome and Constantinople present at that era! Neither was what it had been. But they had changed in opposite directions. Both had been the seat of Imperial Power; Rome, where heresy never throve, had exchanged its Emperor for the succession of St. Peter and St. Paul; Constantinople had passed from secular supremacy into schism, and thence into a blasphemous apostacy. The unhappy city, which, with its subject provinces had been successively the seat of Arianism, of Nestorianism, of Photianism, now had become the metropolis of the false Prophet, and, while in the West, the great edifice of the Vatican Basilica was rising anew in its wonderful proportions and its costly materials, the Temple of St. Sophia in

---

[1] [These two sentences are the late Mr. Bowden's, from a review of whose work on the "Life and Pontificate of Gregory VII." this extract

the East was degraded into a Mosque! O the strange contrast in the state of the inhabitants of each place! Here, in the city of Constantine, a God-denying misbelief was accompanied by an impure, man-degrading rule of life, by the slavery of woman, and the corruption of youth. But there, in the city which Apostles had consecrated with their blood, the great and true reformation of the age was in full progress. There, the determinations, in doctrine and discipline, of the great Council of Trent had lately been promulgated. There, for twenty years past, had laboured our own dear Saint, St. Philip, till he earned the title of Apostle of Rome, and yet had still nearly thirty years of life and work in him. There, too, the romantic royal-minded Saint, Ignatius Loyola, had but lately died. And there, when the Holy See fell vacant, and a Pope had to be appointed in the great need of the Church, a Saint was present in the Conclave to find in it a brother Saint, and to recommend him for the Chair of St. Peter, to the suffrages of the Fathers and Princes of the Church. ("Hist. Sketches," vol. I. p. 150.)

THE ELECTION OF ST. PIUS V.

ST. CARLO BORROMEO, the Cardinal Archbishop of Milan, was the nephew of the Pope who was just dead, and though he was only twenty-five years of age at the time, nevertheless, by the various influences arising out of the position which he held, and from the weight attached to his personal character, he might be considered to sway the votes of the College of Cardinals, and to determine the election of a new Pontiff. It is remarkable that Cardinal

Alessandrino, as St. Pius was then called (from Alexandria in North Italy, near which he was born), was not the first object of his choice. His eyes were first turned on Cardinal Morone, who was in many respects the most illustrious of the Sacred College, and had served the Church, on various occasions, with great devotion, and with distinguished success. From his youth he had been reared up in public affairs; he had held many public offices, he had great influence with the German Emperor; he had been Apostolical Legate at the Council of Trent. He had great virtue, judgment, experience, and sagacity. Such, then, was the choice of St. Carlo, and the votes were taken; but it seemed otherwise to the Holy Ghost. He wanted four to make up the sufficient number of votes. St. Carlo had to begin again; and again, strange to say, the Cardinal Alessandrino still was not his choice. He chose Cardinal Sirleto, a man most opposite in character, in history, to Morone. He was not nobly born, he was no man of the world, he had ever been urgent with the late Pope not to make him Cardinal. He was a first-rate scholar in Hebrew, Greek, and Latin; versed in the Scriptures, ready as a theologian. Moreover, he was of a character most unblemished, of most innocent life, and of manners most popular and winning. St. Pius, as well as St. Carlo, advocated the cause of Cardinal Sirleto, and the votes were given a second time; a second time they came short. It was like holy Samuel choosing Eliab instead of David. Then matters were in confusion; one name and another were mentioned, and no progress was made.

At length, and at last, and not till all others were thought of who could enter into the minds of the electors, the Cardinal Alessandrino himself began to attract attention. He seems not to have been known to the Fathers of the Conclave in general; a Dominican Friar, of humble rank, ever taken up in the duties of his rule, and his special employment, living in his cell, knowing little or nothing of mankind. Such a one, St. Carlo, the son of a prince, and the nephew of a Pope, had no means of knowing; and the intimacy, consequent on their co-operation in behalf of Cardinal Sirleto, was the first real introduction which the one Saint had to the other. It was just at this moment that our own St. Philip was in his small room, at St. Giralamo, with Marcello Ferro, one of his spiritual children, when, lifting up his eyes to heaven, and going almost into an ecstacy, he said, " The Pope will be elected on Monday." On one of the following days, as they were walking together, Marcello asked him who was to be Pope. Philip answered, " Come, I will tell you. The Pope will be one whom you have never thought of, and whom no one has spoken of as likely, and that is Cardinal Alessandrino; and he will be elected on Monday evening, without fail." The event accomplished the prediction; the statesman and the man of the world, the accomplished and exemplary and amiable scholar, were put aside to make way for the Saint. He took the name of Pius.

I am far from denying that St. Pius was stern and severe, as far as a heart burning within, and melting with the fulness of divine love, could be so; and this was the reason that the Conclave was so slow in electing him. Yet such energy and vigour as his was necessary for his time. He was emphatically a soldier of Christ, in a time of insurrection and rebellion, when, in a spiritual sense, martial law was proclaimed. St. Philip, a private priest, might follow his vent in casting his net for souls, as he expressed himself, and enticing them to the truth; but the Vicar of Christ had to right and steer the vessel when it was in rough waters, and among breakers. A Protestant historian on this point does justice to him. " When Pope," he says, "he lived in all the austerity of his monastic life, fasted with the utmost rigour and punctuality; would wear no finer garments than before, . . arose at an early hour in the morning, and took no *siesta*. If we doubted the depth of his religious earnestness, we may find a proof of it in his declaration, that the Papacy was unfavourable to his advance in piety; that it did not contribute to his salvation, and to his attainment of Paradise; and that, but for prayer, the burden had been too heavy for him. The happiness of a fervent devotion, which often moved him to tears, was granted him to the end of his life. The people were incited to enthusiasm when they saw him walking in procession, bare-footed and bare-headed, with the expression of unaffected piety in his countenance, and with his long snow-white beard falling on his breast. They thought there had never been so pious a Pope. They told each other how his very look had converted heretics. Pius was kind, too, and affable; his intercourse with his old servants was of the most confidential kind. At a former period, before he was Pope, the Count Della Trinità had threatened to have him thrown into a well; and he had replied, that it must be as God pleased. How beautiful was his greeting to this same Count, who was now sent as ambassador to his Court! 'See,' said he, when he recognized him, 'how God preserves the innocent.' This was the only way in which he made him feel that he recollected his enmity. He had ever been most charitable and bounteous; he kept a list of the poor of Rome, whom he regularly assisted according to their station and their wants." The writer, after proceeding to condemn what he considers his severity, ends thus: "It is certain that his deportment and mode of thinking exercised an incalculable influence on his contemporaries, and on the general development of the Church, of which he was the head. After so many circumstances had concurred to excite and foster a religious spirit, after so many resolutions and measures had been taken to exalt it to universal dominion, a Pope like this was needed, not only to proclaim it to the world, but also to reduce it to practice. His zeal and his example combined produced the most powerful effect."[1] ("Hist. Sketches," vol. I. p. 151.)

THE BATTLE OF LEPANTO.

IT is not to be supposed that a Saint upon whom lay " the solicitude of all the Churches " should neglect the tradition, which his predecessors of so many centuries had bequeathed to him, of zeal and hostility against the Turkish power. He was only six years on the Pontifical throne, and the achievement of which I am going to speak was among his last; he died the following year. At this time the Ottoman armies were continuing their course of victory; they had just taken Cyprus, with the active co-operation of the Greek population of the island, and were massacring the Latin nobility and clergy, and mutilating and flaying alive the Venetian governor; yet the Saint found it impossible to move Christendom to its own defence. How, indeed, was that to be done, when half Christendom had become Protestant, and secretly, perhaps, felt as the Greeks felt, that the Turk was its friend and ally? In such a quarrel, England, France, and Germany were out of the question. At length, however, with great effort, he succeeded in

[1] Ranke's Hist. of the Popes.

forming a holy league between himself, King Philip of Spain, and the Venetians; Don John of Austria, King Philip's half brother, was appointed commander-in-chief of the forces; and Colonna admiral. The treaty was signed on the 24th of May; but such was the cowardice and jealousy of the parties concerned, that the autumn had arrived and nothing of importance was accomplished. With difficulty were the armies united; with difficulty were the dissensions of the commanders brought to a settlement. Meanwhile the Ottomans were scouring the Gulf of Venice, blockading the ports, and terrifying the city itself.

But the holy Pope was securing the success of his cause by arms of his own, which the Turks understood not. He had been appointing a Triduo of supplication at Rome, and had taken part in the procession himself. He had proclaimed a jubilee to the whole Christian world, for the happy issue of the war. He had been interesting the Holy Virgin in his cause. He presented to his admiral, after High Mass in his chapel, a standard of red damask, embroidered with a crucifix, and with the figures of St. Peter and St. Paul, and the legend, *In hoc signo vinces*. Next, sending to Messina, where the allied fleet lay, he assured the general-in-chief and the armament, that "if, relying on divine, rather than on human help, they attacked the enemy, God would not be wanting to His own cause. He augured a prosperous and happy issue; not on any light or random hope, but on a divine guidance, and by the anticipations of many holy men." Moreover, he enjoined the officers to look to the good conduct of their troops; to repress swearing, gaming, riot, and plunder, and thereby to render them more deserving of victory. Accordingly, a fast of three days was proclaimed for the fleet, beginning with the nativity of Our Lady; all the men went to confession and communion, and appropriated to themselves the plentiful indulgences which the Pope attached to the expedition. Then they moved across the foot of Italy to Corfu, with the intention of presenting themselves at once to the enemy; being disappointed in their expectations, they turned back to the Gulf of Corinth; and there at length, on the 7th of October, they found the Turkish fleet, halfway between Lepanto and the Echiniades on the north, and Patras in the Morea on the south; and, though it was towards evening, strong in faith and zeal, they at once commenced the engagement.

The night before the battle, and the day itself, aged as he was, and broken with a cruel malady, the Saint had passed in the Vatican in fasting and prayer. All through the Holy City the Monasteries and the Colleges were in prayer too. As the evening advanced, the Pontifical Treasurer asked an audience of the Sovereign Pontiff on an important matter. Pius was in his bed-room and began to converse with him; when suddenly he stopped the conversation, left him, threw up the window, and gazed up into heaven. Then closing it again, he looked gravely at his official, and said, "This is no time for business; go, return thanks to the Lord God. In this very hour our fleet has engaged the Turkish, and is victorious!" As the Treasurer went out, he saw him fall on his knees before the altar in thankfulness and joy.

And a most memorable victory it was; upwards of 30,000 Turks are said to have lost their lives in the engagement, and three thousand five hundred were made prisoners. Almost their whole fleet was taken. I quote from Protestant authorities when I say that the Sultan, on the news of the calamity, neither ate, nor drank, nor showed himself, nor saw any-one for three days; that it was the greatest blow which the Ottomans had had since Timour's victory over Bajazet, a century and a half before; nay, that it was the turning-point in the Turkish history, and that though the Sultans have had isolated successes since, yet from that day they undeniably and constantly declined; that they have lost their prestige and their self-confidence; and that the victories gained over them since, are but the complements and the reverberations of the overthrow at Lepanto. ("Hist. Sketches," vol. I. p. 155.)

THE RELIGIOUS HISTORY OF ENGLAND.

TIME was when the forefathers of our race were a savage tribe, inhabiting a wild district beyond the limits of this quarter of the earth. Whatever brought them thither, they had no local attachments there or political settlement; they were a restless people, and whether urged forward by enemies or by desire of plunder, they left their place, and passing through the defiles of the mountains on the frontiers of Asia, they invaded Europe, setting out on a journey towards the farther West. Generation after generation passed away, and still this fierce and haughty race moved forward. On, on they went; but travel availed them not; the change of place could bring them no truth, or peace, or hope, or stability of heart; they could not flee from themselves. They carried with them their superstitions and their sins, their gods of iron and of clay, their savage sacrifices, their lawless witchcrafts, their hatred of their kind, and their ignorance of their destiny. At length they buried themselves in the deep forests of Germany, and gave themselves up to indolent repose; but they had not found their rest; they were still heathens, making the fair trees, the primeval work of God, and the innocent beasts of the chase, the objects and the instruments of their idolatrous worship. And, last of all, they crossed over the strait and made themselves masters of this island, and gave their very name to it; so that, whereas it had hitherto been called Britain, the southern part, which was their main seat, obtained the name of England. And now they had proceeded forward nearly as far as they could go, unless they were prepared to look across the great ocean, and anticipate the discovery of the world which lies beyond it.

What, then, was to happen to this restless race, which had sought for happiness and peace across the globe, and had not found it? Was it to grow old in its place, and dwindle away, and consume in the fever of its own heart, which admitted no remedy? or was it to become great by being overcome, and to enjoy the only real life of man, and rise to his only true dignity, by being subjected to a Master's yoke? Did its Maker and Lord see any good thing in it, of which, under His divine nurture, profit might come to His elect, and glory to His name? He looked upon it, and He saw nothing there to claim any visitation of His grace, or to merit any relaxation of the awful penalty which its lawlessness and impiety had incurred. It was a proud race, which feared neither God nor man—a race ambitious, self-willed, obstinate, and hard of belief, which would dare everything, even the eternal pit, if it was challenged to do so. I say, there was nothing there of a nature to reverse the destiny which His righteous decrees have assigned to those who sin wilfully and despise Him. But the Almighty Lover of souls looked once again; and He saw in that poor, forlorn, and ruined nature, which He had in the beginning filled with grace and light, He saw in it, not what merited His favour, not what would adequately respond to His influences, not what was a necessary instrument of His purposes, but what would illustrate and preach abroad His grace, if He took pity on it. He saw in it a natural nobleness, a simplicity, a frankness of character, a love of truth, a zeal for justice, an indignation at wrong, an admiration of purity, a reverence for law, a keen appreciation of the beautifulness and majesty of order, nay, further, a tenderness and an affectionateness of heart, which He knew would become the glorious instruments of His high will, when illuminated and vivified by His supernatural gifts. And so He who, did it so please Him, could raise up children to Abraham out of the very stones of the earth, nevertheless determined in this instance in His free mercy to unite what was beautiful in nature with what was radiant in grace; and, as if those poor Anglo-Saxons had been too fair to be heathen, therefore did He rescue them from the devil's service and the devil's doom, and bring them into the house of His holiness and the mountain of His rest.

It is an old story and a familiar, and I need not go through it. I need not tell you, how suddenly the word of truth came to our ancestors in this island and subdued them to its gentle rule; how the grace of God fell on them, and, without compulsion, as the historian tells us, the multitude became Christian; how, when all was tempestuous, and hopeless, and dark, Christ like a vision of glory came walking to them on the waves of the sea. Then suddenly there was a great calm; a change came over the pagan people in that quarter of the country where the gospel was first preached to them; and from thence the blessed influence went forth; it was poured out over the whole land, till, one and all, the Anglo-Saxon people were converted by it. In a hundred years the work was done; the idols, the sacrifices, the mummeries of paganism flitted away and were not, and the pure doctrine and heavenly worship of the Cross were found in their stead. The fair form of Christianity rose up and grew and expanded like a beautiful pageant from north to south; it was majestic, it was solemn, it was bright, it was beautiful and pleasant, it was soothing to the griefs, it was indulgent to the hopes of man; it was at once a teaching and a worship; it had a dogma, a mystery, a ritual of its own; it had an hierarchical form. A brotherhood of holy pastors, with mitre and crosier and uplifted hand, walked forth and blessed and ruled a joyful people. The crucifix headed the procession, and simple monks were there with hearts in prayer, and sweet chants resounded, and the holy Latin tongue was heard, and boys came forth in white, swinging censers, and the fragrant cloud arose, and mass was sung, and the saints were invoked; and day after day, and in the still night, and over the woody hills and in the quiet plains, as constantly as sun and moon and stars go forth in heaven, so regular and solemn was the stately march or blessed services on earth, high festival, and gorgeous procession, and soothing dirge, and passing bell, and the familiar evening call to prayer: till he who recollected the old pagan time, would think it all unreal that he beheld and heard, and would conclude he did but see a vision, so marvellously was heaven let down upon earth, so triumphantly were chased away the fiends of darkness to their prison below.

Such was the change which came over our forefathers; such was the Religion bestowed upon them, bestowed on them, as a second grant, after the grant of the territory itself; nay, it might almost have seemed as the divine guarantee or pledge of its occupation. And you know its name;

there can be no mistake; you know what that Religion was called. It was called by no modern name—for modern religions then were not. You know *what* religion has priests and sacrifices, and mystical rites, and the monastic rule, and care for the souls of the dead, and the profession of an ancient faith, coming, through all ages, from the Apostles. There is one, and only one religion such: it is known every where; every poor boy in the street knows the name of it; there never was a time, since it first was, that its name was not known, and known to the multitude. It is called *Catholicism*—a world-wide name, and incommunicable; attached to us from the first; accorded to us by our enemies; in vain attempted, never stolen from us, by our rivals. Such was the worship which the English people gained when they emerged out of paganism into gospel light. In the history of their conversion, Christianity and Catholicism are one; they are in that history, as they are in their own nature, convertible terms. It was the Catholic faith which that vigorous young race heard and embraced—that faith which is still found, the further you trace back towards the age of the Apostles, which is still visible in the dim distance of the earliest antiquity, and to which the witness of the Church, when investigated even in her first startings and simplest rudiments, "sayeth not the contrary." Such was the religion of the noble English; they knew not heresy; and, as time went on, the work did but sink deeper and deeper into their nature, into their social structure and their political institutions; it grew with their growth, and strengthened with their strength, till a sight was seen—one of the most beautiful which ever has been given to man to see—what was great in the natural order, made greater by its elevation into the supernatural. The two seemed as if made for each other; that natural temperament and that gift of grace; what was heroic, or generous, or magnanimous in nature, found its corresponding place or office in the divine kingdom. Angels in heaven rejoiced to see the divinely wrought piety and sanctity of penitent sinners: Apostles, Popes, and Bishops, long since taken to glory, threw their crowns in transport at the foot of the throne, as saints, and confessors, and martyrs, came forth before their wondering eyes out of a horde of heathen robbers; guardian spirits no longer sighed over the disparity and contrast which had so fearfully intervened between themselves and the souls given to them in charge. It did indeed become a peculiar, special people, with a character and genius of its own; I will say a bold thing—in its staidness, sagacity, and simplicity, more like the mind that rules, through all time, the princely line of Roman pontiffs, than perhaps any other Christian people whom the world has seen. And so things went on for many centuries. Generation followed generation; revolution came after revolution; great men rose and fell: there were bloody wars, and invasions, conquests, changes of dynasty, slavery, recoveries, civil dissensions, settlements Dane and Norman overran the land; and yet all along Christ was upon the waters; and if they rose in fury, yet at His word they fell again and were in calm. The bark of Peter was still the refuge of the tempest-tost, and ever solaced and recruited those whom it rescued from the deep.

But at length a change came over the land: a thousand years had well-nigh rolled, and this great people grew tired of the heavenly stranger who sojourned among them. They had had enough of blessings and absolutions, enough of the intercession of saints, enough of the grace of the sacraments, enough of the prospect of the next life. They thought it best to secure this life in the first place, because

they were in possession of it, and then to go on to the
next, if time and means allowed. And they saw that
to labour for the next world was possibly to lose this;
whereas, to labour for this world might be, for what they
knew, the way to labour for the next also. Any how,
they would pursue a temporal end, and they would account any one their enemy who stood in the way of their
pursuing it. It was a madness; but madmen are strong
and madmen are clever; so with the sword and the halter,
and by mutilation and fine and imprisonment, they cut
off, or frightened away from the land, as Israel did in the
time of old, the ministers of the Most High, and their
ministrations: they "altogether broke the yoke, and
burst the bonds." "They beat one, and killed another,
and another they stoned," and at length they altogether
cast out the Heir from His vineyard, and killed Him,
"that the inheritance might be theirs." And as for the
remnant of His servants whom they left, they drove them
into corners and holes of the earth, and there they bade
them die out; and then they rejoiced and sent gifts either
to other, and made merry, because they had rid themselves
of those "who had tormented them that dwelt upon the
earth." And so they turned to enjoy this world, and to
gain for themselves a name among men, and it was given
unto them according to their wish. They preferred the
heathen virtues of their original nature, to the robe of
grace which God had given them: they fell back, with
closed affections, and haughty reserve, and dreariness
within, upon their worldly integrity, honour, energy,
prudence, and perseverance; they made the most of the
natural man, and they "received their reward." Forthwith they began to rise to a station higher than the
heathen Roman, and have, in three centuries, attained a
wider range of sovereignty; and now they look down in

contempt on what they were, and upon the Religion which reclaimed them from paganism.

Yes, such was the temptation of the evil one, such the fall of his victim, such the disposition of the Most High. The tempter said, "All these will I give thee, if, falling down, thou wilt adore me;" and their rightful Lord and Sovereign permitted the boast to be fulfilled. He permitted it for His greater glory: He might have hindered it, as He might hinder all evil; but He saw good, He saw it best, to let things take their course. He did not interfere, He kept silence, He retired from the land which would be rid of Him. And there were those at that crisis who understood not His providence, and would have interfered in His behalf with a high hand. Holy men and true they were, zealous for God, and tender towards His sheep; but they divined not His will. It was His will to leave the issue to time, and to bring things round slowly and without violence, and to conquer by means of His adversaries. He willed it that their pride should be its own correction; that they should be broken without hands, and dissolve under their own insufficiency. He who might have brought myriads of Angels to the rescue, He who might have armed and blessed the forces of Christendom against His persecutors, wrought more wondrously. He deigned not to use the carnal weapon: He bade the drawn sword return to its sheath: He refused the combinations and the armaments of earthly kings. He who sees the end from the beginning, who is "justified in His words, and overcomes when He is judged," did but wait. He waited patiently; He left the world to itself, nor avenged His Church, but stayed till the fourth watch of the night, when His faithful sons had given up hope, and thought His mercy towards them at an end. He let the winds and the waves insult Him and His own; He suffered meekly the jeers and blasphemies which rose on every side, and pronounced the downfall of His work. "All things have an end," men said; "there is a time for all things; a time to be born, and a time to die. All things have their course and their term; they may last a long time, but after all, a period they have, and not an immortality. So is it with man himself; even Mathusala and Noe exhausted the full fountain of their being, and the pitcher was at length crushed, and the wheel broken. So is it with nations; they rise, and they flourish, and they fall; there is an element in them, as in individuals, which wears out and perishes. However great they may be in their day, at length the moment comes, when they have attained their greatest elevation, and accomplished their full range, and fulfilled their scope. So is it with great ideas and their manifestations; they are realized, they prevail, and they perish. As the constituents of the animal frame at length refuse to hold together, so nations, philosophies, and religions one day lose their unity and undergo the common law of decomposition. Our nation, doubtless, will find its term at length, as well as others, though not yet; but that ancient faith of ours has come to nought already. We have nothing, then, to fear from the past; the past is not, the past cannot revive; the dead tell no tales; the grave cannot open. New adversaries we may have, but with the Old Religion we have parted once for all."

Thus speaks the world, deeming Christ's patience to be feebleness, and His loving affection to be enmity. And the faithful, on the other hand, have had their own misgivings too, whether Catholicism could ever flourish in this country again. Has it yet happened any where in the history of the Church, that a people which once lost its faith ever regained it? It is a gift of grace, a special mercy to receive it once, and not to be expected a second time. Many nations have never had it at all; from some it has been taken away, apparently without their fault, nay, in spite of their meritorious use of it. So was it with the old Persian Church, which, after enduring two frightful persecutions, had scarcely emerged from the second, when it was irretrievably corrupted by heresy. So was it with the famous Church of Africa, whose great saint and doctor's dying moments were embittered by the ravages around him of those fierce barbarians who were destined to be its ruin. What are we better than they? It is then surely against the order of Providence hitherto, that the gift once given should be given again; the world and the Church bear a concordant testimony here.

And the just Judge of man made as though He would do what man anticipated. He retired, as I have said, from the field; He yielded the battle to the enemy;— but He did so that He might in the event more signally triumph. He interfered not for near three hundred years, that His enemies might try their powers of mind in forming a religion instead of His own. He gave them three hundred years' start, bidding them to do something better than He, or something at all, if so be they were able, and He put Himself to every disadvantage. He suffered the daily sacrifice to be suspended, the hierarchy to be driven out, education to be prohibited, religious houses to be plundered and suppressed, cathedrals to be desecrated, shrines to be rifled, religious rites and duties to be interdicted by the law of the land. He would owe the world nothing in that revival of the Church which was to follow. He wrought, as in the old time by His prophet Elias, who, when he was to light the sacrifice with fire from heaven, drenched the burnt-offering with water the first time, the second time, and the third time; "and the water ran round about the altar, and the trench was filled up with water." He wrought as He Himself had done in the raising of Lazarus; for when He heard that His friend was sick, "He remained in the same place two days:" on the third day He "said plainly, Lazarus is dead, and I am glad, for your sake, that I was not there, that you may believe ;" and then, at length, He went and raised him from the grave. So too was it in His own resurrection; He did not rise from the cross; He did not rise from His mother's arms; He rose from the grave, and on the third day.

So is it now; "He hath taken us, and He will heal us; He will strike, and He will cure us. He will revive us after two days; on the third day He will raise us up, and we shall live in His sight." Three ages have passed away; the bell has tolled once, and twice, and thrice; the intercession of the saints has had effect; the mystery of Providence is unravelled; the destined hour is come. And, as when Christ arose, men knew not of His rising, for He rose at midnight and in silence, so when His mercy would do His new work among us, He wrought secretly, and was risen ere men dreamed of it. He sent not His Apostles and preachers, as at the first, from the city where He has fixed His throne. His few and scattered priests were about their own work, watching their flocks by night, with little time to attend to the souls of the wandering multitudes around them, and with no thoughts of the conversion of the country. But He came as a spirit upon the waters; He walked to and fro Himself over that dark and troubled deep; and, wonderful to behold, and inexplicable to man, hearts were stirred, and eyes were raised in hope, and feet began to move towards the Great

Mother, who had almost given up the thought and the seeking of them. First one, and then another, sought the rest which she alone could give. A first, and a second, and a third, and a fourth, each in his turn, as grace inspired him,—not altogether, as by some party understanding or political call,—but drawn by divine power, and against his will, for he was happy where he was, yet with his will, for he was lovingly subdued by the sweet mysterious influence which called him on. One by one, little noticed at the moment, silently, swiftly, and abundantly, they drifted in, till all could see at length that surely the stone was rolled away, and that Christ was risen and abroad. And as He rose from the grave, strong and glorious, as if refreshed with His sleep, so, when the prison doors were opened, the Church came forth, not changed in aspect or in voice, as calm and keen, as vigorous and as well furnished, as when they closed on her. It is told in legends of that great saint and instrument of God, St. Athanasius, how that when the apostate Julian had come to his end, and persecution with him, the saintly confessor, who had been a wanderer over the earth, was found, to the surprise of his people, in his cathedral at Alexandria, seated on his episcopal throne, and clad in the vestments of religion. So is it now; the Church is coming out of prison, as collected in her teaching, as precise in her action, as when she went into it. She comes out with pallium, and cope, and chasuble, and stole, and wonder-working relics, and holy images. Her bishops are again in their chairs, and her priests sit round, and the perfect vision of a majestic hierarchy rises before our eyes.

What an awful vitality is here! What a heavenly-sustained sovereignty! What a self-evident divinity! She claims, she seeks, she desires no temporal power, no secular station; she meddles not with Cæsar or the things of Cæsar; she obeys him in his place, but she is independent of him. Her strength is in her God; her rule is over the souls of men; her glory is in their willing subjection and loving loyalty. She hopes and fears nothing from the world; it made her not, nor can it destroy her. She can benefit it largely, but she does not force herself upon it. She may be persecuted by it, but she thrives under the persecution. She may be ignored, she may be silenced and thrown into a corner, but she is thought of the more. Calumniate her, and her influence grows; ridicule her,—she does but smile upon you more awfully and persuasively. What will you do with her, ye sons of men, if you will not love her, if at least you will not suffer her? Let the last three hundred years reply. Let her alone, refrain from her; for if her counsel or her work be of men, it will come to nought; but if it be of God, you cannot overthrow it, lest perhaps you be found even to fight against God. ("Occasional Sermons," p. 124.)

CATHOLICISM IN ENGLAND FROM THE SIXTEENTH TO THE NINETEENTH CENTURY.

THREE centuries ago, and the Catholic Church, that great creation of God's power, stood in this land in pride of place. It had the honours of near a thousand years upon it; it was enthroned in some twenty sees up and down the broad country; it was based in the will of a faithful people; it energized through ten thousand instruments of power and influence, and it was ennobled by a host of saints and martyrs. The churches, one by one, recounted and rejoiced in the line of glorified intercessors who were the respective objects of their grateful homage. Canterbury alone numbered perhaps some sixteen, from St. Augustine to St. Dunstan and St. Elphege, from St. Anselm and St. Thomas down to St. Edmund. York had its St. Paulinus, St. John, St. Wilfrid, and St. William; London, its St. Erconwald; Durham, its St. Cuthbert; Winton, its St. Swithun. Then there were St. Aidan of Lindisfarne, and St. Hugh of Lincoln, and St. Chad of Lichfield, and St. Thomas of Hereford, and St. Oswald and St. Wulstan of Worcester, and St. Osmund of Salisbury, and St. Birinus of Dorcester, and St. Richard of Chichester. And then, too, its religious orders, its monastic establishments, its universities, its wide relations all over Europe, its high prerogatives in the temporal state, its wealth, its dependencies, its popular honours—where was there in the whole of Christendom a more glorious hierarchy? Mixed up with the civil institutions, with king and nobles, with the people, found in every village and in every town—it seemed destined to stand so long as England stood, and to outlast, it might be, England's greatness.

But it was the high decree of Heaven that the majesty of that presence should be blotted out. It is a long story, my Fathers and Brothers; you know it well. I need not go through it. The vivifying principle of truth, the shadow of St. Peter, the grace of the Redeemer, left it. That old Church in its day became a corpse (a marvellous, an awful change!), and then it did but corrupt the air which once it refreshed, and cumber the ground which once it beautified. So all seemed to be lost, and there was a struggle for a time, and then its priests were cast out or martyred. There were sacrileges innumerable. Its temples were profaned or destroyed; its revenues seized by covetous nobles, or squandered upon the ministers of a new faith. The presence of Catholicism was at length simply removed—its grace disowned, its power despised—its name, except as a matter of history, at length almost unknown. It took a long time to do this thoroughly; much time, much thought, much labour, much expense; but at last it was done. Oh, that miserable day, centuries before we were born! What a martyrdom to live in it, and see the fair form of Truth, moral and material, hacked piecemeal, and every limb and organ carried off, and burned in the fire, or cast into the deep! But at last the work was done. Truth was disposed of, and shovelled away, and there was a calm, a silence, a sort of peace—and such was about the state of things when we were born into this weary world.

My Fathers and Brothers, *you* have seen it on one side, and some of us on another; but one and all of us can bear witness to the fact of the utter contempt into which Catholicism had fallen by the time that we were born. You, alas, know it far better than I can know it; but it may not be out of place, if by one or two tokens, as by the strokes of a pencil, I bear witness to you from without, of what you can witness so much more truly from within. No longer the Catholic Church in the country—nay, no longer, I may say, a Catholic community; but a few adherents of the old religion, moving silently and sorrowfully about, as memorials of what had been. "The Roman Catholics,"—not a sect, not even an interest, as men conceived of it; not a body, however small, representative of the great communion abroad—but a mere handful of individuals, who might be counted like the pebbles and *detritus* of the great deluge, and who, forsooth, merely happened to retain a creed which, in its day indeed, was the profession of a Church. Here, a set of poor Irishmen, coming and going at harvest time, or a colony of them lodged in a miserable quarter of the vast metropolis. There, perhaps, an elderly person seen walking in the streets, grave and solitary, and strange, though noble in bearing, and said to be of good family, and a "Roman Catholic." An old-fashioned house of gloomy appearance, closed in with high walls, with an iron gate and yews, and the report attaching to it that "Roman Catholics" lived there; but who they were, or what they did, or what was meant by calling them Roman Catholics, no one could tell—though it had an unpleasant sound, and told of form and superstition. And then, perhaps, as we went to and fro, looking with a boy's curious eyes through the great city, we might come to-day upon some Moravian chapel, or Quakers' meeting-house, and to-morrow on a chapel of the "Roman Catholics;" but nothing was to be gathered from it, except that there were lights burning there, and some boys in white, swinging censers; and what it all meant could only be learned from books, from Protestant histories and sermons, and they did not report well of "the Roman Catholics," but, on the contrary, deposed that they had once had power and had abused it. And then again we might, on one occasion, hear it pointedly put out by some literary man, as the result of his careful investigation, and as a recondite point of information, which few knew, that there was this difference between the Roman Catholics of England and the Roman Catholics of Ireland, that the latter had bishops, and the former were governed by four officials, called Vicars-Apostolic.

Such was about the sort of knowledge possessed of Christianity by the heathen of old time, who persecuted its adherents from the face of the earth, and then called them a *gens lucifuga*, a people who shunned the light of day. Such were Catholics in England, found in corners, and alleys, and cellars, and the housetops, or in the recesses of the country; cut off from the populous world around them, and dimly seen, as if through a mist, or in twilight, as ghosts flitting to and fro, by the high Protestants, the lords of the earth. At length so feeble did they become, so utterly contemptible, that contempt gave birth to pity, and the more generous of their tyrants actually began to wish to bestow on them some favour, under the notion that their opinions were simply too absurd ever to spread again, and that they themselves, were they but raised in civil importance, would soon unlearn and be ashamed of them. And thus, out of mere kindness to us, they began to vilify our doctrines to the Protestant world, that so our very idiotcy, or our secret unbelief, might be our plea for mercy. ("Occasional Sermons," p. 169.)

THE RE-ESTABLISHMENT OF THE HIERARCHY.

A GREAT change, an *awful* contrast, between the time-honoured Church of St. Augustine and St. Thomas, and the poor remnant of their children in the beginning of the nineteenth century! It was a miracle, I might say, to have pulled down that lordly power; but there was a greater and a truer one in store. No one could have prophesied its fall, but still less would any one have ventured to prophesy its rise again. The fall was wonderful; still, after all, it was in the order of nature; all things come to nought: its rise again would be a different sort of wonder, for it is in the order of grace,—and who can hope for miracles, and such a miracle as this? Has the whole course of history a like to show? I must speak cautiously and according to my knowledge, but I recollect no parallel to it. Augustine, indeed, came to the same island to which the early missionaries had come already; but they came to Britons, and he to Saxons. The Arian Goths and Lombards, too, cast off their heresy in St. Augustine's age, and joined the Church; but they had never fallen away from her. The inspired word seems to imply the almost impossibility of such a grace as the renovation of those who have crucified to themselves again, and trodden underfoot, the Son of God. Who then could have dared to hope that, out of so sacrilegious a nation as this is, a people would have been formed again unto their Saviour? What signs did it show that it was to be singled out from among the nations? Had it been prophesied some fifty years ago, would not the very notion have seemed preposterous and wild?

My Fathers, there was one of your own order[1] then in the maturity of his powers and his reputation. His name is the property of this diocese; yet is too great, too venerable, too dear to all Catholics, to be confined to any part of England, when it is rather a household word in the mouths of all of us. What would have been the feelings of that venerable man, the champion of God's ark in an evil time, could *he* have lived to see this day? It is almost presumptuous for one who knew him not, to draw pictures about him, and his thoughts, and his friends, some of whom are even here present; yet am I wrong in fancying that a day such as this in which we stand would have seemed to him a dream, or, if he prophesied of it, to his hearers nothing but a mockery? Say that one time, rapt in spirit, he had reached forward

[1] [Bp. Milner.]

to the future, and that his mortal eye had wandered from that lowly chapel in the valley,[1] which had been for centuries in the possession of Catholics, to the neighbouring height, then waste and solitary. And let him say to those about him: "I see a bleak mount, looking upon an open country, over against that huge town, to whose inhabitants Catholicism is of so little account. I see the ground marked out, and an ample enclosure made; and plantations are rising there, clothing and circling in the space. And there on that high spot, far from the haunts of men, yet in the very centre of the island, a large edifice,[2] or rather pile of edifices, appears, with many fronts and courts, and long cloisters and corridors, and story upon story. And there it rises, under the invocation of the same sweet and powerful name which has been our strength and consolation in the Valley. I look more attentively at that building, and I see it is fashioned upon that ancient style of art which brings back the past, which had seemed to be perishing from off the face of the earth, or to be preserved only as a curiosity, or to be imitated only as a fancy. I listen, and I hear the sound of voices, grave and musical, renewing the old chant, with which Augustine greeted Ethelbert in the free air upon the Kentish strand. It comes from a long procession, and it winds along the cloisters. Priests and religious, theologians from the schools, and canons from the Cathedral, walk in due precedence. And then there comes a vision of well-nigh twelve mitred heads; and last I see a Prince of the Church, in the royal dye of empire and of martyrdom, a pledge to us from Rome of Rome's unwearied love, a token that that goodly company is firm in Apostolic faith and hope. And the shadow of the Saints is

---

[1] [Maryvale.]   [2] [St. Mary's College, Oscott.]

there;—St. Benedict is there, speaking to us by the voice of bishop and of priest, and counting over the long ages through which he has prayed, and studied, and laboured; there, too, is St. Dominic's white wool, which no blemish can impair, no stain can dim;—and if St. Bernard be not there, it is only that his absence may make him be remembered more. And the princely patriarch, St. Ignatius, too, the St. George of the modern world, with his chivalrous lance run through his writhing foe, he, too, sheds his blessing upon that train. And others, also, his equals or his juniors in history, whose pictures are above our altars, or soon shall be, the surest proof that the Lord's arm has not waxen short, nor his mercy failed,—they, too, are looking down from their thrones on high upon the throng. And so that high company moves on into the holy place; and there, with august rite and awful sacrifice, inaugurates the great act which brings it thither." What is that act? it is the first Synod[1] of a new Hierarchy; it is the resurrection of the Church. .

O my Fathers, my Brothers, had that revered Bishop spoken then, who that had heard him but would have said that he spoke what could not be? What! those few scattered worshippers, *the* Roman Catholics, to form a Church! Shall the past be rolled back? Shall the grave open? Shall the Saxons live again to God? Shall the shepherds, watching their poor flocks by night, be visited by a multitude of the heavenly army, and hear how their Lord has been new-born in their own city? Yes; for grace can, where nature cannot. The world grows old, but the Church is ever young. She can, in any time, at her Lord's will, "inherit the Gentiles, and inhabit the desolate cities." "Arise, Jerusalem, for thy light is come, and the glory of

---

[1] [The Synod of Oscott.]

the Lord is risen upon thee. Behold, darkness shall cover the earth, and a mist the people; but the Lord shall arise upon thee, and His glory shall be seen upon thee. Lift up thine eyes round about, and see; all these are gathered together, they come to thee; thy sons shall come from afar, and thy daughters shall rise up at thy side." "Arise, make haste, my love, my dove, my beautiful one, and come. For the winter is now past, and the rain is over and gone. The flowers have appeared in our land .. the fig-tree hath put forth her green figs; the vines in flower yield their sweet smell. Arise, my love, my beautiful one, and come." It is the time for thy Visitation. Arise, Mary, and go forth in thy strength into that north country, which once was thine own, and take possession of a land which knows thee not! Arise, Mother of God, and with thy thrilling voice, speak to those who labour with child, and are in pain, till the babe of grace leaps within them! Shine on us, dear Lady, with thy bright countenance, like the sun in his strength, *O stella matutina*, O harbinger of peace, till our year is one perpetual May! From thy sweet eyes, from thy pure smile, from thy majestic brow, let ten thousand influences rain down, not to confound or overwhelm, but to persuade, to win over thine enemies. O Mary, my hope, O Mother undefiled, fulfil to us the promise of this spring! A second temple rises on the ruins of the old. Canterbury has gone its way, and York is gone, and Durham is gone, and Winchester is gone. It was sore to part with them. We clung to the vision of past greatness, and would not believe it could come to nought; but the Church in England has died, and the Church lives again. Westminster and Nottingham, Beverley and Hexham, Northampton and Shrewsbury, if the world lasts, shall be names as musical to the ear, as stirring to the heart, as the glories we have lost; and saints shall rise out of them, if God so will, and doctors once again shall give the law to Israel, and preachers call to penance and to justice, as at the beginning.

Yes, my Fathers and Brothers, and if it be God's blessed will, not saints alone, not doctors only, not preachers only, shall be ours—but martyrs, too, shall re-consecrate the soil to God. We know not what is before us, ere we win our own; we are engaged in a great, a joyful work, but in proportion to God's grace is the fury of His enemies. They have welcomed us as the lion greets his prey. Perhaps they may be familiarized in time with our appearance, but perhaps they may be irritated the more. To set up the Church again in England is too great an act to be done in a corner. We have had reason to expect that such a boon would not be given to us without a cross. It is not God's way that great blessings should descend without the sacrifice first of great sufferings. If the truth is to be spread to any wide extent among this people, how can we dream, how can we hope, that trial and trouble shall not accompany its going forth? And we have already, if it may be said without presumption, to commence our work withal, a large store of merits. We have no slight outfit for our opening warfare. Can we religiously suppose that the blood of our martyrs three centuries ago and since, shall never receive its recompence? Those priests, secular and regular, did they suffer for no end? or rather, for an end which is not yet accomplished? The long imprisonment, the fetid dungeon, the weary suspense, the tyrannous trial, the barbarous sentence, the savage execution, the rack, the gibbet, the knife, the caldron, the numberless tortures of those holy victims, O my God, are they to have no reward? Are Thy martyrs to cry from under Thine altar for their loving vengeance on this guilty people, and to cry in vain? Shall they lose life, and not gain a better life for the children of those who persecuted them? Is this Thy way, O my God, righteous and true? Is it according to Thy promise, O King of Saints, if I may dare talk to Thee of justice? Did not Thou Thyself pray for Thine enemies upon the cross, and convert them? Did not Thy first martyr win Thy great Apostle, then a persecutor, by his loving prayer? And in that day of trial and desolation for England, when hearts were pierced through and through with Mary's woe, at the crucifixion of Thy body mystical, was not every tear that flowed, and every drop of blood that was shed, the seeds of a future harvest, when they who sowed in sorrow were to reap in joy?

And as that suffering of the martyrs is not yet recompensed, so, perchance, it is not yet exhausted. Something, for what we know, remains to be undergone, to complete the necessary sacrifice. May God forbid it, for this poor nation's sake. But still, could we be surprised, my Fathers and my Brothers, if the winter even now should not yet be quite over? Have we any right to take it strange, if, in this English land, the spring-time of the Church should turn out to be an English spring—an uncertain, anxious time of hope and fear, of joy and suffering—of bright promise and budding hopes, yet withal, of keen blasts, and cold showers, and sudden storms?

One thing alone I know, that according to our need, so will be our strength. One thing I am sure of, that the more the enemy rages against us, so much the more will the saints in heaven plead for us; the more fearful are our trials from the world, the more present to us will be our Mother Mary and our good Patrons and Angel Guardians; the more malicious are the devices of men against us, the louder cry of supplication will ascend from the bosom of the whole Church to God for us. We shall not be left orphans; we shall have within us the strength of the Para-

clete, promised to the Church and to every member of it.
My Fathers, my Brothers in the priesthood, I speak from
my heart when I declare my conviction, that there is no
one among you here present but, if God so willed, would
readily become a martyr for His sake. I do not say you
would wish it; I do not say that the natural will would not
pray that that chalice might pass away; I do not speak of
what you can do by any strength of yours; but in the
strength of God, in the grace of the Spirit, in the armour
of justice, by the consolations and peace of the Church, by
the blessing of the Apostles Peter and Paul, and in the
name of Christ, you would do what nature cannot do. By
the intercession of the Saints on high, by the penances and
good works and the prayers of the people of God on earth,
you would be forcibly borne up as upon the waves of the
mighty deep, and carried on out of yourselves by the fulness of grace, whether nature wished it or no. I do not
mean violently, or with unseemly struggle, but calmly,
gracefully, sweetly, joyously, you would mount up and
ride forth to the battle, as on the rush of Angels' wings, as
your fathers did before you, and gained the prize. You,
who day by day offer up the Immaculate Lamb of God,
you who hold in your hands the Incarnate Word under the
visible tokens which He has ordained, you who again and
again drain the chalice of the Great Victim; who is to
make you fear? What is to startle you? what to seduce
you? Who is to stop you, whether you are to suffer or to
do, whether to lay the foundations of the Church in tears,
or to put the crown upon the work in jubilation. ("Occasional Sermons," p. 173.)

PART IV.

RELIGIOUS.

Section I.—PROTESTANTISM.

PROTESTANTISM AND HISTORICAL CHRISTIANITY.

WHATEVER be historical Christianity, it is not Protestantism. If ever there were a safe truth, it is this. And Protestantism has ever felt it. I do not mean that every Protestant writer has felt it; for it was the fashion at first, at least as a rhetorical argument against Rome, to appeal to past ages, or to some of them; but Protestantism, as a whole, feels it, and has felt it. This is shown in the determination of dispensing with historical Christianity altogether, and of forming a Christianity from the Bible alone; men never would have put it aside, unless they had despaired of it. It is shown by the long neglect of ecclesiastical history in England, which prevails even in the English Church. Our popular religion scarcely recognizes the fact of the twelve long ages which lie between the Councils of Nicæa and Trent, except as affording one or two passages to illustrate its wild interpretations of certain prophecies of St. Paul and St. John. It is melancholy to say it, but the chief, perhaps the only English writer who has any claim to be considered an ecclesiastical historian, is the infidel Gibbon. German Protestantism, on the other hand, has been of a bolder character; it has calmly faced and carefully surveyed the

Christianity of eighteen hundred years, and it frankly avows that it is a mere religion of man, and the accident of a period. It considers it a syncretism of various opinions, springing up in time and place, and forming such combinations, one with another, as their respective characters admitted. It considers it as the religion of the childhood of the human mind, and curious to the philosopher as a phenomenon. And the utter incongruity between Protestantism and historical Christianity is true, whether the latter be regarded in its earlier or in its later centuries. Protestants can as little bear its ante-Nicene, as its post-Tridentine period. I have elsewhere observed on this circumstance: "So much must the Protestant grant, that if such a system of doctrine as he would now introduce ever existed in early times, it has been clean swept away as if by a deluge, suddenly, silently, and without memorial; by a deluge coming in a night, and utterly soaking, rotting, heaving up, and hurrying off every vestige of what it found in the Church, before cock-crowing: so that 'when they rose in the morning' her true seed 'were all dead corpses'—nay, dead and buried —and without grave-stone. 'The waters went over them; there was not one of them left; they sunk like lead in the mighty waters.' Strange antitype, indeed, to the early fortunes of Israel!—then the enemy was drowned, and 'Israel saw them dead upon the seashore.' But now, it would seem, water proceeded as a flood 'out of the serpent's mouth,' and covered all the witnesses, so that not even their dead bodies 'lay in the streets of the great city.' Let him take which of his doctrines he will, his peculiar view of self-righteousness, of formality, of superstition; his notion of faith, or of spirituality in religious worship; his denial of the virtues of the Sacraments, or of the ministerial commission, or of the visible Church;

or his doctrine of the divine efficacy of the Scriptures as the one appointed instrument of religious teaching; and let him consider how far antiquity, as it has come down to us, will countenance him in it. No; he must allow that the alleged deluge has done its work; yes, and has in turn disappeared itself; it has been swallowed in the earth mercilessly as itself was merciless."[1]

That Protestantism, then, is not the Christianity of history, it is easy to determine. ("Essay on Development," p. 5.)

BIBLE RELIGION.

THERE is in the literary world just now an affectation of calling religion a "sentiment;" and it must be confessed that usually it is nothing more with our own people, educated or rude. Objects are barely necessary to it. I do not say so of old Calvinism, or Evangelical religion; I do not call the religion of Leighton, Beveridge, Wesley, Thomas Scott, or Cecil, a mere sentiment, nor do I so term the high Anglicanism of the present generation. But these are only denominations, parties, schools, compared with the national religion of England in its length and breadth. "Bible Religion" is both the recognized title and the best description of English religion.

It consists, not in rites or creeds, but mainly in having the Bible read in church, in the family, and in private. Now I am far indeed from undervaluing that mere knowledge of Scripture which is imparted to the population

---

[1] ["Hist. Sketches," vol. I. p. 418.]

thus promiscuously. At least in England, it has to a certain point made up for great and grievous losses in its Christianity. The reiteration again and again in fixed course in the public service of the words of inspired teachers under both Covenants, and that in grave majestic English, has in matter of fact been to our people a vast benefit. It has attuned their minds to religious thoughts; it has given them a high moral standard; it has served them in associating religion with compositions which, even humanly considered, are among the most sublime and beautiful ever written; especially, it has impressed upon them the series of Divine Providences in behalf of man from his creation to his end, and, above all, the words, deeds, and sacred sufferings of Him in whom all the Providences of God centre.

So far the indiscriminate reading of Scripture has been of service; still, much more is necessary than the benefits which I have enumerated, to answer to the idea of a Religion; whereas our national form professes to be little more than thus reading the Bible and living a correct life. It is not a religion of persons and things, of acts of faith and of direct devotion; but of sacred scenes and pious sentiments. It has been comparatively careless of creed and catechism; and has in consequence shown little sense of the need of consistency in the matter of its teaching. Its doctrines are not so much facts, as stereotyped aspects of facts; and it is afraid, so to say, of walking round them. It induces its followers to be content with this meagre view of revealed truth; or, rather, it is suspicious, and protests, or is frightened, as if it saw a figure in a picture move out of its frame, when our Lord, the Blessed Virgin, or the Holy Apostles, are spoken of as real beings, and really such as Scripture implies them to be. I am not denying that the assent which it inculcates and elicits is genuine as regards its contracted range of **doctrine, but** it is **at best** notional. What Scripture especially illustrates from its first page to its last, **is God's** Providence; and that is nearly the only doctrine held with a real assent[1] by the mass of religious Englishmen. Hence the Bible is so great a solace and refuge to them in trouble. I repeat, I am not speaking of particular schools and parties in England, whether of the High Church **or** the Low, but of the mass of piously-minded and well-living people in all ranks of the community. ("**Grammar of Assent**," p. 53.)

PURITANISM.

PURITANISM [2] is a very peculiar creed, **as** being based on no one principle, but propping itself up upon several, and those not very concordant. . . And thus it contains within it the seeds of ruin, which time only is required to develop. At present, not **any** one principle does it carry out logically; nor does it try to adjust **and limit one** by the **other; but** as the English language is partly **Saxon, partly Latin,** with some **German,** some French,

---

[1] ["Real" and "Notional" are here used in a technical sense, which Dr. Newman explains thus:—"In Notional Assent .. the mind contemplates its own creations, instead of things; in Real, it is directed towards things, represented by the impressions which they have left upon the imagination." ("Grammar of Assent," p. 72.)]

[2] [Dr. Newman **uses** this term to denote the system of opinion received by the **party in** the Anglican Church known as "Evangelical."]

some Dutch, and some Italian, so this religious creed is made up of the fragments of religion, which the course of events has brought together and has embedded in it, something of Lutheranism, and something of Calvinism, something of Erastianism, and something of Zwinglianism, a little Judaism, and a little dogmatism, and not a little secularity, as if by hazard. It has no straightforward view on any one point on which it professes to teach; and, to hide its poverty, it has dressed itself out in a maze of words, which all enquirers feel and are perplexed with, yet few are able to penetrate. It cannot pronounce plainly what it holds about the Sacraments, what it means by unity, what it thinks of Antiquity, what fundamentals are, what the Church; what again it means by faith. It has no intelligible rule for interpreting Scripture, beyond that of submission to the arbitrary comments which have come down to it, though it knows it not, from Zwingle or Melancthon. "Unstable as water it cannot excel." It is but the inchoate state or stage of a doctrine, and its final resolution is in Rationalism. This it has ever shown when suffered to work itself out without interruption. ("Essays, Crit. and Hist.," vol I. p. 293.)

MUSCULAR CHRISTIANITY.

There are few religions which have no points in common; and these, whether true or false, when embraced with an absolute conviction, are the pivots on which changes take place in that collection of credences, opinions, prejudices, and other assents, which make up what is called a man's selection and adoption of a form of religion, a denomination, or a Church. There have been Protestants whose idea of enlightened Christianity has been a strenuous antagonism to what they consider the unmanliness and unreasonableness of Catholic morality, an antipathy to the precepts of patience, meekness, forgiveness of injuries, and chastity. All this they have considered a woman's religion, the ornament of monks, of the sick, the feeble, and the old. Lust, revenge, ambition, courage, pride—these, they have fancied, made the man, and want of them the slave. No one could fairly accuse such men of any great change of their convictions, if they were one day found to have taken up the profession of Islam. ("Grammar of Assent," p. 241.)

ENGLISH RELIGIOUS IDEAS.

(I.)

Now let me attempt to trace out how the English mind, in these last centuries, has come to think there is nothing good in that Religion which it once thought the very teaching of the Most High. Consider, then, this: most men, by nature, dislike labour and trouble; if they labour, as they are obliged to do, they do so *because* they are obliged. They exert themselves under a stimulus or excitement, and just as long as it lasts. Thus they labour for their daily bread, for their families, or for some temporal object which they desire; but they do not take on them the trouble of doing so without some such motive cause.

Hence, in religious matters, having no urgent appetite after truth, or desire to please God, or fear of the consequences of displeasing Him, or detestation of sin, they take what comes, they form their notions at random, they are moulded passively from without, and this is what is commonly meant by "private judgment." "Private judgment" commonly means passive impression. Most men in this country like opinions to be brought to them, rather than to be at the pains to go out and seek for them. They like to be waited on, they like to be consulted for, they like to be their own centre. As great men have their slaves or their body servants for every need of the day, so, in an age like this, when every one reads and has a voice in public matters, it is indispensable that they should have persons to provide them with their ideas, the clothing of their mind, and that of the best fashion. Hence the extreme influence of periodical publications at this day, quarterly, monthly, or daily; they teach the multitude of men what to think and what to say. And thus it is that, in this age, every one is intellectual, a sort of absolute king, though his realm is confined to himself or to his family; for at least he can think and say, though he cannot do, what he will, and that with no trouble at all, because he has plenty of intellectual servants to wait on him. Is it to be supposed that a man is to take the trouble of finding out truth, when he can pay for it? So his only object is to have cheap knowledge; that he may have his views of revelation, and dogma, and policy, and conduct—in short, of right and wrong—ready to hand, as he has his table-cloth laid for his breakfast, and the materials provided for the meal. Thus it is, then, that the English mind grows up into its existing character. There are nations naturally so formed for speculation, that individuals, almost as they eat and drink and work, will originate doctrines and follow out ideas; they, too, of course have their own difficulties in submitting to the Church, but such is not the Englishman. He is in his own way the creature of circumstances; he is bent on action; but as to opinion he takes what comes, only he bargains not to be teased or troubled about it. He gets his opinions any how, some from the nursery, some at school, some from the world, and has a zeal for them, because they are his own. Other men, at least, exercise a judgment upon them, and prove them by a rule. He does not care to do so, but he takes them as he finds them, whether they fit together or not, and makes light of the incongruity, and thinks it a proof of common sense, good sense, strong shrewd sense, to do so. All he cares for is, that he should not be put to rights; of that he is jealous enough. He is satisfied to walk about, dressed just as he is. As opinions come, so they must stay with him; and, as he does not like trouble in his acquisition of them, so he resents criticism in his use.

When, then, the awful form of Catholicism, of which he has already heard so much good and so much evil—so much evil which revolts him, so much good which amazes and troubles him—when this great vision, which hitherto he has known from books and from rumour, but not by sight and hearing, presents itself before him, it finds in him a very different being from the simple Anglo-Saxon to whom it originally came. It finds in him a being, not of rude nature, but of formed habits, averse to change and resentful of interference; a being who looks hard at it, and repudiates and loathes it, first of all, because, if listened to, it would give him much trouble. He wishes to be let alone; but here is a teaching which purports to be revealed, which would mould his mind on new ideas, which he has to learn, and which, if he cannot learn thoroughly, he must borrow from others. The very notion of a theology or a ritual frightens and oppresses him; it is a yoke, because it makes religion difficult, not easy. There is enough of labour in learning matters of this life, without concerning oneself with the revelations of another. He does not choose to believe that the Almighty has told us so many things, and he readily listens to any person or argument maintaining the negative. And, moreover, he resents the idea of interference itself; "an Englishman's house is his castle;" a maxim most salutary in politics, most dangerous in moral conduct. He cannot bear the thought of not having a will of his own, or an opinion of his own, on any given subject of enquiry, whatever it be. It is intolerable, as he considers, not to be able, on the most awful and difficult of subjects, to think for oneself; it is an insult to be told that God has spoken and superseded investigation.

(II.)

And, further still, consider this: strange as it may be to those who do not know him, he really believes in that accidental collection of tenets, of which I have been speaking; habit has made it all natural to him, and he takes it for granted; he thinks his own view of things as clear as day, and every other view irrational and ludicrous. In good faith and in sincerity of heart, he thinks the Englishman knows more about God's dealings with men then any one else; and he measures all things in heaven and earth by the floating opinions which have been drifted into his mind. And especially is he satisfied and sure of his *principles;* he conceives them to be the dictates of the simplest and most absolute sense, and it does not occur to him for a moment that objective truth claims to be sought, and a revealed doctrine requires to be ascertained. He himself is the ultimate sanction and appellate authority of all that he holds. Putting aside, then, the indignation which, under these circumstances, he naturally feels, in being invited to go to school again, his present opinions are an effectual bar to his ever recognizing the divine mission of Catholicism, for he criticises Catholicism simply by those opinions themselves which are antagonists of it, and takes his notes of truth and error from a source already committed against it. And thus you see that frequent occurrence, of really worthy persons unable to reconcile their minds, do what they will, to the teaching and the ways of the Catholic Church. The more they see of her members, the more their worst suspicions are confirmed. They did not wish, they say, to believe the popular notions of her anti-Christian character; but really, after what they have seen of her authorities and her people, nothing is left to them but an hostility to her, which they are loth to adopt. They wish to think the best of every one, but this ecclesiastical measure, that speech, that book, those persons, those expressions, that line of thought, those realized results, all tend one way, and force them to unlearn a charitableness which is as pernicious as it is illusory. Thus they speak; alas, they do not see that they are assuming the very point in dispute; for the original question is, whether Catholics or they are right in their respective principles and views, and to decide it merely by what is habitual to themselves is to exercise the double office of accuser and judge. Yet multitudes of sober and serious minds and well-regulated lives look out upon the Catholic Church and shrink back again from her presence, on no better reasons than these. They cannot endure her; their whole being revolts from her; she leaves, as they speak, a bad taste in their mouths; all is so novel, so strange so unlike what is familiar to them, so unlike the Anglican Prayer-Book, so unlike some favourite author of their own, so different from what they would do or say themselves, requires so much explanation, is so strained and unnatural, so unreal and extravagant, so unquiet, nay, so disingenuous, so unfeeling, that they cannot even tolerate it. The Mass is so difficult to follow, and we say prayers so very quickly, and we sit when we should stand, and we talk so freely when we should be reserved, and we keep Sunday so differently from them, and we have such notions of our own about marriage and celibacy, and we approve of vows, and we class virtues and sins on so unreasonable a standard; these and a thousand such details are, in the case of numbers, decisive proofs that we deserve the hard names which are heaped on us by the world.

(III.)

Recollect too, that a great part of the actions of every day, when narrowly looked into, are neither good nor bad in themselves, but only in relation to the persons who do them, and the circumstances or motives under which they are done. There are actions, indeed, which no circumstances can alter; which, at all times and in all places, are duties or sins. Veracity, purity, are always virtues—blasphemy always a sin; but to speak against another, for instance, is not always detraction, and swearing is not always taking God's name in vain. What is right in one person, may be wrong in another; and hence the various opinions which are formed of public men, who, for the most part, cannot be truly judged, except with a knowledge of their principles, characters, and motives. Here is another source of misrepresenting the Church and her servants; much of what they do admits both of a good interpretation and a bad; and when the world, as I have supposed, starts with the hypothesis that we are hypocrites or tyrants, that we are unscrupulous, crafty, and profane, it is easy to see how the very same actions which it would extol in its friends, it will unhesitatingly condemn in the instance of the objects of its hatred or suspicion. When men live in their own world, in their own habits and ways of thought, as I have been describing, they contract, not only a narrowness, but what may be called a one-sidedness of mind. They do not judge of us by the rules they apply to the conduct of themselves and each other; what they praise or allow in those they admire, is an offence to them in us. Day by day, then, as it passes, furnishes, as a matter of course, a series of charges against us, simply because it furnishes a succession of our sayings and doings. Whatever we do, whatever we do not do, is a demonstration against us. Do we argue? men are surprised at our insolence or effrontery. Are we silent? we are underhand and deep. Do we appeal to the law? it is in order to evade it. Do we obey the Church? it is a sign of our disloyalty. Do we state our pretensions? we blaspheme. Do we conceal them? we are liars and hypocrites. Do we display the pomp of our ceremonial, and the habits of our Religious? our presumption has become intolerable. Do we put them aside and dress as others? we are ashamed of being seen, and skulk about as conspirators. Did a Catholic priest cherish doubts of his faith, it would be an interesting and touching fact, suitable for public meetings. Does a Protestant minister, on the other hand, doubt of the Protestant opinions? he is but dishonestly eating the bread of the Establishment. Does a Protestant exclude Catholic books from his house? he is a good father and master. Does a Catholic do the same with Protestant tracts? he is afraid of the light. Protestants may ridicule a portion of our Scriptures under the name of the Apocrypha: we may not denounce the mere Protestant translation of the Bible. Protestants are to glory in their obedience to their ecclesiastical head; we may not be faithful to ours. A Protestant layman may determine and propound all by himself the terms of salvation: we are bigots and despots if we do but proclaim what a thousand years have sanctioned. The Catholic is insidious, when the Protestant is prudent; the Protestant frank and honest, when the Catholic is rash or profane. Not a word that we say, not a deed that we do, but is viewed in the medium of that one idea, by the light of that one prejudice, which our enemies cherish concerning us; not a word or a deed but is grafted on the original assumption that we certainly come from below, and are the servants of Antichrist. ("Occasional Sermons," p. 148.)

A PROTESTANT VIEW OF CONVERSIONS.

ONE word here as to the growth of Catholicism, of conversions, and converts—the Prejudiced Man has his own view of it all. First, he denies that there are any conversions or converts at all. This is a bold game, and will not succeed in England, though I have been told that in Ireland it has been strenuously maintained. However, let him grant the fact, that converts there are, and he has a second ground to fall back upon; the converts are weak and foolish persons—notoriously so; all their friends think so; there is not a man of any strength of character or force of intellect among them. They have either been dreaming over their folios, or have been caught with the tinsel embellishments of Popish worship. They are lack-a-daisical women, or conceited young persons, or silly squires, or the very dregs of our large towns, who have nothing to lose, and no means of knowing one thing from another. Thirdly, in corroboration:—they went over, he says, on such exceedingly wrong motives; not any one of them but you may trace his conversion to something distinctly wrong; it was love of notoriety; it was restlessness; it was resentment; it was lightness of mind; it was self-will. There was trickery in his mode of taking the step, or inconsiderateness towards the feelings of others. They went too soon, or they ought to have gone sooner. They ought to have told every one their doubts as soon as ever they felt them, and before they knew whether or not they should overcome them or no: if they had clerical charges in the Protestant Church, they ought to have flung them up at once, even at the risk of afterwards finding they had made a commotion for nothing. Or, on the other hand, what, forsooth, must these men do when a doubt came on their mind, but at once abandon all their clerical duty and go to Rome, as if it were possible anywhere to be absolutely certain? In short, they did not become Catholics at the right moment; so that, however numerous they may be, no weight whatever attaches to their conversion. As for him, it does not affect him at all; he means to die just where he is; indeed, these conversions are a positive argument in favour of Protestantism; he thinks still worse of Popery, in consequence of these men going over, than he did before. His fourth remark is of this sort: they are sure to come back. He prophesies that by this time next year, not one of them will be a Catholic. His fifth is as bold as the first—they *have* come back. This argument, however, of the Prejudiced Man, admits at times of being shown to great advantage, should it so happen that the subjects of his remarks have, for some reason or other, gone abroad; for then there is nothing to restrain his imagination. Hence, directly a new Catholic is safely lodged two or three thousand miles away, out comes the confident news that he has returned to Protestantism; when no friend has the means to refute it. When this argument fails, as fail it must, by the time a letter can be answered, our Prejudiced Man falls back on his sixth commonplace, which is to the effect that the converts are very unhappy. He knows this on the first authority; he has seen letters declaring or showing it. They are quite altered men, very much disappointed with Catholicism; restless, and desirous to come back except from false shame. Seventhly, they are altogether deteriorated in character; they have become harsh, or overbearing, or conceited, or vulgar. They speak with extreme bitterness against Protestantism; have cast off their late friends, or seem to forget that they ever were Protestants themselves. Eighthly, they have become infidels;—alas! heedless of false witness, the Prejudiced Man spreads the news about, right and left, in a tone of great concern and distress; he considers it very awful. Lastly, when every resource has failed, and in spite of all that can be said, and surmised, and expressed, and hoped, about the persons in question, Catholics they have become and Catholics they remain, the Prejudiced Man has a last resource, he simply forgets that Protestants they ever were. They cease to have antecedents; they cease to have any character, any history to which they may appeal; they merge in the great fog, in which, to his eyes, everything Catholic is enveloped; they are dwellers in the land of romance and fable; and, if he dimly contemplates them plunging and floundering amid the gloom, it is as griffins, wiverns, salamanders, the spawn of Popery, such as are said to sport in the depths of the sea, or to range amid the central sands of Africa. He forgets that he ever heard of them; he has no duties to their name; he is released from all anxiety about them. They die to him. ("Present Position of Catholics," p. 243.)

PROTESTANT TEXTS.

PROTESTANTS judge of the Apostles' doctrine, by "texts," as they are commonly called, taken from Scripture, and nothing more; and they judge of our doctrine too, by "texts" taken from our writings, and nothing more. Picked verses, bits torn from the context, half-sentences, are the warrant of the Protestant Idea of what is Apostolic truth on the one hand, and, on the other, of what is Catholic falsehood. As they have their chips and fragments of St. Paul and St. John, so have they their chips and fragments of Suarez and Bellarmine; and out of the former they make to themselves their own Christian religion, and out of the latter our Anti-Christian superstition. They do not ask themselves sincerely, as a matter of fact and history, *What* did the Apostles teach then? Nor do they ask sincerely, and as a matter of fact, *What* do Catholics teach now? They judge of the Apostles, and they judge of us, by scraps, and on these scraps they exercise their private judgment,—that is, their Prejudice, . . . and their Assumed Principles, . . . and the process ends in their bringing forth, out of their scraps from the

Apostles, what they call "Scriptural Religion," and out of their scraps from our theologians, what they call Popery.

The first Christians were a living body; they were thousands of zealous, energetic men, who preached, disputed, catechised, and conversed from year's end to year's end. They spoke by innumerable tongues, with one heart, and one soul, all saying the same thing. All this multitudinous testimony about the truths of Revelation, Protestants narrow down into one or two meagre sentences, which at their own will and pleasure they select from St. Paul, and at their own will and pleasure they explain, and call the Gospel. They do just the same thing with us. Catholics, at least, have a lively illustration and evidence of the absurdity of Protestant private judgment as exercised on the Apostolic writings, in the visible fact of its absurdity as exercised on themselves. They, as their forefathers, the first Christians, are a living body; they, too, preach, dispute, catechise, converse with innumerable tongues, saying the same thing, as our adversaries confess, all over the earth. Well, then, you would think the obvious way was, if they would know what we really teach, to come and ask us, to talk with us, to try to enter into our views, and to attend to our teaching. Not at all; they do not dream of doing so; they take their "texts;" they have got their cut-and-dried specimens from our divines, which the Protestant tradition hands down from generation to generation, and, as by the aid of their verses from Scripture, they think they understand the Gospel better than the first Christians, so by the help of these choice extracts from our works, they think they understand our doctrine better than we do ourselves. They will not allow us to explain our own books. So sure are they of their knowledge, and so superior to us, that they have no difficulty in setting us right, and in accounting for our contradicting them. Sometimes Catholics are "evasive and shuffling," which, of course, will explain everything; sometimes they simply "have never been told what their creed really is;" the priest keeps it from them, and cheats them; as yet, too, perhaps they are "recent converts," and do not know the actual state of things, though they will know in time. Thus Protestants judge us by their "texts;" and by "texts" I do not mean only passages from our writers, but all those samples of whatever kind, historical, ecclesiastical, biographical, or political, carefully prepared, improved, and finished off by successive artists for the occasion, which they think so much more worthy of credit and reliance as to facts, than us and our word, who are in the very communion to which those texts relate. Some good personal knowledge of us, and intercourse with us, not in the way of controversy or criticism, but what is prior—viz. in the way of sincere enquiry, in order to ascertain how things really lie—such knowledge and intercourse would be worth all the conclusions, however elaborate and subtle, from rumours, false witnessings, suspicions, romantic scenes, morsels of history, morsels of theology, morsels of our miraculous legends, morsels of our devotional writers, morsels from our individual members, whether unlearned or intemperate, which are the "text" of the traditional Protestant view against us. . . Yet any one is thought qualified to attack or to instruct a Catholic in matters of his religion; a country gentleman, a navy captain, a half-pay officer, with time on his hands, never having seen a Catholic, or a Catholic ceremonial, or a Catholic treatise in his life, is competent, by means of one or two periodicals and tracts, and a set of Protestant extracts against Popery, to teach the Pope his own religion, and to refute a Council. ("Present Position of Catholics," p. 322.)

PROTESTANT IMAGE WORSHIP.

A PROTESTANT blames Catholics for showing honour to images; yet he does it himself. And first, he sees no difficulty in a mode of treating them, quite as repugnant to his own ideas of what is rational as the practice he abominates, and that is the offering insult and mockery to them. Where is the good sense of showing dishonour, if it be stupid and brutish to show honour? Approbation and criticism, praise and blame, go together. I do not mean, of course, that you dishonour what you honour; but that the two ideas of honour and dishonour so go together, that where you *can* apply (rightly or wrongly, but still) where it is *possible* to apply, the one, it is possible to apply the other. Tell me, then, what is meant by burning Bishops, or Cardinals, or Popes in *effigy*? Has it no meaning? Is it not plainly intended for an insult? Would any one who was burned in effigy feel it no insult? Well, then, how is it *not* absurd to feel pain at being dishonoured in effigy, *yet* absurd to feel pleasure at being honoured in effigy? How is it childish to honour an image, if it is not childish to dishonour it? This only can a Protestant say in defence of the act which he allows and practises, that he is used to it, whereas to the other he is not used. Honour is a new idea, it comes strange to him, and, wonderful to say, he does not see that he has admitted it in principle already in admitting dishonour, and after preaching against the Catholic, who crowns an image of the Madonna, he complacently goes his way and sets light to a straw effigy of Guy Fawkes.

But this is not all; **Protestants** actually set up images

to represent their heroes, and they show them honour without any misgiving. The very flower and cream of Protestantism used to glory in the statue of King William, on College Green, Dublin; and, though I cannot make any reference in print, I recollect well what a shriek they raised some years ago, when the figure was unhorsed. Some profane person one night applied gunpowder, and blew the King right out of his saddle, and he was found by those who took interest in him, like Dagon, on the ground. You might have thought the poor senseless block had life to see the way people took on about it, and how they spoke of his face, and his arms, and his legs; yet those same Protestants, I say, would at the same time be horrified had I used "he" and "him" of a crucifix, and would call me one of the monsters described in the Apocalypse did I but honour my living Lord as they their dead King. ("Present Position of Catholics," p. 180.)

THE RIGHT OF PRIVATE JUDGMENT OR THE PRIVATE RIGHT OF JUDGMENT?

FOR all the haranguing and protesting which goes on in Exeter and other halls, this great people is not such a conscientious supporter of the sacred right of Private Judgment as a good Protestant would desire. Why should we go out of our way, one and all of us, to impute personal motives in explanation of the conversion of every individual convert, as he comes before us, if there were in us, the public, an adhesion to that absolute, and universal, and unalienable principle, as its titles are set forth in heraldic style, high and broad, sacred and awful, the right and the duty, and the possibility of Private Judgment? Why should we confess it in the general, yet promptly and pointedly deny it in every particular, if our hearts retained more than the "magni nominis umbra," when we preached up the Protestant principle? Is it not sheer wantonness and cruelty in Baptist, Independent and Irvingite, Wesleyan, Establishmentman, Jumper, and Mormonite, to delight in trampling on and crushing these manifestations of their own pure and precious charter, instead of dutifully and reverently exalting, at Bethel, or at Dan, each instance of it, as it occurs, to the gaze of its professing votaries? If a staunch Protestant's daughter turns Roman, and betakes herself to a convent, why does he not exult in the occurrence? Why does he not give a public breakfast, or hold a meeting, or erect a memorial, or write a pamphlet in honour of her, and of the great undying principle she has so gloriously vindicated? Why is he in this base, disloyal style muttering about priests, and Jesuits, and the horror of nunneries, in solution of the phenemenon, when he has the fair and ample form of Private Judgment rising before his eyes, and pleading with him, and bidding him impute good motives, not bad, and in very charity ascribe to the influence of a high and holy principle, to a right and a duty of every member of the family of man, what his poor human instincts are fain to set down as a folly or a sin? All this would lead us to suspect that the doctrine of Private Judgment in its simplicity, purity, and integrity—Private Judgment, all Private Judgment, and nothing but Private Judgment—is held by very few persons indeed, and that the great mass of the population are either stark unbelievers in it, or deplorably dark about it; and that even the minority, who are in a manner faithful to it, have glossed and corrupted the true sense of it by a miserably faulty reading, and hold not the Right of Private Judgment, but the Private Right of Judgment; in other words, their own private right, and no one's else. ("Essays, Crit. and Hist.," vol. II. p. 339.)

THE RATIONALE OF PROTESTANT PERSECUTION.

I MIGHT leave Protestants to unravel the mystery how it is that, after all their solemn words against persecution, they have persecuted, whenever, wherever, and however they could, from Elizabeth down to Victoria, from the domestic circle up to the Legislature, from black looks to the extremity of the gibbet and stake; I might leave them, but I am tempted to make them one parting suggestion. I observe, then, it is no accident that they unite in their history this abjuration with this practice of religious coercion; the two go together. I say it boldly and decidedly, and do not flinch from the avowal—Protestants attempt too much, and they end in doing nothing; they go too far: they attempt what is against nature, and therefore impossible. I am not proving this; it is a separate subject; it would require a treatise. I am only telling the Protestant world why it is they ever persecute in spite of their profession. It is because their doctrine of private judgment, as they hold it, is extreme and unreal, and necessarily leads to excesses in the opposite direction. They are attempting to reverse nature, with no warrant for doing so; and nature has its ample revenge upon them. They altogether ignore a principle which the Creator has put into our breasts, the duty of maintaining the truth, and, in consequence, they deprive themselves of the opportunity of controlling, restraining, and directing it. So it was with the actors in the first French Revolution; never were there such extravagant praises of the rights of reason; never so signal, so horrible a profanation of them. They cried "Liberty, Equality, Fraternity," and they proceeded to massacre the priests, and to hurry the laity by thousands to the scaffold or the river-side.

Far other is the conduct of the Church. Not to put the matter on higher and doctrinal grounds, it is plain, if only to prevent the occurrence of injustice and cruelty, she must—to use a phrase of the day—direct impulses which it is impossible from the nature of man to destroy. And in the course of eighteen hundred years, though her children have been guilty of various excesses, though she herself is responsible for isolated acts of most solemn import, yet for one deed of severity with which she can be charged, there have been hundreds of her acts, repressive of the persecutor and protective of his victims. She has been a never-failing fount of humanity, equity, forbearance, and compassion, in consequence of her very recognition of national ideas and instincts, which Protestants would vainly ignore and contradict; and this is the solution of the paradox stated by a distinguished author,[1] to the effect that the Religion which forbids private judgment in matters of Revelation, is historically more tolerant than the Religion which upholds it. His words will bear repetition. "We find in all parts of Europe scaffolds prepared to punish crimes against religion. Scenes which sadden the soul were everywhere witnessed. Rome is one exception to the rule; Rome, which it has been attempted to represent a monster

---

[1] Balmez' Protestantism, trans., p. 166.

of intolerance and cruelty. It is true, that the Popes have not preached, like the Protestants, universal toleration; but the facts show the difference between the Protestants and the Popes. The Popes, armed with a tribunal of intolerance, have scarce spilt a drop of blood; Protestants and Philosophers have shed it in torrents." ("Present Position of Catholics," p. 220.)

PROTESTANTISM DRIFTING INTO SCEPTICISM.

DISPUTANTS may maintain, if they please, that religious doubt is our natural, our normal state; that to cherish doubts is our duty; that to complain of them is impatience; that to dread them is cowardice; that to overcome them is inveracity; that it is even a happy state, a state of philosophic enjoyment, to be conscious of them; —but after all, unavoidable or not, such a state is not natural and not happy, if the voice of mankind is to decide the question. English minds, in particular, have too much of a religious temper in them, as a natural gift, to acquiesce for any long time in positive, active doubt. For doubt and devotion are incompatible with each other; every doubt, be it greater or less, stronger or weaker, involuntary as well as voluntary, acts upon devotion, so far forth, as water sprinkled, or dashed, or poured upon a flame. Real and proper doubt kills faith and devotion with it; and even involuntary or half-deliberate doubt, though it does not actually kill faith, goes far to kill devotion; and religion without devotion is little better than a burden, and soon becomes a superstition. Since, then, this is a day of objection and of doubt about the intellectual basis of Revealed Truth, it follows that there is a great deal of secret discomfort and distress in the religious portion of the community, the result of that general curiosity in speculation and enquiry which has been the growth among us of the last twenty or thirty years.[1]

The people of this country, being Protestants, appeal to Scripture, when a religious question arises, as their ultimate informant and decisive authority in all such matters; but who is to decide for them the previous question, that Scripture is really such an authority? When, then, as at this time, its divine authority is the very point to be determined, that is the character and extent of its inspiration and of its component parts, then they find themselves at sea, without the means of directing their course. Doubting about the authority of Scripture, they doubt about its substantial truth; doubting about its truth, they have doubts about the object which it sets before their faith, about the historical accuracy and objective reality of the picture which it presents to us of our Lord. We are not speaking of wilful doubting, but of those painful misgivings, greater or less, to which we have already referred. Religious Protestants, when they think calmly on the subject, can hardly conceal from themselves that they have a house without logical foundation, which contrives, indeed, for the present to stand, but which may go any day—and where are they then?

Of course Catholics will bid them receive the Canon of Scripture on the authority of the Church, in the spirit of St. Augustine's well-known words: "I should not believe the Gospel, were I not moved by the authority of the Catholic Church." But who, they ask, is to be voucher in

[This passage was written in 1866.]

turn for the Church and for St. Augustine? Is it not as difficult to prove the authority of the Church and her doctors as the authority of the Scriptures? We Catholics answer, and with reason, in the negative; but since they cannot be brought to agree with us here, what argumentative ground is open to them? Thus they seem drifting, slowly, perhaps, but surely, in the direction of scepticism. ("Discussions and Arguments," p. 366.)

Section II.—Anglicanism.

THE ANGLICAN VIEW OF THE VISIBLE CHURCH.

THE high school of Anglicans . . upholds the existence of a visible Church as firmly as Catholics, and the only question between the two parties is, what and where the Church is; in what it consists; and on this point it is that they differ. This Church, this spiritually endowed body, this minister of the Sacraments, teacher of Gospel truth, possessor of that power of binding and loosing, commonly called the power of the keys, is this Divine creation coincident, as Catholics hold, with the whole extended body of Christians everywhere, so as to be in its essence one and only one organized association? or, on the other hand, as [Anglicans insist,] is every separate bishopric, every diocesan unit, of which that whole is composed, properly and primarily the Church which has the promises, each of them being, like a crystallization, only a repetition of the rest, each of them, in point of privileges, as much the perfect Church as all together, each equal to each, each independent of each, each invested with full spiritual powers, *in solidum*, as St. Cyprian speaks, none subject to any, none bound to union with other by any law of its being, or condition of its prerogatives, but all free from all, except as regards the duty of mutual love, and only called one Church when taken in the aggregate, or in its Catholicity, though really multiform, by a conversational misnomer or figure of speech, or abstraction of the mind, as when all men, viewed as one, are called " man." . .

Now it is very intelligible to deny that there is any divinely established, divinely commissioned, Church at all; but to hold that the one Church is realized and perfected in each of a thousand independent corporate units, co-ordinate, bound by no necessary intercommunion, adjusted into no divine organized whole, is a tenet not merely unknown to Scripture, but so plainly impossible to carry out practically, as to make it clear that it never would have been devised except by men, who, conscientiously believing in a visible Church, and who, conscientiously opposed to Rome, had nothing left for them, whether they would or would not, but to entrench themselves in the paradox, that the Church was one indeed, and the Church was Catholic indeed, but that the one Church was not the Catholic, and the Catholic Church was not the one. . .

If it be asked of me how, with my present views of the inherent impracticability of the Anglican theory of Church polity, I could ever have held it myself, I answer, that, though swayed by great names, I never was without misgivings about the difficulties which it involved, and that as early as 1837, in my volume in defence of "Anglicanism, as contrasted with Romanism and Popular Protestantism," I expressed my sense of these difficulties.[1] ("Essays, Crit and Hist.," vol. II. pp. 90-99.)

[1] [See p. 37.]

THE "BRANCH THEORY."

WHAT is called the "Branch Theory" is, that the Roman, Greek, and Anglican Communions make up the one visible, indivisible Church of God which the Apostles founded, to which the promise of perseverance was made; a view which is as paradoxical when regarded as a fact, as it is heterodox when regarded as a doctrine. Such surely is the judgment which must be pronounced upon it in itself, and as considered apart from the motives which have led Anglicans to its adoption, for these, when charitably examined, . . are far from reprehensible; on the contrary, they betoken a goodwill towards Catholics, a Christian spirit, and a religious earnestness, which Catholics ought to be the last to treat with slight or unkindness.

Let it once be admitted that in certain minds misconceptions and prejudices may exist, such as to make it their duty in conscience (though it be a false conscience) to remain in Anglicanism, and then this paradoxical view of the Catholic Church is in them better, nearer the truth, and more hopeful than any other erroneous view of it. First, because it is the view of men deeply impressed with the great doctrine and precept of unity. Such men cannot bear to think of the enormous scandal—the loss of faith, the triumph to infidels, the obstacle to heathen conversion—resulting from the quarrels of Christians with each other; and they cannot rest until they can form some theory by which they can alleviate it to the imagination. They recollect our Lord's most touching words, just before His passion, in which He made unity the great note and badge of His religion, and they wish to be provided with some explanation of this apparent broad reversal of it, both for their own sake, and for that of others. As there are Protestants whose expedient for this purpose is to ignore all creeds and all forms of worship, and to make unity consist in a mere union of hearts, an intercourse of sentiment and work, and an agreement to differ on theological points, so the persons in question endeavour to discern the homogeneity of the Christian name in a paradoxical and compulsory resolution of the doctrines and rites of Rome, Greece, and Canterbury, to some general form common to all three.

Nor is this all; the kindliness of the theory is shown by the strong contrast which it presents to a persuasion, very strong and widely prevalent in the English Establishment, in regard to the Catholic Church. The palmary, the most effective argument of the Reformers against us, was that Rome was Antichrist. It was Mr. Keble's idea that without this tenet the Reformers would have found it impossible to make head against the prestige, the imposing greatness, the establishment, the momentum of Catholicism. There was no medium; it was either from God or from the Evil One. Is it too much to say, that wherever Protestantism has been earnest, and (what is called) spiritual, there this odious imagination has been vigorous? Is it too much to say that it is the received teaching of Anglican bishops and divines, from Latimer down to Dr. Wordsworth? Have Catholics then no bowels of compassion for [those who] adopt such a *Via media* towards the Church as I have been describing? . .

The third motive which leads religious Anglicans to hold the doctrine in question is one of a personal nature, but of no unworthy sort. Though they think it a duty to hold off from us, they cannot be easy at their own separation from the *orbis terrarum*, and from the Apostolic See.

which is the consequence of it; and the pain it causes them, and the expedient they take to get relieved of it, should interest us in their favour, since these are the measures of the real hold, which, in spite of their still shrinking from the Church, Catholic principles and ideas have upon their intellects and affections.

These remarks, however, in favour of the advocates of what may be called the Anglican paradox are quite consistent with a serious apprehension that there are those among them, known of course only to God, who make that paradox the excuse for stifling an enquiry which conscience tells them they ought to pursue, and turning away from the light which otherwise would lead them to the Church. And, then, as to this paradox itself, all the learning, all the argumentative skill of its ablest champions, would fail in proving that two sovereign states were numerically one state, even although they happened to have the same parentage, the same language, the same form of government; and yet the gulf between Rome and England, which is greater than this demarcation between state and state . . [Anglicans] merely call "an interruption of external union!" ("Essays, Crit. and Hist.," vol. I. pp. 181-184.)

THE CHURCH OF ENGLAND.

WE must not indulge our imagination in the view we take of the National Establishment. If, indeed, we dress it up in an ideal form, as if it were something real, with an independent and a continuous existence, and a proper history, as if it were in deed and not only in name a

Church, then indeed we may feel interest in it, and reverence towards it, and affection for it, as men have fallen in love with pictures, or knights in romance do battle for high dames whom they have never seen. Thus it is that students of the Fathers, antiquarians, and poets, begin by assuming that the body to which they belong is that of which they read in times past, and then proceed to decorate it with that majesty and beauty of which history tells, or which their genius creates. Nor is it by an easy process or a light effort that their minds are disabused of this error. It is an error for many reasons too dear to them to be readily relinquished. But at length, either the force of circumstances or some unexpected accident dissipates it; and, as in fairy tales, the magic castle vanishes when the spell is broken, and nothing is seen but the wild heath, the barren rock, and the forlorn sheep-walk, so is it with us as regards the Church of England, when we look in amazement on that we thought so unearthly, and find so commonplace or worthless. Then we perceive, that aforetime we have not been guided by reason, but biassed by education and swayed by affection. We see in the English Church, I will not merely say no descent from the first ages, and no relationship to the Church in other lands, but we see no body politic of any kind; we see nothing more or less than an Establishment, a department of Government, or a function or operation of the State,—without a substance,—a mere collection of officials, depending on and living in the supreme civil power. Its unity and personality are gone, and with them its power of exciting feelings of any kind. It is easier to love or hate an abstraction, than so commonplace a framework or mechanism. We regard it neither with anger, nor with aversion, nor with contempt, any more than with respect or interest. It is but one aspect of the State, or mode of civil governance;

it is responsible for nothing; it can appropriate neither praise nor blame ; but, whatever feeling it raises is to be referred on, by the nature of the case, to the Supreme Power whom it represents, and whose will is its breath. And hence it has no real identity of existence in distinct periods, unless the present Legislature or the present Court can affect to be the offspring and disciple of its predecessor. Nor can it in consequence be said to have any antecedents, or any future; or to live, except in the passing moment. As a thing without a soul, it does not contemplate itself, define its intrinsic constitution, or ascertain its position. It has no traditions; it cannot be said to think; it does not know what it holds, and what it does not;[1] it is not even conscious of its own existence. It has no love for its members, or what are sometimes called its children, nor any instinct whatever, unless attachment to its master, or love of its place, may be so called. Its fruits, as far as they are good, are to be made much of, as long as they last, for they are transient, and without succession; its former champions of orthodoxy are no earnest of orthodoxy now; they died, and there was no reason why they should be reproduced. Bishop is not like bishop, more than king is like king, or ministry like ministry; its Prayer-Book is

---

[1] This fact is strikingly brought out in Archbishop Sumner's correspondence with Mr. Maskell. "You ask me," he says, "whether you are to conclude that you ought not to teach, and have not *authority* of the Church to teach, any of the doctrines spoken of in your five former questions, in the *dogmatical* terms there stated? To which I reply, *Are* they contained in the Word of God? St. Paul says, 'Preach the word.' . . Now, whether the doctrines concerning which you enquire are contained in the Word of God, and can be proved thereby, you have the same means of discovering as myself, and I have no special authority to declare." The Archbishop at least would quite allow what I have said in the text, even though he might express himself differently.

an Act of Parliament of two centuries ago, and its cathedrals and its chapter-houses are the spoils of Catholicism.

I have said all this, not in declamation, but to bring out clearly why I cannot feel interest of any kind in the National Church, nor put any trust in it at all from its past history, as if it were, in however narrow a sense, a guardian of orthodoxy. It is as little bound by what it said or did formerly, as this morning's newspaper by its former numbers, except as it is bound by the Law; and while it is upheld by the Law it will not be weakened by the subtraction of individuals, nor fortified by their continuance. Its life is an Act of Parliament. It will not be able to resist the Arian, Sabellian, or Unitarian heresies now, because Bull or Waterland resisted them a century or two before; nor, on the other hand, would it be unable to resist them, though its more orthodox theologians were presently to leave it. It will be able to resist them while the State gives the word; it would be unable, when the State forbids it. Elizabeth boasted that she "tuned her pulpits;" Charles forbade dicussions on Predestination; George on the Holy Trinity; Victoria allows differences on Holy Baptism.[1] While the nation wishes an Establishment, it will remain, whatever individuals are for it or against it; and that which determines its existence will determine its voice. Of course the presence or departure of individuals will be one out of various disturbing causes, which may delay or accelerate by a certain number of years a change in its teaching; but, after all, the change

---

[1] [Since this was written, in 1850, similar "differences" have been allowed by the Supreme Court of Appeal in Ecclesiastical Causes with regard to various other important matters, such as the eternal reprobation of the finally impenitent, the inspiration of Scripture, and the Real and Adorable Presence in the Eucharist.]

itself depends on events broader and deeper than these; it depends on changes in the nation. As the nation changes its political, so may it change its religious views; the causes which carried the Reform Bill and Free Trade may make short work with orthodoxy. ("Anglican Difficulties," p. 4.)

ANGLICAN ORDERS.

As to Anglican Orders, I certainly do think them doubtful and untrustworthy, and that independent of any question arising out of Parker's consecration, into which I will not enter. Granting, for argument's sake, that that consecration was in all respects what its defenders say it was, still I feel a large difficulty in accepting the Anglican Succession and Commission of the Ministry, arising out of the historical aspect of the Anglican Church and of its prelates, an aspect which suggests a grave suspicion of their acts from first to last. I had occasion to make some remarks on this subject several years ago;[1] but I left them unfinished, as feeling that I was distressing, without convincing, men whom I love and respect by impugning an article of their belief, which to them is sacred, in proportion as it is vital. Now, however, when time has passed, and I am opposing, not them but my former self, I may be allowed, *pace charissimorum virorum*, to explain myself, and leave my explanations on record, as regards some points to which exception was then taken. And, in so

[1] [See p. 66.]

doing, I do but profess to be setting down a view of the subject which is very clear to my own mind, and which, as I think, ought to be clear to them; but of course I am not laying down the law on a point on which the Church has not directly and distinctly spoken, nor implying that I am not open to arguments on the other side, if such are forthcoming, which I do not anticipate.

First of all, I will attempt to set right what I thought I had set right at the time. A misstatement was made some time ago in Notes and Queries, to the effect that I had expressed "doubts about Machyn's Diary." In spite of my immediate denial of it in that publication, it has been repeated in a recent learned work on Anglican Orders. Let me then again declare that I know nothing whatever about Machyn, and that I have never mentioned his name in anything I have ever written, and that I have no doubts whatever, because I have no opinion whatever, favourable or unfavourable, about him and his Diary. Indeed, it is plain that, since, in the letter in which I was supposed to have spoken on the subject, I had dismissed altogether what is called the "antiquarian" question concerning the consecrations of 1559, as one which I felt to be dreary and interminable, I should have been simply inconsistent, had I introduced Machyn or his Diary into it, and should, in point of logic, have muddled my argument.

That argument, which I maintain now as then, is as follows:—That the consecrations of 1559 were not only facts, they were acts; that those acts were not done and over once for all, but were only the first of a series of acts done in a long course of years; that these acts too, all of them, were done by men of certain positive opinions and intentions, and none of these opinions and views, from first to last, of a Catholic complexion, but, on the contrary, erroneous and heretical. And I questioned whether men of these opinions could by means of a mere rite or formulary, however correct in itself, start and continue in a religious communion, such as the Anglican, a ministerial succession which could be depended upon as inviolate. I do not see what guarantee is producible for the faithful observance of a sacred rite, in form, matter and intention, through so long a period, in the hands of such administrators. And again, the existing state of the Anglican body, so ignorant of fundamental truth, so overrun with diversified error, would be but a sorry outcome of Apostolical ordinances and graces. "By their fruits shall ye know them." Revelation involves in its very idea a teaching and a hearing of Divine Truth. What clear and steady light of Truth is there in the Church of England? What candlestick upright and firm on which it has been set? This seems to me what Leslie calls "a short and easy method;" it is drawn out from one of the Notes of the Church. When we look at the Anglican Communion, not in the books, in the imagination, or in the affections of its champions, but as it is in fact, its claims to speak in Christ's name are refuted by its very condition. An Apostolical Ministry necessarily involves an Apostolical teaching. This practical argument was met at the time by two objections; first, that it was far-fetched, and next, that in a Catholic, it was suicidal. I do not see that it is either, and I proceed to say why:—

1. As to its being far-fetched or unreasonable; if so, it is strange that it should have lately approved itself to a writer placed in very different circumstances, who has used it, not indeed against Anglican Orders, for he firmly upholds them, but against Swedish;—I mean Dr. Littledale. This learned and zealous man, in his late Lecture at Oxford, decides that a certain uncatholic act, which he specifies, of the Swedish Ecclesiastical Establishment, done

at a particular time and place, has so bad a look as to suffice, independent of all investigation into documents of past history, at once to unchurch it,—which is to go much further in the use of my argument than I should think it right to go myself. "Sweden," he says, "*professes* to have retained an Apostolical Succession; I am satisfied from historical evidence that she has nothing of the kind; *but* the late Chaplain to the Swedish embassy in London has been good enough to supply me with *an important disproof of his own orders.* During a long illness, from which he was suffering some time ago, he entrusted the entire charge of his flock to a Danish pastor, until such time as his own successor was at length sent from Sweden. His *official position* must have made the *sanction of the authorities*, both in Church and State, necessary for a delegation of his duties, so that the *act* cannot be classed with that of an obscure Yorkshire incumbent, the other day, who invited an Anabaptist minister to fill his pulpit. And thus we gather that the *quasi* Episcopal Church of Sweden treats Presbyterian ministers on terms of perfect equality."

Here then, a writer, whose bias is towards the Church of England, distinctly lays down the principle, that a lax ecclesiastical practice, ascertained by even one formal instance, apart from documentary evidence, or ritual observance, is sufficient in itself to constitute an important disproof of the claim advanced by a nation to the possession of an Apostolical Sucession in its clergy. I speak here only of the principle involved in Dr. Littledale's argument, which is the same as my own principle, though, for myself, I do not say more than that Anglican ordinations are doubtful, whereas he considers the Swedish to be simply null. Nor again should I venture to assert that one instance of irregularity, such as that which he adduces, is sufficient to carry on me or (much less) him, to our respective conclusions. To what indeed does his "disproof" of Swedish orders come but to this; that the Swedish authorities think that Presbyterianism, as a religion, has in its doctrines and ordinances what is called "the root of the matter," and that the Episcopal form is nothing more than what I have [elsewhere][1] called "the extra twopence?" Do the highest living authorities in the Anglican Church, Queen or Archbishop, think very differently from this? Would they not, if they dared, do just what the late Swedish Chaplain did, and think it a large wisdom and a true charity to do so?

So much on the reasonableness of my argument. I conceive there is nothing evasive in refusing to decide the question of Orders by the mere letter of an Ordination Service, to the neglect of more elementary and broader questions; nothing far-fetched in taking into account the opinions and practices of its successive administrators, unless Anglicans may act towards the Swedes as Catholics may not act towards Anglicans. Such is the common sense of the matter, and that it is the Catholic sense, too, a few words will show.

It will be made clear in three propositions:—First, the Anglican Bishops for three centuries have lived and died in heresy (I am not questioning their good faith and invincible ignorance, which is an irrelevant point); next, it is far from certain, it is at the utmost only probable, that orders conferred by heretics are valid; lastly, in administering the Sacraments, the safer side, not merely the more probable, must ever be taken. And as to the proof of

[1] ["Men speak as if 'Apostolical Order' were (to use a homely illustration) like. . . the 'politeness,' the charge for which in some dame's schools, used to be an extra twopence." Essays, Crit. and Hist., vol. 1. p. 365.]

these three points:—as regards the first of them, I ask, how many Anglican Bishops have believed in transubstantiation, or in the necessity of sacramental penance? yet to deny these dogmas is to be a heretic. Secondly, as to orders conferred by heretics, there is, I grant, a strong case for their validity, but then there is also a strong case against it (vid. "Bingham Antiq." IV. 7); so that, at most, heretical ordination is not certainly but only probably valid. As to the third point, viz. that in conferring Sacraments, not merely the more probable, but the safer side must be taken, and that they must practically be considered invalid when they are not certainly valid, this is the ordinary doctrine of the Church. "Opinio probabilis," says St. Alfonso Liguori, "est illa, quæ gravi aliquo innititur fundamento, apto ad hominis prudentis assensum inclinandum. In sacramentorum collatione, *non potest minister uti opinione probabili*, aut probabiliori, de sacramenti valore; sed tutiores sequendæ sunt, aut moraliter certæ."[1] Pope Benedict XIV. supplies us with an illustration of this principle, even as regards a detail of the rite itself. In his time, an answer was given from Rome, in the case of a candidate for the priesthood, who in the course of his ordination had received the imposition of hands, but accidentally neglected to receive from the Bishop the Paten and Chalice. It was to the effect that

[1] The principle of the "tutior" opinion applies also to the rule of three bishops for a consecration, about which Hallier says:—"An consecratio episcopi, omnino nulla, irrita, et invalida sit, vel solum illegitima, quæ a paucioribus tribus episcopis peracta fuerit; Caietanus, Bellarminus, Vasquez et alii affirmantem partem sequuntur (nisi ecclesiæ dispensatio acciderit); negantem vero Paludanus .. Sylvester... et alii... Difficilis utique hæc controversia est, in qua tamen posterior et longe probabilior, et fortioribus innixa mihi videtur argumentis... Tamen prior communis est, et hocce tempore magis recepta." De S. Ordin. T. II. pp. 299-308.

he was bound to be ordained over again, *sub conditione*.¹
What Anglican candidate for the priesthood has ever
touched physically or even morally Paten or Chalice in his
ordination, from Archbishop Parker to Archbishop Tait?
In truth, the Catholic rite, whether it differs from itself or
not in different ages, still in every age, age after age, is
itself, and nothing but itself. It is a concrete whole, one
and indivisible, and acts per *modum unius*; and having
been established by the Church, and being in possession,
it cannot be cut up into bits, be docked and twisted, or
split into essentials and non-essentials, genus and species,
matter and form, at the heretical will of a Cranmer or
a Ridley, or turned into a fancy ordinal by a royal commission of divines, without a sacrilege perilous to its vitality.
Though the delivery of the sacred vessels was not primitive, it was part of the existing rite, three centuries ago,

¹ Benedict says, Syn. Diœc. VIII. 10:—"Quidam sacerdotio
initiandus, etsi omnes consuetas manus impositiones ab episcopo
accepsisset, ad episcopum tamen, solita patenæ cum hostiâ et calicis
cum vino instrumenta porrigentem, ad alia tunc temporis distractus,
non accessit. Re postea detectâ, quid facto opus esset, dubitatum,
atque a Sacra Congregatione petitum est." After giving his own
opinion, "Nihil esse iterandum, sed cauté supplendum, quod per
errorem prætermissum," he states the decision of the Sacred Congregation: "Sacra Congregatio totam Ordinationem sub conditione iterandam rescripsit." And Scavini Theol. Mor. b. III. p. 278, referring to
the passage in Benedict, says of the "libri traditio," as well as the
"manuum impositio," in the ordination of a deacon; "Probabile est
libri traditionem de essentia. . . quare pro praxi concludimus,
utramque esse adhibendam, cum agatur de Sacramentis ; et, si quidpiam, ex istis fuerit omissam, sub conditione ordinationem iterandam
esse." It is true that Father Perrone, in 1863, on his asking as to the
necessity of the "physicus tactus" (as Father Ephrem before him in
1661), received for answer as Ephrem did, that to insist on it was a
scruple (Gury de Ord.) ; but we are here concerned not with the mere
physical "tactus," but the moral "traditio instrumentorum."

as it is now, and could not, and cannot be omitted, without prejudice to the ecclesiastical status of those who are ordained without it.

Whether indeed, as time goes on, the Pope, in the plenitude of his power, could, with the aid of his theologians, obtain that clearer light, which the Church has not at present, on the whole question of ordination, for which St. Leo IX. so earnestly prayed, and thereby determine what is at present enveloped in such doubtfulness, viz. the validity of heretical ordinations, and, what is still more improbable than the abstract proposition, the validity of Anglican Orders in particular, is a subject on which I do not enter. As the matter stands, all we see is a hierarchical body, whose opinions through three hundred years compromise their acts, who do not themselves believe that they have the gifts which their zealous adherents ascribe to them, who in their hearts deny those sacramental formulas which their country's law obliges them to use, who conscientiously shudder at assuming real episcopal or sacerdotal power, who resolve "Receive the Holy Ghost" into a prayer, "Whose sins ye remit are remitted" into a license to preach, and "This is My Body, this is My Blood" into an allegory.

And then, supposing if ever these great difficulties were overcome, after all would follow the cardinal question which Benedict XIV. opens, as I have shown, about the sufficiency of the rite itself.

Any how, as things now stand, it is clear no Anglican bishop or priest can by Catholics be recognized as such. If, indeed, earnestness of mind and purity of purpose could ever be a substitute for the formal conditions of a Sacrament, which Apostles have instituted and the Church maintains, certainly in that case one might imagine it to be so accepted in many an Anglican ordination. I do believe that, in the case of many men, it is the one great day of their lives, which cannot come twice, the day on which, in their fresh youth, they freely dedicated themselves and all their powers to the service of the Redeemer,—solemn and joyful at the time, and ever after fragrant in their memories: —it is so; but devotion cannot reverse the past, nor good faith fulfil its own aspirations; and it is because I feel this, and in no temper of party, that I refuse to entertain an imagination which is neither probable in fact, nor Catholic in spirit. If we do not even receive the baptism of Anglicans, how can we receive their ordinations?

2. But now, secondly, comes the question, whether the argument, used above against Anglican, may not be retorted on Catholic ordinations;—for it may be objected that, however Catholics may claim to themselves the tradition of doctrine and rite, they do not profess to be secure against bad ecclesiastics any more than Protestants; that there have been times of ignorance, violence, unscrupulousness, in the history of the Catholic Church; and that if Anglican Orders are untrustworthy, because of the chance mistakes in three hundred years, much more so are Catholic, which have run a whole eighteen hundred; in short, that I have but used against the Anglican ministry the old, notorious argument of Chillingworth and Macaulay, an argument which is of a sceptical character in them, and in a Catholic suicidal also.

Now I do not know what is meant by calling such an argument sceptical. It seems to me a very fair argument. Scepticism is the refusal to be satisfied with reasons which ought to satisfy. To be sceptical is to be unreasonable. But what is there unreasonable, what extravagant in idea, or inconsistent with experience, in recognizing the chance of important mistakes, here or there, in a given succession of acts? I do certainly think it most probable, that an intricate series of ordinations through three hundred years, and much more through eighteen hundred, will have flaws in it. Who does not think so? It will have them to a certainty, and is in itself untrustworthy. By "untrustworthy in itself," I mean, humanly speaking; for if indeed there be any special protection promised to it, beyond nature, to secure it against errors and accidents, that, of course, is another matter; and the simple question is whether this or that particular Succession has such a promise, or, in other words, whether this or that Succession is or is not Apostolical. It is usual for Anglicans to say, as we say, that they have "the Apostolical Succession;" but that is begging the question; if a Succession be Apostolical, then indeed it is protected from errors; but it has to be proved Apostolical before such protection can be claimed for it; that is, we and they, both of us, must give reasons in our own case respectively for this our critical assumption of our *being* Apostolical. We, Catholics, do produce our reasons,—that is, we produce what are commonly called the "Notes of the Church;"—by virtue of those reasons, we consider that we belong to that Apostolical Church, in which were at the beginning stored the promises, and, therefore, our Succession has the Apostolical promise of protection, and is preserved from accidents, or is Apostolic; on the other hand, Anglicans must give reasons on their part for maintaining that they too belong to the Apostolic Church, and that their Succession is Apostolic. There is, then, nothing unfair in Macaulay's argument, viewed in itself; it is fair to both of us; nor is it suicidal in the hands of a Catholic to use it against Anglicans, if, at the same time, he gives reasons why it cannot be used against himself. Let us look, then, at the objection, more closely.

Lord Macaulay's remarks on the "Apostolic Succession"

contained in one of his reviews, written with the force and brilliancy for which he is so well known, are far too extended to admit of insertion here; but I will quote a few words of his argument from its beginning and ending. He begins by laying down, first, that whether an Anglican clergyman "be a priest by succession from the Apostles, depends on the question, whether, during that long period, some thousands of events took place, any one of which may, without any gross impropriety, be supposed not to have taken place;" and next, "that there is not a tittle of evidence for any one of those events." Then, after various vivid illustrations of his argument, he ends by a reference to Chillingworth's "very remarkable words," as he calls them. "That of ten thousand requisites, whereof any one may fail, not one should be wanting, this to me is extremely improbable, and even cousin-german to impossible."

I cannot deny, certainly, that Catholics, as well as the High Anglican school, do believe in the Apostolic Succession of ministry, continued through eighteen hundred years; nor that they both believe it to be necessary to an Apostolic ministry; nor that they act upon their belief. But, as I have said, though so far the two parties agree, still they differ materially in their respective positions relatively towards that Succession, and differ, in consequence, in their exposure respectively to the force of the objection on which I have been dwelling. The difference of position between the two may be expressed in the following antithesis:—Catholics believe their Orders are valid, because they are members of the true Church; and Anglicans believe they belong to the true Church, because their Orders are valid. And this is why Macaulay's objection tells against Anglicans, and does not tell against Catholics. In other words, our Apostolic descent is to us a theological inference, and not primarily a doctrine of faith;

theirs, necessarily is a first principle in controversy, and a patent matter of fact, the credentials of their mission. That they can claim to have God's ministers among them, depends directly and solely upon the validity of their Orders; and to prove their validity, they are bound to trace their Succession through a hundred intermediate steps, till at length they reach the Apostles; till they do this, their claim is in abeyance. If it is improbable that the Succession has no flaws in it, they have to bear the brunt of the improbability; if it is presumable that a special Providence precludes such flaws, or compensates for them, they cannot take the benefit of that presumption to themselves; for to do so would be claiming to belong to the true Church, to which that high Providence is promised, and this they cannot do without arguing in a circle, first proving that they are of the true Church because they have valid Orders, and then that their Orders are valid because they are of the true Church.

Thus the Apostolical Succession is to Anglican divines a *sine quâ non*, not "necessitate præcepti," sed "necessitate medii." Their Succession is indispensable to their position, as being the point from which they start, and therefore it must be unimpeachable, or else they do not belong to the Church: and to prove it is unimpeachable by introducing the special Providence of God over His Church, would be like proving the authority of Scripture by those miracles of which Scripture alone is the record It must be unimpeachable before, and without taking that special Providence into account, and this, I have said above, cannot be. We, on our side, on the contrary, are not in such a dilemma as this. Our starting-point is not the fact of a faithful transmission of Orders, but the standing fact of the Church, the Visible and One Church, the reproduction and succession of herself, age after age. It is the Church herself that vouches for our Orders, while she authenticates herself to be the Church not by our Orders, but by her Notes. It is the great Note of an ever-enduring *cœtus fidelium*, with a fixed organization, a unity of jurisdiction, a political greatness, a continuity of existence in all places and times, a suitableness to all classes, ranks, and callings, an ever-energizing life, an untiring, ever-evolving history, which is her evidence that she is the creation of God, and the representative and home of Christianity. She is not based upon her Orders; she is not the subject of her instruments; they are not necessary for her idea. We could even afford, for argument's sake, to concede to Lord Macaulay the uncertainty of our Succession. If Providence had so willed, she might have had her ministers without any lineal descent from the Apostles at all. Her mere nomination might have superseded any rite of ordination; there might have been no indelible character in her ministers; she might have commissioned them, used them, and recalled them at her pleasure. She might have been like a civil state, in which there is a continuation of office but not a propagation of official life. The occupant of the See of St. Peter, himself made such by mere election, might have made Bishops and unmade them. Her Divine Founder has chosen a better way, better because He has chosen it. Transmission of ministerial power ever has been, and ever shall be; and He who has so ordained, will carry out His ordinance, preserve it from infraction, and make good any damage to it, because it is His ordinance; but still that ordinance is not simply of the essence of the Church: it is not more than an inseparable accident and a necessary instrument. Nor is the Apostolic descent of her priests the direct warrant of their power in the eyes of the faithful. Their warrant is her immediate, present, living **authority; it is the word of the Church** which marks them out as the ministers of God, not any historical or antiquarian research, or genealogical table; and while she is most cautious and jealous that they should be ordained aright, yet it is sufficient in proof of their ordination that they belong to her.

Thus it would appear that to Catholics the certainty of Apostolical Orders is not a point of prime necessity, yet they possess it; and for Anglicans it is absolutely indispensable, yet they have it not.

On such grounds as these it is, that I consider the line of argument which I have adopted against Anglican Orders, is neither open to the charge of scepticism, nor suicidal in the hands of a Catholic. ("Essays, Crit. and Hist.," vol. II. p. 76.)

ANGLICAN ORDINANCES.

(I).

YOU tell me, my [Anglican] brethren, that you have the clear evidence of the influences of grace in your hearts, by its effects sensible at the moment or permanent in the event. You tell me, that you have been converted from sin to holiness, or that you have received great support and comfort under trial, or that you have been carried over very special temptations, though you have not submitted yourselves to the Catholic Church. More than this, you tell me of the peace, and joy, and strength which you have experienced in your own ordinances. You tell me, that when you began to go weekly to communion, you found yourselves wonderfully advanced in purity. You tell me that you went to confession, and you never will believe that the hand of God was not over you at the moment when you received absolution. You were ordained, and a fragrance breathed around you; you hung over the dead, and you all but saw the happy spirit of the departed. This is what you say, and the like of this; and I am not the person, my dear brethren, to quarrel with the truth of what you say. I am not the person to be jealous of such facts, nor to wish you to contradict your own memory and your own nature; nor am I so ungrateful to God's former mercies to myself, to have the heart to deny them in you. As to miracles, indeed, if such you mean, that of course is a matter which might lead to dispute; but if you merely mean to say that the supernatural grace of God, as shown either at the time or by consequent fruits, has overshadowed you at certain times, has been with you when you were taking part in the Anglican ordinances, I have no wish, and a Catholic has no anxiety, to deny it.

Why should I deny to your memory what is so pleasant in mine? Cannot I, too, look back on many years past, and many events, in which I myself experienced what is now your confidence? Can I forget the happy life I have led all my days, with no cares, no anxieties worth remembering; without desolateness, or fever of thought, or gloom of mind, or doubt of God's love to me, and providence over me? Can I forget,—I never can forget, —the day when, in my youth, I first bound myself to the ministry of God in that old church of St. Frideswide, the patroness of Oxford? nor how I wept most abundant and most sweet tears, when I thought what I then had become; though I looked on ordination as no sacramental rite, nor even to baptism ascribed any supernatural virtue? Can I wipe out from my memory, or wish to wipe out, those happy Sunday mornings, light or dark, year after year, when I celebrated your communion-rite, in my own church of St. Mary's; and in the pleasantness and joy of it heard nothing of the strife of tongues which surrounded its walls? When, too, shall I not feel the soothing recollection of those dear years which I spent in retirement, in preparation for my deliverance from Egypt, asking for light, and by degrees gaining it, with less of temptation in my heart, and sin on my conscience, than ever before? O my dear brethren, my Anglican friends! I easily give you credit for what I have experienced myself. Provided you be in good faith, if you are not trifling with your conscience, if you are resolved to follow whithersoever God shall lead, if the ray of conviction has not fallen on you, and you have shut your eyes to it; then, anxious as I am about you for the future, and dread as I may till you are converted, that perhaps, when conviction comes, it will come in vain; yet still, looking back at the past years of my own life, I recognize what you say, and bear witness to its truth. Yet what has this to do with the matter in hand? I admit your fact; do you admit, in turn, my explanation of it. It is the explanation ready provided by the Catholic Church, provided in her general teaching, quite independently of your particular case, not made for the occasion, only applied when it has arisen;—listen to it, and see, whether you admit it or not as true, if it be not sufficiently probable, or possible if you will, to invalidate the argument on which you so confidently rely.

(II).

Surely you ought to know the Catholic teaching on the subject of grace, in its bearing on your argument, without my insisting on it:—*Spiritus Domini replevit orbem terrarum.* Grace is given for the merits of Christ all over the earth; there is no corner, even of Paganism, where it is not present, present in each heart of man in real sufficiency for his ultimate salvation. Not that the grace presented to each is such as at once to bring him to heaven; but it is sufficient for a beginning. It is sufficient to enable him to plead for other grace; and that second grace is such as to impetrate a third grace; and thus the soul may be led from grace to grace, and from strength to strength, till at length it is, so to say, in very sight of heaven, if the gift of perseverance does but complete the work. Now here observe, it is not certain that a soul which has the first grace will have the second; for the grant of the second at least depends on its use of the first. Again, it may have the first and second, and yet not the third; from the first on to the nineteenth, and not the twentieth. We mount up by steps towards God, and alas! it is possible that a soul may be courageous and bear up for nineteen steps, and stop and faint at the twentieth. Nay, further than this, it is possible to conceive a soul going forward till it arrives at the very grace of contrition—a contrition so loving, so sin-renouncing, as to bring it at once into a state of reconciliation, and clothe it in the vestment of justice; and yet it may yield to the further trials which beset it, and fall away.

Now all this may take place even outside the Church; and consider what at once follows from it. This follows, in the first place, that men there may be, not Catholics, yet really obeying God and rewarded by Him—nay, I might say (at least by way of argument), in His favour, with their sins forgiven, and in the enjoyment of a secret union with that heavenly kingdom to which they do not visibly belong—who are, through their subsequent failure, never to reach it. There may be those who are increasing in grace and knowledge, and approaching nearer to the Catholic Church every year, who are not in the Church, and never will be. The highest gifts and graces are compatible with ultimate reprobation. As regards, then, the evidence of sanctity in members of the National Establishment, on which you insist, Catholics are not called on to deny them. We think such instances are few, nor so eminent as you are accustomed to fancy; but we do not wish to deny, nor have any difficulty in admitting, such facts as you have to adduce, whatever they be. We do not think it necessary to carp at every instance of supernatural excellence among Protestants when it comes before us, or to explain it away; all we know is, that the grace given them is intended ultimately to bring them into the Church, and if it is not tending to do so, it will not ultimately profit them; but we as little deny its presence in their souls as they do themselves; and as the fact is no perplexity to us, it is no triumph to them.

And, secondly, in like manner, whatever be the comfort or the strength attendant upon the use of the national ordinances of religion, in the case of this or that person, a Catholic may admit it without scruple, for it is no evidence to him in behalf of those ordinances themselves. It is the teaching of the Catholic Church from time immemorial, and independently of the present controversy, that grace is given in a sacred ordinance in two ways, viz. to use the scholastic distinction, *ex opere operantis*, and *ex opere operato*.

Grace is given *ex opere operato*, when, the proper dispositions being supposed in the recipient, it is given through the ordinance itself; it is given *ex opere operantis*, when, whether there be outward sign or no, the inward energetic act of the recipient is the instrument of it. Thus Protestants say that justification, for instance, is gained by faith as by an instrument—*ex opere operantis;* thus Catholics also commonly believe that the benefit arising from the use of holy water accrues, not *ex opere operato*, or by means of the element itself, but *ex opere operantis*, through the devout mental act of the person using it, and the prayers of the Church. So again, the Sacrifice of the Mass benefits the person for whom it is offered *ex opere operato*, whatever be the character of the celebrating Priest; but it benefits him more or less, *ex opere operantis*, according to the degree of sanctity which the Priest has attained, and the earnestness with which he offers it. Again, baptism, whether administered by man or woman, saint or sinner, heretic or Catholic, regenerates an infant *ex opere operato;* on the other hand, in the case of the baptism of blood, as it was anciently called (that is, the martyrdom of unbaptized persons desiring the Sacrament, but unable to obtain it), a discussion has arisen, whether the martyr was justified *ex opere operato* or *ex opere operantis*—that is, whether by the physical act of his dying for the faith, considered in itself, or by the mental act of supreme devotion to God, which caused and attended it. So again, contrition of a certain kind is sufficient as a disposition or condition, or what is called matter, for receiving absolution in Penance *ex opere operato*, or by virtue of the Sacrament; but it may be heightened and purified into so intense an act of divine love, of hatred and sorrow for sin, and of renunciation of it, as to cleanse and justify the soul, without the sacrament at all, or *ex opere operantis*. It is plain from this distinction, that, if we would determine whether the Anglican ordinances are attended by divine grace, we must first determine whether the effects which accompany them arise *ex opere operantis* or *ex opere operato*—whether out of the religious acts, the prayers, aspirations, resolves of the recipient, or by the direct power of the ceremonial act itself,—a nice and difficult question, not to be decided by means of those effects themselves, whatever they be.

Let me grant to you, then, that the reception of your ordinances brings peace and joy to the soul; that it permanently influences or changes the character of the recipient. Let me grant, on the other hand, that their profanation, when men have been taught to believe in them, and in profaning are guilty of contempt of that God to whom they ascribe them, is attended by judgments; this properly shows nothing more than that, by a general law, lying, deceit, presumption, or hypocrisy are punished, and prayer, faith, contrition rewarded. There is nothing to show that the effects would not have been precisely the same on condition of the same inward dispositions, though another ordinance, a love-feast or a washing of the feet, with no pretence to the name of a Sacrament, had been in good faith adopted. And it is obvious to any one that, for a member of the Establishment to bring himself to confession, especially some years back, required dispositions of a very special character, a special contrition, and a special desire of the Sacrament, which as far as we may judge by outward signs, were a special effect of grace, and would fittingly receive from God's bounty a special reward, some further and higher grace, and even, at least I am not bound to deny it, remission of sins. And again, when a member of the Establishment, surrounded by those who scoffed at the doctrine, accepted God's word that He would make Bread His Body, and honoured Him by the fact that he accepted it, is it wonderful, is it not suitable to God's mercy, if He rewards such a special faith with a *quasi* sacramental grace, though the worshipper unintentionally offered to a material substance that adoration which he intended to pay to the present, but invisible, Lamb of God?

(III.)

BUT this is not all, my dear brethren; I must allow to others what I allow to you. If I let you plead the sensible effects of supernatural grace, as exemplified in yourselves, in proof that your religion is true, I must allow the plea to others to whom by your theory you are bound to deny it. Are you willing to place yourselves on the same footing with Wesleyans? yet what is the difference? or rather, have they not more remarkable phenomena in their history, symptomatic of the presence of grace among them, than you can show in yours? Which, then, is the right explanation of your feelings and your experience,— mine, which I have extracted from received Catholic teaching; or yours, which is an expedient for the occasion, and cannot be made to tell for your own Apostolical authority without telling for those who are rebels against it? Survey the rise of Methodism, and say candidly, whether those who made light of your ordinances, abandoned them, or at least disbelieved their virtue, have not had among them evidences of that very same grace which you claim for yourselves, and which you consider a proof of your acceptance with God. Really I am obliged in candour to allow, whatever part the evil spirit had in the work, whatever gross admixture of earth polluted it, whatever extravagance there was to excite ridicule or disgust, whether it was Christian virtue or the excellence of unaided man, whatever was the spiritual state of the subjects of it, whatever their end and their final account, yet there were higher and nobler vestiges or semblances of grace and truth in Methodism than there have been among you. I give you credit for what you are, grave, serious, earnest, modest, steady, self-denying, consistent; you have the praise of such virtues; and you have a clear perception of many of the truths, or of portions of the truths, of Revelation. In these points you surpass the Wesleyans; but if I wished to find what was striking, extraordinary, suggestive of Catholic heroism—of St. Martin, St. Francis, or St. Ignatius—I should betake myself far sooner to them than to you. . . The Established Church may have preserved in the country the idea of sacramental grace, and the [High Church] movement . . may have spread it; but if you wish to find the shadow and the suggestion of the supernatural qualities which made up the notion of a Catholic Saint, to Wesley you must go, and such as him. Personally I do not like him, if it were merely for his deep self-reliance and self-conceit; still I am bound, in justice to him, to ask, and you, in consistency, to answer, what historical personage in the Establishment, during its whole three centuries, has approximated in force and splendour of conduct and achievements to one who began by innovating on your rules, and ended by contemning your authorities? He and his companions, starting amid ridicule at Oxford, with fasting and praying in the cold night air, then going about preaching, reviled by the rich and educated, and pelted and dragged to prison by the populace, and converting their thousands from sin to God's service—were it not for their pride and eccentricity, their fanatical doctrine and untranquil devotion, they would startle us, as if the times of St. Vincent Ferrer or St. Francis Xavier were come again in a Protestant land.

Or, to turn to other communions, whom have you with you with those capabilities of greatness in them, which show themselves in the benevolent zeal of Howard the philanthropist, or Elizabeth Fry? Or consider the almost miraculous conversion and subsequent life of Col. Gardiner. Why, even old Bunyan, with his vivid dreams when a child, his conversion, his conflicts with Satan, his preachings and imprisonments, however inferior to you in discipline of mind and knowledge of the truth, is, in the outline of his history, more Apostolical than you. "Weep not for me," were his last words," as if he had been a Saint, "but for yourselves. I go to the Father of our Lord Jesus Christ, who doubtless, through the mediation of His Son, will receive me, though a sinner, when we shall ere long meet, to sing the new song and be happy for ever!" Consider the death-beds of the thousands of those, in and out of the Establishment, who, with scarcely one ecclesiastical sentiment in common with you, die in confidence of the truth of their doctrine, and of their personal safety. Does the peace of their deaths testify to the divinity of their creed or of their communion? Does the extreme earnestness and reality of religious feeling, exhibited in the sudden seizure and death of one who was as stern in his hatred of your opinions as admirable in his earnestness, who one evening protested against the Sacramental principle, and next morning died nobly with the words of Holy Scripture in his mouth—does it give any sanction to that hatred and that protest?[1] And there is another, a Cal-

---

[1] Dr. Arnold.

vinist, one of whose special and continual prayers in his last illness was for perseverance in grace, who cried, "O Lord, abhor me not, though I be abhorrible, and abhor myself!" and who, five minutes before his death, by the expression of his countenance, changing from prayer to admiration and calm peace, impressed upon the bystanders that the veil had been removed from his eyes, and that, like Stephen, he saw things invisible to sense—did he, by the circumstances of his death-bed, bear evidence to the truth of what you, as well as I, hold to be an odious heresy?[1] "Mr. Harvey resigned his meek soul into the hands of his Redeemer, saying, 'Lord, now lettest Thou Thy servant depart in peace.'" "Mr. Walker, before he expired, spoke nearly these words: 'I have been on the wings of the cherubim; heaven has in a manner been opened to me; I shall be there soon.'" "Mr. Whitfield rose at four o'clock on the Sabbath-day, went to his closet, and was unusually long in private; laid himself on his bed for about ten minutes, then went on his knees and prayed most fervently he might that day finish his Master's work." Then he sent for a clergyman, "and before he could reach him, closed his eyes on this world without a sigh or groan, and commenced a Sabbath of everlasting rest."[2] Alas! there was another, who for three months "lingered," as he said, "in the face of death." "O my God," he cried, "I know Thou dost not overlook any of Thy creatures. Thou dost not overlook me. So much torture . . to kill a worm! Have mercy on me! I cry to Thee, knowing I cannot alter Thy ways. I cannot if I would, and I would not if I could. If a word would remove these sufferings, I would not utter it." "Just life enough to suffer," he continued;

---

[1] Mr. Scott, of Ashton Sandford.
[2] Sidney's Life of Hill.

"but I submit, and not only submit, but rejoice." One morning he woke up, "and with firm voice and great sobriety of manner, spoke only these words: 'Now I die!' He sat as one in the attitude of expectation, and, about two hours afterwards, it was as he had said." And he was a professed infidel, and worse than an infidel—an apostate priest!

(IV.)

No, my dear brethren, these things are beyond us. Nature can do so much, and go so far; can form such rational notions of God and of duty, without grace or merit, or a future hope; good sense has such an instinctive apprehension of what is fitting; intellect, imagination, and feeling, can so take up, develop, and illuminate, what nature has originated; education and intercourse with others can so insinuate into the mind what really does not belong to it; grace, not effectual, but inchoate, can so plead, and its pleadings look so like its fruits; and its mere visitations may so easily be mistaken for its indwelling presence, and its vestiges, when it has departed, may gleam so beautifully on the dead soul, that it is quite impossible for us to conclude, with any fairness of argument, that a certain opinion is true, or a religious position safe, simply on account of the confidence or apparent excellence of those who adopt it. Of course we think as tenderly of them as we can, and may fairly hope that what we see is, in particular instances, the work of grace, wrought in those who are not responsible for their ignorance;[1] but the claim in their behalf is unreasonable and

---

[1] [See "Invincible Igorance and Anglicanism," p. 313.]

exorbitant if it is to the effect that their state of mind is to be taken in evidence, not only of promise in the individual, but of truth in his creed.

And should this view of the subject unsettle and depress you, as if it left you no means at all of ascertaining whether God loves you, or whether anything is true, or anything to be trusted, then let this feeling answer the purpose for which I have impressed it on you. I wish to deprive you of your undue confidence in self; I wish to dislodge you from that centre in which you sit so self-possessed and self-satisfied. Your fault has been to be satisfied with but a half-evidence of your safety; you have been too well contented with remaining where you found yourselves, not to catch at a line of argument so indulgent yet so plausible. You have thought that position impregnable, and growing confident, as time went on, you have not only said it was a sin to ascribe your good thoughts, and purposes, and aspirations, to any but God (which you were right in saying), but you have presumed to pronounce it blasphemy against the Holy Ghost to doubt that they came into your hearts by means of your Church and by virtue of its ordinances. Learn, my dear brethren, a more sober, a more cautious tone of thought. Learn to fear for your souls. It is something, indeed, to be peaceful within, but it is not everything. It may be the stillness of death. The Catholic, and he alone, has within him that union of external with internal notes of God's favour, which sheds the light of conviction over his soul, and makes him both fearless in his faith, and calm and thankful in his hope. ("Anglican Difficulties," p. 70.)

THE HIGH CHURCH PARTY.

CONFIDENT, indeed, and with reason, of the truth of its great principles, having a perception and certainty of its main tenets, which is like the evidence of sense compared with the feeble, flitting, and unreal views of doctrine held by the Evangelical body, still, as to their application, their adaptation, their combination, their development, [the High Church party] has been miserably conscious that it has had nothing to guide it but its own private and unaided judgment. Dreading its own interpretation of Scripture and the Fathers, feeling its need of an infallible guide, yet having none; looking up to its own Mother, as it called her, and finding her silent, ambiguous, unsympathetic, sullen, and even hostile to it; with ritual mutilated, sacraments defective, precedents inconsistent, articles equivocal, canons obsolete, courts Protestant, and synods suspended; scouted by the laity, scorned by men of the world, hated and blackened by its opponents; and moreover at variance with itself, hardly two of its members taking up the same position—nay, all of them, one by one, shifting their own ground as time went on, and obliged to confess that they were in progress; is it wonderful . . that these men have exhibited "a conduct and a rule of a religious life," "full of shifts, and compromises, and evasions, a rule of life, based upon the acceptance of half one doctrine, all the next, and none of the third, upon the belief entirely of another, but not daring to say so"? After all, they have not been nearly so guilty "of shifts, and compromises, and evasions," as the national formularies themselves; but they have had none to support them, or, if I may use a familiar word, to act the bully for them, under the imputation. There was no one, with confident air and loud voice, to retort upon their opponents the charges urged against them, and no public to applaud though there had been. Whether they looked above or below, behind or before, they found nothing, indeed, to shake or blunt their faith in Christ, in His establishment of a Church, in its visibility, continuance, catholicity, and gifts, and in the necessity of belonging to it: they despised the hollowness of their opponents, the inconsequence of their arguments, the shallowness of their views, their disrelish of principle, and their carelessness about truth; but their heart sunk within them, under the impossibility, on the one hand, of their carrying out their faith into practice, *there*, where they found themselves, and of realizing their ideas in fact,—and the duty, on the other, as they were taught it, of making the best of the circumstances in which they were placed. Such were they; I trust they are so still: I will not allow myself to fancy that secret doubts on the one hand, that self-will, disregard of authority, an unmanly, disingenuous bearing, and the spirit of party on the other, have deformed a body of persons whom once I loved, revered, and sympathized in. I speak of those many persons whom I admired ; who, like the hero in the epic, did not want courage, but encouragement; who looked out in vain for the approbation of authority ; who felt their own power, but shrank from the omen of evil, the hateful raven, which flapped its wings over them ; who seemed to say with the poet—

> ——— Non me tua fervida terrent
> Dicta, ferox ; Dii me terrent, et Jupiter hostis.

But their very desire of realities, and their fear of deceiving themselves with dreams, was their insurmountable difficulty here. They could not make the Establishment what it was not. ("Anglican Difficulties," p. 14.)

THE CHRISTIAN YEAR.

MUCH certainly came of the Christian Year: it was the most soothing, tranquillizing, subduing work of the day; if poems can be found to enliven in dejection, and to comfort in anxiety, to cool the over-sanguine, to refresh the weary, and to awe the worldly; to instil resignation into the impatient, and calmness into the fearful and agitated— they are these.

> Tale tuum carmen nobis, divine poeta,
> Quale sopor fessis in gramine ; quale per æstum
> Dulcis aquæ saliente sitim restinguere rivo.

Or like the Shepherd's pipe, in the Oriental Vision, of which we are told, that "the sound was exceedingly sweet, and wrought into a variety of tunes that were inexpressibly melodious, and altogether different from anything I had ever heard. They put me in mind of those heavenly airs which are played to the departing souls of good men upon their first arrival in Paradise, to wear out the impressions of the last agonies, and to qualify them for the pleasures of that happy place. I drew near with the reverence which is due to a superior nature; and as my heart was entirely subdued by the captivating strains I had heard, I fell down at his feet and wept."

Such was the gift of the author of the Christian Year, and he used it in attaching the minds of the rising generation to the Church of his predecessors Ken and Herbert. He did that for the Church of England which none but a poet could do; he made it poetical. It is sometimes asked whether poets are not more commonly found external to the Church than among her children; and it would not surprise us to find the question answered in the affirmative. Poetry is the refuge of those who have not the Catholic Church to flee to, and repose upon; for the Church herself is the most sacred and august of poets. 'Poetry,'[1] as Mr. Keble lays it down in his University Lectures on the subject, is a method of relieving the over-burdened mind. It is a channel through which emotion finds expression, and that a safe, regulated expression. Now, what is the Catholic Church viewed in her human aspect, but a discipline of the affections and passions? What are her ordinances and practices, but the regulated expression of keen, or deep, or turbid feeling, and thus a "cleansing," as Aristotle would word it, of the sick soul? She is the poet of her children; full of music to soothe the sad and control the wayward—wonderful in story for the imagination of the romantic; rich in symbol and imagery, so that gentle and delicate feelings, which will not bear words, may in silence intimate their presence or commune with themselves. Her very being is poetry; every psalm, every petition, every collect, every versicle, the cross, the mitre, the thurible, is a fulfilment of some dream of childhood, or aspiration of youth. Such poets as are born under her shadow, she takes into her service; she sets them to write hymns, or to compose chants, to embellish shrines, or to determine ceremonies, or to marshal processions; nay, she can even make schoolmen of them, as she made of St. Thomas, till

---

[1] [Æstuantibus eam affectibus parcere et indulgere paulisper intelligimus, atque id saltem nobis solatii contigisse, quod negatum olim Didoni nocuit. "Prælectiones Academicæ," vol. I. p. 11.]

logic becomes poetical. Now the author of the Christian Year found the Anglican system all but destitute of this divine element, which is an essential property of Catholicism; a ritual dashed upon the ground, trodden on and broken piecemeal; prayers, clipped, pieced, torn, shuffled about at pleasure, until the meaning of the composition perished, and offices which had been poetry were no longer even good prose; antiphons, hymns, benedictions, invocations, shovelled away; Scripture lessons turned into chapters; heaviness, feebleness, unwieldiness, where the Catholic rites had had the lightness and airiness of a spirit; vestments chucked off, lights quenched, jewels stolen, the pomp and circumstances of worship annihilated, a dreariness which could be felt, and which seemed the token of an incipient Socinianism, forcing itself upon the eye, the ear, the nostrils, of the worshipper, a smell of dust and damp, not of incense; a sound of ministers preaching Catholic prayers, and parish clerks droning out Catholic canticles; the royal arms for the crucifix; ugly huge boxes of wood, sacred to preachers, frowning upon the congregation in the place of the mysterious altar; and the long cathedral aisles unused, railed off, like the tombs (as they were) of what had been and was not; and for orthodoxy, a frigid, inelastic, inconsistent, dull, helpless dogmatic, which could give no just account of itself, yet was intolerant of all teaching which contained a doctrine more, or a doctrine less, and resented every attempt to give it a meaning;—such was the religion of which this gifted author was, not the judge and denouncer (a deep spirit of reverence hindered it), but the renovator, so far as it has been renovated. Clear as was his perception of the degeneracy of his times, he attributed nothing of it to his Church, over which he threw the poetry of his own mind, and the memory of better days.

His happy magic made the Anglican Church seem what Catholicism was and is. The established system found to its surprise, that it had been all its life talking, not prose, but poetry,

"Miraturque novas frondes, et non sua poma."

Beneficed clergymen used to go to rest as usual on Christmas-eve, and leave to ringers, or sometimes to carollers, the observance which was paid, not without creature comforts, to the sacred night; but now, they suddenly found themselves, to their great surprise, to be "wakeful shepherds," and "still as the day came round," "in music and in light," the new-born Saviour "dawned upon their prayer." Anglican bishops had not only lost the habit of blessing, but had sometimes been startled and vexed when asked to do so; but now they were told of their "gracious arm stretched out to bless;" moreover, what they had never dreamed when they were gazetted or did homage, they were taught that each of them was "an Apostle true, a crowned and robed seer." The parish church had been shut up, except for vestry meetings and occasional services, all days of the year but Sundays, and one or two other sacred days; but church-goers were now assured that "Martys and Saints" dawned on their way, that the absolution in the Common Prayer Book was "the Golden Key each morn and eve;" and informed, moreover, at a time too when the Real Presence was all but utterly forgotten or denied, of "the dear feast of Jesus dying, upon that altar ever lying, while Angels prostrate fall." They learned, besides, that what their pastors had spoken of, and churchwardens had used at vestry meetings, as a mere table, was "the dread altar;" and that "holy lamps were blazing: perfumed embers quivering bright," while "stoled priests minister at them," while the "floor was by knees of sinners worn."

Such doctrine coming from one who had such claims on his readers from the weight of his name, the depth of his devotional and ethical tone, and the special gift of consolation, of which his poems themselves were the evidence, wrought a great work in the Establishment. The Catholic Church speaks for itself, the Anglican needs external assistance; his poems became a sort of comment upon its formularies and ordinances, and almost elevated them into the dignity of a religious system. It kindled hearts towards his Church, it gave a something for the gentle and forlorn to cling to; and it raised up advocates for it among those, who otherwise, if God and their good Angel had suffered it, might have wandered away into some sort of philosophy, and acknowledged no Church at all. Such was the influence of his Christian Year. ("Essays, Crit. and Hist.," vol. II. p. 441.)

THE TRACTARIAN MOVEMENT.

[THE Tractarian] movement started on the ground of maintaining ecclesiastical authority, as opposed to the Erastianism of the State. It exhibited the Church as the one earthly object of religious loyalty and veneration, the source of all spiritual power and jurisdiction, and the channel of all grace. It represented it to be the interest, as well as the duty, of Churchmen, the bond of peace and the secret of strength, to submit their judgment in all things to her decision. And it taught that this divinely founded Church was realized and brought into effect in our country in the National Establishment, which was the outward form or development of a continuous dynasty and hereditary power which descended from the Apostles. It gave, then, to that Establishment, in its officers, its laws, its usages, and its worship, that devotion and obedience which are correlative to the very idea of the Church. It set up on high the bench of Bishops and the Book of Common Prayer, as the authority to which it was itself to bow, with which it was to cow and overpower an Erastian State. . .

Such . . was the clear unvarying line of thought, as I believe it to be, on which the movement commenced and proceeded, as regards the questions of Church authority and private judgment. It was fancied that no opportunity for the exercise of private judgment could arise in any public or important matter. The Church declared, whether by Prayer Book or Episcopal authority, what was to be said or done, and private judgment either had no objection which it could make good, or only in those minor matters where there was a propriety in yielding to authority. And the present Church declared what her divines had declared; and her divines declared what the Fathers had declared; and what the Fathers had declared was no matter of private at all, but a matter of fact, cognizable by all who chose to read their writings. Their testimony was as decisive and clear as Pope's Bull or Definition of Council, or catechisings or direction of any individual parish priest. There was no room for two opinions on the subject; and, as Catholics consider that the truth is brought home to the soul supernaturally, so that the soul sees it and no longer depends on reason, so in some parallel way it was supposed, in the theology of the movement, that that same truth, as contained in the Fathers, was a natural fact, recognized by the natural and ordinary intelligence of mankind, as soon as that intelligence was directed towards it.

The idea, then, of the divines of the [Tractarian] movement was simply and absolutely submission to an external authority; to such an authority they appealed, to it they betook themselves; there they found a haven of rest; thence they looked out upon the troubled surge of human opinion and upon the crazy vessels which were labouring, without chart or compass, upon it. Judge then of their dismay, when, according to the Arabian tale, on their striking their anchors into the supposed soil, lighting their fires on it, and fixing in it the poles of their tents, suddenly their island began to move, to heave, to splash, to frisk to and fro, to dive, and at last to swim away, spouting out inhospitable jets of water upon the credulous mariners who had made it their home. And such, I suppose, was the undeniable fact: I mean, the time at length came, when first of all turning their minds (some of them, at least) more carefully to the doctrinal controversies of the early Church, they saw distinctly that in the reasonings of the Fathers, elicited by means of them, and in the decisions of authority, in which they issued, were contained at least the rudiments, the anticipation, the justification of what they had been accustomed to consider the corruptions of Rome. And if only one, or a few of them, were visited with this conviction, still even one was sufficient, of course, to destroy that cardinal point of their whole system, the objective perspicuity and distinctness of the teaching of the Fathers. But time went on, and there was no mistaking or denying the misfortune which was impending over them. They had reared a goodly house, but their foundations were falling in. The soil and the masonry both were bad. The Fathers *would* protect "Romanists" as well as extinguish Dissenters. The Anglican divines *would* misquote the Fathers, and shrink from the very doctors to whom they appealed. The Bishops of the seventeenth century were shy of the Bishops of the fourth; and the Bishops of the nineteenth were shy of the Bishops of the seventeenth. The ecclesiastical courts upheld the sixteenth century against the seventeenth, and, regardless of the flagrant irregularities of Protestant clergymen, chastised the mild misdemeanours of Anglo-Catholic. Soon the living rulers of the Establishment began to move. There are those who, reversing the Roman's maxim,[1] are wont to shrink from the contumacious, and to be valiant towards the submissive; and the authorities in question gladly availed themselves of the power conferred on them by the movement against the movement itself. They fearlessly handselled their Apostolic weapons upon the Apostolical party. One after another, in long succession, they took up their song and their parable against it. It was a solemn war-dance, which they executed round victims, who by their very principles were bound hand and foot, and could only eye, with disgust and perplexity, this most unaccountable movement, on the part of their "holy Fathers, the representatives of the Apostles, and the Angels of the Churches." It was the beginning of the end. When it was at length plain that primitive Christianity ignored the National Church, and that the National Church cared little for primitive Christianity, or for those who appealed to it as her foundation; when Bishops spoke against them, and Bishops' courts sentenced them, and Universities degraded them, and the people rose against them,—from that day their "occupation was gone." Their initial principle, their basis, external authority, was cut from under

---

[1] "Parcere subjectis, et debellare superbos." It may be right here to say, that the author never can forget the great kindness which Dr. Bagot, at that time Bishop of Oxford, showed him on several occasions. He also has to notice the courtesy of Dr. Thirlwall's language, a prelate whom he has never had the honour of knowing.

them; they had "set their fortunes on a cast;" they had lost; henceforward they had nothing left for them but to shut up their school, and retire into the country. Nothing else was left for them, unless, indeed, they took up some other theory, unless they changed their ground, unless they ceased to be what they were, and became what they were not; unless they belied their own principles, and strangely forgot their own luminous and most keen convictions; unless they vindicated the right of private judgment, took up some fancy-religion, retailed the Fathers, and jobbed theology. They had but a choice between doing nothing at all, and looking out for truth and peace elsewhere. ("Anglican Difficulties," pp. 114 and 131.)

ANGLO-CATHOLIC OR PATRISTICO-PROTESTANT?

I CAN understand, I can sympathize with, those old-world thinkers, whose commentators are Mant and D'Oyly, whose theologian is Tomlin, whose ritualist is Wheatly, and whose canonist is Burns; who are proud of their Jewells and their Chillingworths, whose works they have never opened, and toast Cranmer and Ridley, and William of Orange, as the founders of their religion. In these times, three hundred years is a respectable antiquity; and traditions, recognized in law-courts, and built into the structure of society, may well, without violence, be imagined to be immemorial. Those also I can understand who take their stand upon the Prayer Book; or those who honestly profess to follow the *consensus* of Anglican divines as the voice of authority and the standard of faith.

Moreover, I can quite enter into the sentiment with which members of the liberal and infidel school investigate the history and the documents of the early Church. They profess a view of Christianity truer than the world has ever had; nor, on the assumption of their principles, is there anything shocking to good sense in this profession. They look upon the Christian Religion as something simply human; and there is no reason at all why a phenomenon of that kind should not be better understood, in its origin and nature, as years proceed. It is, indeed, an intolerable paradox to assert, that a revelation, given from God to man, should lie unknown or mistaken for eighteen centuries, and now at length should be suddenly deciphered by individuals; but it is quite intelligible to assert, and plausible to argue, that a human fact should be more philosophically explained than it was eighteen hundred years ago, and more exactly ascertained than it was a thousand. History is at this day undergoing a process of revolution; the science of criticism, the disinterment of antiquities, the unrolling of manuscripts, the interpretation of inscriptions, have thrown us into a new world of thought; characters and events come forth transformed in the process; romance, prejudice, local tradition, party bias, are no longer accepted as guarantees of truth; the order and mutual relation of events are readjusted; the springs and the scope of action are reversed. Were Christianity a mere work of man, it, too, might turn out something different from what it has hitherto been considered; its history might require re-writing, as the history of Rome, or of the earth's strata, or of languages, or of chemical action. A Catholic neither deprecates nor fears such enquiry, though he abhors the spirit in which it is too often conducted. He is willing that infidelity should do its work against the Church, knowing that she will be found just where she was, when the assault is over. It is nothing to him, though her enemies put themselves to the trouble of denying everything that has hitherto been taught, and begin with constructing her history all over again, for he is quite sure that they will end at length with a compulsory admission of what at first they so wantonly discarded. Free thinkers and broad thinkers, Laudians and Prayer Book Christians, high-and-dry and Establishment-men, all these he would understand; but what he would feel so prodigious is this,—that such as you, my [Anglican] brethren, should consider Christianity given from heaven once for all, should protest against private judgment, should profess to transmit what you have received, and yet, from diligent study of the Fathers, from your thorough knowledge of St. Basil and St. Chrysostom, from living, as you say, in the atmosphere of antiquity, that you should come forth into open day with your new edition of the Catholic faith, different from that held in any existing body of Christians anywhere, which not half-a-dozen men all over the world would honour with their *imprimatur;* and then, withal, should be as positive about its truth in every part, as if the voice of mankind were with you instead of being against you.

You are a body of yesterday; you are a drop in the ocean of professing Christians; yet you would give the law to priest and prophet; and you fancy it an humble office, forsooth, suited to humble men, to testify the very truth of Revelation to a fallen generation, or rather to almost a long bi-millenary, which has been in unalleviated traditionary error. You have a mission to teach the National Church, which is to teach the British Empire, which is to teach the world. You are more learned than Greece; you are purer than Rome; you know more than St. Bernard; you judge how far St. Thomas was right, and where he is to be read with caution, or held up to blame; you can bring to light juster views of grace, or of penance, or of invocation of saints, than St. Gregory or St. Augustine. . . You do not follow the bishops of the National Church; you disown its existing traditions; you are discontented with its divines; you protest against its law-courts; you shrink from its laity; you outstrip its Prayer Book. You have in all respects an eclectic or an original religion of your own. You dare not stand or fall by Andrewes, or by Laud, or by Hammond, or by Bull, or by Thorndike, or by all of them together. There is a *consensus* of divines, stronger than there is for Baptismal Regeneration or the Apostolical Succession, that Rome is, strictly and literally, an anti-Christian power;—Liberals and High Churchmen in your Communion in this agree with Evangelicals; you put it aside. There is a *consensus* against Transubstantiation, besides the declaration of the Article, yet many of you hold it notwithstanding. Nearly all your divines, if not all, call themselves Protestants, and you anathematize the name. Who makes the concessions to Catholics which you do, yet remains separate from them? Who, among Anglican authorities, would speak of Penance as a Sacrament, as you do? Who of them encourages, much less insists upon, auricular confession, as you? Or makes fasting an obligation? Or uses the crucifix and the rosary? Or reserves the consecrated bread? Or believes in miracles as existing in your Communion? Or administers, as I believe you do, Extreme Unction? In some points you prefer Rome, in others Greece, in others England, in others Scotland; and of that preference your own private judgment is the ultimate sanction.

What am I to say in answer to conduct so preposterous? Say you go by any authority whatever, and I shall know where to find you, and I shall respect you. Swear by any school of Religion, old or modern, by Ronge's Church, or the Evangelical Alliance, nay, by yourselves, and I shall know what you mean, and will listen to you. But do not come to me with the latest fashion of opinion which the world has seen, and protest to me that it is the oldest. Do not come to me at this time of day with views palpably new, isolated, original, *sui generis*, warranted old neither by Christian nor unbeliever, and challenge me to answer what I really have not the patience to read. Life is not long enough for such trifles. Go elsewhere, not to me, if you wish to make a proselyte. Your inconsistency, my dear brethren, is on your very front. Nor pretend that you are but executing the sacred duty of defending your own Communion; your Church does not thank you for a defence which she has no dream of appropriating. You innovate on her professions of doctrine, and then you bid us love her for your innovations. You cling to her for what she denounces; and you almost anathematize us [converts to Catholicism] for taking a step which you would please her best by taking also. You call it restless, impatient, undutiful in us, to do what she would have us do; and you think it a loving and confiding course in her children to believe, not her, but you. She is to teach, and we are to hear, only according to your own private researches into St. Chrysostom and St. Augustine. "I began myself with doubting and enquiring," you seem to say; "I departed from the teaching I received; I was educated in some older type of Anglicanism; in the school of Newton, Cecil, and Scott, or in the Bartlett's-Building school, or in the Liberal Whig school. I was a Dissenter, or a Wesleyan, and by study and thought I became an Anglo-Catholic. And then I read the Fathers, and I have determined what works are genuine, and what are not; which of them apply to all times, which are occasional;

which historical, and which doctrinal; what opinions are private, what authoritative; what they only seem to hold, what **they ought to** hold; what **are** fundamental, what ornamental. Having thus measured and **cut and put together my creed by my** own proper intellect, by my **own** lucubrations, and differing from the whole world in my results, I distinctly bid you, I solemnly warn you, not **to do as I** have done, but to **accept** what I have found, to revere **that,** to use that, **to** believe that, for **it is the teaching of the** old Fathers, **and of your** Mother, the Church **of England.** Take my word for it, **that this is the** very truth **of Christ; deny** your own reason, for I know better than you, **and it is as** clear as day that some moral fault in you is the **cause of your** differing from me. **It is** pride, or vanity, **or** self-reliance, or fulness of bread. You require some medicine for your soul; you must fast; you must make a general confession; and look very sharp to yourself, **for you** are already **next door to a** rationalist or an infidel."

Surely I have not exaggerated: but can a party formed on such principles be, in any sense, called a genuine continuation **of the** Apostolical party of twenty years ago? The basis of that party was the professed abnegation of private **judgment;** your basis is the professed exercise of it. ("Anglican Difficulties," p. 136.)

THE NON-JURORS AND THE LESSON THEY TEACH.

IN the commencement of the [Tractarian] movement much interest was felt in the Non-jurors. It was natural that enquirers who **had drawn their principles** from the primitive

Church, should be attracted by the exhibition of any portion of those principles anywhere in, or about, an Establishment which was so emphatically opposed to them. Therefore, in their need, they fixed their eyes on a body of men who were not only sufferers for conscience' sake, but held, in connection with their political principles, a certain portion of Catholic truth. But, after all, what *is*, in a word, the history of the Non-jurors; for it does not take long to tell it? A party composed of seven Bishops and some hundred Clergy, virtuous and learned, and, as regards their leaders, even popular, for political services lately rendered to the nation, is hardly formed, but it begins to dissolve and come to nought, and that simply because it had no sufficient object, represented no idea, and proclaimed no dogma. What should keep it together? why should it exist? To form an association is to go out of the way, and ever requires an excuse or an account of so pretentious a proceeding. Such were the ancient apologies put forward for the Church in her first age; such the apologies of the Anglican Jewell, and the Quaker Barclay. What was the apology of the Non-jurors? Now their secession, properly speaking, was based on no theological truth at all; it arose simply because, as their name signifies, certain Bishops and Clergy could not take the oaths to a new King. There is something very venerable and winning in Bishop Ken; but this arises in part from the very fact that he was so little disposed to defend any position, or oppose things as they were. He could not take the oaths, and was dispossessed; but he had nothing special to say for himself; he had no message to deliver; his difficulty was of a personal nature, and he was unwilling that the Non-juring Succession should be continued. It was against his judgment to perpetuate his own communion. But look at the body in its more theological aspect, and its negative and external character is brought out even more strikingly. Its members had much more to say against the Catholic Church, like Protestants in general, than for themselves. They are considered especially high in their Doctrine of the Holy Eucharist; yet I do not know anything in Dr. Brett's whole Treatise on the Ancient Liturgies, which fixes itself so vividly on the reader's mind, as his assertion, that the rubrics of the Roman Missal are "corrupt, dangerous, superstitious, abominably idolatrous, theatrical, and utterly unworthy the gravity of so sacred an institution."

The Non-jurors were far less certain what they did hold than what they did not. They were great champions of the Sacrifice, and wished to restore the ancient Liturgies; yet they could not raise their minds to anything higher than the sacrifice of the material bread and wine, as representatives of One who was not literally present but absent; as symbols of His Body and Blood, not in truth and fact, but in virtue and effect. Yet, while they had such insufficient notions of the heavenly gift committed to the ordinance, they could, as I have said, be very jealous of its outward formalities, and laid the greatest stress on a point, important certainly in its place, but not when separated from that which gave it meaning and life, the mixing of the water with the wine; and upon this, and other questions, of higher moment indeed, but not of a character specifically different, they soon divided into two communions. They broke into pieces, not from external causes, not from the hostility or the allurements of a court, but simply because they had no common heart and life in them. They were safe from the civil sword, from their insignificancy; they had no need of falling back on a distant centre for support; all they needed was an idea, an object, a work to make them one.

But I have another remark to make on the Non-jurors.

You recollect that they are the continuation and heirs of the traditions, so to call them, of the High Church divines of the seventeenth century. Now, how high and imposing do the names sound of Andrewes, Laud, Taylor, Jackson, Pearson, Cosin, and their fellows! I am not speaking against them as individuals, but viewing them as theological authorities. How great and mysterious are the doctrines which they teach! and how proudly they appeal to primitive times, and claim the ancient Fathers! Surely, as some one says, "in Laud is our Cyprian, and in Taylor is our Chrysostom, and all we want is our Athanasius." Look on, my brethren, to the history of the Non-jurors, and you will see what these Anglican divines were worth. There you will see that it was simply their position, their temporal possessions, their civil dignities, as standing round a King's throne, or seated in his great council, and not their principles, which made them what they were. Their genius, learning, faith, whatever it was, would have had no power to stand by themselves; these qualities had no substance; for, as we see, when the State abandoned them, they shrank at once and collapsed, and ceased to be. These qualities were not the stuff out of which a Church is made, though they looked well and bravely when fitted *upon* the Establishment. And, indeed, they did not, in the event, wear better in the Establishment than out of it; for since the Establishment at the Revolution had changed its make and altered its position, the old vestments would not fit it, and fell out of fashion. The nation and the National Church had got new ideas, and the language of the ancient Fathers could not express them. There were those who, at the era in question, took the oaths; they could secure their positions—could they secure their creed? The event answers the question. There is some story of Bull and Beveridge, who were two of the number, meeting together,

I think in the House of Lords, and mourning together over the degeneracy of the times. The times certainly *were* degenerate; and if learning could have restored them, there was enough in those two heads to have done the work of Athanasius, Leo, and the seventh Gregory; but learning never made a body live. The High Church party died out within the Establishment, as well as outside of it, for it had neither dogma to rest upon, nor object to pursue.

All this is your warning, my [Anglican] brethren; you too, when it comes to the point, will have nothing to profess, to teach, to transmit. At present you do not know your own weakness. You have the life of the Establishment in you, and you fancy it is your own life; you fancy that the accidental *congeries* of opinions, which forms your creed, has that unity, individuality, and consistency, which allows of its developing into a system, and perpetuating a school. Look into the matter more steadily; it is very pleasant to decorate your chapels, oratories, and studies now, but you cannot be doing this for ever. It is pleasant to adopt a habit or a vestment; to use your office-book or your beads; but it is like feeding on flowers, unless you have that objective vision in your faith, and that satisfaction in your reason, of which devotional exercises and ecclesiastical regulations are the suitable expression. Such will not last in the long run, as are not commanded and rewarded by divine authority; they cannot be made to rest on the influence of individuals. It is well to have rich architecture, curious works of art, and splendid vestments, when you have a present God; but oh! what a mockery, if you have not! If your externals surpass what is within, you are, so far, as hollow as your Evangelical opponents, who baptize, yet expect no grace; or, as the latitudinarian, who would make Christ's kingdom not of this world, in order to do little more than the world's work. Thus your Church becomes, not a home, but a sepulchre; like those high cathedrals, once Catholic, which you do not know what to do with, which you shut up and make monuments of, sacred to the memory of what has passed away. ("Anglican Difficulties," p. 193.)

THE ANGLICAN ARGUMENT FROM DIFFERENCES AMONG CATHOLICS.

THE primary question, with every serious enquirer, is the question of salvation. I am speaking to those who feel this to be so; not to those who make religion a sort of literature or philosophy, but to those who desire, both in their creed and in their conduct, to approve themselves to their Maker, and to save their souls. This being taken for granted, it immediately follows to ask, "What must I *do* to be saved?" and "Who is to *teach* me?" and next, Can Protestantism, can the National Church, teach me? No, is the answer of common sense, for this simple reason, because of the variations and discordances in teaching of both the one and the other. The National Church is no guide into the truth, because no one knows what it holds, and what it commands: one party says this, and a second party says that, and a third party says neither this nor that. I must seek the truth then elsewhere; and then the question follows, Shall I seek it in the Communion of Rome? In answer, this objection is instantly made, "You cannot find the truth in Rome, for there are as many divisions there as in the National Communion."

Who would not suppose the objection to mean, that these divisions were such as to make it difficult or impossible to ascertain what it was that the Roman Communion taught? Who would not suppose it to mean that there was within the Communion of Rome a difference of creed and of dogmatic teaching? whereas the state of the case is just the reverse. No one can pretend that the quarrels in the Catholic Church are questions of faith, or have tended in any way to obscure or impair what she declares to be such, and what is acknowledged to be such by the very parties in those quarrels. That Dominicans and Franciscans have been zealous respectively for certain doctrinal views, which they declare at the same time to be beyond and in advance of the promulgated faith of the Church, throws no doubt upon that faith itself; how does it follow that they differ in questions of faith, because they differ in questions not of faith? Rather, I would say, if a number of parties distinct from each other give the same testimony on certain points, their differences on other points do but strengthen the evidence for the truth of those matters in which they all are agreed; and the greater the difference, the more remarkable is the unanimity. The question is, "*Where* can I be taught, who cannot be taught by the National Communion, because it does *not* teach?" and the Protestant warning runs, "Not in the Catholic Church, because she, in spite of differences on subordinate points amongst her members, *does* teach."

In truth, she not only teaches in spite of those differences, but she has ever taught by means of them. Those very differences of Catholics on further points have themselves implied and brought out their absolute faith in the doctrines which are previous to them. The doctrines of faith are the common basis of the combatants, the ground on which they contend, their ultimate authority, and their arbitrating rule. They are assumed, and introduced, and commented on, and enforced, in every stage of the alternate disputation; and I will venture to say, that, if you wish to get a good view of the unity, consistency, solidity, and reality of Catholic teaching, your best way is to get up the controversy on Grace, or on the Immaculate Conception. No one can do so without acquiring a mass of theological knowledge, and sinking in his intellect a foundation of dogmatic truth, which is simply antecedent and common to the rival schools, and which they do but exhibit and elucidate. To suppose that they perplex an enquirer or a convert, is to fancy that litigation destroys the principles and the science of law, or that spelling out words of five syllables makes a child forget his alphabet. On the other hand, place your unfortunate enquirer between Luther and Calvin, if the Holy Eucharist is his subject; or, if he is determining the rule of faith, between Bramhall and Chillingworth, Bull and Hoadley, and what residuum will be left, when you have eliminated their contrarieties? ("Anglican Difficulties," p. 271.)

ANGLICAN OBJECTIONS FROM ANTIQUITY.

(1).

IF I am to say something, not directly in answer to the particular objections in detail brought from antiquity against the doctrine and discipline of the present Catholic Church, but by way of appeasing and allaying that general misgiving and perplexity which these objections excite, what can I do better than appeal to a fact,—though I cannot do so without some indulgence on the part of my hearers,—a fact connected with myself? And it is the less unfair to do so, because, as regards the history of the early Church and the writings of the Fathers, so many must go by the testimony of others, and so few have opportunity to use their own experience. I say, then, that the writings of the Fathers, so far from prejudicing at least one man against the modern Catholic Church, have been simply and solely the one intellectual cause of his having renounced the religion in which he was born and submitted himself to her. What other causes there may be, not intellectual, unknown, unsuspected by himself, though freely imputed on mere conjecture by those who would invalidate his testimony, it would be unbecoming and impertinent to discuss; for himself, if he is asked why he became a Catholic, he can only give that answer which experience and consciousness bring home to him as the true one, viz. that he joined the Catholic Church simply because he believed it, and it only, to be the Church of the Fathers; —because he believed that there was a Church upon earth till the end of time, and one only; and because, unless it was the Communion of Rome, and it only, there was none; —because, to use language purposely guarded, because it was the language of controversy, "all parties will agree that, of all existing systems, the present Communion of Rome is the nearest approximation in fact to the Church of the Fathers; possible though some may think it, to be still nearer to it on paper;"—because, "did St. Athanasius or St. Ambrose come suddenly to life, it cannot be doubted what Communion they would mistake," that is, would recognize, "for their own;"—because "all will agree that these Fathers, with whatever differences of opinion, whatever protests if you will, would find themselves more at home with such men as St. Bernard or St. Ignatius Loyola, or with the lonely priest in his lodgings, or the holy sisterhood of charity, or the unlettered crowd before the altar, than with the rulers or the members of any other religious community."[1]

This is the great, manifest, historical phenomenon which converted me—to which all particular enquiries converged. Christianity is not a matter of opinion, but an external fact, entering into, carried out in, indivisible from, the history of the world. It has a bodily occupation of the world; it is one continuous fact or thing, the same from first to last, distinct from everything else: to be a Christian is to partake of, to submit to, this thing; and the simple question was, Where, what is this thing in this age, which in the first age was the Catholic Church? The answer was undeniable; the Church called Catholic now, is that very same thing in hereditary descent, in organization, in principles, in position, in external relations, which was called the Catholic Church then; name and thing have ever gone together, by an uninterrupted connection and succession, from then till now. Whether it had been corrupted in its teaching was, at best, a matter of opinion. It was indefinitely more evident a fact, that it stood on the ground and in the place of the ancient Church, as its heir and representative, than that certain peculiarities in its teaching were really innovations and corruptions. Say there is no Church at all, if you will, and at least I shall understand you; but do not meddle with a fact attested by mankind. I am almost ashamed to insist upon so plain

---

[1] [Essay on Doctrinal Development, p. 138. This Essay, it will be remembered, was "written and partly printed" while Dr. Newman was still an Anglican. It was as he "advanced in it" that his "difficulties cleared away," and he resolved to be received into the Catholic Church. See p. 59 of the present volume.]

a point, which in many respects is axiomatically true, except that there are persons who wish to deny it. Of course, there are and have been such persons, and men of deep learning; but their adverse opinion does not interfere with my present use of what I think so plain. Observe, I am not insisting on it as an axiom, though that is my own view of the matter; nor proving it as a conclusion, nor forcing it on your acceptance as *your* reason for joining the Catholic Church, as it was mine. Let every one have his own reason for becoming a Catholic; for reasons are in plenty, and there are enough for you all, and moreover all of them are good ones and consistent with each other. I am not assigning reasons why you should be Catholics; you have them already: from first to last I am doing nothing more than removing difficulties in your path, which obstruct the legitimate effect of those reasons which have, as I am assuming, already convinced you. And to-day I am answering the objection, so powerfully urged upon those who have no means of examining it for themselves, that, as a matter of fact, the modern Church has departed from the teaching of the ancient. Now even one man's contrary testimony obscures the certainty of this supposed matter of fact, though it is not sufficient to establish any opposite matter of fact of his own. I say, then, the Catholicism of to-day is not likely to be really very different from the Catholicism of antiquity, if its agreement, or rather its identity, with antiquity forms the very reason on which even one educated and reflecting person was induced, much against every natural inducement, to submit to its claims. Ancient Catholicity cannot supply a very conclusive argument against modern Catholicity, if the ancient has furnished even one such person with a conclusive argument in favour of the modern. . .

(II.)

Yet this was but one head of argument, which the history of the early Church afforded against the National Establishment, and in favour of the Roman See. I have already alluded to the light which the schism of the African Donatists casts on the question between the two parties in the controversy; it is clear, strong, and decisive, but perfectly distinct from the proof derivable from the Arian, Nestorian, and Monophysite histories.[1]

Then again, after drawing out from antiquity the outlines of the ecclesiastical structure, and its relations to bodies and powers external to it, when we go on, as it were, to colour it with the thousand tints which are to be found in the same ancient records, when we consider the ritual of the Church, the ceremonial of religion, the devotions of private Christians, the opinions generally received, and the popular modes of acting, what do we find but a third and most striking proof of the identity between primitive Christianity and modern Catholicism? No other form of Christianity but this present Catholic Communion, has a pretence to resemble, even in the faintest shadow, the Christianity of antiquity, viewed as a living religion on the stage of the world. This has ever attached me to such works as Fleury's Church History; because, whatever may be its incidental defects or mistakes, it brings before the reader so vividly the Church of the Fathers, as a fact and a reality, instead of speculating, after the manner of most histories, on the principles, or of making views upon the facts, or cataloguing the heresies,

[1] [See pp. 44, 46, and 50.]

rites, or writers, of those ancient times. You may make ten thousand extracts from the Fathers, and not get deeper into the state of their times than the paper you write upon; to imbibe into the intellect the ancient Church as a fact, is either to be a Catholic or an infidel.

Recollect, my brethren, I am going into these details, not as if I thought of convincing you on the spot by a view of history which convinced me after careful consideration, nor as if I called on you to be convinced by what convinced me at all (for the methods of conviction are numberless, and one man approaches the Church by this road, another by that), but merely in order to show you how it was that antiquity, instead of leading me from the Holy See as it leads many, on the contrary drew me on to submit to its claims. But, even had I worked out for you these various arguments ever so fully, I should have brought before you but a secondary portion of the testimony which the ancient Church seemed to me to supply to its own identity with the modern. What was far more striking to me than the ecclesiastical phenomena which I have been drawing out, remarkable as they are, is a subject of investigation which is not of a nature to introduce into a popular lecture; I mean, the history of the doctrinal definitions of the Church. It is well known that, though the creed of the Church has been one and the same from the beginning, yet it has been so deeply lodged in her bosom as to be held by individuals more or less implicitly, instead of being delivered from the first in those special statements, or what are called definitions, under which it is now presented to us, and which preclude mistake or ignorance. These definitions, which are but the expression of portions of the one dogma which has ever been received by the Church, are the work of time; they have grown to their present shape and number in the course of eighteen centuries, under the exigency of successive events, such as heresies and the like, and they may, of course, receive still further additions as time goes on. Now this process of doctrinal development, as you might suppose, is not of an accidental or random character; it is conducted upon laws, as everything else which comes from God; and the study of its laws and of its exhibition, or, in other words, the science and history of the formation of theology, was a subject which had interested me more than anything else from the time I first began to read the Fathers, and which had engaged my attention in a special way. Now it was gradually brought home to me, in the course of my reading, so gradually, that I cannot trace the steps of my conviction, that the decrees of later Councils, or what Anglicans call the Roman corruptions, were but instances of that very same doctrinal law which was to be found in the history of the early Church; and that in the sense in which the dogmatic truth of the prerogatives of the Blessed Virgin may be said, in the lapse of centuries, to have grown upon the consciousness of the faithful, in that same sense did, in the first age, the mystery of the Blessed Trinity also gradually shine out and manifest itself more and more completely before their minds. Here was at once an answer to the objections urged by Anglicans against the present teaching of Rome; and not only an answer to objections, but a positive argument in its favour; for the immutability and uninterrupted action of the laws in question throughout the course of Church history is a plain note of identity between the Catholic Church of the first ages and that which now goes by that name;—just as the argument from the analogy of natural and revealed religion is at once an answer to difficulties in the latter, and a direct proof that Christianity has the same Author as the physical and moral world. But the force of this, to me, ineffably cogent argument, I cannot hope to convey to another. ("Anglican Difficulties," p. 320.)

INVINCIBLE IGNORANCE AND ANGLICANISM.

(I.)

I SUPPOSE, as regards this country, .. we may entertain most reasonable hopes that vast multitudes are in a state of invincible ignorance; so that those among them who are living a life really religious and conscientious, may be looked upon with interest and even pleasure, though a mournful pleasure, in the midst of the pain which a Catholic feels at their ignorant prejudices against what he knows to be true. Amongst the most bitter railers against the Church in this country, may be found those who are influenced by divine grace, and are at present travelling towards heaven, whatever be their ultimate destiny. Among the most irritable disputants against the Sacrifice of the Mass or Transubstantiation, or the most impatient listeners to the glories of Mary, there may be those for whom she is saying to her Son, what He said on the cross to His Father, "Forgive them, for they know not what they do." Nay, while such persons think as at present, they are bound to act accordingly, and only so far to connect themselves with us as their conscience allows. "When persons who have been brought up in heresy," says a Catholic theologian, "are persuaded from their childhood that we are the enemies of God's word, are idolaters, pestilent deceivers, and therefore, as pests, to be avoided, they cannot, while this persuasion lasts, hear us with a safe conscience, and they labour under invincible ignorance, inasmuch as they doubt not that they are in a good way."[1]

Nor does it suffice, in order to throw them out of this irresponsible state, and to make them guilty of their ignorance, that there are means actually in their power of getting rid of it. For instance, say they have no conscientious feeling against frequenting Catholic chapels, conversing with Catholics, or reading their books; and say they are thrown into the neighbourhood of the one or the company of the other, and do not avail themselves of their opportunities; still these persons do not become responsible for their present ignorance till such time as they actually feel it, till a doubt crosses them upon the subject, and the thought comes upon them that inquiry is a duty. And thus Protestants may be living in the midst of Catholic light, and labouring under the densest and most stupid prejudices; and yet we may be able to view them with hope, though with anxiety, with the hope that the question has never occurred to them, strange as it may seem, whether we are not right and they wrong. Nay, I will say something further still; they may be so circumstanced that it is quite certain that, in course of time, this ignorance will be removed, and doubt will be suggested to them, and the necessity of enquiry consequently imposed, and according to our best judgment, fallible of course as it is, we may be quite certain too, that, when that time comes, they will refuse to enquire, and will quench the doubt; yet should it so happen that they are cut off by death before that time

---

[1] Busenbaum, vol. I. p. 54.

has arrived (I am putting an hypothetical case), we may have as much hope of their salvation as if we had had no such foreboding about them on our mind; for there is nothing to show that they were not taken away on purpose, in order that their ignorance might be their excuse.

As to the prospect of those countless multitudes of a country like this, who apparently have no supernatural vision of the next world at all, and die without fear, because they die without thought, with these, alas! I am not here concerned. But the remarks I have been making suggest much of comfort, when we look out into what is called the religious world in all its varieties, whether it be the High Church section, or the Evangelical, whether it be in the Establishment, or in Methodism, or in Dissent, so far as there seems to be real earnestness and invincible prejudice. One cannot but hope that that written Word of God, for which they desire to be jealous, though exhibited to them in a mutilated form and in a translation unsanctioned by Holy Church, is of incalculable blessing to their souls, and may be, through God's grace, the divine instrument of bringing many to contrition and to a happy death who have received no sacrament since they were baptized in their infancy. One cannot hope but that the Anglican Prayer Book, with its Psalter and Catholic prayers, even though these, in the translation, have passed through heretical intellects, may retain so much of its old virtue as to co-operate with divine grace in the instruction and salvation of a large remnant. In these and many other ways, even in England, and much more in Greece, the difficulty is softened which is presented to the imagination by the view of such large populations, who, though called Christian, are not Catholic or orthodox in creed.

(II.)

There is but one set of persons, indeed, who inspire the Catholic with special anxiety, as much so as the open sinner, who is not peculiar to any Communion, Catholic or schismatic, and who does not come into the present question. There is one set of persons in whom every Catholic must feel intense interest, about whom he must feel the gravest apprehensions; viz. those who have some rays of light vouchsafed to them as to their heresy or as to their schism, and who seem to be closing their eyes upon it; or those who have actually gained a clear view of the nothingness of their own Communion, and the reality and divinity of the Catholic Church, yet delay to act upon their knowledge. You, my dear brethren, if such are here present, are in a very different state from those around you. You are called by the inscrutable grace of God to the possession of a great benefit, and to refuse the benefit is to lose the grace. You cannot be as others: they pursue their own way, they walk over this wide earth, and see nothing wonderful or glorious in the sun, moon, and stars of the spiritual heavens; or they have an intellectual sense of their beauty, but no feeling of duty or of love towards them; or they wish to love them, but think they ought not, lest they should get a distaste for that mire and foulness which is their present portion. They have not yet had the call to enquire, and to seek, and to pray for further guidance, infused into their hearts by the gracious Spirit of God; and they will be judged according to what is given them, not by what is not. But on you the thought has dawned that possibly Catholicism may be true; you have doubted the safety of your present position, and the present pardon of your sins, and the completeness of your present faith. You, by means of that very system in which you find yourselves, have been led to doubt that system. If the Mosaic law, given from above, was a schoolmaster to lead souls to Christ, much more is it true that an heretical creed, when properly understood, warns us against itself, and frightens us from it, and is forced against its will to open for us with its own hands its prison gates, and to show us the way to a better country. So has it been with you. You set out in simplicity and earnestness intending to serve it, and your very serving taught you to serve another. You began to use its prayers and act upon its rules, and they did but witness against it, and made you love it, not more but less, and carried off your affections to one whom you had not loved. The more you gazed upon your own communion the more unlike it you grew; the more you tried to be good Anglicans, the more you found yourselves drawn in heart and spirit to the Catholic Church. It was the destiny of the false prophetess that she could not keep the little ones who devoted themselves to her; and the more simply they gave up their private judgment to her, the more sure they were of being thrown off by her, against their will, into the current of attraction which led straight to the true Mother of their souls. So month has gone on after month, and year after year; and you have again and again vowed obedience to your own Church, and you have protested against those who left her, and you have thought you found in them what you liked not, and you have prophesied evil about them and good about yourselves; and your plans seemed prospering and your influence extending, and great things were to be; and yet, strange to say, at the end of the time you have found yourselves steadily advanced in the direction which you feared, and never were nearer to the promised land than you are now.

O, look well to your footing that you slip not; be very much afraid lest the world should detain you; dare not in anything to fall short of God's grace, or to lag behind when that grace goes forward. Walk with it, co-operate with it, and I know how it will end. You are not the first persons who have trodden that path; yet a little time, and, please God, the bitter shall be sweet, and the sweet bitter, and you will have undergone the agony, and will be lodged safely in the true home of your souls and the valley of peace. Yet but a little while, and you will look out from your resting-place upon the wanderers outside; and will wonder why they do not see that way which is now so plain to you, and will be impatient with them that they do not come on faster. And, whereas you are now so perplexed in mind that you seem to yourselves to believe nothing, then you will be so full of faith, that you will almost see invisible mysteries, and will touch the threshold of eternity. And you will be so full of joy that you will wish all around you to be partakers of it, as if for your own relief; and you will suddenly be filled with yearnings, deep and passionate, for the salvation of those dear friends whom you have outstripped; and you will not mind their coolness, or stiffness, or distance, or constrained gravity, for the love you bear to their souls. And, though *they* will not hear you, you will address yourselves to those who will; I mean, you will weary Heaven with your novenas for them, and you will be ever getting Masses for their conversion, and you will go to communion for them, and you will not rest till the bright morning comes, and they are yours once again. ("Anglican Difficulties," p. 309.)

FUNDAMENTAL DIFFERENCE BETWEEN CATHOLICISM AND ANGLICANISM.

THE idea of worship is different in the Catholic Church from the idea of it in [Anglicanism]; for, in truth, the *religions* are different. . . It is not that ours is your religion, carried a little further,—a little too far, as you would say. No, they differ in kind, not in degree; ours is one religion, yours another. And when the time comes, and come it will, for you, alien as you are now, to submit yourself to the gracious yoke of Christ, then, .. it will be *faith* which will enable you to bear the ways and usages of Catholics, which else might perhaps startle you. Else the habits of years, the associations in your mind of a certain outward behaviour with real inward acts of devotion, might embarrass you, when you had to conform yourself to other habits, and to create for yourself other associations. But this faith, of which I speak, the great gift of God, will enable you in that day to overcome yourself, and to submit, as your judgment, your will, your reason, your affections, so your tastes and likings, to the rule and usage of the Church. Ah, that faith should be necessary in such a matter! ("Loss and Gain," p. 289.)

Section III.—CATHOLICISM.

CATHOLICISM AND THE RELIGIONS OF THE WORLD.

HOW different are all religions that ever were, from the lofty and unchangeable Catholic Church! They depend on time and place for their existence, they live in periods or in regions. They are children of the soil, indigenous plants, which readily flourish under a certain temperature, in a certain aspect, in moist or in dry, and die if they are transplanted. Their *habitat* is one article of their scientific description. Thus the Greek schism, Nestorianism, the heresy of Calvin, and Methodism, each has its geographical limits. Protestantism has gained nothing in Europe since its first outbreak. Some accident gives rise to these religious manifestations; some sickly season, the burning sun, the vapour-laden marsh, breeds a pestilence, and there it remains, hanging in the air over its birthplace perhaps for centuries; then some change takes place in the earth or in the heavens, and it suddenly is no more. Sometimes, however, it is true, such scourges of God have a course upon earth, and affect a Catholic range. They issue as from some poisonous lake or pit in Ethiopia or in India, and march forth with resistless power to fulfil their mission

of evil, and walk to and fro over the face of the world
Such was the Arabian imposture of which Mahomet was
the framer; and you will ask, perhaps, whether it has not
done that which I have said the Catholic Church alone
can do, and proved thereby that it had in it an internal
principle, which, depending not on man, could subdue him
in any time or place? No; look narrowly, and you will
see the marked distinction which exists between the religion of Mahomet and the Church of Christ. For Mahometanism has done little more than the Anglican communion is doing at present. That communion is found
in many parts of the world; its primate has a jurisdiction
even greater than the Nestorian Patriarch of old; it has
establishments in Malta, in Jerusalem, in India, in China,
in Australia, in South Africa, and in Canada. Here, at
least, you will say, is Catholicity, even greater than that
of Mahomet. Oh, be not beguiled by words: will any
thinking man say for a moment, whatever this objection
be worth, that the established Religion *is* superior to time
and place? well, if not, why set about proving that it is?
rather, does not its essence lie in its recognition by the
State? is not its establishment its very *form?* what would
it be, would it last ten years, if abandoned to itself? It is
its establishment which erects it into a unity and individuality; can you contemplate it, though you stimulate
your imagination to the task, abstracted from its churches
palaces, colleges, parsonages, revenues, civil precedence,
and national position? Strip it of this world, and you
have performed a mortal operation upon it, for it has
ceased to be. Take its bishops out of the legislature, tear
its formularies from the Statute Book, open its universities
to Dissenters, allow its clergy to become laymen again,
legalize its private prayer-meetings, and what would be
its definition? You know that, did not the State compel

it to be one, it would split at once into three several bodies, each bearing within it the elements of further divisions. Even the small party of Non-jurors, a century and a half since, when released from the civil power, split into two. It has then no internal consistency, or individuality, or soul, to give it the capacity of propagation. Methodism represents some sort of an idea, Congregationalism an idea; the Established Religion has in it no idea beyond establishment. Its extension has been, for the most part, passive, not active; it is carried forward into other places by State policy, and it moves because the State moves; it is an appendage, whether weapon or decoration, of the sovereign power; it is the religion, not even of a race, but of the ruling portion of a race. The Anglo-Saxon has done in this day what the Saracen did in a former. He does grudgingly for expedience, what the other did heartily from fanaticism. This is the chief difference between the two; the Saracen, in his commencement, converted the heretical East with the sword; but at least in India the extension of his faith has been by immigration, as the Anglo-Saxon's now; he grew into other nations by commerce and colonization; but, when he encountered the Catholic of the West, he made as little impression upon Spain, as the Protestant Anglo-Saxon makes on Ireland.

There is but one form of Christianity possessed of that real internal unity which is the primary condition of independence. Whether you look to Russia, England, or Germany, this note of divinity is wanting. In this country, especially, there is nothing broader than class religions; the established form itself is but the religion of a class. There is one persuasion for the rich, and another for the poor; men are born in this or that sect; the enthusiastic go here, and the sober-minded and rational go there. They make money, and rise in the world, and then they profess to belong to the Establishment. This body lives in the world's smile, that in its frown; the one would perish of cold in the world's winter, and the other would melt away in the summer. Not one of them undertakes human nature: none compasses the whole man; none places all men on a level; none addresses the intellect and the heart, fear and love, the active and the contemplative. It is considered, and justly, as an evidence for Christianity, that the ablest men have been Christians; not that all sagacious or profound minds have taken up its profession, but that it has gained victories among them, such and so many, as to show that it is not the mere fact of ability or learning which is the reason why all are not converted. Such too is the characteristic of Catholicity; not the highest in rank, not the meanest, not the most refined, not the rudest, is beyond the influence of the Church; she includes specimens of every class among her children. She is the solace of the forlorn, the chastener of the prosperous, and the guide of the wayward. She keeps a mother's eye for the innocent, bears with a heavy hand upon the wanton, and has a voice of majesty for the proud. She opens the mind of the ignorant, and she prostrates the intellect of even the most gifted. These are not words; she has done it, she does it still, she undertakes to do it. All she asks is an open field, and freedom to act. She asks no patronage from the civil power; in former times and places she has asked it; and, as Protestantism also, has availed herself of the civil sword. It is true she did so, because in certain ages it has been the acknowledged mode of acting, the most expeditious, and open at the time to no objection, and because, where she has done so, the people clamoured for it and did it in advance of her; but her history shows that she needed it not, for she has extended and flourished without it. She is ready for any service which occurs; she will take the world as it comes; nothing but force can repress her. See, my brethren, what she is doing in this country now; for three centuries the civil power has trodden down the goodly plant of grace, and kept its foot upon it; at length circumstances have removed that tyranny, and lo! the fair form of the Ancient Church rises up at once, as fresh and as vigorous as if she had never intermitted her growth. She is the same as she was three centuries ago, ere the present religions of the country existed; you know her to be the same; it is the charge brought against her that she does not change; time and place affect her not, because she has her source where there is neither time nor place, because she comes from the throne of the Illimitable, Eternal God. ("Discourses to Mixed Congregations," p. 250.)

FAITH IN THE CATHOLIC CHURCH.

(I.)

IT is perfectly true that the Church does not allow her children to entertain any doubt of her teaching; and that, first of all, simply for this reason, because they are Catholics only while they have faith, and faith is incompatible with doubt. No one can be a Catholic without a simple faith, that what the Church declares in God's name, is God's word, and therefore true. A man must simply believe that the Church is the oracle of God; he must be as certain of her mission as he is of the mission of the Apostles. Now, would any one ever call him certain that the Apostles came from God, if, after professing his certainty, he added, that, for what he knew, he might doubt one day about their mission? Such an anticipation would be a real, though latent doubt, betraying that he was not certain of it at present. A person who says, "I believe just at this moment, but perhaps I am excited without knowing it, and I cannot answer for myself that I shall believe to-morrow," does not believe. A man who says, "Perhaps I am in a kind of delusion, which will one day pass away from me, and leave me as I was before;" or, "I believe as far as I can tell, but there may be arguments in the background which will change my view," such a man has not faith at all. When, then, Protestants quarrel with us for saying that those who join us must give up all ideas of ever doubting the Church in time to come, they do nothing else but quarrel with us for insisting on the necessity of faith in her. Let them speak plainly; our offence is that of demanding faith in the Holy Catholic Church; it is this, and nothing else. I must insist upon this: faith implies a confidence in a man's mind, that the thing believed is really true; but, if it is once true, it never can be false. If it is true that God became man, what is the meaning of my anticipating a time when perhaps I shall not believe that God became man? This is nothing short of anticipating a time when I shall disbelieve a truth. And if I bargain to be allowed in time to come not to believe, or to doubt, that God became man, I am but asking to be allowed to doubt, or to disbelieve, what is an eternal truth. I do not see the privilege of such a permission at all, or the meaning of wishing to secure it:—if at present I have no doubt whatever about it, then I am but asking leave to fall into error; if at present I have doubts about it, then I do not believe it at present, that is, I have not faith. But I cannot both really believe it now, and yet look forward to a time when, perhaps, I shall not believe it; to make provision for future doubt, is to doubt at present. It proves I am not in a fit state to become a Catholic now. I may love by halves, I may obey by halves; I cannot believe by halves: either I have faith, or I have it not.

And so, again, when a man has become a Catholic, were he to set about following out a doubt which has occurred to him, he has already disbelieved. *I* have not to warn him against losing his faith, he is not merely in danger of losing it, he has lost it; from the nature of the case, he has already lost it; he fell from grace at the moment when he deliberately determined to pursue his doubt. No one can determine to doubt what he is sure of; but if he is not sure that the Church is from God, he does not believe it. It is not I who forbid him to doubt; he has taken the matter into his own hands when he determined on asking for leave; he has begun, not ended, in unbelief; his very wish, his purpose, is his sin. I do not make it so, it is such from the very state of the case. You sometimes hear, for example, of Catholics falling away, who will tell you it arose from reading the Scriptures, which opened their eyes to the "unscripturalness," so they speak, of the Church of the Living God. No, Scripture did not make them disbelieve (impossible!); they disbelieved *when* they opened the Bible; they opened it in an unbelieving spirit, and for an unbelieving purpose; they would not have opened it had they not anticipated—I might say, hoped—that they should find things there inconsistent with Catholic teaching. They begin in self-will and disobedience, and they end in apostasy. This, then, is the direct and obvious reason why the Church cannot allow her children the liberty of doubting the truth of her word. He who really believes in it now, cannot imagine the future discovery of reasons to shake his faith; if he imagines it, he has not faith; and that so many Protestants think it a sort of tyranny in the Church to forbid any children of hers to doubt about her teaching, only shows they do not know what faith is—which is the case; it is a strange idea to them. Let a man cease to inquire, or cease to call himself her child.

(II.)

This is my first remark, and now I go on to a second. You may easily conceive, that they who are entering the Church, or at least those who have entered it, have more than faith; that they have some portion of Divine love also. They have heard in the Church of the charity of Him who died for them, and who has given them His Sacraments as the means of conveying the merits of His death to their souls, and they have felt more or less in those poor souls of theirs, the beginnings of a responsive charity drawing them to Him. Now, does it stand with a loving trust, better than with faith, for a man to anticipate the possibility of doubting or denying the great mercies in which he is rejoicing? Take an instance; what would you think of a friend whom you loved, who could bargain that, in spite of his present trust in you, he might be allowed some day to doubt you? who, when a thought came into his mind that you were playing a game with him, or that you were a knave, or a profligate, did not drive it from him with indignation, or laugh it away for its absurdity, but considered that he had an evident right to indulge it, nay, should be wanting in duty to himself, unless he did? Would you think that your friend trifled with truth, that he was unjust to his reason, that he was wanting in manliness, that he was hurting his mind, if he shrank from it, or would you call him cruel and miserable if he did not? For me, if he took the latter course, may I never be intimate with so unpleasant a person; suspicious, jealous minds, minds that keep at a distance from me, that insist on their rights, fall back on their own centre, are ever fancying offences, and are cold, censorious, wayward, and uncertain, these are often to be borne as a cross; but give me for my friend, one who will unite heart and hand with me, who will throw himself into my cause and interest, who will take my part when I am attacked, who will be sure beforehand that I am in the right, and, if he is critical, as he may have cause to be towards a being of sin and imperfection, will be so from very love and loyalty, from anxiety that I should always show to advantage, and a wish that others should love me as heartily as he. I should not say a friend trusted me, who listened to every idle story against me; and I should like his absence better than his company, if he gravely told me that it was a duty he owed to himself to encourage his misgivings of my honour.

Well, pass on to a higher subject;—could a man be said to trust in God, and to love God, who was familiar with doubts whether there was a God at all, or who bargained that, just as often as he pleased, he might be at liberty to doubt whether God was good, or just, or almighty; and who maintained that, unless he did this, he was but a poor slave, that his mind was in bondage, and could render no free acceptable service to his Maker;—that the very worship which God approved, was one attended with a *caveat*, on the worshipper's part, that he did not promise to render it to-morrow, that he would not answer for himself that some argument might not come to light, which he had never heard before, which would make it a grave moral duty in him to suspend his judgment and his devotion? Why, I should say, that that man was worshipping his own mind, his own dear self, and not God; that his idea of God was a mere accidental form, which his thoughts took at this time or that, for a long period or a short one, as the case might be, not an image of the great Eternal Object, but a passing sentiment or imagination, which meant nothing at all. I should say, and most men would agree with me, did they choose to give attention to the matter, that the person in question was a very self-conceited, self-wise man, and had neither love, nor faith, nor fear, nor anything supernatural about him; that his pride must be broken, and his heart new-made, before he was capable of any religious act at all. The argument is the same, in its degree, when applied to the Church; she comes to us as a messenger from God,—how can a man who feels this, who comes to her, who falls at her feet as such, make a reserve, that he may be allowed to doubt her at some future day? Let the world cry out, if it will, that his reason is in fetters; let it pronounce that he is a bigot, if he does not reserve his right of doubting; but he knows full well himself that he would be an ingrate and a fool, if he did. Fetters, indeed! yes, "the cords of Adam," the fetters of love, these are what bind him to the Holy Church; he is, with the Apostle, the slave of Christ, the Church's Lord; united, never to part, as he trusts, while life lasts, to her Sacraments, to her Sacrifices, to her Saints, to the Blessed Mary her advocate, to Jesus, to God.

The truth is, that the world, knowing nothing of the blessings of the Catholic faith, and prophesying nothing but ill concerning it, fancies that a convert, after the first fervour is over, feels nothing but disappointment, weariness, and offence in his new religion, and is secretly desirous of retracing his steps. This is at the root of the alarm and irritation which it manifests at hearing that doubts are incompatible with a Catholic's profession, because it is sure that doubts will come upon him, and then how pitiable will be his state! That there can be peace, and joy, and knowledge, and freedom, and spiritual strength in the Church, is a thought far beyond its imagination; for it regards her simply as a frightful conspiracy against the happiness of man, seducing her victims by specious professions, and, when they are once hers, caring nothing for the misery which breaks upon them, so that by any means she may detain them in bondage. Accordingly, it conceives we are in perpetual warfare with our own reason, fierce objections ever rising within us, and we forcibly repressing them. It believes that, after the likeness of a vessel which has met with some accident at sea, we are ever baling out the water which rushes in upon us, and have hard work to keep afloat; we just manage to linger on, either by an unnatural strain on our minds, or by turning them away from the subject of religion. The world disbelieves our doctrines itself, and cannot understand our own believing them. It considers them so strange, that it is quite sure, though we will not confess it, that we are haunted day and night with doubts, and tormented with the apprehension of yielding to them. I really do think it is the world's judgment, that one principal part of a confessor's work is the putting down such misgivings in his penitents. It fancies that the reason is ever rebelling, like the flesh; that doubt, like concupiscence, is elicited by every sight and sound, and that temptation insinuates itself in every page of letter-press, and through the very voice of a Protestant polemic. When it sees a Catholic Priest, it looks hard at him, to make out how much there is of folly in his composition, and how much of hypocrisy. But, my dear brethren, if these are your thoughts, you are simply in error. Trust me, rather than the world, when I tell you, that it is no difficult thing for a Catholic to believe; and that unless he grievously mismanages himself, the difficult thing is for him to doubt. He has received a gift which makes faith easy; it is not without an effort, a miserable effort, that any one who has received that gift, unlearns to believe. He does violence to his mind, not in exercising, but in withholding his faith. When objections occur to him, which they may easily do if he lives in the world, they are as odious and unwelcome to him as impure thoughts are to the virtuous. He does certainly shrink from them, he flings them away from him, but why? not in the first instance, because they are dangerous, but because they are cruel and base. His loving Lord has done everything for him, and has he deserved such a return? *Popule meus, quid feci tibi?* "O My people, what have I done to thee, or in what have I molested thee? answer thou Me. I brought thee out of the land of Egypt, and delivered thee out of the house of slaves; and I sent before thy face Moses, and Aaron, and Mary; I fenced thee in, and planted thee with the choicest vines; and what is there that I ought to do more to My vineyard that I have not done to it?" He has poured on us His grace, He has been with us in our perplexities, He has led us on from one truth to another, He has forgiven us our sins, He has satisfied our reason, He has made faith easy, He has given us His Saints, He shows before us day by day His own Passion; why should I leave Him? What has He ever done to me but good? Why must I re-examine what I have examined once for all? Why must I listen to every idle word which flits past me against Him, on pain of being called a bigot and a slave, when I should be behaving to the Most High, as you yourselves, who so call me, would not behave towards a human friend or benefactor? If I am convinced in my reason, and persuaded in my heart, why may I not be allowed to remain unmolested in my worship? ("Discourses to Mixed Congregations," p. 216.)

FAITH IN ANY OTHER RELIGIOUS BODY THAN THE CATHOLIC CHURCH IMPOSSIBLE.

It is very evident that no other religious body has a right to demand such an exercise of faith in them, and a right to forbid you further enquiry, but the Catholic Church; and for this simple reason, that no other body even claims to be infallible, let alone the proof of such a claim. Here is the defect at first starting, which disqualifies them, one and all, from ever competing with the Church of God. The sects about us, so far from demanding your faith, actually call on you to enquire and to doubt freely about their own merits; they protest that they are but voluntary associations, and would be sorry to be taken for anything else; they beg and pray you not to mistake their preachers for anything more than mere sinful men, and they invite you to take the Bible with you to their sermons, and to judge for yourselves whether their doctrine is in accordance with it. Then, as to the Established Religion, grant that there are those in it who forbid enquiry into its claims; yet still dare they maintain that it is infallible? If they do not (and no one does), how can they forbid enquiry about it, or claim for it the absolute faith of any of its members? Faith under these circumstances is not really faith, but obstinacy. Nor do they commonly venture to demand it; they will say, negatively, "Do not enquire;" but they cannot say positively, "Have faith;" for in whom are their members to have faith? of whom can they say, whether individual or collection of men, "He or they are gifted with infallibility, and cannot mislead us?" Therefore, when pressed to explain themselves, they ground their duty of continuance in their communion, not on faith in it, but on attachment to it, which is a very different thing; utterly different, for there are very many reasons why they should feel a very great liking for the religion in which they have been brought up. Its portions of Catholic teaching, its "decency and order," the pure and beautiful English of its prayers, its literature, the piety found among its members, the influence of superiors and friends, its historical associations, its domestic character, the charm of a country life, the remembrance of past years,—there is all this and much more to attach the mind to the national worship. But attachment is not trust, nor is to obey the same as to look up to, and to rely upon; nor do I think that any thoughtful or educated man can simply believe or confide in the *word* of the Established Church. I never met any such person who did, or said he did, and I do not think that such a person is possible. Its defenders would believe if they could; but their highest confidence is qualified by a misgiving. They obey, they are silent before the voice of their superiors, but they do not profess to believe. Nothing is clearer than this, that if faith in God's word is required of us for salvation, the Catholic Church is the only medium by which we can exercise it. ("Discourses to Mixed Congregations," p. 230.)

DISPOSITIONS FOR JOINING THE CATHOLIC CHURCH

No one should enter the Church without a firm purpose of taking her word in all matters of doctrine and morals, and that on the ground of her coming directly from the God of Truth. If you do not come in this spirit, you may as well not come at all: high and low, learned and ignorant, must come to learn. If you are right as far as this, you cannot go very wrong; you have the foundation; but, if you come in any other temper, you had better wait till you have got rid of it. You must come, I say, to the Church to learn; you must come, not to bring your own notions to her, but with the intention of ever being a learner; you must come with the intention of taking her for your portion and of never leaving her. Do not come as an experiment; do not come as you would take sittings in a chapel, or tickets for a lecture-room; come to her as to your home, to the school of your souls, to the Mother of Saints, and to the vestibule of heaven. On the other hand, do not distress yourselves with thoughts whether, when you have joined her, your faith will last; this is a suggestion of your Enemy to hold you back. He who has begun a good work in you, will perfect it; He who has chosen you, will be faithful to you; put your cause into His hand, wait upon Him, and you will surely persevere. What good work will you ever begin, if you bargain first to see the end of it? If you wish to do all at once, you will do nothing; he has done half the work, who has begun it well; you will not gain your Lord's praise at the final reckoning by hiding His talent. No; when He brings you from error to truth, He will have done the more difficult work (if aught is difficult to Him), and surely He will preserve you from returning from truth to error. Take the experience of those who have gone before you in the same course; they had many fears that their faith would fail them, before taking the great step, but those fears vanished on their taking it; they had fears, before the grace of faith, lest, after receiving it, they should lose it again, but no fears (except on the ground of their general frailness) after it was actually given.

Be convinced in your reason that the Catholic Church is a teacher sent to you from God, and it is enough. I do not wish you to join her till you are. If you are half convinced, pray for a full conviction, and wait till you have it. It is better, indeed, to come quickly, but better slowly than carelessly; and sometimes, as the proverb goes, the more haste, the worse speed. Only make yourselves sure that the delay is not from any fault of yours which you can remedy. God deals with us very differently; conviction comes slowly to some men, quickly to others; in some it is the result of much thought and many reasonings, in others of a sudden illumination. One man is convinced at once, as in the instance described by St. Paul: "If all prophesy," he says, speaking of exposition of doctrine, "and there come in one that believeth not, or one unlearned, he is convinced of all, he is judged of all. The secrets of his heart are made manifest; and so, falling down on his face, he will worship God, and say that God is among you of a truth." The case is the same now; some men are converted merely by entering a Catholic Church; others are converted by reading one book; others by one doctrine. They feel the weight of their sins, and they see that that religion must come from God which alone has the means of forgiving them. Or they are touched and overcome by the evident sanctity, beauty, and (as I may say) fragrance of the Catholic Religion. Or they long for a guide amid the strife of tongues; and the very doctrine of the Church about faith, which is so hard to many, is conviction to them. Others, again, hear many objections to the Church, and follow out the whole subject far and wide; conviction can scarcely come to them except as at the end of a long enquiry. As in a court of justice, one man's innocence may be proved at once, another's is the result of a careful investigation; one has nothing in his conduct or character to explain, another has many presumptions against him at first sight; so Holy Church presents herself very differently to different minds who are contemplating her from without. God deals with them differently; but, if they are faithful to their light, at last, in their own time, though it may be a different time to each, He brings them to that one and the same state of mind, very definite and not to be mistaken, which we call *conviction*. They will have no doubt, whatever difficulties may still attach to the subject, that the Church is from God; they may not be able to answer this objection or that, but they will be certain in spite of it.

This is a point which should ever be kept in view: conviction is a state of mind, and it is something beyond and distinct from the mere arguments of which it is the result; it does not vary with their strength or their number. Arguments lead to a conclusion, and when the arguments are stronger, the conclusion is clearer; but conviction may be felt as strongly in consequence of a clear conclusion, as of one which is clearer. A man may be so sure upon six reasons, that he does not need a seventh, nor would feel surer if he had it. And so as regards the Catholic Church: men are convinced in very various ways,—what convinces one, does not convince another; but this is an accident; the time comes anyhow, sooner or later, when a man ought to be convinced, and is convinced, and then he is bound not to wait for any more arguments, though more arguments be producible. He will find himself in a condition when he may even refuse to hear more arguments in behalf of the Church; he does not wish to read or think more on the subject, his mind is quite made up. In such a case it is his duty to join the Church at once; he must not delay; let him be cautious in counsel, but prompt in execution. This it is that makes Catholics so anxious about him: it is not that they wish him to be precipitate; but knowing the temptations which the evil one ever throws in our way, they are lovingly anxious for his soul, lest he has come to the point of conviction, and is passing it, and is losing his chance of conversion. If so, it may never return; God has not chosen every one to salvation; it is a rare gift to be a Catholic; it may be offered to us once in our lives and never again; and, if we have not seized on the "accepted time," nor known "in our day the things which are for our peace," oh, the misery for us! .. Oh, the awful thought for all eternity! oh, the remorseful sting, "I was called, I might have answered, and I did not!" And oh, the blessedness, if we can look back on the time of trial, when friends implored and enemies scoffed, and say,—The misery for me, which would have been, had I not followed on, had I hung back, when Christ called! Oh, the utter confusion of mind, the wreck of faith and opinion, the blackness and void, the dreary scepticism, the hopelessness which would have been my lot, the pledge of the outer darkness to come had I been afraid to follow Him! I have lost friends, I have lost the world, but I have gained Him, who gives in Himself houses and brethren and sisters and mothers and children and lands a hundred-fold; I have lost the perishable, and gained the Infinite; I have lost time, and I have gained eternity. ("Discourses to Mixed Congregations," p. 232.)

NO LOGICAL ALTERNATIVE BETWEEN CATHOLICISM AND SCEPTICISM.

. . TURN away from the Catholic Church, and to whom will you go? it is your only chance of peace and assurance in this turbulent, changing world. There is nothing between it and scepticism, when men exert their reason freely. Private creeds, fancy religions, may be showy and imposing to the many in their day; national religions may lie huge and lifeless, and cumber the ground for centuries, and distract the attention or confuse the judgment of the learned; but on the long run it will be found that either the Catholic Religion is verily and indeed the coming in of the unseen world into this, or that there is nothing positive, nothing dogmatic, nothing real in any of our notions as to whence we come and whither we are going. Unlearn Catholicism, and you become Protestant, Unitarian, Deist, Pantheist, Sceptic, in a dreadful, but infallible succession, only not infallible, by some accident of your position, of your education, and of your cast of mind; only not infallible, if you dismiss the subject of religion from your mind, deny yourself your reason, devote your thoughts to moral duties, or dissipate them in engagements of the world. Go, then, and do your duty to your neighbour, be just, be kindly-tempered, be hospitable, set a good example, uphold religion as good for society, pursue your business, or your profession, or your pleasure, eat and drink, read the news, visit your friends, build and furnish, plant and sow, buy and sell, plead and debate, work for the world, settle your children, go home and die, but eschew religious enquiry, if you will not have faith, nor hope that you can have faith, if you will not join the Church.

Avoid, I say, enquiry else, for it will but lead you thither, where there is no light, no peace, no hope; it will lead you to the deep pit, where the sun, and the moon, and the stars, and the beauteous heavens are not, but chilliness, and barrenness, and perpetual desolation. Oh, perverse children of men, who refuse truth when offered you, because it is not truer! Oh, restless hearts and fastidious intellects, who seek a gospel more salutary than the Redeemer's, and a creation more perfect than the Creator's! God, forsooth, is not great enough for you; you have those high aspirations and those philosophical notions, inspired by the original Tempter, which are content with nothing that is, which determine that the Most High is too little for your worship, and His attributes too narrow for your love. Satan fell by pride; and what was said of old as if of him, may surely now, by way of warning, be applied to all who copy him:—" Because thy heart is lifted up, and thou hast said, I am God, and I sit in the chair of God, . . whereas thou art a man and not God, and hast set thy heart as if it were the heart of God, therefore . . I will bring thee to nothing, and thou shalt not be, and if thou be sought for, thou shalt not be found any more for ever." ("Discourses to Mixed Congregations," p. 283.)

A CONVERT.

A CONVERT comes to learn, and not to pick and choose. He comes in simplicity and confidence, and it does not occur to him to weigh and measure every proceeding, every practice which he meets with among those whom he has joined. He comes to Catholicism as to a living system, with a living teaching, and not to a mere collection of decrees and canons, which by themselves are of course but the framework, not the body and substance of the Church. And this is a truth which concerns, which binds, those also who never knew any other religion, not only the convert. By the Catholic system, I mean that rule of life, and those practices of devotion, for which we shall look in vain in the Creed of Pope Pius. The convert comes, not only to believe the Church, but also to trust and obey her priests, and to conform himself in charity to her people. It would never do for him to resolve that he never would say a Hail Mary, never avail himself of an indulgence, never kiss a crucifix, never accept the Lent dispensations, never mention a venial sin in confession. All this would not only be unreal, but would be dangerous too, as arguing a wrong state of mind, which could not look to receive the divine blessing. Moreover, he comes to the ceremonial, and the moral theology, and the ecclesiastical regulations, which he finds on the spot where his lot is cast. And again, as regards matters of politics, of education, of general expedience, of taste, he does not criticize or controvert. And thus surrendering himself to the influences of his new religion, and not risking the loss of revealed truth altogether by attempting by a private rule to discriminate every moment its substance from its accidents, he is gradually indoctrinated in Catholicism. ("Anglican Difficulties," p. 370.)

FAITH AND DEVOTION.

By "faith" I mean the Creed and assent to the Creed; by "devotion" I mean such religious honours as belong to the objects of our faith, and the payment of those honours. Faith and devotion are as distinct in fact, as they are in idea. We cannot, indeed, be devout without faith, but we may believe without feeling devotion. Of this phenomenon every one has experience both in himself and in others; and we bear witness to it as often as we speak of realizing a truth or not realizing it. It may be illustrated, with more or less exactness, by matters which come before us in the world. For instance, a great author, or public man, may be acknowledged as such for a course of years; yet there may be an increase, an ebb and flow, and a fashion, in his popularity. And if he takes a lasting place in the minds of his countrymen, he may gradually grow into it, or suddenly be raised to it. The idea of Shakespeare as a great poet, has existed from a very early date in public opinion; and there were at least individuals then who understood him as well, and honoured him as much, as the English people can honour him now; yet, I think, there is a national devotion to him in this day such as never has been before. This has happened, because, as education spreads in the country, there are more men able to enter into his poetical genius, and, among these, more capacity again for deeply and critically understanding him; and yet, from the first, he has exerted a great insensible influence over the nation, as is seen in the circumstance that his phrases and sentences, more than can be numbered, have become almost proverbs among us. And so again in philosophy, and in the arts and sciences, great truths and principles have sometimes been known and acknowledged for a course of years; but, whether from feebleness of intellectual power in the recipients, or external circumstances of an accidental kind, they have not been turned to account. Thus the Chinese are said to have known of the properties of the magnet from time immemorial, and to have used it for land expeditions, yet not on the sea. Again, the ancients knew of the principle that water finds its own level, but seem to have made little application of their knowledge. And Aristotle was familiar with the principle of induction; yet it was left for Bacon to develop it into an experimental philosophy. Illustrations such as these, though not altogether apposite, serve to convey that distinction between faith and devotion on which I am insisting. It is like the distinction between objective and subjective truth. The sun in the spring-time will have to shine many days before he is able to melt the frost, open the soil, and bring out the leaves; yet he shines out from the first notwithstanding, though he makes his power felt but gradually. It is one and the same sun, though his influence day by day becomes greater; and so in the Catholic Church it is the one Virgin Mother, one and the same from first to last, and Catholics may have ever acknowledged her; and yet, in spite of that acknowledgment, their devotion to her may be scanty in one time and place, and overflowing in another.

This distinction is forcibly brought home to a convert, as a peculiarity of the Catholic Religion, on his first introduction to its worship. The faith is everywhere one and the same, but a large liberty is accorded to private judgment and inclination as regards matters of devotion. Any large church, with its collections and groups of people, will illustrate this. The fabric itself is dedicated to Almighty God, and that, under the invocation of the Blessed Virgin, or some particular Saint ; or again, of some mystery belonging to the divine Name or the Incarnation, or of some mystery associated with the Blessed Virgin. Perhaps there are seven altars or more in it, and these again have their several Saints. Then there is the Feast proper to the particular day ; and during the celebration of Mass, of all the worshippers who crowd around the Priest, each has his own particular devotions, with which he follows the rite. No one interferes with his neighbour ; agreeing, as it were, to differ, they pursue independently a common end, and by paths distinct, but converging, present themselves before God. Then there are confraternities attached to the Church,—of the Sacred Heart, or of the Precious Blood; associations of prayer for a good death, or for the repose of departed souls, or for the conversion of the heathen ; devotions connected with the brown, blue, or red scapular; —not to speak of the great ordinary Ritual observed through the four seasons, or of the constant Presence of the Blessed Sacrament, or of its ever-recurring rite of Benediction, and its extraordinary forty hours' Exposition. Or, again, look through such manuals of prayers as the *Raccolta*, and you at once will see both the number and the variety of devotions which are open to individual Catholics to choose from, according to their religious taste and prospect of personal edification.

Now these diversified modes of honouring God did not come to us in a day, or only from the Apostles ; they are the accumulations of centuries ; and, as in the course of years some of them spring up, so others decline and die.

Some are local, in memory of some particular Saint, who happens to be the Evangelist, or Patron or pride of the nation, or who lies entombed in the church or in the city where it is found; and these devotions, necessarily, cannot have an earlier date than the Saint's day of death or interment there. The first of these sacred observances, long before such national memories, were the devotions paid to the Apostles, then those which were paid to the Martyrs; yet there were Saints nearer to our Lord than either Martyrs or Apostles; but, as if these sacred persons were immersed and lost in the effulgence of His glory, and because they did not manifest themselves, when in the body, in external works separate from Him, it happened that for a long while they were less dwelt upon. However, in process of time, the Apostles, and then the Martyrs, exerted less influence than before over the popular mind, and the local Saints, new creations of God's power, took their place, or again, the Saints of some religious order here or there established. Then, as comparatively quiet times succeeded, the religious meditations of holy men and their secret intercourse with heaven gradually exerted an influence out of doors, and permeated the Christian populace, by the instrumentality of preaching and by the ceremonial of the Church. Hence at length those luminous stars rose in the ecclesiastical heavens, which were of more august dignity than any which had preceded them, and were late in rising, for the very reason that they were so specially glorious. Those names, I say, which at first sight might have been expected to enter soon into the devotions of the faithful, with better reason might have been looked for at a later date, and actually were late in their coming. St. Joseph furnishes the most striking instance of this remark; here is the clearest of instances of the distinction between doctrine and devotion. Who, from his prerogatives and the testimony on which they come to us, had a greater claim to receive an early recognition among the faithful than he? A Saint of Scripture, the foster-father of our Lord, he was an object of the universal and absolute faith of the Christian world from the first, yet the devotion to him is comparatively of late date. When once it began, men seemed surprised that it had not been thought of before; and now, they hold him next to the Blessed Virgin in their religious affection and veneration.—("Anglican Difficulties," p. 378.)

PRIVATE JUDGMENT AMONG CATHOLICS.

THE very idea of the Catholic Church, as an instrument of supernatural grace, is that of an institution which innovates upon, or rather superadds to nature. She does something for nature above or beyond nature. When, then, it is said that she makes her members one, this implies that by nature they are not one, and would not become one. Viewed in themselves, the children of the Church are not of a different nature from the Protestants around them; they are of the very same nature. What Protestants are, such would they be, but for the Church, which brings them together forcibly, though persuasively, "fortiter et suaviter," and binds them into one by her authority. Left to himself, each Catholic likes and would maintain his own opinion and his private judgment just as much as a Protestant; and he has it, and he maintains it, just so far as the Church does not, by the authority of Revelation, supersede it. The very moment the Church ceases to speak, at the very point at which she, that is, God who speaks by her, circumscribes her range of teaching, there private judgment of necessity starts up; there is nothing to hinder it. The intellect of man is active and independent: he forms opinions about everything; he feels no deference for another's opinion, except in proportion as he thinks that that other is more likely than he to be right; and he never absolutely sacrifices his own opinion, except when he is sure that that other knows for certain. He *is* sure that God knows; therefore, if he is a Catholic, he sacrifices his opinion to the Word of God, speaking through His Church. But, from the nature of the case, there is nothing to hinder his having his own opinion, and expressing it, whenever, and so far as, the Church, the oracle of Revelation, does not speak.

But again, human nature likes, not only its own opinion, but its own way, and will have it whenever it can, except when hindered by physical or moral restraint. So far forth, then, as the Church does not compel her children to do one and the same thing (as, for instance, to abstain from work on Sunday, and from flesh on Friday), they will do different things; and still more so, when she actually allows or commissions them to act for themselves, gives to certain persons or bodies privileges and immunities, and recognizes them as centres of combination, under her authority, and within her pale.

And further still, in all subjects and respects whatever, whether in that range of opinion and of action which the Church has claimed to herself, and where she has superseded what is private and individual, or, on the other hand, in those larger regions of thought and of conduct, as to which she has not spoken, though she might speak, the natural tendency of the children of the Church, as men, is to resist her authority. Each mind naturally is self-willed, self-dependent, self-satisfied; and, except so far as grace has subdued it, its first impulse is to rebel. Now this tendency, through the influence of grace, is not often exhibited in matters of faith; for it would be incipient heresy, and would be contrary, if knowingly indulged, to the first element of Catholic duty; but in matters of conduct, of ritual, of discipline, of politics, of social life, in the ten thousand questions which the Church has not formally answered, even though she may have intimated her judgment, there is a constant rising of the human mind against the authority of the Church, and of superiors, and that in proportion as each individual is removed from perfection. For all these reasons, there ever has been, and ever will be, a vast exercise and a realized product, partly praiseworthy, partly barely lawful, of private judgment within the Catholic Church. The freedom of the human mind is "in possession" (as it is called), and it meddles with every question, and wanders over heaven and earth, except so far as the authority of the Divine Word, as a superincumbent weight, presses it down, and restrains it within limits.—("Anglican Difficulties," p. 263.)

THE AIM OF THE CATHOLIC CHURCH.

(I.)

THE world believes in the world's ends as the greatest of goods; it wishes society to be governed simply and entirely for the sake of this world. Provided it could gain one little islet in the ocean, one foot upon the coast, if it could cheapen tea by sixpence a pound, or make its flag respected among the Esquimaux or Otaheitans, at the cost of a hundred lives and a hundred souls, it would think it a very good bargain. What does it know of hell? it disbelieves it; it spits upon, it abominates, it curses its very name and notion. Next, as to the devil, it does not believe in him either. We next come to the flesh, and it is "free to confess" that it does not think there is any great harm in following the instincts of that nature which, perhaps it goes on to say, God has given. How could it be otherwise? who ever heard of the world fighting against the flesh and the devil? Well, then, what is its notion of evil? Evil, says the world, is whatever is an offence to me, whatever obscures my majesty, whatever disturbs my peace. Order, tranquillity, popular contentment, plenty, prosperity, advance in arts and sciences, literature, refinement, splendour, this is my millennium, or rather my elysium, my swerga; I acknowledge no whole, no individuality, but my own; the units which compose me are but parts of me; they have no perfection in themselves; no end but in me; in my glory is their bliss, and in the hidings of my countenance they come to nought.

(II.)

Such is the philosophy and practice of the world—now the Church looks and moves in a simply opposite direction. It contemplates, not the whole, but the parts; not a nation, but the men who form it; not society in the first place, but in the second place, and in the first place individuals; it looks beyond the outward act, on and into the thought, the motive, the intention, and the will; it looks beyond the world, and detects and moves against the devil, who is sitting in ambush behind it. It has, then, a foe in view, nay, it has a battle-field, to which the world is blind; its proper battle-field is the heart of the individual, and its true foe is Satan.

Do not think I am declaiming in the air, or translating the pages of some old worm-eaten homily; I bear my own testimony to what has been brought home to me most closely and vividly, as a matter of fact, since I have been a Catholic, viz. that that mighty world-wide Church, like her Divine Author, regards, consults for, labours for, the individual soul; she looks at the souls for whom Christ died, and who are made over to her; and her one object, for which everything is sacrificed—appearances, reputation, worldly triumph—is to acquit herself well of this most awful responsibility. Her one duty is to bring forward the elect to salvation, and to make them as many as she can:—to take offences out of their path, to warn them of sin, to rescue them from evil, to convert them, to teach them, to feed them, to protect them, and to perfect them. . . . She overlooks everything in comparison of the immortal soul. Good and evil to her are not lights and shades passing over the surface of society, but living powers, springing from the depths of the heart. Actions, in her sight, are not mere outward deeds and words, committed by hand or tongue, and manifested in effects over a range of influence wider or narrower, as the case may be; but they are the thoughts, the desires, the purposes, of the solitary responsible spirit. She knows nothing of space or time, except as secondary to will; she knows no evil but sin, and sin is a something personal, conscious, voluntary. She knows no good but grace, and grace again is something personal, private, special, lodged in the soul of the individual. She has one and one only aim—to purify the heart; she recollects who it is who has turned our thoughts from the external crime to the inward imagination; who said, that "unless our justice abounded more than that of Scribes and Pharisees, we should not enter into the kingdom of Heaven;" and that "out of the heart proceed evil thoughts, murders, adulteries, fornications, thefts, false testimonies, blasphemies. These are the things that defile a man."

Now I would have you take up the sermons of any preacher, or any writer on moral theology, who has a name among Catholics, and see if what I have said is not strictly fulfilled, however little you fancied so before you make trial. Protestants, I say, think that the Church aims at appearance and effect; she must be splendid, and majestic, and influential: fine services, music, lights, vestments; and then, again, in her dealings with others, courtesy, smoothness, cunning, dexterity, intrigue, management—these, it seems, are the weapons of the Catholic Church. Well, she cannot help succeeding, she cannot help being strong, she cannot help being beautiful; it is her gift; as she moves, the many wonder and adore;—"Et vera incessu patuit Dea." It cannot be otherwise, certainly; but it is not her aim; she goes forth on the one errand, as I have said, of healing the diseases of the soul. Look, I say, into any book of moral theology you will; there is much there which may startle you: you will find principles hard to digest; explanations which seem to you subtle; details which distress you; you will find abundance of what will make excellent matter of attack at Exeter Hall; but you will find from first to last this one idea—(nay, you will find that very matter of attack upon her is occasioned by her keeping it in view; she would be saved the odium, she would not have thus bared her side to the sword, but for her fidelity to it)—the one idea, I say, that sin is the enemy of the soul; and that sin especially consists, not in overt acts, but in the thoughts of the heart.

(III.)

This, then, is the point I insist upon. . . The Church aims, not at making a show, but at doing a work. She regards this world, and all that is in it, as a mere shadow, as dust and ashes, compared with the value of one single soul. She holds that, unless she can, in her own way, do good to souls, it is no use her doing anything; she holds that it were better for sun and moon to drop from heaven, for the earth to fail, and for all the many millions who are upon it to die of starvation in extremest agony, so far as temporal affliction goes, than that one soul, I will not say, should be lost, but should commit one single venial sin, should tell one wilful untruth, though it harmed no one, or steal one poor farthing without excuse. She considers the action of this world and the action of the soul simply incommensurate, viewed in their respective spheres; she would rather save the soul of one single wild bandit of Calabria, or whining beggar of Palermo, than draw a hundred lines of railroad through the length and breadth of Italy, or carry out a sanitary reform, in its fullest details, in every city of Sicily, except so far as these great national works tended to some spiritual good beyond them.

Such is the Church, O ye men of the world, and now you know her. Such she is, such she will be; and though she aims at your good, it is in her own way,—and if you oppose her, she defies you. She has her mission, and do it she will, whether she be in rags or in fine linen; whether with awkward or with refined carriage; whether by means of uncultivated intellects, or with the grace of accomplishments. Not that, in fact, she is not the source of numberless temporal and moral blessings to you also; the history of ages testifies it; but she makes no promises; she is sent to seek the lost; that is her first object, and she will fulfil it, whatever comes of it. . .

(IV.)

I may say the Church aims at three special virtues, as reconciling and uniting the soul to its Maker;—faith, purity, and charity; for two of which the world cares little or nothing. The world, on the other hand, puts in the foremost place, in some states of society, certain heroic qualities; in others, certain virtues of a political or mercantile character. In ruder ages, it is personal courage, strength of purpose, magnanimity; in more civilized, honesty, fairness, honour, truth, and benevolence:—virtues, all of which, of course, the teaching of the Church comprehends, all of which she expects in their degree in all her consistent children, and all of which she exacts in their fulness in her saints; but which, after all, most beautiful as they are, admit of being the fruit of nature as well as of grace; which do not necessarily imply grace at all; which do not reach so far as to sanctity, or unite the soul by any supernatural process to the source of supernatural perfection and supernatural blessedness. Again, as I have already said, the Church contemplates virtue and vice in their first elements, as conceived and existing in thought, desire, and will, and holds that the one or the other may be as complete and mature, without passing forth from the home of the secret heart, as if it had ranged forth in profession and in deed all over the earth. Thus, at first sight, she seems to ignore bodies politic, and society, and temporal interests: whereas the world, on the contrary, talks of religion as being a matter of such private concern, so personal, so sacred, that it has no opinion at all about it: it praises public men, if they are useful to itself, but simply ridicules enquiry into their motives, thinks it impertinent in others to attempt it, and out of taste in themselves to sanction it. All public men it considers to be pretty much the same at bottom; but what matter is that to it, if they do its work? It offers high pay, and it expects faithful service; but, as to its agents, overseers, men of business, operatives, journeymen, figure-servants, and labourers, what they are personally, what are their principles and aims, what their creed, what their conversation; where they live, how they spend their leisure time, whither they are going, how they die—I am stating a simple matter of fact, I am not here praising or blaming, I am but contrasting,—I say, all questions implying the existence of the soul, are as much beyond the circuit of the world's imagination, as they are intimately and primarily present to the apprehension of the Church.

The Church, then, considers the momentary, fleeting act of the will, in the three subject matters I have mentioned, to be capable of guiltiness of the deadliest character, or of the most efficacious and triumphant merit. Moreover, she holds that a soul laden with the most enormous offences, in deed as well as thought, a savage tyrant, who delighted in cruelty, an habitual adulterer, a murderer, a blasphemer, who has scoffed at religion through a long life, and corrupted every soul which he could bring within his influence, who has loathed the Sacred Name, and cursed his Saviour, —that such a man can under circumstances, in a moment, by one thought of the heart, by one true act of contrition, reconcile himself to Almighty God (through His secret grace), without Sacrament, without priest, and be as clean, and fair, and lovely, as if he had never sinned. Again, she considers that in a moment also, with eyes shut and arms folded, a man may cut himself off from the Almighty by a deliberate act of the will, and cast himself into perdition. With the world it is the reverse; a member of society may go as near the line of evil, as the world draws it, as he will; but, till he has passed it, he is safe. Again, when he has once transgressed it, recovery is impossible; let honour of man or woman be sullied, and to restore its splendour is simply to undo the past; it is impossible.

Such being the extreme difference between the Church and the world, both as to the measure and the scale of moral good and evil, we may be prepared for those vast differences in matters of detail, which I hardly like to mention, lest they should be out of keeping with the gravity of the subject, as contemplated in its broad principle. For instance, the Church pronounces the momentary wish, if conscious and deliberate, that another should be struck down dead, or suffer any other grievous misfortune, as a blacker sin than a passionate, unpremeditated attempt on the life of the Sovereign. She considers direct unequivocal consent, though as quick as thought, to a single unchaste desire, as indefinitely more heinous than any lie which can possibly be fancied, that is, when that lie is viewed, of course, in itself, and apart from its causes, motives, and consequences. Take a mere beggar-woman, lazy, ragged, and filthy, and not over-scrupulous of truth—(I do not say she had arrived at perfection)—but if she is chaste, and sober, and cheerful, and goes to her religious duties (and I am supposing not at all an impossible case), she will, in the eyes of the Church, have a prospect of heaven, which is quite closed and refused to the State's pattern-man, the just, the upright, the generous, the honourable, the conscientious, if he be all this, not from a supernatural power— (I do not determine whether this is likely to be the fact, but I am contrasting views and principles)—not from a supernatural power, but from mere natural virtue. Polished, delicate-minded ladies, with little of temptation around them, and no self-denial to practise, in spite of their refinement and taste, if they be nothing more, are objects of less interest to her, than many a poor outcast who sins, repents, and is with difficulty kept just within the territory of grace. Again, excess in drinking is one of the world's most disgraceful offences; odious it ever is in the eyes of the Church, but if it does not proceed to the loss of reason, she thinks it a far less sin than one deliberate act of detraction, though the matter of it be truth. And again, not unfrequently does a priest hear a confession of thefts, which he knows would sentence the penitent to transportation, if brought into a court of justice, but which he knows, too, in the judgment of the Church, might be pardoned on the man's private contrition, without any confession at all. Once more, the State has the guardianship of property, as the Church is the guardian of the faith:—in the middle ages, as is often objected, the Church put to death for heresy; well but, on the other hand, even in our own times, the State has put to death for forgery, nay, I suppose for sheep-stealing. How distinct must be the measure of crime in Church and in State, when so heterogeneous is the rule of punishment in the one and in the other!

You may think it impolitic in me thus candidly to state what may be so strange in the eyes of the world;—but not so, just the contrary. The world already knows quite enough of our difference of judgment from it on the whole; it knows that difference also in its results; but it does not know that it is based on principle; it taunts the Church with that difference, as if nothing could be said for her,—as if it were not, as it is, a mere question of a balance of evils,—as if the Church had nothing to show for herself, were simply ashamed of her evident helplessness, and pleaded guilty to the charge of her inferiority to the world in the moral effects of her teaching. The world points to the children of the Church, and asks if she acknowledges them as her own. It dreams not that this contrast arises out of a difference of principle, and that she claims to act upon a principle higher than the world's. Principle is always respectable; even a bad man is more respected, though he may be more hated, if he owns and justifies his actions, than if he is wicked by accident; now the Church professes to judge after the judgment of the Almighty; and it cannot be imprudent or impolitical to bring this out clearly and boldly. His judgment is not as man's: "I judge not according to the look of man," He says, "for man seeth those things which appear, but the Lord beholdeth the heart." The Church aims at realities, the world at decencies; she dispenses with a complete work, so she can but make a thorough one. Provided she can do for the soul what is necessary, if she can but pull the brands out of the burning, if she can but extract the poisonous root which is the death of the soul, and expel the disease, she is content, though she leaves in it lesser maladies, little as she sympathizes with them. ("Anglican Difficulties," p. 206.)

THE RELIGION OF CATHOLICS.

THE energetic, direct apprehension of an unseen Lord and Saviour has not been peculiar to Prophets and Apostles; it has been the habit of His Holy Church and of her children, down to this day. Age passes after age, and she varies her discipline, and she adds to her devotions, and all with the one purpose of fixing her own and their gaze more fully upon the person of her unseen Lord. She has adoringly surveyed Him, feature by feature, and has paid a separate homage to Him in every one. She has made us honour His Five Wounds, His Precious Blood, and His Sacred Heart. She has bid us meditate on His infancy, and the acts of His ministry; His agony, His scourging, and His crucifixion. She has sent us on a pilgrimage to His birthplace and His sepulchre, and the mount of His ascension. She has sought out and placed before us, the memorials of His life and death; His crib and holy house, His holy tunic, the handkerchief of St. Veronica, the cross and its nails, His winding-sheet, and the napkin for His head.

And so, again, if the Church has exalted Mary or Joseph, it has been with a view to the glory of His sacred humanity. If Mary is proclaimed as immaculate, it illustrates the doctrine of her Maternity. If she is called the Mother of God, it is to remind Him that, though He is out of sight, He, nevertheless, is our possession, for He is of the race of man. If she is painted with Him in her arms, it is because we will not suffer the Object of our love to cease to be human, because He is also divine. If she is the Mater Dolorosa, it is because she stands by His cross. If she is Maria Desolata, it is because His dead body is on her lap. If, again, she is the Coronata, the crown is set upon her head by His dear hand. And, in like manner, if we are devout to Joseph, it is as to His foster-father; and if he is the saint of happy death, it is because he dies in the hands of Jesus and Mary.

And what the Church urges on us down to this day saints and holy men down to this day have exemplified, Is it necessary to refer to the lives of the Holy Virgins, who were and are His very spouses, wedded to Him by a mystical marriage, and in many instances visited here by the earnests of that ineffable celestial benediction which is in heaven their everlasting portion? The martyrs, the confessors of the Church, bishops, evangelists, doctors, preachers, monks, hermits, ascetical teachers,—have they not, one and all, as their histories show, lived on the very name of Jesus, as food, as medicine, as fragrance, as light, as life from the dead?—as one of them says, "in aure dulce canticum, in ore mel mirificum, in corde nectar cœlicum."

Nor is it necessary to be a saint tnus to feel: this intimate, immediate dependence on Emmanuel, God with us, has been in all ages the characteristic, almost the definition, of a Christian. It is the ordinary feeling of Catholic populations; it is the elementary feeling of every one who has but a common hope of heaven. I recollect, years ago, hearing an acquaintance, not a Catholic, speak of a work of devotion, written as Catholics usually write, with wonder and perplexity, because (he said) the author wrote as if he had "a sort of personal attachment to our Lord;" "it was as if he had seen Him, known Him, lived with Him, instead of merely professing and believing the great doctrine of the Atonement." It is this same phenomenon which strikes those who are not Catholics, when they enter our churches. They themselves are accustomed to do religious acts simply as a duty; they are serious at prayer time, and behave with decency, because it is a duty. But you know, my brethren, mere duty, a sense of propriety, and good behaviour, these are not the ruling principles present in the minds of our worshippers. Wherefore, on the contrary, those spontaneous postures of devotion? why those unstudied gestures? why those abstracted countenances? why that heedlessness of the presence of others? why that absence of the shamefacedness which is so sovereign among professors of other creeds? The spectator sees the effect; he cannot understand the cause of it. *Why* is this simple earnestness of worship? *we* have no difficulty in answering. It is because the Incarnate Saviour is present in the tabernacle; and then, when suddenly the hitherto silent church is, as it were, illuminated with the full piercing burst of voices from the whole congregation, it is because He now has gone up upon His throne over the altar, there to be adored. It is the visible Sign of the Son of Man which thrills through the congregation, and makes them overflow with jubilation. ("Occasional Sermons," p. 40.)

THE PRIVILEGES OF CATHOLICS.

OH, my dear brethren, what joy and what thankfulness should be ours, that God has brought us into the Church of His Son! What gift is equal to it in the whole world, in its preciousness, and in its rarity? In this country in particular, where heresy ranges far and wide, where uncultivated nature has so undisputed a field all her own, where grace is given to such numbers only to be profaned and quenched, where baptisms only remain in their impress and character, and faith is ridiculed for its very firmness, for us to find ourselves here, in the region of light, in the home of peace, in the presence of Saints, to find ourselves where we can use every faculty of the mind, and affection of the heart, in its perfection, because in its appointed place and office, to find ourselves in the possession of certainty, consistency, stability, on the highest and holiest subjects of human thought, to have hope here, and heaven hereafter, to be on the Mount with Christ, while the poor world is guessing and quarrelling at its foot,—who among us shall not wonder at his own blessedness, who shall not be awe-struck at the inscrutable grace of God, which has brought him, not others, where he stands? As the Apostle says, "Through our Lord Jesus Christ we have, through faith, access into this grace wherein we stand, and glory in the hope of the glory of the sons of God. And hope confoundeth not; because the charity of God is poured out into our hearts by the Holy Ghost who is given to us." And as St. John says, still more exactly to our purpose, "Ye have an unction from the Holy One;" your eyes are anointed by Him who put clay on the eyes of the blind man; "from Him have you an unction, and ye know," not conjecture, or suppose, or opine, but "know," see, "all things." "So let the unction which you have received of Him abide in you. Nor need ye that any one teach you, but as His unction teaches you of all things, and is true, and no lie, and hath taught you, so abide in Him." You can abide in nothing else; opinions change, conclusions are feeble, enquiries run their course, reason stops short, but faith alone reaches to the end, faith only endures. Faith and prayer alone will endure in that last dark hour, when Satan urges all his powers and resources against the sinking soul. What will it avail[1] us, then, to have devised some subtle argument, or to have led some

[1] Te maris et terræ, numeroque carentis arenæ
    Mensorem cohibent Archyta,
Pulveris exigui prope littus parva Matinum,
    Munera; nec quicquam tibi prodest
Aerias tentasse domos, animoque rotundum
    Percurrisse polum, morituro!

brilliant attack, or to have mapped out the field of history, or to have numbered and sorted the weapons of controversy, and to have the homage of friends and the respect of the world for our successes,—what will it avail to have had a position, to have followed out a work, to have re-animated an idea, to have made a cause to triumph, if after all, we have not the light of faith to guide us on from this world to the next? Oh, how fain shall we be in that day to exchange our place with the humblest, and dullest, and most ignorant of the sons of men, rather than to stand before the judgment-seat in the lot of him who has received great gifts from God, and used them for self and for man, who has shut his eyes, who has trifled with truth, who has repressed his misgivings, who has been led on by God's grace, but stopped short of its scope, who has neared the land of promise, yet not gone forward to take possession of it! ("Discourses to Mixed Congregations," p. 190.)

INTEGRITY OF CATHOLIC DOCTRINE.

THE Catholic doctrines .. are members of one family, and suggestive, or correlative, or confirmatory, or illustrative of each other. In other words, one furnishes evidence to another, and all to each of them; if this is proved, that becomes probable; if this and that are both probable, but for different reasons, each adds to the other its own probability. The Incarnation is the antecedent of the doctrine of Mediation, and the archetype both of the Sacramental principle, and of the merits of Saints. From the doctrine of Mediation follow the Atonement, the Mass, the merits of Martyrs and Saints, their invocation and cultus. From the Sacramental principle come the Sacraments properly so called, the unity of the Church, and the Holy See as its type and centre; the authority of Councils; the sanctity of rites; the veneration of holy places, shrines, images, vessels, furniture, and vestments. Of the Sacraments, Baptism is developed into Confirmation on the one hand, into Penance, Purgatory, and Indulgences, on the other; and the Eucharist into the Real Presence, adoration of the Host, Resurrection of the Body, and the virtue of Relics. Again, the doctrine of the Sacraments leads to the doctrine of Justification; Justification to that of Original Sin; Original Sin to the merit of Celibacy. Nor do these separate developments stand independent of each other, but by cross relations they are connected, and grow together while they grow from one. The Mass and Real Presence are parts of one; the veneration of Saints and their Relics are parts of one; their intercessory power, and the Purgatorial State, and, again, the Mass and that State are correlative; Celibacy is the characteristic mark of Monachism and the Priesthood. You must accept the whole, or reject the whole; reduction does but enfeeble, and amputation mutilate. It is trifling to receive all but something which is as integral as any other portion; and, on the other hand, it is a solemn thing to receive any part, for, before you know where you are, you may be carried by a stern logical necessity to accept the whole. ("Essay on Development," p. 154.)

TRANSUBSTANTIATION.

People say that the doctrine of Transubstantiation is difficult to believe; I did not believe the doctrine till I was a Catholic. I had no difficulty in believing it, as soon as I believed that the Catholic Roman Church was the oracle of God, and that she had declared this doctrine to be part of the original revelation. It is difficult, impossible to imagine, I grant;—but how is it difficult to believe? Yet Macaulay thought it so difficult to believe that he had need of a believer in it, of talents as eminent as Sir Thomas More, before he could bring himself to conceive that the Catholics of an enlightened age could resist the overwhelming force of the argument against it. "Sir Thomas More," he says, "is one of the choice specimens of wisdom and virtue; and the doctrine of Transubstantiation is a kind of proof charge. A faith which stands that test, will stand any test." But, for myself, I cannot indeed prove it, I cannot tell *how* it is; but I say, "Why should it not be? What's to hinder it? What do I know of substance or matter? Just as much as the greatest philosophers, and that is nothing at all." So much is this the case, that there is a rising school of philosophy now, which considers phenomena to constitute the whole of our knowledge in physics. The Catholic doctrine leaves phenomena alone. It does not say that the phenomena go; on the contrary, it says that they remain; nor does it say that the same phenomena are in several places at once. It deals with what no one on earth knows anything about; the material substances themselves. And, in like manner, of that majestic article of the Anglican as well as of the

Catholic Creed,—the doctrine of the Trinity in Unity. What do I know of the Essence of the Divine Being? I know that my abstract idea of three is simply incompatible with my idea of one; but when I come to the question of concrete fact, I have no means of proving that there is not a sense in which one and three can equally be predicated of the Incommunicable God. ("Apologia," p. 239.)

MASS.

To me nothing is so consoling, so piercing, so thrilling, so overcoming, as the Mass, said as it is among us. I could attend Masses for ever, and not be tired. It is not a mere form of words—it is a great action, the greatest action that can be on earth. It is, not the invocation merely, but, if I dare use the word, the evocation of the Eternal. He becomes present on the altar in flesh and blood, before whom angels bow and devils tremble. This is that awful event which is the scope, and the interpretation, of every part of the solemnity. Words are necessary, but as means, not as ends; they are not mere addresses to the throne of grace, they are instruments of what is far higher, of consecration, of sacrifice. They hurry on, as if impatient to fulfil their mission. Quickly they go, the whole is quick, for they are all parts of one integral action. Quickly they go, for they are awful words of sacrifice, they are a work too great to delay upon, as when it was said in the beginning, "What thou doest, do quickly." Quickly they pass, for the Lord Jesus goes with them, as He passed along the lake in the days of his flesh, quickly calling first one and then another; quickly they pass, because as the lightning which shineth from one part of the heaven unto the other, so is the coming of the Son of Man. Quickly they pass, for they are as the words of Moses, when the Lord came down in the cloud, calling on the Name of the Lord as he passed by, "The Lord, the Lord God, merciful and gracious, long suffering, and abundant in goodness and truth." And as Moses on the mountain, so we too "make haste and bow our heads to the earth, and adore." So we, all around, each in his place, look out for the great Advent, "waiting for the moving of the water," each in his place, with his own heart, with his own wants, with his own thoughts, with his own intentions, with his own prayers, separate but concordant, watching what is going on, watching its progress, uniting in its consummation; not painfully and hopelessly, following a hard form of prayer from beginning to end, but, like a concert of musical instruments, each different, but concurring in a sweet harmony, we take our part with God's priest, supporting him, yet guided by him. There are little children there, and old men, and simple labourers, and students in seminaries, priests preparing for Mass, priests making their thanksgiving, there are innocent maidens, and there are penitent sinners; but out of these many minds rises one Eucharistic hymn, and the great action is the measure and the scope of it. ("Loss and Gain," p. 290.)

BENEDICTION.

THE Benediction of the Blessed Sacrament is one of the simplest rites of the Church. The Priests enter and kneel down; one of them unlocks the Tabernacle, takes out the Blessed Sacrament, inserts it upright in a Monstrance of precious metal, and sets it in a conspicuous place above the altar, in the midst of lights, for all to see. The people then begin to sing; meanwhile the Priest twice offers incense to the King of heaven, before whom he is kneeling. Then he takes the Monstrance in his hands, and turning to the people blesses them with the Most Holy, in the form of a cross, while the bell is sounded by one of the attendants to call attention to the ceremony. It is our Lord's solemn benediction of His people, as when He lifted up His hands over the children, or when He blessed His chosen ones when He ascended up from Mount Olivet. As sons might come before a parent before going to bed at night, so, once or twice a week, the great Catholic family comes before the eternal Father, after the bustle or toil of the day, and He smiles upon them, and sheds upon them the light of His countenance. It is a full accomplishment of what the Priest invoked upon the Israelites, "The Lord bless thee and keep thee; the Lord show His face to thee and have mercy on thee; the Lord turn His countenance to thee and give thee peace." Can there be a more touching rite, even in the judgment of those who do not believe in it? How many a man, not a Catholic, is moved, on seeing it, to say, "Oh, that I did but believe it!" when he sees the Priest take up the Fount of Mercy, and the people bent low in adoration!

It is one of the most beautiful, natural, and soothing actions of the Church. (Present Position of Catholics, p. 255.)

CONFESSION.

How many are the souls in distress, anxiety, or loneliness, whose one need is to find a being to whom they can pour out their feelings unheard by the world? Tell them out they must; they cannot tell them out to those whom they see every hour. They want to tell them and not to tell them; and they want to tell them out, yet be as if they be not told; they wish to tell them to one who is strong enough to bear them, yet not too strong to despise them; they wish to tell them to one who can at once advise and can sympathize with them; they wish to relieve themselves of a load, to gain a solace, to receive the assurance that there is one who thinks of them, and one to whom in thought they can recur, to whom they can betake themselves, if necessary, from time to time, while they are in the world. How many a Protestant's heart would leap at the news of such a benefit, putting aside all distinct ideas of a sacramental ordinance, or of a grant of pardon and the conveyance of grace! If there is a heavenly idea in the Catholic Church, looking at it simply as an idea, surely, next after the Blessed Sacrament, Confession is such. And such is it ever found in fact,—the very act of kneeling, the low and contrite voice, the sign of the cross hanging, so to say, over the head bowed low, and the words of peace and blessing. Oh, what a soothing charm is there, which the world can neither give nor take away! Oh, what piercing, heart-subduing tranquillity, provoking tears of joy, is poured almost substantially and physically upon the soul, the oil of gladness, as Scripture calls it, when the penitent at length rises, his God reconciled to him, his sins rolled away for ever! This is Confession as it is in fact. (Present Position of Catholics, p. 351.)

COUNSELS OF PERFECTION.

THE world judges of God's condescension as it judges of His bounty. We know from Scripture that the "teaching of the cross" was in the beginning "foolishness" to it; grave, thinking men scoffed at it as impossible, that God, who was so high, should humble Himself so low, and that One who died a malefactor's death should be worshipped on the very instrument of His execution. Voluntary[1] humiliation they did not understand then, nor do they now. They do not, indeed, express their repugnance to the doctrine so openly now, because what is called public opinion does not allow them; but you see what they really think of Christ, by the tone which they adopt towards

[1] ["If an instance can be imagined of voluntary suffering, it is the mission and death of our Lord. He came to die, when He need not have died; He died to satisfy for what might have been pardoned without satisfaction; He paid a price which need not have been asked, nay, which needed not to be accepted when paid; . . He died, not in order to exert a peremptory claim on the divine justice, if I may so speak—as if He were bargaining in the market-place . .— but in a more loving, generous, munificent way." "Discourses to Mixed Congregations," p. 307.]

those who in their measure follow Him. Those who are partakers of His fulness are called on, according as the gift is given them, whether by His ordinary suggestion, or by particular inspiration, to imitate His pattern; they are carried on to the sacrifice of self, and thus they come into collision with the maxims of the world. A voluntary or gratuitous mortification, in one shape or another, voluntary chastity, voluntary poverty, voluntary obedience, vows of perfection, all this is the very point of contest between the world and the Church, the world hating it, and the Church counselling it. "Why cannot they stop with me?" says the world; "why will they give up their station or position, when it is certain they might be saved where they are? Here is a lady of birth; she might be useful at home, she might marry well, she might be an ornament to society, she might give her countenance to religious objects, and she has perversely left us all; she has cut off her hair, and put on a coarse garment, and is washing the feet of the poor. There is a man of name and ability, who has thrown himself out of his sphere of influence, and he lives in a small room, in a place where no one knows who he is, and he is teaching little children their catechism." The world is touched with pity, and shame, and indignation, at the sight, and moralizes over persons who act so unworthily of their birth or education, and are so cruel towards themselves. And, worse still, here is a Saint, and what must he do but practise eccentricities?—as, indeed, they would be in others, though in him they are but the necessary antagonists to the temptations which otherwise would come on him from the "greatness of the revelations," or are but tokens of the love with which he embraces the feet of his Redeemer. And here again is another, and she submits her flesh to penances shocking to think of, and wearies herself out in the search after misery, and all from some notion that she is assimilating her condition to the voluntary self-abasement of the Word. Alas, for the world! which is simply forgetful that God is great in all He does, great in His sufferings, and that He makes Saints and holy men in their degree partakers of that greatness. ("Discourses to Mixed Congregations," p. 313.)

RELICS AND MIRACLES.

(I.)

I SUPPOSE there is nothing which prejudices us more in the minds of Protestants of all classes than our belief in the miracles wrought by the relics and the prayers of the Saints. They inspect our churches, or they attend to our devotions, or they hear our sermons, or they open our books, or they read paragraphs in the newspapers, and it is one and the same story—relics and miracles. Such a belief, such a claim, they consider a self-evident absurdity; they are too indignant even to laugh; they toss the book from them in the fulness of anger and contempt, and they think it superfluous to make one remark in order to convict us of audacious imposture, and to fix upon us the brand of indelible shame. I shall show, then, that this strong feeling arises simply from their assumption of a First Principle, which ought to be proved, if they would be honest reasoners, before it is used to our disadvantage.

You observe, we are now upon a certain question of controversy, in which the argument is *not* directly about *fact*. . . We accuse our enemies of untruth in most cases; we do not accuse them, on the whole, of untruth here. I know it is very difficult for prejudice such as theirs to open its mouth at all without some misstatement or exaggeration; still, on the whole, they do bear true, not false witness, in the matter of miracles. We do certainly abound, we are exuberant, we overflow, with stories which cause our enemies, from no fault of ours, the keenest irritation, and kindle in them the most lively resentment against us. Certainly the Catholic Church, from east to west, from north to south, is, according to our conceptions, hung with miracles. The store of relics is inexhaustible; they are multiplied through all lands, and each particle of each has in it at least a dormant, perhaps an energetic virtue, of supernatural operation.[1] At Rome there is the true cross, the crib of Bethlehem, and the chair of St. Peter; portions of the crown of thorns are kept at Paris; the holy coat is shown at Trèves; the winding-sheet at Turin; at Monza, the iron crown is formed out of a Nail of the Cross; and another Nail is claimed for the Duomo of Milan; and

---

[1] (The following verses, written eighteen years before this passage, may, perhaps, be fitly introduced here:—

RELICS OF SAINTS.

> The Fathers are in dust, yet live to God:
>   So says the Truth; as if the motionless clay
> Still held the seeds of life beneath the sod,
>   Smouldering and struggling till the judgment-day.
>
> And hence we learn with reverence to esteem
>   Of these frail houses, though the grave confines;
> Sophist may urge his cunning tests, and deem
>   That they are earth;—but they are heavenly shrines.
>
>   "Verses on Various Occasions," p. 131.]

pieces of our Lady's habit are to be seen in the Escurial. The Agnus Dei, blessed medals, the scapular, the cord of St. Francis, all are the medium of Divine manifestations and graces. Crucifixes have bowed the head to the suppliant, and Madonnas have bent their eyes upon assembled crowds. St. Januarius's blood liquefies periodically at Naples, and St. Winifred's well is the scene of wonders even in our unbelieving country. Women are marked with the sacred stigmata, blood has flowed on Fridays from their five wounds, and their heads are crowned with a circle of lacerations. Relics are ever touching the sick, the diseased, the wounded; sometimes with no result at all, at other times with marked and undeniable efficacy. Who has not heard of the abundant favours gained by the intercession of the Blessed Virgin, and of the marvellous consequences which have attended the invocation of St. Antony of Padua? These phenomena are sometimes reported of Saints in their lifetime, as well as after their death, especially if they were evangelists or martyrs. The wild beasts crouched before their victims in the Roman amphitheatre; the axe-man was unable to sever St. Cecilia's head from her body; and St. Peter elicited a spring of water for his jailer's baptism in the Mamertine. St. Francis Xavier turned salt water into fresh for five hundred travellers; St. Raymond was transported over the sea on his cloak; St. Andrew shone brightly in the dark; St. Scholastica gained by her prayers a pouring rain; St. Paul was fed by ravens; and St. Frances saw her guardian Angel. I need not continue the catalogue; here what one party urges, the other admits; they join issue over a fact; that fact is the claim of miracles on the part of the Catholic Church; it is the Protestants' charge, and it is our glory.

Observe, then, **we** affirm that the Supreme Being has

wrought miracles on earth since the time of the Apostles. Protestants deny it. Why do we affirm? Why do they deny? We affirm it on a First Principle; they deny it on a First Principle; and on either side the First Principle is made to be decisive of the question. . . Both they and we start with the miracles of the Apostles,[1] and then their First Principle, or presumption against our miracles, is, "What God did once, He is *not* likely to do again;" while our First Principle, or presumption for our miracles, is this: "What God did once, He *is* likely to do again." They say, "It cannot be supposed He will work *many* miracles;" we, "It cannot be supposed that He will work *few*." . . The two parties, you see, start with contradictory principles, and they determine the particular miracles which are the subject of dispute by their respective principles, without looking to such testimony as may be brought in their favour. They do not say, "St. Francis, or St. Antony, or St. Philip Neri, did no miracles, for the *evidence* for them is worth nothing;" or "because what *looked* like a miracle was not a miracle;" no, but they say, "It is *impossible* they should have wrought miracles." Bring before the Protestant the largest mass of evidence and testimony in proof of the miraculous liquefaction of St. Januarius's blood at Naples, let him be urged by witnesses of the highest character, chemists of the first fame, circumstances the most favourable for the detection of imposture, coincidences and confirmations the most close, and minute, and indirect, he will not believe it; his First Principle *blocks* belief. . . He laughs at the very idea of miracles or supernatural acts, as occurring at this present day, he

---

[1] I am arguing with Protestants; if unbelievers are supposed, then they generally use Hume's celebrated argument, which still is a presumption of First Principle, viz. it is impossible to fancy the order of nature interrupted [as to which see p. 139].

laughs at the notion of evidence for them; one is just as likely as another, they are all false. Why? Because of his First Principle: there are no miracles since the Apostles. . .

(II.)

Now, on the other hand, let us take our own side of the question, and consider how we ourselves stand, relatively to the charge made against us. Catholics, then, hold the mystery of the Incarnation; and the Incarnation is the most stupendous event which ever can take place on earth; and after it, and henceforth, I do not see how we can scruple at any miracle on the mere ground of its being unlikely to happen. No miracle can be so great as that which took place in the Holy House at Nazareth; it is indefinitely more difficult to believe than all the miracles of the Breviary, of the Martyrology, of Saints' lives, of legends, of local traditions, put together; and there is the grossest inconsistency, on the very face of the matter, for any one so to strain out the gnat, and to swallow the camel, as to profess what is inconceivable, yet to protest against what is surely within the limits of intelligible hypothesis. If, through divine grace, we once are able to accept the solemn truth that the Supreme Being was born of a mortal woman, what is there to be imagined which can offend us on the ground of its marvellousness? Thus, you see, it happens that, though First Principles are commonly assumed, not proved, ours in this case admits, if not of proof, yet of recommendation, by means of that fundamental truth which Protestants profess as well as we. When we start with assuming that miracles are not unlikely, we are putting forth a position which lies imbedded, as it were, and involved in the great revealed fact of the Incarnation.

So much is plain at starting, but more is plain too. Miracles are not only not unlikely, they are positively likely, and for this simple reason, because, for the most part, when God begins, He goes on. We conceive that when He first did a miracle, He began a series; what He commenced, He continued; what has been, will be. Surely this is good and clear reasoning. To my own mind, certainly, it is incomparably more difficult to believe that the Divine Being should do one miracle and no more, than that He should do a thousand; that He should do one great miracle only, than that He should do a multitude of less besides. This beautiful world of nature, His own work, He broke its harmony, He broke through His own laws, which he had imposed on it; He worked out His purposes, not simply through it, but in violation of it. If He did this only in the lifetime of the Apostles; if He did it but once, eighteen hundred years ago and more, that isolated infringement looks as the mere infringement of a rule; if Divine Wisdom would not leave an infringement, an anomaly, a solecism, on His work, He might be expected to introduce a series of miracles, and to turn the apparent exception into an additional law of His Providence. If the Divine Being does a thing once, He is, judging by human reason, likely to do it again. This surely is common sense... Suppose you yourselves were once to see a miracle, would you not feel that experience to be like passing a line? should you, in consequence of it, declare, "I never will believe another if I hear of one"? would it not, on the contrary, predispose you to listen to a new report? would you scoff at it, and call it priestcraft, for the reason that you had actually seen one with your own eyes? I think you would not; then, I ask, what is the difference of the argument, whether you have seen one or believe one? You believe the Apostolic miracles, therefore be inclined, beforehand, to believe later ones. Thus you see, our First Principle, that miracles are not unlikely now, is not at all a strange one in the mouths of those who believe that the Supreme Being came miraculously into this world, miraculously united Himself to man's nature, passed a life of miracles, and then gave His Apostles a greater gift of miracles than He exercised Himself. So far on the principle itself; and now, in the next place, see what comes of it. This comes of it,—that there are two systems going on in the world, one of nature and one above nature; and two histories, one of common events, and one of miracles; and each system and each history has its own order. When I hear of the miracle of a Saint, my first feeling would be of the same kind as if it were a report of any natural exploit or event. Supposing, for instance, I heard a report of the death of some public man, it would not startle me, even if I did not at once credit it, for all men must die. Did I read of any great feat of valour, I should believe it, if imputed to Alexander or Cœur de Lion. Did I hear of any act of baseness, I should disbelieve it, if imputed to a friend whom I knew and loved. And so, in like manner, were a miracle reported to me as wrought by a member of Parliament, or a Bishop of the Establishment, or a Wesleyan preacher, I should repudiate the notion: were it referred to a Saint, or the relic of a Saint, or the intercession of a Saint, I should not be startled at it, though I might not at once believe it. And I certainly should be right in this conduct, supposing my First Principle to be true. Miracles to the Catholic are facts of history and biography, and nothing else; and they are to be regarded and dealt with as other facts; and as natural facts, under circumstances, do not startle Protestants, so supernatural, under circumstances, do not startle the Catholic.[1] They may or may not have taken place in particular cases; he may be unable to determine which; he may have no distinct evidence; he may suspend his judgment; but he will say, "It is very possible;" he never will say, "I cannot believe it."[2]..

(III.)

Such, then, is the answer I would make to those who urge against us the multitude of miracles recorded in our Saints' Lives. We think them true in the sense in which

---

[1] Douglas, succeeding Middleton, lays down the sceptical and Protestant First Principle thus: "The history of miracles (to make use of the words of an author whose authority you will think of some weight), is of a kind totally *different* from that of common events; *the one to be suspected always of course*, without the *strongest* evidence to *confirm* it; the other to be admitted of course, without as *strong* reason to *suspect* it," &c. "Criterion," p. 26.

[2] ["Though it is a matter of faith with Catholics that miracles never cease in the Church, still that this or that professed miracle really took place, is for the most part only a matter of opinion, and when it is believed, whether on testimony or tradition, it is not believed to the exclusion of all doubt, whether about the fact or its miraculousness. Thus I may believe in the liquefaction of St. Pantaleon's blood, and believe it to the best of my judgment to be a miracle, yet, supposing a chemist offered to produce exactly the same phenomena under exactly similar circumstances by the materials put at his command by his science, so as to reduce what seemed beyond nature within natural laws, I should watch with some suspense of mind and misgiving the course of his experiment, as having no Divine Word to fall back upon as a ground of certainty that the liquefaction was miraculous." "Grammar of Assent," p. 193.]

Protestants think the details of English history true... If, indeed, miracles never can occur, then, indeed, impute the narratives to fraud; but, till you prove they are not likely, we shall consider the histories which have come down to us true on the whole, though in particular cases they may be exaggerated or unfounded. Where, indeed, they can certainly be proved to be false, there we shall be bound to do our best to get rid of them; but till that is clear, we shall be liberal enough to allow others to use their private judgment in their favour, as we use ours in their disparagement. For myself, lest I appear to be in any way shrinking from a determinate judgment on the claims of those miracles and relics, which Protestants are so startled at, and to be hiding particular questions in what is vague and general, I will avow distinctly, that, putting out of the question the hypothesis of unknown laws of nature (that is, of the professed miracle being not miraculous), I think it impossible to withstand the evidence which is brought for the liquefaction of the blood of St. Januarius at Naples, and for the motion of the eyes of the pictures of the Madonna in the Roman States. I see no reason to doubt the material of the Lombard Crown at Monza; and I do not see why the Holy Coat at Trèves may not have been what it professes to be. I firmly believe that portions of the true Cross are at Rome, and elsewhere, that the crib of Bethlehem is at Rome, and the bodies of St. Peter and St. Paul also. I believe that at Rome, too, lies St. Stephen, that St. Matthew lies at Salerno, and St. Andrew at Amalfi. I firmly believe that the relics of the Saints are doing innumerable miracles and graces daily, and that it needs only for a Catholic to show devotion to any Saint in order to receive special benefits from his intercession. I firmly believe that the Saints in their lifetime have before now raised the dead to life, crossed the sea without vessels multiplied grain and bread, cured incurable diseases, and superseded the operation of the laws of the universe in a multitude of ways. Many men, when they hear an educated man so speak, will at once impute the avowal to insanity, or to an idiosyncrasy, or to imbecility of mind, or to decrepitude of powers, or to fanaticism, or to hypocrisy. They have a right to say so, if they will; and we have a right to ask them why they do not say it of those who bow down before the Mystery of mysteries, the Divine Incarnation. If they do not believe this, they are not yet Protestants; if they do, let them grant that He who has done the greater may do the less.—("Present Position of Catholics," p. 298.)

THE EARLIEST RECORDED APPARITION OF THE BLESSED VIRGIN.

I KNOW of no instance to my purpose earlier than A.D. 234, but it is a very remarkable one. . . St. Gregory Nyssen,[1] then, a native of Cappadocia in the fourth century, relates that his namesake, Bishop of Neo-Cæsarea, surnamed Thaumaturgus, in the century preceding, shortly before he was called to the priesthood, received in a vision a Creed, which is still extant, from the Blessed Mary at the hands of St. John. The account runs thus:—He was deeply pondering theological doctrine, which the heretics of the day depraved. "In such thoughts," says his namesake of Nyssa, "he was passing the night, when one appeared,

[1] [See "Essay on Doctrinal Development," p. 386.]

as if in human form, aged in appearance, saintly in the fashion of his garments, and very venerable both in grace of countenance and general mien. Amazed at the sight, he started from his bed, and asked who it was, and why he came; but, on the other calming the perturbation of his mind with his gentle voice, and saying he had appeared to him by divine command on account of his doubts, in order that the truth of the orthodox faith might be revealed to him, he took courage at the word, and regarded him with a mixture of joy and fright. Then, on his stretching his hand straight forward and pointing with his fingers at something on one side, he followed with his eyes the extended hand, and saw another appearance opposite to the former, in shape of a woman, but more than human. . . When his eyes could not bear the apparition, he heard them conversing together on the subject of his doubts; and thereby not only gained a true knowledge of the faith, but learned their names, as they addressed each other by their respective appellations. And thus he is said to have heard the person in woman's shape bid 'John the Evangelist' disclose to the young man the mystery of godliness; and he answered that he was ready to comply in this matter with the wish of 'the Mother of the Lord,' and enunciated a formulary, well-turned and complete, and so vanished. He, on the other hand, immediately committed to writing that divine teaching of his mystagogue, and henceforth preached in the Church according to that form, and bequeathed to posterity, as an inheritance, that heavenly teaching, by means of which his people are instructed down to this day, being preserved from all heretical evil." He proceeds to rehearse the Creed thus given, "There is One God, Father of a Living Word," &c. Bull, after quoting it in his work on the Nicene Faith, alludes to this history of its origin, and adds, "No one should think it incredible that such a providence should befall a man whose whole life was conspicuous for revelations and miracles, as all ecclesiastical writers who have mentioned him (and who has not?) witness with one voice."

Here our Lady is represented as rescuing a holy soul from intellectual error. This leads me to a reflection. . . It is said of her in the Antiphon, "All heresies thou hast destroyed alone." Surely the truth of it is verified in this age, as in former times. . . She is the great exemplar of prayer in a generation which emphatically denies the power of prayer *in toto*, which determines that fatal laws govern the universe, that there cannot be any direct communication between earth and heaven, that God cannot visit His earth, and that man cannot influence His providence. ("Anglican Difficulties," p. 423.)

THE ANTECEDENT ARGUMENT FOR AN INFALLIBLE ARBITER OF FAITH AND MORALS.

THE common sense of mankind . . feels that the very idea of revelation implies a present informant and guide, and that an infallible one; not a mere abstract declaration of truths not before known to man, or a record of history, or the result of an antiquarian research, but a message and a lesson speaking to this man and that. This is shown by the popular notion which has prevailed among us since the Reformation, that the Bible itself is such a guide; and which succeeded in overthrowing the

Supremacy of Church and Pope, for the very reason that it was a rival authority, not resisting merely, but supplanting it. In proportion, then, as we find, in matter of fact, that the inspired volume is not calculated or intended to subserve that purpose, are we forced to revert to that living and present guide, which, at the era of her rejection, had been so long recognized as the dispenser of Scripture, according to times and circumstances, and the arbiter of all true doctrine and holy practice to her children. We feel a need, and she alone, of all things under heaven, supplies it. We are told that God has spoken. Where? In a book? We have tried it, and it disappoints; it disappoints, that most holy and blessed gift, not from fault of its own, but because it is used for a purpose for which it was not given. The Ethiopian's reply, when St. Philip asked him if he understood what he was reading, is the voice of nature, " How can I, unless some man shall guide me?" The Church undertakes that office; . . she alone . . dares claim it, as if a secret instinct and involuntary misgivings restrained those rival communions which go so far towards affecting it. The most obvious answer, then, to the question, why we yield to the authority of the Church in the questions and developments of faith is, that some authority there must be if there is a revelation, and other authority there is none but she; in the words of St. Peter to her Divine Master and Lord, "To whom shall we go?" Nor must it be forgotten, in confirmation, that Scripture expressly calls the Church "the Pillar and Ground of the Truth," and promises her as by covenant that, "the Spirit of the Lord which is upon her, and His words which He has put in her mouth, shall not depart out of her mouth, nor out of the mouth of her seed, nor out of the mouth of her seed's seed, from henceforth and for ever."

And if the very claim to infallible arbitration in religious disputes is of so weighty importance and interest in all ages of the world, much more is it welcome at a time like the present, when the human intellect is so busy, and thought so fertile, and opinion so indefinitely divided. The absolute need of a spiritual supremacy is at present the strongest of arguments in favour of its supply. Surely, either an objective revelation has not been given, or it has been provided with means for impressing its objectiveness on the world. If Christianity be a social religion, as it certainly is, and if it be based on certain ideas acknowledged as divine, or a creed, which shall here be assumed, and if these ideas have various aspects, and make distinct impressions on different minds, and issue in consequence in a multiplicity of developments, true, or false, or mixed, as has been shown, what influence will suffice to meet and to do justice to these conflicting conditions, but a supreme authority ruling and reconciling individual judgments, by a divine right and a recognized wisdom? In barbarous times the will is reached through the senses; but in an age in which reason, as it is called, is the standard of truth and right, it is abundantly evident to any one who mixes ever so little with the world, that, if things are left to themselves, every individual will have his own view of things, and take his own course; that two or three agree together to-day to part to-morrow; that Scripture will be read in contrary ways, and history will be analyzed into subtle but practical differences; that philosophy, taste, prejudice, passion, party, caprice, will find no common measure, unless there be some supreme power to control the mind, and to compel agreement. There can be no combination on the basis of truth without an organ of truth. As cultivation brings out the colours of flowers, and domestication the hues of animals, so does education of necessity develop differences of opinion; and while it is impossible to lay down first principles in which all will unite, it is utterly unreasonable to expect that this man should yield to that, or all to one. I do not say there are no eternal truths, such as the poet speaks of,[1] which all acknowledge in private, but that there are none sufficiently commanding to be the basis of public union and action. The only general persuasive in matters of conduct is authority; that is, when truth is in question, a judgment which we consider superior to our own. If Christianity is both social and dogmatic, and intended for all ages, it must, humanly speaking, have an infallible expounder. Else you will secure unity of form, at the loss of unity of doctrine, or unity of doctrine at the loss of unity of form; you will have to choose between a comprehension of opinions, and a resolution into parties, between latitudinarian and sectarian error; you may be tolerant or intolerant of contrarieties of thought, but contrarieties you will have. By the Church of England, a hollow uniformity is preferred to an infallible chair, and by the sects of England, an interminable division. Germany and Geneva began with persecution and have ended in scepticism. The doctrine of infallibility is a less violent hypothesis than this sacrifice either of faith or of charity. ("Essay on Development," p. 125.)

[1] Οὐ γάρ τι νῦν γε κἀχθές. κ.τ.λ.

THE PRACTICAL WISDOM OF THE HOLY SEE.

In the midst of our difficulties[1] I have one ground of hope, just one stay, but, as I think, a sufficient one, which serves me in the stead of all other argument whatever, which hardens me against criticism, which supports me if I begin to despond, and to which I ever come round, when the question of the possible and the expedient is brought into discussion. It is the decision of the Holy See; St. Peter has spoken; it is he who has enjoined that which seems to us so unpromising. He has spoken, and has a claim on us to trust him. He is no recluse, no solitary student, no dreamer about the past, no doter upon the dead and gone, no projector of the visionary. He for eighteen hundred years has lived in the world; he has seen all fortunes, he has encountered all adversaries, he has shaped himself for all emergencies. If ever there was a power on earth who had an eye for the times, who has confined himself to the practicable, and has been happy in his anticipations, whose words have been facts, and whose commands prophecies, such is he in the history of ages, who sits from generation to generation in the Chair of the Apostles, as the Vicar of Christ, and the Doctor of his Church.

These are not the words of rhetoric, but of history. All who take part with the Apostle, are on the winning side. He has long since given warrants for the confidence which he claims. From the first he has looked through the wide world, of which he has the burden; and, accord-

[1] [Attending the foundation of the Catholic University in Dublin.]

ing to the need of the day, and the inspirations of his Lord, he has set himself now to one thing, now to another; but to all in season, and to nothing in vain. He came first upon an age of refinement and luxury like our own, and, in spite of the persecutor, fertile in the resources of his cruelty, he soon gathered, out of all classes of society, the slave, the soldier, the high-born lady, and the sophist, materials enough to form a people to his Master's honour. The savage hordes came down in torrents from the north, and Peter went out to meet them, and by his very eye he sobered them, and backed them in their full career. They turned aside and flooded the whole earth, but only to be more surely civilized by him, and to be made ten times more his children even than the older populations which they had overwhelmed. Lawless kings arose, sagacious as the Roman, passionate as the Hun, yet in him they found their match, and were shattered, and he lived on. The gates of the earth were opened to the east and west, and men poured out to take possession; but he went with them by his missionaries, to China, to Mexico, carried along by zeal and charity, as far as those children of men were led by enterprize, covetousness, or ambition. Has he failed in his successes up to this hour? Did he, in our fathers' day, fail in his struggle with Joseph of Germany and his confederates, with Napoleon, a greater name, and his dependent kings, that, though in another kind of fight, he should fail in ours? What grey hairs are on the head of Judah, whose youth is renewed like the eagle's, whose feet are like the feet of harts, and underneath the Everlasting arms? ("Idea of a University," p. 13.)

THE OBLIGATIONS OF CATHOLICS TO THE HOLY SEE

OUR duty to the Holy See, to the Chair of St. Peter, is to be measured by what the Church teaches us concerning that Holy See and concerning him who sits in it. Now St. Peter, who first occupied it, was the Vicar of Christ. You know well, our Lord and Saviour Jesus Christ, who suffered on the Cross for us, thereby bought for us the kingdom of heaven. "When Thou hadst overcome the sting of death," says the hymn, "Thou didst open the kingdom of heaven to those who believe." He opens, and He shuts; He gives grace, He withdraws it; He judges, He pardons, He condemns. Accordingly He speaks of Himself in the Apocalypse as "Him who is the Holy and the True, Him that hath the key of David (the key, that is, of the chosen king of the chosen people), Him that openeth and no man shutteth, that shutteth and no man openeth." And what our Lord, the Supreme Judge, is in heaven, that was St. Peter on earth; he had those keys of the kingdom, according to the text, "Thou art Peter, and upon this rock I will build My Church, and the gates of hell shall not prevail against it. And I will give to thee the keys of the kingdom of heaven; and whatsoever thou shalt bind upon earth, shall be bound also in heaven; and whatsoever thou shalt loose on earth, shall be loosed also in heaven."

Next, let it be considered, the kingdom which our Lord set up, with St. Peter at its head, was decreed in the counsels of God to last to the end of all things, according to the words I have just quoted, "The gates of hell shall not prevail against it." And again, "Behold, I am with you all days, even to the consummation of the world." And in the words of the prophet Isaias, speaking of that divinely established Church, then in the future, "This is My covenant with them, My Spirit that is in thee, and My words which I have put in thy mouth, shall not depart out of thy mouth, nor out of the mouth of thy seed, nor out of the mouth of thy seed's seed, saith the Lord, from henceforth and for ever." And the prophet Daniel says, "The God of heaven will set up a kingdom that shall never be destroyed . . and it shall break in pieces and shall consume all those kingdoms (of the earth, which went before it), and itself shall stand for ever."

That kingdom our Lord set up when He came on earth, and especially after His resurrection; for we are told by St. Luke that this was His gracious employment, when He visited the Apostles from time to time, during the forty days which intervened between Easter Day and the day of His Ascension. "He showed Himself alive to the Apostles," says the Evangelist, "after His passion by many proofs, for forty days appearing to them and speaking of the kingdom of God." And accordingly, when at length He had ascended on high, and had sent down "the promise of His Father," the Holy Ghost, upon His Apostles, they forthwith entered upon their high duties, and brought that kingdom or Church into shape, and supplied it with members, and enlarged it, and carried it into all lands. As to St. Peter, he acted as the head of the Church, according to the previous words of Christ; and, still according to his Lord's supreme will, he at length placed himself in the see of Rome, where he was martyred. And what was then done, in its substance cannot be undone. "God is not as a man that He should lie, nor as the son of man, that He should change. Hath He said then, and shall He not do? hath He spoken, and will He not fulfil?" And, as St. Paul says, "the gifts and the calling of God are without repentance." His Church, then, in all necessary matters, is as unchangeable as He. Its framework, its polity, its ranks, its offices, its creed, its privileges, the promises made to it, its fortunes in the world, are ever what they have been.

Therefore, as it was *in* the world, but not *of* the world in the Apostles' times, so it is now:—as it was "in honour and dishonour, in evil report and good report, as chastised but not killed, as having nothing and possessing all things," in the Apostles' times, so it is now:—as then it taught the truth, so it does now; as then it had the sacraments of grace, so has it now; as then it had a hierarchy or holy government of Bishops, priests, and deacons, so has it now; and as it had a Head then, so must it have a Head now. Who is that visible Head now? who is now the Vicar of Christ? who has now the keys of the kingdom of heaven, as St. Peter had then? Who is it who binds and looses on earth, that our Lord may bind and loose in heaven? Who, I say, if a successor to St. Peter there must be, who is that successor in his sovereign authority over the Church? It is he who sits in St. Peter's Chair: it is the Bishop of Rome. We all know *this;* it is part of our *faith;* I am not proving it to you, my brethren. The visible headship of the Church, which was with St. Peter while he lived, has been lodged ever since in his Chair: the successors in his headship are the successors in his Chair, that continuous line of Bishops of Rome, or Popes, as they are called, one after another, as years have rolled on, one dying and another coming, down to this day, when we see Pius the Ninth sustaining the weight of the glorious Apostolate, and that for twenty years past—a tremendous weight, a ministry involving momentous duties, innumerable anxieties, and immense responsibilities, as it ever has done.

And now, though I might say much more about the prerogatives of the Holy Father, the visible Head of the Church, I have said more than enough for the purpose which has led to my speaking about him at all. I have said that, like St. Peter, he is the Vicar of his Lord. He can judge, and he can acquit; he can pardon, and he can condemn; he can command, and he can permit; he can forbid, and he can punish. He has a supreme jurisdiction over the people of God. He can stop the ordinary course of sacramental mercies; he can excommunicate from the ordinary grace of redemption; and he can remove again the ban which he has inflicted. It is the rule of Christ's providence, that what His Vicar does in severity or in mercy upon earth, He Himself confirms in heaven. And in saying all this, I have said enough for my purpose, because that purpose is to define our obligations to him. That is the point on which our attention is fixed; "our obligations to the Holy See;" and what need I say more to measure our own duty to it and to him who sits in it, than to say that, in his administration of Christ's kingdom, in his religious acts, we must never oppose his will, or dispute his word, or criticise his policy, or shrink from his side? There are kings of the earth who have despotic authority, which their subjects obey in deed but disown in their hearts; but we must never murmur at that absolute rule which the Sovereign Pontiff has over us, because it is given to him by Christ, and in obeying him we are obeying his Lord. We must never suffer ourselves to doubt that, in his government of the Church, he is guided by an intelligence more than human. His yoke is the yoke of Christ; *he* has the responsibibity of his own acts, not we; and to his *Lord* must he render account, not to us. Even in secular matters it is ever safe to be on his side, dangerous to be on the side of his enemies. Our duty is,—not indeed to mix up Christ's Vicar with this or that party of men, because he in his high station is above all parties,—but to look at his formal deeds, and to follow him whither he goeth, and never to desert him, however we may be tried, but to defend him at all hazards, and against all comers, as a son would a father, and as a wife a husband, knowing that his cause is the cause of God. And so as regards his successors, if we live to see them; it is our duty to give *them* in like manner our dutiful allegiance and our unfeigned service, and to follow them also whithersoever they go, having that same confidence that each in his turn and in his own day will do God's work and will, which we felt in their predecessors, now taken away to their eternal reward. ("Occasional Sermons," p. 264.)

ENGLISH CATHOLICS AND PIUS IX.

AND if I am to pass on to speak of the present Pontiff, and of our own obligations to him, then I would have you recollect that it is he who has taken the Catholics of England out of their unformed state and made them a Church. He it is who has redressed a misfortune of nearly three hundred years' standing. Twenty years ago we were a mere collection of individuals; but Pope Pius has brought us together, has given us Bishops, and created out of us a body politic, which (please God), as time goes on, will play an important part in Christendom, with a character, an intellect, and a power of its own, with schools of its own, with a definite influence in the counsels of the Holy Church Catholic, as England had of old time.

This has been his great act towards our country; and then specially, as to his great act towards us here, towards me. One of his first acts after he was Pope was, in his great condescension, to call me to Rome; then, when I got there, he bade me send for my friends to be with me; and he formed us into an Oratory. And thus it came to pass that, on my return to England, I was able to associate myself with others who had not gone to Rome, till we were so many in number, that not only did we establish our own Oratory here,[1] whither the Pope had specially sent us, but we found we could throw off from us a colony of zealous and able priests into the metropolis, and establish there, with the powers with which the Pope had furnished me, and the sanction of the late Cardinal, that Oratory which has done and still does so much good among the Catholics of London.

Such is the Pope now happily reigning in the Chair of St. Peter; such are our personal obligations to him; such has he been towards England, such towards us, towards you, my Brethren. Such he is in his benefits, and great as are the claims of those benefits upon us, great equally are the claims on us of his personal character and of his many virtues. He is one whom to see is to love; one who overcomes even strangers, even enemies, by his very look and voice; whose presence subdues, whose memory haunts, even the sturdy, resolute mind of the English Protestant. Such is the Holy Father of Christendom, the worthy successor of a long and glorious line. Such is he; and, great as he is in office, and in his beneficent acts and virtuous life, as great is he in the severity of his trials, in the complication of his duties, and in the gravity of his perils. ("Occasional Sermons," p. 271.)

---

[1] [In Birmingham.]

SCANDALS IN THE CATHOLIC CHURCH.

No Catholic will deny [that the Church has scandals]. She has ever had the reproach and shame of being the mother of children unworthy of her. She has good children;—she has many more bad. Such is the will of God as declared from the beginning. He might have formed a pure Church; but He has expressly predicted that the cockle, sown by the enemy, shall remain with the wheat, even to the harvest at the end of the world. He pronounced that His Church should be like a fisher's net, gathering of every kind, and not examined till the evening Nay, more than this, He declared that the bad and imperfect should far surpass the good. "Many are called," He said, "but few are chosen;" and His Apostle speaks of "a remnant saved according to the election of grace." There is ever, then, an abundance of materials in the lives and the histories of Catholics, ready to the use of those opponents who, starting with the notion that the Holy Church is the work of the devil, wish to have some corroboration of their leading idea. Her very prerogative gives special opportunity for it; I mean, that she is the Church of all lands and of all times. If there was a Judas among the Apostles, and a Nicholas among the deacons, why should we be surprised that in the course of eighteen hundred years there should be flagrant instances of cruelty, of unfaithfulness, of hypocrisy, or of profligacy, and that not only in the Catholic people, but in high places, in royal palaces, in bishops' households, nay, in the seat of St. Peter itself? Why need it surprise, if in barbarous ages, or in ages of luxury, there have been bishops, or abbots, or priests, who have forgotten themselves and their God, and served the world or the flesh, and have perished in that evil service? What triumph is it, though in a long line of between two and three hundred popes, amid martyrs, confessors, doctors, sage rulers, and loving fathers of their people, one, or two, or three are found who fulfil the Lord's description of the wicked servant, who began "to strike the manservants and maidservants, and to eat and drink and be drunk"? What will come of it, though we grant that at this time or that, here or there, mistakes in policy, or ill advised measures, or timidity, or vacillation in action, or secular maxims, or inhumanity, or narrowness of mind, have seemed to influence the Church's action or her bearing towards her children? I can only say that, taking man as he is, it would be a miracle were such offences altogether absent from her history. Consider what it is to be left to oneself and one's conscience, without others' judgment on what we do, which at times is the case with all men; consider what it is to have easy opportunities of sinning; and then cast the first stone at churchmen who have abused their freedom from control or independence of criticism. With such considerations before me, I do not wonder that these scandals take place; which, of course, are the greater in porportion as the field on which they are found is larger and wider, and the more shocking in proportion as the profession of sanctity, under which they exhibit themselves, is more prominent. What religious body can compare with us in duration or in extent? There are crimes enough to be found in the members of all denominations: if there are passages in our history, the like of which do not occur in the annals of Wesleyanism or of Independency, or the other religions of the day, recollect there have been no Anabaptist pontiffs, no Methodist kings, no Congregational monasteries, no Quaker populations.

Let the tenets of Irving or Swedenborg spread, as they never can, through the world, and we should see if, amid the wealth, and power, and station which would accrue to their holders, they would bear their faculties more meekly than Catholics have done. ("Occasional Sermons," p. 144.)

"POPULAR" CATHOLICS.

HERE is a grave matter against you, that you are so well with the Protestants about you; I do not mean to say that you are not bound to cultivate peace with all men, and to do them all the offices of charity in your power. Of course you are, and if they respect, esteem, and love you, it redounds to your praise and will gain you a reward; but I mean more than this; they do *not* respect you, but they like you, because they think of you as of themselves, they see no difference between themselves and you. This is the very reason why they so often take your part, and assert or defend your political rights. Here, again, there is a sense of course in which our civil rights may be advocated by Protestants without any reflection on us, and with honour to them. We are like others in this, that we are men; that we are members of the same state with them, subjects, contented subjects, of the same Sovereign; that we have a dependence on them, and have them dependent on us; that, like them, we feel pain when illused, and are grateful when well-treated. We need not be ashamed of a fellowship like this, and those who recognize it in us are generous in doing so. But we have much cause to be ashamed, and much cause to be anxious what God thinks of us, if we gain their support by giving them a false impression in our persons of what the Catholic Church is, and what Catholics are bound to be, what bound to believe and to do; and is not this the case often, that the world takes up your interests, because you share its sins?

Nature is one with nature, grace with grace; the world then witnesses against you by being good friends with you; you could not have got on with the world so well, without surrendering something which was precious and sacred. The world likes you, all but your professed creed; distinguishes you from your creed in its judgment of you, and would fain separate you from it in fact. Men say, "These persons are better than their Church; we have not a word to say for their Church; but Catholics are not what they were; they are very much like other men now. Their creed certainly is bigoted and cruel, but what would you have of them? You cannot expect them to confess this; let them change quietly, no one changes in public, be satisfied that they are changed. They are as fond of the world as we are; they take up political objects as warmly; they like their own way just as well; they do not like strictness a whit better; they hate spiritual thraldom, and they are half ashamed of the Pope and his Councils. They hardly believe any miracles now, and are annoyed when their own brethren officiously proclaim them; they never speak of purgatory; they are sore about images; they avoid the subject of Indulgences; and they will not commit themselves to the doctrine of exclusive salvation. The Catholic doctrines are now mere badges of party. Catholics think for themselves and judge for themselves, just as we do; they are kept in their Church by a point of honour, and a reluctance at seeming to abandon a fallen cause."

Such is the judgment of the world, and you, my brethren, are shocked to hear it;—but may it not be that the world knows more about you than you know about yourselves? "If ye had been of the world," says Christ, "the world would love its own; but because ye are not of the world, but I have chosen you out of the world, therefore the world hateth you." So speaks Christ of His Apostles. How run His words when applied to you? "If ye be of the world, the world will love its own; therefore ye *are* of the world, and I have *not* chosen you out of the world, because the world loveth you." Do not complain of the world's imputing to you more than is true; those who live as the world give colour to those who think them of the world, and seem to form but one party with them. In proportion as you put off the yoke of Christ, so does the world by a sort of instinct recognize you, and think well of you accordingly. Its highest compliment is to tell you that you disbelieve. Oh, my brethren, there is an eternal enmity between the world and the Church. The Church declares by the mouth of an Apostle, "Whoso will be a friend of the world, becomes an enemy of God;" and the world retorts, and calls the Church apostate, sorceress, Beelzebub, and Antichrist. She is the image and the mother of the predestinate, and, if you would be found among her children when you die, you must have part in her reproach while you live. Does not the world scoff at all that is glorious, all that is majestic, in our holy religion? Does it not speak against the special creations of God's grace? Does it not disbelieve the possibility of purity and chastity? Does it not slander the profession of celibacy? Does it not deny the virginity of Mary? Does it not cast out her very name as evil? Does it not scorn her as a dead woman, whom you know to be the Mother of all living, and the great Intercessor of the faithful? Does it not ridicule the Saints? Does it not make light of their relics? Does it not despise the Sacraments? Does it not blaspheme the awful Presence which dwells upon our altars, and mock bitterly and fiercely at our believing that what it calls bread and wine is that very same Body and Blood of the Lamb which lay in Mary's womb and hung on the Cross? What are we, that we should be better treated than our Lord, and His Mother, and His servants, and His works? Nay, what are we, if we *be* better treated, but the friends of those who treat us well, and who ill-treat Him? ("Discourses to Mixed Congregations," p. 165.)

A BAD CATHOLIC.

[BY how many] a Catholic have the very mercies of God been perverted to his [own] ruin! He has rested on the Sacraments, without caring to have the proper dispositions for attending them. At one time he had lived in neglect of religion altogether; but there was a date when he felt a wish to set himself right with his Maker; so he began, and has continued ever since, to go to Confession and Communion at convenient intervals. He comes again and again to the Priest; he goes through his sins; the Priest is obliged to take his account of them, which is a very defective account, and sees no reason for not giving him absolution. He is absolved, as far as words can absolve him; he comes again to the Priest when the season comes round; again he confesses, and again he has the form pronounced over him. He falls sick, he receives the last Sacraments: he receives the last rites of the Church, and he is lost. He is lost, because he has never really turned his heart to God; or, if he had some poor measure of contrition for awhile, it did not last beyond his first or second confession. He soon taught himself to come to the Sacraments without any contrition at all; he deceived himself, and left out his principal and most important sins. Somehow he deceived himself into the notion that they were not sins, or not mortal sins; for some reason or other he was silent, and his confession became as defective as his contrition. Yet this scanty show of religion was sufficient to soothe and stupefy his conscience: so he went on year after year, never making a good confession, communicating in mortal sin, till he fell ill; and then, I say, the viaticum and holy oil were brought to him, and he committed sacrilege for his last time,—and so he went to his God.

Oh, what a moment for the poor soul, when it comes to itself, and finds itself suddenly before the judgment-seat of Christ! Oh, what a moment, when, breathless with the journey, and dizzy with the brightness, and overwhelmed with the strangeness of what is happening to him, and unable to realize where he is, the sinner hears the voice of the accusing spirit, bringing up all the sins of his past life, which he has forgotten, or which he has explained away, which he would not allow to be sins, though he suspected they were; when he hears him detailing all the mercies of God which he has despised, all His warnings which he has set at nought, all His judgments which he has outlived; when that evil one follows out into detail the growth and progress of a lost soul,—how it expanded and was confirmed in sin,—how it budded forth into leaves and flowers, grew into branches, and ripened into fruit,—till nothing was wanted for its full condemnation! And, oh! still more terrible, still more distracting, when the Judge speaks, and consigns it to the jailors, till it shall pay the endless debt which lies against it! "Impossible, I a lost soul! I separated from hope and from peace for ever! It is not I of whom the Judge so spake! There is a mistake somewhere; Christ, Saviour, hold Thy hand,—one minute to explain it! My name is Demas: I am but Demas, not Judas, or Nicholas, or Alexander, or Philetus, or Diotrephes. What? hopeless pain! for me! impossible, it shall not be!" And the poor soul struggles and wrestles in the grasp of the mighty demon which has hold of it, and whose every touch is torment. "Oh, atrocious!" it shrieks in agony, and in anger too, as if the very keenness of the infliction were a proof of its injustice. "A second! and a third! I can bear no more! stop, horrible fiend, give over; I am a man, and not such as thou! I am not food for thee, or sport for thee! I never was in hell as thou; I have not on me the smell of fire, nor the taint of the charnel-house! I know what human feelings are; I have been taught religion; I have had a conscience; I have a cultivated mind; I am well versed in science and art; I have been refined by literature; I have had an eye for the beauties of nature; I am a philosopher, or a poet, or a shrewd observer of men, or a hero, or a statesman, or an orator, or a man of wit and humour. Nay,—I am a Catholic: I am not an unregenerate Protestant; I have received the grace of the Redeemer; I have attended the Sacraments for years; I have been a Catholic from a child; I am a son of the Martyrs; I died in communion with the Church: nothing, nothing which I have ever been, which I have ever seen, bears any resemblance to thee, and to the flame and stench which exhale from thee; so I defy thee, and abjure thee, O enemy of man!"

Alas! poor soul; and whilst it thus fights with that destiny which it has brought upon itself, and with those companions whom it has chosen, the man's name perhaps is solemnly chanted forth, and his memory decently cherished among his friends on earth. His readiness in speech, his fertility in thought, his sagacity, or his wisdom, are not forgotten. Men talk of him from time to time; they appeal to his authority; they quote his words; perhaps they even raise a monument to his name, or write his history. "So comprehensive a mind! such a power of throwing light on a perplexed subject, and bringing conflicting ideas or facts into harmony!" "Such a speech it was that he made on such and such an occasion; I happened to be present, and never shall forget it;" or, "It was the saying of a very sensible man;" or, "A great personage, whom some of us knew;" or, "It was a rule with a very worthy and excellent friend of mine, now no more;" or, "Never was his equal in society, so just in his remarks, so versatile, so unobtrusive;" or, "I was fortunate to see him once when I was a boy;" or, "So great a benefactor to his country and to his kind;" "His discoveries so great;" or, "His philosophy so profound." Oh, vanity! vanity of vanities, all is vanity! What profiteth it? What profiteth it? His soul is in hell. Oh, ye children of men, while thus ye speak, his soul is in the beginning of those torments in which his body will soon have part, and which will never die. ("Discourses to Mixed Congregations," p. 37.)

THE IDEA OF A SAINT.

WORLDLY-MINDED men, however rich, if they are Catholics, cannot, till they utterly lose their faith, be the same as those who are external to the Church; they have an instinctive veneration for those who have the traces of heaven upon them, and they praise what they do not imitate.

Such men have an idea before them which a Protestant nation has not; they have the idea of a Saint; they believe they realize the existence of those rare servants of God, who rise up from time to time in the Catholic Church like Angels in disguise, and shed around them a light as they walk on their way heavenward. They may not in practice do what is right and good, but they know what is true; they know what to think and how to judge. They have a standard for their principles of conduct, and it is the image, the pattern of Saints which forms it for them. . . Very various are the Saints, their very variety is a token of God's workmanship; but however various, and whatever was their special line of duty, they have been heroes in it; they have attained such noble self-command, they have so crucified the flesh, they have so renounced the world; they are so meek, so gentle, so tender-hearted, so merciful, so sweet, so cheerful, so full of prayer, so diligent, so forgetful of injuries; they have sustained such great and continued pains, they have persevered in such vast labours, they have made such valiant confessions, they have wrought such abundant miracles, they have been blessed with such strange successes, that they have set up a standard before us of truth, of magnanimity, of holiness, of love. They are not always our examples, we are not always bound to follow them; not more than we are bound to obey literally some of our Lord's precepts, such as turning the cheek or giving away the coat; not more than we can follow the course of the sun, moon, or stars in the heavens; but, though not always our examples, they are always our standard of right and good; they are raised up to be monuments and lessons, they remind us of God, they introduce us into the unseen world, they teach us what Christ loves, they track out for us the way which leads heavenward. They are to us who see them, what wealth, notoriety, rank, and name are to the multitude of men who live in darkness, —objects of our veneration and of our homage. ("Discourses to Mixed Congregations," p. 94.)

LINGERING IMPERFECTIONS OF SAINTS; PERSONAL AND TEMPORARY ERRORS OF POPES.

THE lingering imperfections of the Saints surely make us love them more, without leading us to reverence them less, and act as a relief to the discouragement and despondency which may come over those, who, in the midst of much error and sin, are striving to imitate them;—according to the saying of St. Gregory, on a graver occasion, "Plus nobis Thomæ infidelitas ad fidem, quam fides credentium discipulorum profuit."

And in like manner, the dissatisfaction of Saints, of St. Basil, or again of our own St. Thomas, with the contemporary policy or conduct of the Holy See, while it cannot be taken to justify ordinary men, bishops, clergy or laity, in feeling the same, is no reflection either on those Saints or on the Vicar of Christ. Nor is his infallibility in dogmatic decisions compromised by any personal or temporary error into which he may have fallen, in his estimate, whether of a heretic such as Pelagius, or of a Doctor of the Church such as Basil. Accidents of this nature are unavoidable in the state of being which we are allotted here below. ("Historical Sketches," vol. II. p. xiii.)

ST. JOHN BAPTIST.

WHOM can we conceive of such majestic and severe sanctity as the Holy Baptist? He had a privilege which reached near upon the prerogative of the Most Blessed Mother of God; for, if she was conceived without sin, at least without sin he was born. She was all-pure, all-holy, and sin had no part in her; but St. John was in the beginning of his existence a partaker of Adam's curse: he lay under God's wrath, deprived of that grace which Adam had received, and which is the life and strength of human nature. Yet as soon as Christ, his Lord and Saviour, came to him, and Mary saluted his own mother, Elizabeth, forthwith the grace of God was given to him, and the original guilt was wiped away from his soul. And therefore it is that we celebrate the nativity of St. John: nothing unholy does the Church celebrate; not St. Peter's, nor St. Paul's, nor St. Augustine's, nor St. Gregory's, nor St. Bernard's, nor St. Aloysius's, nor the nativity of any other Saint, however glorious, because they were all born in sin. She celebrates their conversions, their prerogatives, their martyrdoms, their deaths, their translations, but not their birth, because in no case was it holy. Three nativities alone does she commemorate, our Lord's, His Mother's, and, lastly, St. John's. What a special gift was this, my brethren, separating the Baptist off, and distinguishing him from all prophets and preachers, who ever lived, however holy, except perhaps the prophet Jeremias! And such as was his commencement, was the course of his life. He was carried away by the Spirit into the desert, and there he lived on the simplest fare, in the rudest clothing, in the caves of wild beasts, apart from men, for thirty years, leading a life of mortification and of meditation, till he was called to preach penance, to proclaim the Christ, and to baptize Him; and then having done his work, and having left no act of sin on record, he was laid aside as an instrument which had lost its use, and languished in prison till he was suddenly cut off by the sword of the executioner. Sanctity is the one idea of him impressed upon us from first to last; a most marvellous Saint, a hermit from his childhood, then a preacher to a fallen people, and then a Martyr. Surely such a life fulfils the expectation which the salutation of Mary raised concerning him before his birth. ("Discourses to Mixed Congregations," p. 63.)

ST. JOHN EVANGELIST.

YET still more beautiful, and almost as majestic, is the image of his namesake, that great Apostle, Evangelist, and Prophet of the Church, who came so early into our Lord's chosen company, and lived so long after all his fellows. We can contemplate him in his youth and in his venerable age; and on his whole life, from first to last, as his special gift, is marked purity. He is the virgin Apostle, who on that account was so dear to his Lord, "the disciple whom Jesus loved," who lay on His Bosom, who received His Mother from Him when upon the Cross, who had the vision of all the wonders which were to come to pass in the world to the end of time. "Greatly to be honoured," says the Church, "is blessed John, who on the Lord's Breast lay at supper, to whom, a virgin, did Christ on the Cross commit His Virgin Mother. He was chosen a virgin by the Lord, and was more beloved than the rest. The special prerogative of chastity had made him meet for his Lord's larger love, because being chosen by Him a virgin, a virgin he remained unto the end." He it was who in his youth professed his readiness to drink Christ's chalice with Him, who wore away a long life as a desolate stranger in a foreign land, who was at length carried to Rome, and plunged into the hot oil, and then was banished to a far island until his days drew near their close. ("Discourses to Mixed Congregations," p. 65.)

ST. MARY MAGDALEN.

LOVE is presented to us as the distinguishing grace of those who were sinners before they were saints. . . [and] who . . so fully instances [it] as the woman who "was a sinner," who watered the Lord's feet with her tears, and dried them with her hair, and anointed them with precious ointment? What a time for such an act! She, who had come into the room as if for a festive purpose, to go about an act of penance! It was a formal banquet, given by a rich Pharisee, to honour, yet to try, our Lord. Magdalen came, young and beautiful, and "rejoicing in her youth," "walking in the ways of her heart and the gaze of her eyes:" she came as if to honour that feast, as women were wont to honour such festive doings, with her sweet odours and cool unguents for the forehead and hair of the guests. And he, the proud Pharisee, suffered her to come, so that she touched not him; let her come, as we might suffer inferior animals to enter our apartments, without caring for them; suffered her as a necessary embellishment of the entertainment, yet as having no soul, or as destined to perdition, but any how as nothing to him. He, proud being, and his brethren like him, might "compass sea and land to make one proselyte;" but, as to looking into that proselyte's heart, pitying its sin, and trying to heal it, this did not enter into the circuit of his thoughts. No, he thought only of the necessities of his banquet, and he let her come to do her part, such as it was, careless what her life was, so that she did that part well, and confined herself to it. But, lo, a wondrous sight! was it a sudden inspiration, or a mature resolve? was it an act of the moment, or the result of a long conflict?—but behold, that poor, many-coloured child of guilt approaches to crown with her sweet ointment the head of Him to whom the feast was given; and see, she has stayed her hand. She has looked, and she discerns the Immaculate, the Virgin's Son, "the brightness of the Eternal Light, and the spotless mirror of God's majesty." She looks, and she recognizes the Ancient of Days, the Lord of life and death, her Judge; and again she looks, and she sees in His face and in His mien a beauty, and a sweetness, awful, serene, majestic, more than that of the sons of men, which paled all the splendour of that festive room. Again she looks, timidly yet eagerly, and she discerns in His eye, and in His smile, the loving-kindness, the tenderness, the compassion, the mercy of the Saviour of man. She looks at herself, and oh! how vile, how hideous is she, who but now was so vain of her attractions!—how withered is that comeliness, of which the praises ran through the mouths of her admirers!—how loathsome has become the breath, which hitherto she thought so fragrant, savouring only of those seven bad spirits which dwell within her! And there she would have stayed, there she would have sunk on the earth, wrapped in her confusion and in her despair, had she not cast once glance again on that all-loving, all-forgiving Countenance. He is looking at her: it is the Shepherd looking at the lost sheep, and the lost sheep surrenders herself to Him. He speaks not, but He eyes her; and she draws nearer to Him. Rejoice, ye Angels, she draws near, seeing nothing but Him, and caring neither for the scorn of the proud, nor the jests of the profligate. She draws near, not knowing whether she shall be saved or not, not knowing whether she shall be received, or what will become of her; this only knowing, that He is the Fount of holiness and truth, as of mercy, and to whom should she go, but to Him who hath the words of eternal life? "Destruction is thine own, O Israel; in Me only is thy help. Return unto Me, and I will not turn away My face from thee: for I am holy, and will not be angry for ever." "Behold, we come unto Thee; for Thou art the Lord our God. Truly the hills are false, and the multitude of the mountains: truly the Lord our God is the salvation of Israel." Wonderful meeting between what was most base and what is most pure! Those wanton hands, those polluted lips, have touched, have kissed the feet of the Eternal, and He shrank not from the homage. And as she hung over them, and as she moistened them from her full eyes, how did her love for One so great, yet so gentle, wax vehement within her, lighting up a flame which never was to die from that moment even for ever! and what excess did it reach, when He recorded before all men her forgiveness, and the cause of it! "Many sins are forgiven her, for she loved much; but to whom less is forgiven, the same loveth less. And He said unto her, Thy sins are forgiven thee; thy faith hath made thee safe; go in peace."

Henceforth love was to her, as to St. Augustine and to St. Ignatius Loyola afterwards (great penitents in their own time), as a wound in the soul so full of desire as to become anguish. She could not live out of the presence of Him in whom her joy lay; her spirit languished after Him, when she saw Him not; and waited on Him silently, reverently, wistfully, when she was in His blissful Presence. We read of her, on one occasion, sitting at His feet, and listening to His words; and He testified to her that she had chosen that best part which should not be taken away from her. And, after His resurrection, she, by her perseverance, merited to see Him even before the Apostles. She would not leave the sepulchre, when

Peter and John retired, but stood without, weeping; and when the Lord appeared to her, and held her eyes that she should not know Him, she said piteously to the supposed keeper of the garden, "Tell me where thou hast laid Him, and I will take Him away." And when at length He made Himself known to her, she turned herself, and rushed to embrace His feet, as at the beginning, but He, as if to prove the dutifulness of her love, forbade her: "Touch Me not," He said, "for I have not yet ascended to My Father; but go to My brethren, and say to them, I ascend to My Father and your Father, to My God and your God." And so she was left to long for the time when she should see Him, and hear His voice, and enjoy His smile, and be allowed to minister to Him, for ever in Heaven. ("Discourses to Mixed Congregations," p. 75.)

ST. AUGUSTINE.

LET me speak of another celebrated conquest of God's grace in an after age, and you will see how it pleases Him to make a Confessor, a Saint, a Doctor of His Church, out of sin and heresy both together. It was not enough that the Father of the Western Schools, the author of a thousand works, the triumphant controversialist, the especial champion of grace, should have been once a poor slave of the flesh, but he was the victim of a perverted intellect also. He who, of all others, was to extol the grace of God, was left more than others to experience the helplessness of nature. The great St. Augustine (I am not speaking of the holy missionary of the same name, who came to England and converted our pagan forefathers, and became the first Archbishop of Canterbury, but of the great African Bishop, two centuries before him)—Augustine, I say, not being in earnest about his soul, not asking himself the question, how was sin to be washed away, but rather being desirous, while youth and strength lasted, to enjoy the flesh and the world, ambitious and sensual, judged of truth and falsehood by his private judgment and his private fancy; despised the Catholic Church because it spoke so much of faith and subjection, thought to make his own reason the measure of all things, and accordingly joined a far-spread sect, which affected to be philosophical and enlightened, to take large views of things, and to correct the vulgar, that is, the Catholic notions of God and Christ, of sin, and of the way to heaven. In this sect of his he remained for some years; yet what he was taught there did not satisfy him. It pleased him for a time, and then he found he had been eating for food what had no nourishment in it; he became hungry and thirsty after something more substantial, he knew not what; he despised himself for being a slave to the flesh, and he found his religion did not help him to overcome it; thus he understood that he had not gained the truth, and he cried out, "Oh, who will tell me where to seek it, and who will bring me into it?"

Why did he not join the Catholic Church at once? I have told you why; he saw that truth was nowhere else, but he was not sure it was there. He thought there was something mean, narrow, irrational, in her system of doctrine; he lacked the gift of faith. Then a great conflict began within him,—the conflict of nature with grace; of nature and her children, the flesh and false reason, against conscience and the pleadings of the Divine Spirit, leading him to better things. Though he was still in a state of perdition, yet God was visiting him, and giving him the first fruits of those influences which were in the event to bring him out of it. Time went on; and looking at him, as his Guardian Angel might look at him, you would have said that, in spite of much perverseness, and many a successful struggle against his Almighty Adversary, in spite of his still being, as before, in a state of wrath, nevertheless grace was making way in his soul,—he was advancing towards the Church. He did not know it himself, he could not recognize it himself; but an eager interest in him, and then a joy, was springing up in heaven among the Angels of God. At last he came within the range of a great Saint in a foreign country; and, though he pretended not to acknowledge him, his attention was arrested by him, and he could not help coming to sacred places to look at him again and again. He began to watch him and speculate about him, and wondered with himself whether he was happy. He found himself frequently in church, listening to the holy preacher, and he once asked his advice how to find what he was seeking. And now a final conflict came on him with the flesh: it was hard, very hard, to part with the indulgences of years, it was hard to part and never to meet again. Oh, sin was so sweet, how could he bid it farewell? how could he tear himself away from its embrace, and betake himself to that lonely and dreary way which led heavenwards? but God's grace was sweeter far, and it convinced him while it won him; it convinced his reason, and prevailed;—and he who without it would have lived and died a child of Satan, became under its wonder-working power, an oracle of sanctity and truth. ("Discourses to Mixed Congregations," p. 53.)

ST. PHILIP NERI.

MY own special Father and Patron, St. Philip Neri, lived in an age as traitorous to the interests of Catholicism as any that preceded it, or can follow it. He lived at a time when pride mounted high, and the senses held rule; a time when kings and nobles never had more of state and homage, and never less of personal responsibility and peril; when mediæval winter was receding, and the summer sun of civilization was bringing into leaf and flower a thousand forms of luxurious enjoyment; when a new world of thought and beauty had opened upon the human mind, in the discovery of the treasures of classic literature and art. He saw the great and the gifted, dazzled by the Enchantress, and drinking in the magic of her song; he saw the high and the wise, the student and the artist, painting, and poetry, and sculpture, and music, and architecture, drawn within her range, and circling round the abyss: he saw heathen forms mounting thence, and forming in the thick air:—all this he saw, and he perceived that the mischief was to be met, not with argument, not with science, not with protests and warnings, not by the recluse or the preacher, but by means of the great counter-fascination of purity and truth. He was raised up to do a work almost peculiar in the Church,—not to be a Jerome Savonarola, though Philip had a true devotion towards him and a tender memory of his Florentine house; not to be a St. Charles, though in his beaming countenance Philip had recognized the aureol of a saint; not to be a St. Ignatius, wrestling with the foe, though Philip was termed the Society's bell of call, so many subjects did he send to it ; not to be a St. Francis Xavier, though Philip had longed to shed his blood for Christ in India with him; not to be a St. Caietan, or hunter of souls, for Philip preferred, as he expressed it, tranquilly to cast in his net to gain them ; he preferred to yield to the stream, and direct the current, which he could not stop, of science, literature, art, and fashion, and to sweeten and to sanctify what God had made very good and man had spoilt.

And so he contemplated as the idea of his mission, not the propagation of the faith, nor the exposition of doctrine, nor the catechetical schools ; whatever was exact and systematic pleased him not ; he put from him monastic rule and authoritative speech, as David refused the armour of his king. No; he would be but an ordinary individual priest as others: and his weapons should be but unaffected humility and unpretending love. All he did was to be done by the light, and fervour, and convincing eloquence of his personal character and his easy conversation. He came to the Eternal City and he sat himself down there, and his home and his family gradually grew up around him, by the spontaneous accession of materials from without. He did not so much seek his own as draw them to him. He sat in his small room, and they in their gay worldly dresses, the rich and the well-born, as well as the simple and the illiterate, crowded into it. In the mid-heats of summer, in the frosts of winter, still was he in that low and narrow cell at San Girolamo, reading the hearts of those who came to him, and curing their souls' maladies by the very touch of his hand. It was a vision of the Magi worshipping the infant Saviour, so pure and innocent, so sweet and beautiful was he; and so loyal and so dear to the gracious Virgin Mother. And they who came remained gazing and listening, till at length, first one and then another threw off their bravery, and took his poor cassock and girdle instead : or, if they kept it, it was to put haircloth under it, or to take on them a rule of life, while to the world they looked as before.

In the words of his biographer, "he was all things to all men. He suited himself to noble and ignoble, young and old, subjects and prelates, learned and ignorant; and received those who were strangers to him with singular benignity, and embraced them with as much love and charity as if he had been a long while expecting them. When he was called upon to be merry, he was so; if there was a demand upon his sympathy, he was equally ready. He gave the same welcome to all: caressing the poor equally with the rich, and wearying himself to assist all to the utmost limits of his power. In consequence of his being so accessible and willing to receive all comers, many went to him every day, and some continued for the space of thirty, nay forty years, to visit him very often both morning and evening, so that his room went by the agreeable nickname of the Home of Christian mirth. Nay, people came to him, not only from all parts of Italy, but from France, Spain, Germany, and all Christendom; and even the infidels and Jews, who had ever any communication with him, revered him as a holy man."[1] The first families of Rome, the Massimi, the Aldobrandini, the Colonnas, the Altieri, the Vitelleschi, were his friends and his penitents. Nobles of Poland, Grandees of Spain,

[1] Bacci, vol. I. p. 192; II. p. 98.

Knights of Malta, could not leave Rome without coming to him. Cardinals, Archbishops, and Bishops were his intimates; Federigo **Borromeo** haunted his room and got the name of "Father Philip's soul." The Cardinal-Archbishops of Verona and Bologna wrote books in his honour. Pope Pius the Fourth died in his arms. Lawyers, painters, musicians, physicians, it was the same too with them. Baronius, Zazzara, and Ricci, left the law at his bidding, and joined his congregation, to do its work, to write the annals of the Church, and to die in the odour of sanctity. Palestrina had Father Philip's ministrations in his last moments. Animuccia hung about him during life, sent him a message after death, and was conducted by him through Purgatory to Heaven. And who was he, I say, all the while, but an humble priest, a stranger in Rome, with no distinction of family or letters, no claim of station or of office, great simply in the attraction with which a Divine Power had gifted him? and yet thus humble, thus unennobled, thus empty-handed, he has achieved the glorious title of Apostle of Rome. ("Idea of a University," p. 234.)

MATER DEI.

MERE Protestants have seldom any real perception of the doctrine of God and man in one Person. They speak in a dreamy, shadowy way of Christ's divinity; but, when their meaning is sifted, you will find them very slow to commit themselves to any statement sufficient to express the Catholic dogma. They will tell you at once, that the subject is not to be enquired into, for that it is impossible to enquire into it at all, without being technical and subtle. Then when they comment on the Gospels, they will speak of Christ, not simply and consistently as God, but as a being made up of God and man, partly one and partly the other, or between both, or as a man inhabited by a special divine presence. Sometimes they even go on to deny that He was the Son of God in heaven, saying that He became the Son when He was conceived of the Holy Ghost; and they are shocked, and think it a mark both of reverence and good sense to be shocked, when they hear the Man spoken of simply and plainly as God. They cannot bear to have it said, except as a figure or mode of speaking, that God had a human body, or that God suffered; they think that the "Atonement," and "Sanctification through the Spirit," as they speak, is the sum and substance of the Gospel, and they are shy of any dogmatic expression which goes beyond them. Such, I believe, is the ordinary character of the Protestant notions among us on the divinity of Christ, whether among members of the Anglican communion, or dissenters from it, excepting a small remnant of them.

Now, if you would witness against these unchristian opinions, if you would bring out, distinctly and beyond mistake and evasion, the simple idea of the Catholic Church that God is man, could you do it better than by laying down in St. John's words that "God *became* man"? and could you express this again more emphatically and unequivocally than by declaring that He was *born* a man, or that He had a *Mother?* The world allows that God *is* man; the admission costs it little, for God is everywhere, and (as it may say) is everything; but it shrinks from confessing that God is the Son of Mary. It shrinks, for it is at once confronted with a severe fact, which violates and shatters its own unbelieving view of things; the revealed doctrine forthwith takes its true shape, and receives an historical reality; and the Almighty is introduced into His own world at a certain time and in a definite way. Dreams are broken and shadows depart; the divine truth is no longer a poetical expression, or a devotional exaggeration, or a mystical economy, or a mythical representation. "Sacrifice and offering," the shadows of the Law, "Thou wouldest not, but a body hast Thou fitted to Me." "That which was from the beginning, which we have heard, which we have seen with our eyes, which we have diligently looked upon, and our hands have handled," "That which we have seen and have heard, declare we unto you;"—such is the record of the Apostle, in opposition to those "spirits" which denied that "Jesus Christ had appeared in the flesh," and which "dissolved" Him by denying either His human nature or His divine. And the confession that Mary is *Deipara*, or the Mother of God is that safeguard wherewith we seal up and secure the doctrine of the Apostle from all evasion, and that test whereby we detect all the pretences of those bad spirits of "Antichrist which have gone out into the world." It declares that He is God; it implies that He is man; it suggests to us that He is God still, though He has become man, and that He is true man though He is God. By witnessing to the *process* of the union, it secures the reality of the two *subjects* of the union, of the divinity and of the manhood. If Mary is the Mother of God, Christ is understood to be Emmanuel, God with us. And hence it was, that, when time went on, and the bad spirits and false prophets grew stronger and bolder and found a way into the Catholic body itself, then the Church, guided by God, could find no more effectual and sure way of expelling them than that of using this word *Deipara* against them; and, on the other hand, when they came up again from the realms of darkness, and plotted the utter overthrow of Christian faith in the sixteenth century, then they could find no more certain expedient for their hateful purpose than that of reviling and blaspheming the prerogatives of Mary, for they knew full sure that, if they could once get the world to dishonour the Mother, the dishonour of the Son would follow close. The Church and Satan agreed together in this, that Son and Mother went together; and the experience of three centuries has confirmed their testimony; for Catholics who have honoured the Mother still worship the Son, while Protestants, who now have ceased to confess the Son, began then by scoffing at the Mother. ("Discourses to Mixed Congregations," p. 346.)

MATER PURISSIMA.

MARY has been made more glorious in her person than in her office; her purity is a higher gift than her relationship to God. This is what is implied in Christ's answer to the woman in the crowd, who cried out, when He was preaching, "Blessed is the womb that bare Thee, and the breasts which Thou hast sucked." He replied by pointing out to His disciples a higher blessedness; "Yea, rather blessed," He said, "are they who hear the word of God and keep it." . . Protestants take these words in disparagement of our Lady's greatness, but they really tell the other way. For consider them; He lays down a principle, that it is more blessed to keep His commandments than to be His Mother; but who even of Protestants will say that she did *not* keep His commandments? She kept them surely, and our Lord does but say that such obedience was in a higher line of privilege than her being His Mother; she was more blessed in her detachment from creatures, in her devotion to God, in her virginal purity, in her fulness of grace, than in her maternity. This is the constant teaching of the Holy Fathers: "More blessed was Mary," says St. Augustine, "in receiving Christ's faith, than in conceiving Christ's flesh;" and St. Chrysostom declares, that she would not have been blessed, though she had borne Him in the body, had she not heard the word of God and kept it. This of course is an impossible case; for she was made holy, that she might be made His Mother, and the two blessednesses cannot be divided. She who was chosen to supply flesh and blood to the Eternal Word, was first filled with grace in soul and body; still, she had a double blessedness, of office and of qualification for it, and the latter was the greater. And it is on this account that the Angel calls her blessed; "*Full of grace,*" he says, "blessed among women;" and St. Elizabeth also, when she cries out, "Blessed thou that hast *believed.*" Nay, she herself bears a like testimony, when the Angel announced to her the favour which was coming on her. Though all Jewish women in each successive age had been hoping to be Mother of the Christ, so that marriage was honourable among them, celibacy a reproach, she alone had put aside the desire and the thought of so great a dignity. She alone, who was to bear the Christ, all but refused to bear Him; He stooped to her, she turned from Him; and why? because she had been inspired, the first of womankind, to dedicate her virginity to God, and she did not welcome a privilege which seemed to involve a forfeiture of her vow. How shall this be, she asked, seeing I am separate from man? Nor, till the Angel told her that the conception would be miraculous and from the Holy Ghost, did she put aside her "trouble" of mind, recognize him securely as God's messenger, and bow her head in awe and thankfulness to God's condescension.

Mary then is a specimen, and more than a specimen, in the purity of her soul and body, of what man was before his fall, and what he would have been, had he risen to his full perfection. It had been hard, it had been a victory for the Evil One, had the whole race passed away, nor any one instance in it occurred to show what the Creator had intended it to be in its original state. Adam, you know, was created in the image and after the likeness of God; his frail and imperfect nature, stamped with a divine seal, was supported and exalted by an indwelling of divine grace. Impetuous passion did not exist in him, except as a latent element and a possible evil; ignorance was dissipated by the clear light of the Spirit; and reason, sovereign over every motion of his soul, was simply subjected to the will of God. Nay, even his body was preserved from every wayward appetite and affection, and was promised immortality instead of dissolution. Thus he was in a supernatural state; and, had he not sinned, year after year would he have advanced in merit and grace, and in God's favour, till he passed from paradise to heaven. But he fell; and his descendants were born in his likeness; and the world grew worse instead of better, and judgment after judgment cut off generations of sinners in vain, and improvement was hopeless, "because man was flesh," and "the thoughts of his heart were bent upon evil at all times." But a remedy had been determined in heaven; a Redeemer was at hand; God was about to do a great work, and he purposed to do it suitably; "where sin abounded, grace was to abound more." Kings of the earth, when they have sons born to them, forthwith scatter some large bounty, or raise some high memorial; they honour the day, or the place, or the heralds of the auspicious event, with some corresponding mark of favour; nor did the coming of Emmanuel innovate on the world's established custom. It was a season of grace and prodigy, and these were to be exhibited in a special manner in the person of His Mother. The course of ages was to be reversed; the tradition of evil was to be broken; a gate of light was to be opened amid the darkness, for the coming of the Just;—a Virgin conceived and bore Him. It was fitting, for His honour and glory, that she, who was the instrument of His bodily presence, should first be a miracle of His grace; it was fitting that she should triumph, where Eve had failed, and should "bruise the serpent's head" by the spotlessness of her sanctity. In some respects, indeed, the curse was not reversed; Mary came into a fallen world, and resigned herself to its laws; she, as also the Son she bore, was exposed to pain of soul and body; she was subjected to death; but she was not put under the power of sin. As grace was infused into Adam from the first moment of his creation, so that he never had experience of his natural poverty, till sin reduced him to it; so was grace given from the first in still ampler measure to Mary, and she never incurred, in fact, Adam's deprivation. She began where others end, whether in knowledge or in love. She was from the first clothed in sanctity, sealed for perseverance, luminous and glorious in God's sight, and incessantly employed in meritorious acts, which continued till her last breath. Hers was emphatically "the path of the just, which, as the shining light, goeth forward and increaseth even to the perfect day;" and sinlessness in thought, word, and deed, in small things as well as great, in venial matter as well as grievous, is surely but the natural and obvious sequel of such a beginning. If Adam might have kept himself from sin in his first state, much more shall we expect immaculate perfection in Mary. ("Discourses to Mixed Congregations," p. 351.)

REFUGIUM PECCATORUM.

SUCH is her prerogative of sinless perfection, and it is, as her maternity, for the sake of Emmanuel; hence she answered the angel's salutation "*Gratia plena,*" with the humble acknowledgment, *Ecce ancilla Domini,* "Behold the handmaid of the Lord." And like to this is her third prerogative, which follows both from her maternity and from her purity, and which I will mention as completing the enumeration of her glories. I mean her intercessory power. For if "God heareth not sinners, but if a man be a worshipper of Him and do His will, him He heareth;" if "the continual prayer of a just man availeth much;" if faithful Abraham was required to pray for Abimelech, "for he was a prophet;" if patient Job was to "pray for his friends," for he had "spoken right things before God;" if meek Moses, by lifting up his hands, turned the battle in favour of Israel, against Amalec; why should we wonder at hearing that Mary, the only spotless child of Adam's seed, has a transcendent influence with the God of grace? And if the Gentiles at Jerusalem sought Philip, because he was an apostle, when they desired access to Jesus, and Philip spoke to Andrew, as still more closely in our Lord's confidence, and then both came to Him, is it strange that the Mother should have power with the Son, distinct in kind from that of the purest angel and the most triumphant saint? If we have faith to admit the Incarnation itself, we must admit it in its fulness; why then should we start at the gracious appointments which arise out of it, or are necessary to it, or are included in it? If the Creator comes on earth in the form of a servant and a creature, why may not his Mother on the other hand rise to be the Queen of heaven, and be clothed with the sun, and have the moon under her feet? ("Discourses to Mixed Congregations," p. 355.)

SINE LABE ORIGINALI CONCEPTA.

WE should be prepared . . to believe that the Mother of God is full of grace and glory, from the very fitness of such a dispensation, even though we had not been taught it; and this fitness will appear still more clear and certain when we contemplate the subject more steadily. Consider, then, that it has been the ordinary rule of God's dealings with us, that personal sanctity should be the attendant upon high spiritual dignity of place or work. The angels, who, as the word imports, are God's messengers, are also perfect in holiness; "without sanctity no one shall see God;" no defiled thing can enter the courts of heaven; and the higher its inhabitants are advanced in their ministry about the throne, the holier are they, and the more absorbed in their contemplation of that Holiness upon which they wait. The Seraphim, who immediately surround the Divine Glory, cry day and night, "Holy,

Holy, Holy, Lord God of Hosts." So is it also on earth; the prophets have ordinarily not only gifts, but graces; they are not only inspired to know and to teach God's will, but inwardly converted to obey it. For surely those only can preach the truth duly, who feel it personally; those only transmit it fully from God to man, who have in the transmission made it their own.

I do not say that there are no exceptions to this rule, but they admit of an easy explanation; I do not say that it never pleases Almighty God to convey any intimation of His will through bad men; of course, for all things can be made to serve Him. By all, even the wicked, He accomplishes His purposes, and by the wicked He is glorified. Our Lord's death was brought about by His enemies, who did His will, while they thought they were gratifying their own. Caiaphas, who contrived and effected it, was made use of to predict it. Balaam prophesied good of God's people in an earlier age, by a divine compulsion, when he wished to prophesy evil. This is true; but in such cases Divine Mercy is plainly overruling the evil, and manifesting his power, without recognizing or sanctioning the instrument. And again, it is true, as He tell us Himself, that in the last day "Many shall say, Lord, Lord, have we not prophesied in Thy Name, and in Thy Name cast out devils, and done many miracles?" and that He shall answer, "I never knew you." This, I say, is undeniable; it is undeniable first, that those who have prophesied in God's Name may *afterwards* fall from God, and lose their souls. Let a man be ever so holy now, he may fall away; and, as present grace is no pledge of perseverance, much less are present gifts; but how does this show that gifts and graces do not commonly go together? Again, it is undeniable that those who have had miraculous gifts may nevertheless have *never* been in God's favour, not even when they exercised them; as I will explain presently. But I am now speaking, not of having gifts, but of being prophets. To be a prophet is something much more personal than to possess gifts. It is a sacred office, it implies a mission, and is the high distinction, not of the enemies of God, but of His friends. Such is the Scripture rule. Who was the first prophet and preacher of justice? Enoch, who walked "by faith," and "pleased God," and was taken from a rebellious world. Who was the second? "Noe," who "condemned the world, and was made heir of the justice which is through faith." Who was the next great prophet? Moses, the lawgiver of the chosen people, who was the "meekest of all men who dwell on the earth." Samuel comes next, who served the Lord from his infancy in the Temple; and then David, who, if he fell into sin, repented, and was "a man after God's heart." And in like manner Job, Elias, Isaias, Jeremias, Daniel, and above them all St. John Baptist, and then again St. Peter, St. Paul, St. John, and the rest, are all especial instances of heroic virtue, and patterns to their brethren. Judas is the exception, but this was by a particular dispensation to enhance our Lord's humiliation and suffering.

Nature itself witnesses to this connection between sanctity and truth. It anticipates that the fountain from which pure doctrine comes should itself be pure; that the seat of divine teaching, and the oracle of faith, should be the abode of angels; that the consecrated home, in which the word of God is elaborated, and whence it issues forth for the salvation of the many, should be holy as that word is holy. Here you see the difference of the office of a prophet and a mere gift, such as that of miracles. Miracles are the simple and direct work of God; the worker of them is but an instrument or organ. And in consequence he need not be holy, because he has not, strictly speaking, a share in the work. So again the power of administering the Sacraments, which also is supernatural and miraculous, does not imply personal holiness; nor is there anything surprising in God's giving to a bad man this gift, or the gift of miracles, any more than in His giving him any natural talent or gift, strength or agility of frame, eloquence, or medical skill. It is otherwise with the office of preaching and prophesying, and to this I have been referring; for the truth first goes into the minds of the speakers, and is apprehended and fashioned there, and then comes out from them as, in one sense, its source and its parent. The divine word is begotten in them, and the offspring has their features and tells of them. They are not like "the dumb animal, speaking with man's voice," on which Balaam rode, a mere instrument of God's word, but they have "received an unction from the Holy One, and they know all things," and "where the Spirit of the Lord is, there is liberty;" and while they deliver what they have received, they enforce what they feel and know. "We have *known and believed*," says St. John, "the charity which God hath to us."

So has it been all through the history of the Church; Moses does not write as David; nor Isaias as Jeremias; nor St. John as St. Paul. And so of the great Doctors of the Church, St. Athanasius, St. Augustine, St. Ambrose, St. Leo, St. Thomas, each has his own manner, each speaks his own words, though he speaks the while the words of God. They speak from themselves, they speak in their own persons, they speak from the heart, from their own experience, with their own arguments, with their own deductions, with their own modes of expression. Now can you fancy such hearts, such feelings to be unholy? how could it be so, without defiling, and thereby nullifying, the word of God? If one drop of corruption makes the purest water worthless, as the slightest savour of bitterness spoils the most delicate viands, how can it be that the word of truth and holiness can proceed profitably from impure lips and an earthly heart? No, as is the tree, so is the fruit; "beware of false prophets," says our Lord; and then He adds, "from their fruits ye shall know them. Do men gather grapes of thorns, or figs of thistles?" Is it not so, my brethren? Which of you would go to ask counsel of another, however learned, however gifted, however aged, if you thought him unholy? nay, though you feel and are sure, as far as absolution goes, that a bad priest could give it as really as a holy priest, yet for advice, for comfort, for instruction, you would not go to one whom you did not respect. "Out of the abundance of the heart, the mouth speaketh;" "a good man out of the good treasure of his heart bringeth good. and an evil man out of the evil treasure bringeth forth evil."

So then is it in the case of the soul; and so is it with the body also; as the offspring of holiness is holy in the instance of spiritual births, so is it in the instance of physical. The child is like the parent. Mary was no mere instrument in God's dispensation; the word of God did not merely come to her and go from her; He did not merely pass through her, as He may pass through us in Holy Communion; it was no heavenly body which the Eternal Son assumed, fashioned by the Angels, and brought down to this lower world: no; He imbibed, He sucked up her blood and her substance into His Divine Person; He became man of her; and received her lineaments and her features, as the appearance and character under which He should manifest Himself to the world.

He was known doubtless, by His likeness to her, to be her Son. Thus His Mother is the first of Prophets, for of her came the Word bodily; she is the sole oracle of Truth, for the Way, the Truth, and the Life, vouchsafed to be her Son; she is the one mould of Divine Wisdom, and in that mould it was indelibly cast. Surely then, if "the first fruit be holy, the mass also is holy; and if the root be holy, so are the branches." It was natural, it was fitting, that so it should be; it was congruous that, whatever the Omnipotent could work in the person of the finite, should be wrought in her. I say, if the Prophets must be holy, "to whom the word of God comes," what shall we say of her, who was so specially favoured, that the true and substantial Word, and not His shadow or His voice, was not merely made in her, but born of her? who was not merely the organ of God's message, but the origin of His human existence, the living fountain from which He drew His most precious blood, and the material of His most holy flesh? Was it not fitting, beseemed it not, that the Eternal Father should prepare her for this ministration by some pre-eminent sanctification? Do not earthly parents act thus by their children? do they put them out to strangers? do they commit them to any chance person to suckle them? Shall even careless parents show a certain tenderness and solicitude in this matter, and shall not God himself show it, when He commits His Eternal Word to the custody of man? It was to be expected then that, if the Son was God, the Mother should be as worthy of Him, as creature can be worthy of Creator; that grace should have in her its "perfect work;" that, if she bore the Eternal Wisdom, she should be that created wisdom in whom "is all the grace of the Way and the Truth;" that if she was the Mother of "fair love, and fear, and knowledge, and holy hope," "she should give an odour like cinnamon and balm, and sweetness like to choice myrrh." Can we set bounds to the holiness of her who was the Mother of the Holiest?

Such, then, is the truth ever cherished in the deep heart of the Church, and witnessed by the keen apprehension of her children, that no limits but those proper to a creature can be assigned to the sanctity of Mary. Did Abraham believe that a son should be born to him of his aged wife? then Mary's faith was greater when she accepted Gabriel's message. Did Judith consecrate her widowhood to God to the surprise of her people? much more did Mary, from her first youth, devote her virginity. Did Samuel, when a child, inhabit the Temple, secluded from the world? Mary, too, was by her parents lodged in the same holy precincts, at the age when children begin to choose between good and evil. Was Solomon on his birth called "dear to the Lord?" and shall not the destined Mother of God be dear to Him, from the moment she was born? But further still; St. John Baptist was sanctified by the Spirit before his birth; shall Mary be only equal to him? is it not fitting that her privilege should surpass his? is it wonderful, if grace, which anticipated his birth by three months, should in her case run up to the very first moment of her being, outstrip the imputation of sin, and be beforehand with the usurpation of Satan? Mary must surpass all the Saints; the very fact that certain privileges are known to have been theirs, proves to us at once, from the necessity of the case, that she had the same and higher.
[1] Her conception then was immaculate, in order that she

---

[1] [On this subject see the Letter to Dr. Pusey, which now forms Part II. of "Anglican Difficulties." I subjoin an extract from it :—" It is to me a most strange phenomenon that so many learned and devout men stumble at this doctrine ; and I can only account for it by supposing that in matter of fact they do not know what we mean

might surpass all Saints in the date as well the fulness of her sanctification. ("Discourses to Mixed Congregations," p. 365.)

by the Immaculate Conception... It has no reference whatever to her parents, but simply to her own person; it does but affirm, that together with the nature she inherited from her own parents, that is, her own nature, she had a superadded fulness of grace, and that from the first moment of her existence... But it may be said, How does this enable us to say that she was conceived without *original sin?* If Anglicans knew what we mean by original sin, they would not ask the question. Our doctrine of original sin is not the same as the Protestant doctrine. 'Original sin,' with us, cannot be called sin, in the mere ordinary sense of the word 'sin;' it is a term denoting Adam's sin as transferred to us, or the state to which Adam's sin reduces his children; but by Protestants it seems to be understood as sin, in much the same sense as actual sin. We, with the Fathers, think of it as something negative, Protestants as something positive. Protestants hold that it is a disease, a radical change of nature, an active poison internally corrupting the soul, infecting its primary elements, and disorganizing it; and they fancy that we ascribe a different nature from ours to the Blessed Virgin, different from that of her parents, and from that of fallen Adam. We hold nothing of the kind; we consider that in Adam she died, as others; that she was included, together with the whole race, in Adam's sentence; that she incurred his debt, as we do; but that, for the sake of Him who was to redeem her and us upon the Cross, to her the debt was remitted by anticipation, on her the sentence was not carried out, except indeed as regards her natural death, for she died when her time came, as others. All this we teach, but we deny that she had original sin; for by original sin we mean, as I have already said, something negative, viz. this only, the *deprivation* of that supernatural unmerited grace which Adam and Eve had on their first formation,—deprivation and the consequences of deprivation. Mary could not merit, any more than they, the restoration of that grace; but it was restored to her by God's free bounty, from the very first moment of her existence, and thereby, in fact, she never came under the original curse, which consisted in the loss of it. And she had this special privilege, in order to fit her to become the Mother of her and our Redeemer, to fit her mentally, spiritually for it; so that, by the aid of the first grace, she

MARIA ASSUMPTA.

IT was surely fitting, it was becoming, that she should be taken up into heaven and not lie in the grave till Christ's second coming, who had passed a life of sanctity and of miracles such as hers. All the works of God are in a beautiful harmony; they are carried on to the end as they begin. This is the difficulty which men of the world find in believing miracles at all; they think these break the order and consistency of God's visible world, not knowing that they do but subserve to a higher order of things, and introduce a supernatural perfection. But at least, when one miracle is wrought, it may be expected to draw others after it for the completion of what is begun. Miracles must be wrought for some great end; and if the course of things fell back again into a natural order before its termination, how could we but feel a disappointment? and if we were told that this certainly was to be, how could we but judge the information improbable and difficult to believe? Now this applies to the history of our Lady. I say, it would be a greater miracle, if, her life being what it was, her death was like that of other men, than if it were such as to correspond to her life. Who can conceive that God should so repay the debt, which He condescended to owe to His Mother, for the elements of His human Body, as to allow the flesh and blood

might so grow in grace, that, when the Angel came and her Lord was at hand, she might be 'full of grace,' prepared as far as a creature could be prepared, to receive Him into her bosom." ("Anglican Difficulties," p. 396.)]

from which It was taken to moulder in the grave? Do the sons of men thus deal with their mothers? do they not nourish and sustain them in their feebleness, and keep them in life while they are able? Or who can conceive that that virginal frame, which never sinned, was to undergo the death of a sinner? Why should she share the curse of Adam, who had no share in his fall? "Dust thou art, and into dust thou shalt return," was the sentence upon sin; she then, who was not a sinner, fitly never saw corruption. She died then because even our Lord and Saviour died; she died, as she suffered, because she was in this world, because she was in a state of things in which suffering and death are the rule. She lived under their external sway; and, as she obeyed Cæsar by coming for enrolment to Bethlehem, so did she, when God willed it, yield to the tyranny of death, and was dissolved into soul and body, as well as others. But though she died as well as others, she died not as others die; for, through the merits of her Son, by whom she was what she was, by the grace of Christ which in her had anticipated sin, which had filled her with light, which had purified her flesh from all defilement, she had been saved from disease and malady, and all that weakens and decays the bodily frame. Original sin had not been found in her, by the wear of her senses, and the waste of her frame, and the decrepitude of years, propagating death. She died, but her death was a mere fact, not an effect; and, when it was over, it ceased to be. She died that she might live; she died as a matter of form or (as I may call it) a ceremony, in order to fulfil, what is called, the debt of nature, —not primarily for herself or because of sin, but to submit herself to her condition, to glorify God, to do what her Son did; not however as her Son and Saviour, with any suffering for any special end; not with a martyr's death, for her martyrdom had been in living; not as an atonement, for man could not make it, and One had made it and made it for all; but in order to finish her course, and to receive her crown.

And therefore she died in private. It became Him who died for the world, to die in the world's sight; it became the Great Sacrifice to be lifted up on high, as a light that could not be hid. But she, the lily of Eden, who had always dwelt out of the sight of man, fittingly did she die in the garden's shade, and amid the sweet flowers in which she had lived. Her departure made no noise in the world. The Church went about her common duties, preaching, converting, suffering; there were persecutions, there was fleeing from place to place, there were martyrs, there were triumphs; at length the rumour spread abroad that the Mother of God was no longer upon earth. Pilgrims went to and fro; they sought for her relics, but they found them not; did she die at Ephesus? or did she die at Jerusalem? reports varied; but her tomb could not be pointed out, or if it was found, it was open; and instead of her pure and fragrant body, there was a growth of lilies from the earth which she had touched. So, enquirers went home marvelling, and waiting for further light. And then it was said how that when her dissolution was at hand, and her soul was to pass in triumph before the judgment-seat of her Son, the Apostles were suddenly gathered together in one place, even in the Holy City, to bear part in the joyful ceremonial; how that they buried her with fitting rites; how that the third day, when they came to the tomb, they found it empty, and angelic choirs with their glad voices were heard singing day and night the glories of their risen Queen. But, however we feel towards the details of this history (nor is there anything in it which will be unwelcome or difficult to piety), so much cannot be doubted, from the consent of the whole Catholic world and the revelations made to holy souls, that, as is befitting, she is, soul and body, with her Son and God in heaven, and that we are enabled to celebrate, not only her death, but her Assumption. (Discourses to Mixed Congregations, p. 375.)

GROWTH OF THE CULTUS OF MARY.

ONE word more, and I have done; I have shown you how full of meaning are the truths themselves which the Church teaches concerning the Most Blessed Virgin, and now consider how full of meaning also has been the Church's dispensation of them.

You will find, then, in this respect, as in Mary's prerogatives themselves, there is the same careful reference to the glory of Him who gave them to her. You know, when first He went out to preach, she kept apart from Him; she interfered not with His work; and even when He was gone up on high, yet she, a woman, went not out to preach or teach, she seated not herself in the Apostolic chair, she took no part in the Priest's office; she did but humbly seek her Son in the daily Mass of those, who, though her ministers in heaven, were her superiors in the Church on earth. Nor, when she and they had left this lower scene, and she was a Queen upon her Son's right hand, not even then did she ask of Him to publish her name to the ends of the world, or to hold her up to the world's gaze, but she remained waiting for the time when her own glory should be necessary for His. He indeed had been from the very first proclaimed by Holy Church, and enthroned in His temple, for He was God; ill had it beseemed the living Oracle of Truth to have withholden from the faithful the very object of their adoration; but it was otherwise with Mary. It became her, as a creature, a mother, and a woman, to stand aside and make way for the Creator, to minister to her Son, and to win her way into the world's homage by sweet and gracious persuasion. So when His Name was dishonoured, then it was that she did Him service; when Emmanuel was denied, then the Mother of God (as it were) came forward; when heretics said that God was not incarnate, then was the time for her own honours. And then, when as much as this had been accomplished, she had done with strife; she fought not for herself. No fierce controversy, no persecuted confessors, no heresiarch, no anathema, marks the history of her manifestation; as she had increased day by day in grace and merit, while the world knew not of it, so has she raised herself aloft silently, and has grown into her place in the Church by a tranquil influence and a natural process. It was as some fair tree, stretching forth her fruitful branches and her fragrant leaves, and overshadowing the territory of the Saints. And thus the Antiphon speaks of her; "Let thy dwelling be in Jacob, and thine inheritance in Israel, and *strike thy roots* in My elect." Again, "And so in Sion was I established, and in the holy city I likewise rested, and in Jerusalem was my power. And I *took root* in an honourable people, and in the glorious company of the Saints was I *detained*. I was exalted like a cedar in Lebanus, and as a cypress in Mount Sion; I have stretched out My branches as the terebinth, and My branches are of honour and of grace." Thus was she reared without hands, and gained a modest victory, and exerts a gentle sway, which she has not claimed. When dispute arose about her among her children, she hushed it;

when objections were urged against her, she waived her claims and waited; till now, in this very day, should God so will, she will win at length her most radiant crown, and, without opposing voice, and amid the jubilation of the whole Church, she will be hailed as immaculate in her conception.[1]

Such art thou, Holy Mother, in the creed and in the worship of the Church, the defence of many truths, the grace and smiling light of every devotion. In thee, O Mary, is fulfilled, as we can bear it, an original purpose of the Most High. He once had meant to come on earth in heavenly glory, but we sinned; and then He could not safely visit us, except with shrouded radiance and a bedimmed majesty, for He was God. So He came Himself in weakness, not in power; and He sent thee a creature in His stead, with a creature's comeliness and lustre suited to our state. And now thy very face and form, dear Mother, speak to us of the Eternal; not like earthly beauty, dangerous to look upon, but like the morning star, which is thy emblem, bright and musical, breathing purity, telling of heaven, and infusing peace. O harbinger of day! O hope of the pilgrim! lead us still as thou hast led; in the dark night, across the bleak wilderness, guide us on to our Lord Jesus, guide us home.

> Maria, mater gratiæ,
> Dulcis parens clementiæ,
> Tu nos ab hoste protege
> Et mortis horâ suscipe.

("Discourses to Mixed Congregations," p. 357.)

---

[1] Since this Sermon was published, 1849, the Immaculate Conception of the Blessed Virgin has been made a dogma of the Church.

INDEX.

A.

	PAGE
Abelard	182
Adam, state of, in Paradise	421
Alexandrian School, the influence of, on Dr. Newman	19
Alison's History of Europe, quoted	88
Alphonso Liguori, St., his Sermons	53
—— on "*probable opinion*," in administering a Sacrament	263
Angels, the	20, 81
Anglicans, and Monophysites, parallel between	44
—— and Semi-Arians, parallel between	50
—— and the "Branch Theory"	252
—— Invincible Ignorance among	313
Anglican Church, the, seen from without	62, 254
—— Orders	258
—— Clergy, the, and the Eucharist	67
—— Ordinances	271
—— view of the visible Church	250
—— paradox, the	254
Anglican, argument from differences among Catholics, the	304
—— objections from Antiquity	306
Anglicanism and Catholicism	319
Anglo-Catholic, or Patristico-Protestant?	294
Apostolical Succession, the	266
—— not an Anglican tradition	67
"Arians of the Fourth Century," the	18
Army, a Constitutional	153
Assumption of Our Lady, the	432
Atheism and Catholicity, no logical medium between	57, 338
Athens	167

B.

Bacon, his mission	120
—— his moral littleness	121
Bede, St., the death of	179
Benediction of the Blessed Sacrament	366, 359
Benedict, St., his rule	175
Benedict XIV., quoted	263
"Bible Religion"	225

	PAGE
Bishop, Dr. Newman's obedience to his	30
Bishops, the Anglican, charge against Dr. Newman	51
—— have for three centuries lived and died in heresy	262
—— shudder at assuming real episcopal power	265
—— have lost the habit of blessing	289
—— are wont to be valiant towards the submissive	293
Bishopric, the Jerusalem	51
Blomfield, Bp., dilutes the high orthodoxy of the Establishment	21
—— on the Apostolical Succession	21
Bowden, John William	10
—— his life of St. Gregory VII., quoted	188
"Branch Theory," the	252
Bunyan, John, his last words	280
Busenbaum, on involuntary ignorance	314
Butler, Bp., his "Analogy"	6
—— Dr. Newman's obligations to	7
—— referred to	112

C.

	PAGE
Carnival, the	32
Catholicism, an incommunicable name	201
—— state of, in England from the sixteenth to the nineteenth century	209
—— re-establishment of its hierarchy in England	213
—— a *different religion* from Anglicanism	319
Catholicism, and the Religions of the World	320
—— and Atheism; no logical alternative between	338
Catholics, Private Judgment among	345
—— the religion of	356
—— the privileges of	359
—— "popular"	395
—— bad	398
Certitude in religious inquiry arrived at by accumulated probabilities	14, 57
Child, a, his apprehension of God	134
Chillingworth, quoted	268
Christianity, "our common"	112
—— "muscular"	228
"Christian Year," the	286
Church, the Catholic, a reality	63
—— and the World, origin of the warfare between	107
—— vitality of	208
—— "resurrection" of	216
—— alone possesses real internal unity	322
—— does not permit her children to doubt her word	324
—— dispositions for joining	334
—— the aim of	347
—— scandals in	393
—— not based upon her Orders	270
Church, the Anglican, what it is	64, 254, 321
—— what it is not	64
—— national jealousy of	153
—— duties of Catholics towards	66
Churches, Catholic, soothing influences of	25, 32

Coleridge, F., Letter to, on
 Anglican Orders . . 66
Condescension . . . 97
Confession, natural to the
 Catholic 105
—— what it is in fact . . 367
—— abuse of . . . 398
Conscience, a connecting
 principle between the creature and his Creator . . 131
—— voice of. . . . 103
Conversions, a Protestant
 view of 236
Convert, a 340
—— the World's view of . 329
Conviction, a state of mind . 336
Copleston, Dr. . . . 9
Corruptions, Roman (so called) 312
Counsels of Perfection. . 368
Culture, ethics of . . . 96
—— and vice . . . 103

D.

Development of Doctrine,
 the principle of . . 55, 311
—— Essay on . . . 59
Devotion, liberty accorded to
 the private judgment and
 inclination of Catholics
 regarding 343
Divine Calls, Sermon on . 48
Doctrine, Catholic, integrity
 of 361
Dogma, the fundamental
 principle of Dr. Newman's
 religion 28
—— growth of definitions of 311
Domenic Father . . . 59
Doubt, difficult for a Catholic 331
Douglas, on Miracles, quoted 377

E.

Education, Intellectual, what
 it is 71
England, Catholicism in, from
 the sixteenth to nineteenth
 century 209
—— the religious history of . 197
England, the Church of 63, 254
—— its life 257
—— its form . . . 321
—— a serviceable breakwater. 66
English horror of Catholicism 233
—— jealousy of Church and
 Army 153
—— religious ideas . . 229
Ex-cathedrâ judgment of the
 Pope, requisites for . . 188

F.

Faith, the Principle of . . 146
—— in the Catholic Church . 324
—— implies a confidence in
 the truth of the thing believed 325
—— in any other Church
 than the Catholic, impossible 332
—— easy to a Catholic . 331
—— and Devotion . . 341
Fouqué, quoted . . . 121
Froude, Hurrell, brings Dr.
 Newman and Mr. Keble
 together 11
—— his high gifts . . 16
—— his religious opinions . 16
—— his influence on Dr.
 Newman . . . 17, 31, 32
—— travels with Dr. Newman in the South of Europe 23

G.

	PAGE
Gentleman, definition of a	100
Gibbon, his "Five Causes"	141
Gilpin, Bernard, quoted	33
God, the idea of	113
—— the, of Monotheism and the God of Rationalism	126
—— easy to use the word, and mean nothing by it	127
—— apprehension of, through the conscience	131
Grace, the Catholic teaching on the subject of	274
Gregory, St., VII., his death	188
Gregory Nyssen, St., his account of an apparition of Our Lady	379

H.

Hallahan, Mother Margaret Mary	89
Hampden, Dr., his "Observations on Religious Dissent"	33
Harmony of the works of God	375, 432
Harvey, Mr., his death	281
Hawkins, Dr., Dr. Newman's obligations to	5
High Church party, the	284
Holy See, the, practical wisdom of	385
—— obligations of Catholics to	387
—— its action with regard to Ireland	161
Hume, his argument against miracles	139
Humility, the virtue of	97

I.

	PAGE
Ignatius, St., his Epistles, quoted	29
Ignatius Loyola, St., his Exercises	52
Ignorance, invincible	313
Illative faculty, the	87
Immaculate Conception, the	431
Incarnation, the, the greatest of miracles	374
Infallibility of the Pope, antecedent argument for the	381
—— not affected by his personal or temporary errors	187, 404
Inaccuracy of mind	72
Intellect, the ordinary sin of the	104
Intellectual education, what it is	71
—— man, popular conception of an	74
—— obstructions	92
Intuition	87
Invincible Ignorance and Anglicanism	313
Ireland, why annexed by the Pope to England	160
Irish discontent	157
—— the, tyrannically oppressed by Protestantism	162

J.

Jerusalem Bishopric, the	51
John Baptist, St.	404
John Evangelist, St.	406
Johnson, Dr., his Rambler	74
Joseph, St., the cultus of	344

Index. 443

	PAGE
Joseph, why exalted by the Catholic Church	357

K.

	PAGE
Keble, John, the true author of the Tractarian Movement	10
—— Dr. Newman's introduction to	11
—— effect of his teaching on Dr. Newman	12
—— his Christian Year	12, 286
—— what he did for the Anglican Church	289

L.

Lacordaire, Dr. Newman's admiration of	8
Liberalism, what Dr. Newman means by the term	8, 28
—— attacks the old orthodoxy of Oxford	33
Liberal view of Christianity	223, 295
Liberius, Pope	187
Littledale, Dr.	260
Lyra Apostolica	24

M.

Macaulay, Lord, on Bacon's philosophy	120
—— on the Apostolical succession	267
—— on Transubstantiation	363
Machyn and his Diary	259
Mary, the Blessed Virgin, Italian devotional manifestations in honour of	53
—— why exalted	357

	PAGE
Mary, the earliest recorded apparition of	379
—— "Mother of God"	416
—— her purity	419
—— her intercessory power	423
—— her Immaculate Conception	424
—— her Assumption	432
—— growth of her cultus	435
Mary Magdalen, St.	407
Maryvale	215
Mass, the	364
Mayers, the Rev. W.	3
Meditation, why prized by Catholics	79
Miller's Bampton Lectures	14
Milner, Joseph, his Church History	5
—— Bp.	214
Mind, the laws of, the expression of the Divine will	93
Miracles	370
Monachism, Early	175
Montalembert	8
More, Sir Thomas	363
Muscular Christianity	228

N.

Napoleon	88
Nativities, the three sinless	405
Newman, John Henry, his early religious impressions	3
—— obligations to Dr. Hawkins	6
—— obligations to Bp. Butler	6
—— obligations to Dr. Whately	7
—— first years of residence at Oriel	9

Index.

	PAGE
Newman, John Henry, introduction to Mr. Keble	10
—— obligations to Mr. Keble	12
—— obligations to Hurrell Froude	17
—— obligations to the Fathers	18
—— travels in the South of Europe	23
—— illness in Sicily	25
—— begins to visit Catholic churches	25
—— begins the "Tracts for the Times"	27
—— his religious principles in 1833	28
—— admiration for Dr. Pusey	34
—— the happiest part of his life in a human point of view	38
—— publishes Tract XC.	39
—— his place in the Tractarian Movement gone	41
—— his first doubts of the tenableness of Anglicanism	44
—— misgivings	44
—— three further blows	50
—— transition state	52
—— what it was that converted him	308, 311
—— reception	60
—— called to Rome by Pius IX.	392
—— establishment of the Birmingham and London Oratories.	392
—— his state of mind since his reception	61
Newton, Sir Isaac	87

	PAGE
Non-jurors, the	299
Northman and Norman	165
Notions, our, of things, only aspects of them	80
—— arithmetical, inapplicable to the Supreme Being	81
Numeration, issues in nonsense unless conducted under conditions	80

O.

Obstructions, intellectual	92
Orders, Anglican	66, 258
Ordinances, Anglican	271
Ordinations, heretical, their doubtfulness	263
"Orley Farm," quoted	86
Oxford	173

P.

Paley, quoted	144, 147
Parnel's Hermit, referred to	110
Passions, the, how apprehended	77
Periodical publications, reason of their influence	230
"Peveril of the Peak," quoted	89
Phaeton in the chariot of the Sun	34
Philip Neri, St.	413
—— predicts the election of St. Pius V.	192
Pius, St., V., his election	190
—— his character	192
—— his reply to the Count della Trinita	193
—— his hostility to the Turkish power	194

Index. 445

	PAGE
Pius, St., V., his supernatural knowledge of the victory of Lepanto	196
Pius IX., obligation of English Catholics to	391
Poetry, what it is	287
Pope, the, thought by Dr. Newman to be Anti-Christ	5, 31
—— this view the only controversial basis of Protestantism	33
—— what is required for an *ex-cathedrâ* judgment of	188
—— antecedent argument for the infallibility of	381
—— his infallibility not affected by personal or temporary errors	404
—— practical wisdom of	160, 202, 385
—— obligations of Catholics to	387
—— English Catholics and the present	391
Popery, Protestant notions of	239
Preacher, the popular, his unworthy use of the Sacred Volume	79
Pride, how utilized by philosophy	99
Principles, First	94
—— Protestant, on miracles	377
—— an Englishman's	232
Private judgment, what it means	230
—— among Catholics	345
—— right of Private Judgment or Private Right of Judgment	243
Protestant, the word, does not denote the profession of any particular religion	37
—— notions of the Divinity of Christ	417
—— view of conversions	236
—— texts	239
—— image worship	242
—— persecution, rationale of	245
Protestants and Eutychians	45
—— and Arians	50
Protestantism, applies the inductive method to Scripture	119
—— the tyrannical oppression of the Irish	162
—— has ever felt that it is not historical Christianity	223
—— drifting into scepticism	247
—— German	223
Punishment, retributive	109
Puritanism	227
—— Pusey, Dr.	9
—— joins the Tractarian Movement	34
—— his distance from the Catholic Church	35

R.

Rationalism, what it is	122
Real apprehension	77
Reality of the Catholic Church	63
Realization	78
Reason, how men reason in concrete matters	82
Relics	370
Religion, fundamental truths of, how commonly held	89

Religion, "Scriptural," how manufactured	. 239
—— of Catholics, the	. 356
Religious life, the, how regarded by men of the world	77, 369
"Reformation," the English	202, 210
—— the True	. 190
Retributive punishment, the doctrine of	. 109
Revolution, the French, profanation of the rights of reason in	. 246
Right of Private Judgment or Private Right of Judgment	243
Rome in 1566	. 189
"Roman Catholics," the	. 211
Russell, Dr.	. 52
Ryder, Bp.	. 22

S.

Saint, the idea of a	. 402
Saints, English	. 210
—— lingering imperfections of	. 403
—— eccentricities of	. 369
—— miracles of	. 377
Scepticism, the "duty of"	. 130
"Scriptural religion"	. 239
Scott, the Rev. Thomas	. 4
—— his death	. 281
Sentiment, the religion of	. 102
Sin, the doctrine of the Catholic Church concerning	. 351
—— original	. 431
Succession, the Apostolical, not an Anglican tradition	. 67
—— Lord Macaulay's remarks on	. 268

Suffering, voluntary	. 368
Sumner, Abp., his "Apostolical Preaching"	. 6
—— his correspondence with Mr. Maskell, quoted	. 256

T.

Texts, Protestant	. 239
Theology, what it is	. 111
—— and physical philosophy	117
—— its instrument, deduction	117
—— physical theology, what it is	. 129
Tracts for the Times, Dr. Newman begins	. 27
Tract XC.	. 39
Tractarian party, the, growth of	. 38
—— Movement, the	. 290
Transubstantiation	. 363
—— mocked at by the World	398
"Trinity," the word	. 81
—— the doctrine of the Most Holy	. 364
"Twopence," the extra	. 262

U.

Usages of Catholics, the, submitted to by *faith*	. 319

V.

"Via media," the	. 36
"Verses on Various Occasions," quoted	. 25, 371
Virgil, medieval opinion about	. 78

W.

	PAGE
Walker, Mr., his last words	281
Watchwords, political and religious, origin of	76
Wesley, John	279
Whately, Abp., Dr. Newman's obligations to	7
Whitfield, Mr., his death	281
William III., statue of, blown out of his saddle	243
Wiseman, Cardinal, visits to, in Rome	24, 25
—— lectures on Catholicism in London	3
Wiseman, Cardinal, his article on the "Anglican Claim"	46
—— places Dr. Newman in Birmingham	60
World, the, religious philosophy of	105
—— its highest idea of man	106
—— its hatred to the Church	397
—— source of its hatred to the Church	108
—— its view of a convert	329
—— its view of a Catholic Priest	330
—— its highest compliment to a Catholic	397

Woodfall & Kinder, Printers, 70 to 76 Long Acre, London, W.C.

www.ingramcontent.com/pod-product-compliance
Lightning Source LLC
Chambersburg PA
CBHW022110300426
44117CB00007B/653